Bible Basics

A Study Manual revealing the joy and peace of true Christianity

Duncan Heaster

First Published 1992
Second Edition 1994
Third Edition 1999
Fourth Edition 2002
Fifth Edition 2008, 2010

ISBN 1 874508 00 3

Carelinks U.S.A.
P.O. Box 1049
Sumner WA 98390
U.S.A.

www.carelinks.net
www.tacomaecclesia.net

Bible   Basics

5

Introduction

A lot of church-going people sense that there's something missing in their experience. And that it's a big 'something'. The idealized worldview preached by so many church leaders just doesn't add up. Health and prosperity don't come because you tithe. There's a big gap between the reality of daily life, and what church leaders preach. We sense that many of the jigsaw puzzle pieces which we have in our possession are real and valid, but all the same, we don't see the big picture. The pieces are all hopelessly jumbled up, even if we hold them in our hands. And we don't even know precisely what the big picture is; we don't have the lid with the picture on it. Although, we *think* we know what that bigger picture roughly is. But of course, it's taken as read that you don't share these doubts with anyone at church. Not a soul. It's an unconscious conspiracy of silence.

What we're crying out for is a systematic, no-nonsense approach to what God is saying to us through the Bible. We want to see the picture on the lid of the jigsaw puzzle, and then fit everything together according to it- both the pieces of understanding of God which we have, and our personal experiences of life.

Now if that's you, as it was me, then read on...

All human beings who have accepted that there *is* a God, and that the Bible is His revelation to man, need to seriously apply themselves to finding out its basic message. Many of those calling themselves 'Christians' seem to make a poor job of this - a few verses from the New Testament on Sundays, a Bible somewhere in the home that is never opened, dimly remembering a handful of Bible stories. Little wonder that with such a laid-back attitude to God's mighty Word of truth, there is so much confusion and uncertainty in the lives and minds of so many.

On the other hand, there are those with little Christian background who decide to try to figure out the Bible's message, but find that everyone they approach tries to offer them a package deal of doctrines and human philosophies which do not *fundamentally* reflect the words of the Bible.

It's the purpose of 'Bible Basics' to analyze the Bible's message in a business-like, systematic way. The main studies are designed to be read straight through as a book, or alternatively to be used as a correspondence course. Answers to the questions at the end of each study can be sent to the address below; your answers will then be passed to a personal tutor who can then correspond with you as you progress further through the Studies. It's appreciated that some readers will shy away from the idea of answering questions, but would rather *ask* questions concerning areas which they are unclear about, or disagree with the interpretation presented here. Again, if such correspondence is directed to the address below, personal answers can be given.

It's my conviction that the basic message of the Bible is crystal clear. However, there will always be some passages and topics which may appear superficially to be at variance with the general theme of Scripture. Some of these, along with other aspects of the Gospel which may only interest some readers, are discussed in the Digressions. It should be possible to understand the Bible's basic message without reading the Digressions, but all readers will have different interests and be on different levels of interest-hopefully all of you will find at least some of them to be relevant and interesting. The Bible translation often used in these studies is the Revised Authorized Version. However, where there is any unclarity in the rendering, other versions are quoted: The Revised Version (R.V.), Revised Standard Version (R.S.V.), Authorized Version (A.V.) and New International Version (N.I.V.).

There are many people who ought to be thanked for their help in producing this book; I am particularly indebted to Clive Rivers for the masterly series of photographs he has contributed, and to those who have commented on the drafts. However, my main debt lies with the hundreds of people in Africa, Asia and Eastern Europe, whose searching questions and thirst for truth have forced me to think through these 'Bible Basics' time and again. Their beauty and strength only increases by being viewed from so many different angles. In crowded taxis, on open trucks and lorries, on endless train journeys across Siberia, in sedate conference rooms to sweltering hotel balconies and starlit bush villages, these topics have been discussed, argued over and enthused about with Bible students from all walks of life. My brethren with whom I have been privileged to work in this have been a ceaseless source of strength and help. The substance of many of the Digressions in this book was often thrashed out between us in hotel rooms, after a gruelling session with a group of interested contacts. The fellowship and unity that comes from being bound together by these basic doctrines of Bible truth is surely unsurpassed in human experience. This 5th edition benefited from contributions, editing and discussion with a number of experienced preachers: Graham Bacon, Robin & Jean Field, Michael Gates, Mark Gilbert, Robin Jones and John Parkes deserve special mention. So to all these "my fellow workers unto the Kingdom of God" I now pay tribute, hoping they will find this volume a help in the great work of publishing the true Gospel "into all nations".

Grasping the real truth of the Gospel as taught in the Bible's pages will affect every part of our lives, leading men and women the world over to properly give glory to God as He intended, both now and for eternity. Every one who finds the truth finds the "pearl of great price", and will know the feelings of Jeremiah for himself: "Your words were found, and I did eat them; your word was unto me the joy and rejoicing of my heart" (Jer.15:16). To achieve this, be sure to pray for God's help in understanding the word before you tackle each of these Studies. "And now...I commend you to God, and to the word of His grace, which *is* able to build you up, and to give you an inheritance among all them which are sanctified" (Acts 20:32).

D.H.

Note: Bible Basics is available in over 50 languages. Contact the publisher for more details, or view online at www.biblebasicsonline.com. Foreign language editions and free distribution of this book are enabled by donations and legacies to the Publishers: The Christadelphian Advancement Trust, Registered Charity No. 1080393, P.O. Box 3034, South Croydon, Surrey CR2 0ZA ENGLAND email: info@carelinks.net.

ABBREVIATIONS USED IN THESE   STUDIES FOR BOOKS OF THE BIBLE

Gen.-Genesis	Jer.-Jeremiah	Rom.-Romans
Ex.-Exodus	Ez.-Ezekiel	1 Cor.-I Corinthians
Lev.-Leviticus	Dan.-Daniel	2 Cor.-2 Corinthians
Num.-Numbers	Hos.-Hosea	Eph.-Ephesians
Dt.-Deuteronomy	Am.-Amos	Phil.-Philippians
Josh.-Joshua	Mic.-Micah	Col.-Colossians
Jud.-Judges	Nah.-Nahum	1 Thes.-1 Thessalonians
1 Sam.-1 Samuel	Hab.-Habakkuk	2 Thes.-2 Thessalonians
2 Sam.-2 Samuel	Zeph.-Zephaniah	1 Tim.-1 Timothy
1 Chron.-1 Chronicles	Hagg.-Haggai	2 Tim.-2 Timothy
2 Chron.-2 Chronicles	Zech.-Zechariah	Tit.-Titus
Neh.-Nehemiah	Mal.-Malachi	Heb.-Hebrews
Ps.-Psalms	Mt.-Matthew	1 Pet.-1 Peter
Prov.-Proverbs	Mk.-Mark	2 Pet.-2 Peter
Ecc.-Ecclesiastes	Lk.-Luke	1 Jn.- 1 John
Isa.-Isaiah	Jn.-John	2 Jn.-2 John
		Rev.-Revelation

The questions at the end of each chapter are of two types: multiple choice (whereby you must choose one of the answers listed as the correct answer to the question), and ordinary questions which require a few sentences in response. Write your answers on a separate piece of paper, not forgetting to write your name and address clearly.

You may send your answers to the addresses below.

Carelinks USA, **P.O.Box 1049, Sumner, WA 98390 U.S.A.**
Or
**Carelinks, P.O. Box 152, Menai NSW 2234 AUSTRALIA
e-mail: info@carelinks.net / www.carelinks.net**

STUDY 1

God

1.1   The Existence Of God

"He who comes to God must believe that He is, and that He is a rewarder of those who diligently seek Him." (Heb. 11:6). The object of these studies is to help those who want to come to God, having first believed "that He is"; therefore we will not concern ourselves with the evidence that confirms faith in God's existence. Examining the intricate structure of our bodies (cf. Ps. 139:14), the evident

design in a flower, gazing up into the vastness of space on a clear night, these and countless other careful reflections on life surely make atheism incredible. To believe that there is no God surely requires more faith than to believe He exists. Without God there is no order, purpose or ultimate explanation in the universe, and this will therefore be reflected in the life of the atheist. Bearing this in mind, it is not surprising that the majority of human beings admit to a certain degree of belief in a God - even in societies where materialism is the prevailing 'god' of people's lives.

But there is a vast difference between having a vague notion that there is a higher power, and actually being certain of what He is offering in return for faithful service to Him. Heb. 11:6 makes this point, we
"must believe that (God) is
AND
that He is a rewarder of those who diligently seek Him".

Much of the Bible is an account of the history of God's people Israel; time and again the point is made that their acceptance of God's existence was not matched by their faith in His promises. They were told by their great leader Moses:

"Therefore know…and consider it in your heart, that the LORD Himself is God in heaven above and on the earth beneath; there is no other. You shall *therefore* keep His statutes and His commandments" (Dt. 4:39,40).

Thus the same point is made - an awareness within us that there is a God does not mean that we are automatically acceptable to God. If we seriously agree that we really do have a Creator, we should *love Him* and "keep *therefore* his...commandments". It is the purpose of this series of studies to explain what these commandments are and how to keep them. As we search the Scriptures to do this, we will find that our faith in God's existence is strengthened.

"Faith comes by hearing, and hearing by the word of God" (Rom. 10:17). Likewise, Is. 43:9-12 shows how an understanding of God's prophecies about the future makes us know "that I am he" (Is. 43:13) - i.e. that God's name 'I am who I am' is perfectly true (Ex. 3:14). The apostle Paul came to a town called Berea, now in Northern Greece. As usual, he preached the gospel ('good news') of God; but instead of the people just accepting Paul's word for it, "they received the word (of God, not Paul) with all readiness, and searched the Scriptures daily to find out whether these things were so. Therefore many of them believed" (Acts 17:11,12). Their belief was due to their open-minded, regular ("daily") and systematic ("those things") searching through the Bible. The gaining of a true faith was therefore not due to God suddenly giving them it by some kind of spiritual heart surgery, unrelated to God's word. So how can people of the world who walk into an Evangelical crusade or Pentecostal revival meeting walk out again as 'believers'? How much daily searching of Scripture has gone on in these cases? This lack of a truly Bible-based faith doubtless accounts for the hollowness which many such 'converts' find in their later Christian experience, and why so many turn away from the evangelical movement.

The purpose of this course of study is to provide a framework for your own systematic searching of Scripture, so that you too may "therefore" believe. The connection between hearing the true Gospel and having a true faith is often highlighted in the record of the Gospel's preaching.

- "Many of the Corinthians *hearing* believed and were baptised" (Acts 18:8)
- People "*hear* the word of the Gospel and believe" (Acts 15:7)
- "So we *preach*, and so you believed" (1 Cor. 15:11)

1.2   The Personality Of God

It is a majestic, glorious theme of the Bible that God is revealed as a real being. It is also a fundamental tenet of Christianity that Jesus is the Son of God. If God is not a real being, then it is impossible for Him to have a Son who was the "image of His person" (Heb. 1:3). The Greek word actually means His "substance" (RV). Further, it becomes difficult to develop a personal, living relationship with 'God', if 'God' is just a concept in our mind. It is tragic that the majority of religions have this unreal, intangible conception of God.

As God is so infinitely greater than we are, it is understandable that many people's faith has balked at the clear promises that ultimately we will see Him. It is impossible for sinful man to see God (Ex. 33:20 RSV) - although this implies that were it not for our sinfulness, God is indeed a being who can 'be seen'. Israel lacked the faith to see God's "shape" (Jn. 5:37). Such faith comes from knowing God and believing His word:

"Blessed are the pure in heart: for they shall see God" (Mt. 5:8).

"His (God's) servants shall serve him: and they shall see his face; and his name (God's name - Rev. 3:12) shall be on their foreheads" (Rev. 22:3,4).

Such a wonderful hope, if we truly believe it, will have a profound practical effect upon our lives: "Pursue peace with all people, and holiness, without which no one will see the Lord" (Heb. 12:14). We should not swear oaths, because "he who swears by heaven, swears by the throne of God and by Him who sits on it." (Mt. 23:22).

In this life our understanding of the heavenly Father is very incomplete, but we can look forward, through the tangled darkness of this life, to meeting Him at last. Our 'seeing' of Him will doubtless be matched by our greater mental comprehension of Him. Thus from the absolute depths of human suffering, Job could rejoice in the totally personal relationship with God which he would fully experience at the last day: "And after my skin is destroyed, this I know, that in my flesh I shall see God, whom I shall see for myself, and my eyes shall behold, and not another." (Job 19:26,27).

And the apostle Paul cried out from another life of pain and turmoil: "Now we look in a glass mirror, with a poor image; but then face to face" (1 Cor. 13:12).

OLD TESTAMENT EVIDENCE

These promises of the New Testament build on a considerable Old Testament backdrop of evidence for a personal God. It cannot be over stressed that it is fundamental to appreciate the nature of God if we are to have any true understanding of what Bible based religion is all about. The Old Testament consistently talks of God as a person; the person-to-person relationship with God of which both Old and New Testaments speak is unique to the true Christian hope. The following are strong arguments in favour of a personal God:

- "God said, Let us make man in our image, after our likeness" (Gen. 1:26). Thus man is made in the image and likeness of God, as manifested through the angels. James 3:9 speaks of "...men, which are made in the similitude of God." Our creation in the image of God surely means that we can infer something about the real object of which we are but an image. Thus God, whom we reflect, is not something nebulous of which we cannot conceive. Ezekiel saw God enthroned above the cherubim, with the silhouette of "the likeness of a man" (Ez. 1:26; 10:20); it is God Himself who is located above the cherubim (2 Kings 19:15 RV). All this has a practical import; because we are in the image of God, because it is imprinted on every part of our bodies, we must give that body to God, just as men were to give the penny which had Caesar's image on it to Caesar (Lk. 20:25). Commenting on this matter in relation to Gen. 1:26,27, Risto Santala writes: "There are two Hebrew words here, *tselem*, 'image' (in modern Hebrew 'photograph'), and *demuth*, 'figure' or 'similitude'... these expressions are very concrete. God is a person and he has a definite form and being" (1).

- "He (God) knows our frame" (Ps. 103:14); He wishes us to conceive of Him as a personal being, a Father to whom we can relate.

- Descriptions of God's dwelling place clearly indicate that He has a personal location: "God is in heaven" (Ecc. 5:2); "For He looked down from the height of His sanctuary; From heaven the LORD viewed the earth" (Ps. 102:19); "Hear in heaven your dwelling place" (1 Kings 8:39). Yet more specifically than this, we read that God has a "throne" (2 Chron. 9:8; Ps. 11:4; Is. 6:1; 66:1). Such language is hard to apply to an undefined essence which exists somewhere in heavenly realms. God is spoken of as "coming down" when He manifests Himself. This suggests a heavenly location of God. It is impossible to understand the idea of 'God manifestation' without appreciating the personal nature of God.

- Is. 45 is full of references by God to His personal involvement in the affairs of His people: "I am the Lord, and there is no other...I the Lord do all these things...I the Lord have created it. Woe unto him who quarrels with his maker... My own hands stretched out the heavens... turn to me and be saved, all you ends of the earth". This last sentence especially shows the personal existence of God - He desires men to look to Him, to conceive of His literal existence with the eye of faith.

- God is revealed to us as a forgiving God, who speaks words to men. Yet forgiveness and speech can only come from a sentient being, they are mental acts. Thus David was a man after God's own heart (1 Sam. 13:14), showing that God has a mind (heart), which is capable of being replicated to some limited degree by man, although man by nature is not after God's heart. Passages like, "The LORD was grieved that he had made man on the earth, and his heart was filled with pain" (Gen. 6:6), reveal God as a feeling, conscious being. This helps us to appreciate how we really can both please and displease Him, as children can a natural father.

IF GOD IS NOT PERSONAL...

If God is not a real, personal being, then the concept of spirituality is hard to grapple with. If God is totally righteous but is not a personal being, then we cannot really conceive of His righteousness manifested in human beings. Once we appreciate that there is a personal being called God, then we can work on our characters, with His help and the influence of His word, to reflect His characteristics in our lives.

God's purpose is to reveal Himself in a multitude of glorified beings. His memorial name, Yahweh Elohim, implies this ('He who shall be revealed in mighty ones', is an approximate translation). The descriptions of the reward of the faithful in God's coming Kingdom on earth show that they will have a tangible, bodily existence, although no longer subject to the weaknesses of human nature. Abraham is one of the "many of them that sleep in the dust of the earth (who) shall awake...to everlasting life" (Dan. 12:2) so that he can receive the promise of eternal inheritance of the land of Canaan, a physical location on this earth (Gen. 17:8). "Saints shall shout aloud for joy... Let the saints be joyful in glory; let them sing aloud on their beds...and execute judgment upon the nations" (Ps. 132:16; 149:5,7). A failure by both Jew and Gentile to appreciate passages like these, as well as the fundamentally literal, physical import of the promises to Abraham, has led to the wrong notion of an "immortal soul" as the real form of human existence. Such an idea is totally devoid of Biblical support. God is an immortal, glorious being, and He is working out His purpose so that men and women might be called to live in His future Kingdom on this earth, to share His attributes, expressed in a bodily form.

The faithful are promised that they will inherit God's nature (2 Pet. 1:4). We will be given a body like that of Jesus (Phil. 3:21), and we know that he will have a physical body in the Kingdom. The doctrine of the personality of God is therefore related to the Gospel of the Kingdom.

There can be no sensible concept of worship, religion or personal relationship with God therefore until it is appreciated that God is a real being and that we are made in His image. We need to develop His mental likeness now so that we may be made fully like Him in the Kingdom of God. So much more sense and comfort can now be gained from the passages which speak of God as a loving Father, chastening us as a Father does his son (e.g. Dt. 8:5). In the context of Christ's sufferings we read that, "it pleased the LORD to bruise Him" (Is. 53:10); although he "cried out to my God; He heard my voice...and my cry came before him, even into his ears" (Ps. 18:6). God's promise to David of a seed who would be God's Son required the miraculous birth of a human being who was truly in the image and likeness of his Father.

A correct understanding of God is a key which opens up many other vital areas of Bible doctrine. But as one lie leads to another lie, so a false concept of God obscures the truth which the Scriptures offer. If you have found this section convincing, or even partly so, the question arises: 'Do you really know God?' We will now further explore Bible teaching about Him.

Notes

(1) Risto Santala, *The Messiah In The Old Testament In The Light Of Rabbinical Writings* (Kukkila, Finland: BGS, 1992), p. 63.

Belief In Practice 1:

Knowing God

PRACTICING THE PRESENCE OF GOD

Believing in God's very existence of itself affects a man's behaviour. "The *living God*" is a phrase often used by men in prayer or desperate straits.

God *is*, He is the living One, and He therefore is a rewarder of those who seek Him. If there is no God, everything is possible. And the reverse is so true: seeing there *is* a God, all aspects of life come under this imperative. All religions apart from the true religion place a mask over God. To claim to be able to know the one true God is too much for them. So they have created false doctrines to cover Him up, to turn Him into what they would like or wish Him to be. Some have claimed that the God people have in their minds is essentially a projection of their own father figure. If their father was abusive and angry, then this is how they see God. If their father was kind and loving, then this, they decide, is what God is like. Freud's theory is probably true for most people in this world who claim a belief in God. The false idea that God is an angry old man appeased by the blood and violent punishment of His son seems to me to be rooted in the poor parental experience of some theologians. They have no experience of practicing the presence of God as Father. This is not the God revealed by open minded Bible study. For those who know and believe the true God of the Bible, God is God, who He is as revealed in His word, and we must resist this temptation to project onto Him our own perceptions of a father.

One of the most tragic misunderstandings of all time is the trinity- which claims that there are three "persons" in a Godhead. Trinitarian theologians borrowed a word- *persona* in Latin, *porsopon* in Greek- which was used for the mask which actors wore on stage. But for us, God doesn't exist in personas. He exists, as God the Father, the real, true God, who isn't acting, projecting Himself through a mask, playing a role to our eyes; the God who is so crucially real and *alive*, there at the other end of our prayers, pulling at the other end of the cord... What we know of Him in His word is what and who He really is. It may not be *all* He is, but it is all the same the truth of the real and living God. And this knowledge should be the most arresting thing in the whole of our existence. So often the prophets use the idea of "knowing God" as an idiom for living a life totally dominated by that knowledge. The new covenant which we have entered is all about 'knowing' God. And Jer. 31:34 comments: "They shall all know me…for I will forgive their iniquity" . The knowledge of God elicits repentance, real repentance; and reveals an equally real forgiveness. It is possible for those in Christ to *in practice* not know God at all. Thus Paul exhorted the Corinthian church: " Awake to righteousness, and do not sin; for some do not have the knowledge of God." (1 Cor. 15:34). The knowledge and practice of the presence of God ought to keep us back from sin.

All too easily we can think that we believe that 'God. But "what we need to know, of course, is not just that God exists, not just that beyond the steely brightness of the stars there is a cosmic intelligence of some kind that keeps the whole show going, but that there is a God right here in the thick of our every-day lives…it is not objective proof of God's existence we want but, whether we use religious language for it or not, the experience of God's presence. That is the miracle we are really after. And that is also, I think, the miracle that we really get". To this I for one can say 'Amen'. For it is in the apparent trivia of life that we see Providence the most clearly, hour by hour.

It can be that we accept God's existence without really believing that He is, therefore, all powerful, and that all His attributes which the Bible reveals are actually functional and real for us today. The unfaithful captain of 2 Kings 7:2 mocked Elisha: " If the Lord should make windows in heaven, might this thing be?" . He forgot that there *are* windows in Heaven (Gen. 7:11; Mal. 3:10) through which blessing can be given. He believed in God's existence. But he didn't think this God could do much, and he doubted whether He would ever practically intervene in human affairs. We must be aware of this same tendency.

FAITH

Many times the idea of "Your father which is in heaven" is used in the context of faith in prayer being answered (Mt. 7:11; 18:19; 21:22; Mk. 11:24; Jn. 14:13; James 1:5,6,17 etc.). It's as if the reality of God actually existing in Heaven in a personal form should be a powerful focus for our prayers. We have the highest imperative to develop into that which bears God's moral image, seeing we are made in His physical image- for God is a personal being. Exactly because "Your hands have made me and fashioned me", David asks for strength to put on God's moral image: "Give me [therefore] understanding, that I may learn your commandments" (Ps. 119:73). The reality that He truly exists in a personal form can be almost terrifying when first grasped.

I think it is worth all of us pausing to ask the most basic question: Do we *really* believe that God exists? Do we believe in a personal God, or merely in the God-idea? The Jews must have been shocked when the Lord Jesus told them to "believe in God" (Jn. 14:1 RVmg.). For there were no atheists amongst them. What Jesus was saying was that their faith was in the God-idea, not in the real God. For if they believed the Father, they would accept His Son. We must ask whether we feel any real passion for Him, any true emotion, any sense of spiritual crisis, of radical motivation... Consider how the prison keeper "rejoiced greatly...having believed in God" (Acts 16:34 RV). He was unlikely to have been an atheist [atheism wasn't very common in the 1st century]. But he grasped for the first time the real import of a real and relevant faith in the one true God as a personal being.

INSPIRATION TO DYNAMIC LIVING

In passing, I would argue that the false trinitarian perception that there are three 'personas' in the [supposed] trinity has led to a denial of God the Father being a real, live person, with all the unique individuality which attaches to a 'person'. The fact that God is a person means that who *we* are as persons, our being as persons, is of the ultimate importance. Having a personal relationship with a personal God means that we in that process develop as persons after His image; for there is something magnetically changing about being in relationship with Him. We are changed from glory to glory, by simply beholding His face and inevitably reflecting the glory there, which glory abides upon us in the same way as it stuck to the face of Moses even after his encounters with the Angel of Yahweh (2 Cor. 3:18-21 RV). And yet we live in a world which increasingly denies us ultimate privacy or isolation; the loudness of the world is all permeating, all intrusive, to the point that we can feel unable to separate ourselves at any time from the world to which we belong. We just can't seem to 'get away from it all' and be with God, no matter where we go on holiday, with whom we go, even if we slip off for an hour to be quite alone in the local park. But ultimately, I believe we *can* separate from the world's endless call and insistent pull, even if we're stuck with an unbelieving or unhelpful partner, sniffly kids, long hours at work, the TV always on, the phone always ringing. Because we as unique and individual persons can *personally* relate to the *personal* God and His Son, thus finding the ultimate privacy and isolation which being human in this world appears to preclude. But further, it's actually in the very razzmatazz of our mundane, frustrated experience in this world that we can come to know God, and in which God reveals Himself to us. And how does all this happen in practice? To experience God is to know Him. So often the prophets speak of 'knowing God' as meaning 'to experience God'. Because God is love, to love is to know God (1 Jn. 4:8). Quite simply, how deeply we have loved [and I am speaking of 'love' in its Biblical sense] is how deeply we have known God- and vice versa. And that love is worked out in the very earthliness and worldliness of human life in practice.

Belief In Practice 2:

The Supremacy Of Love

Robin Jones

It's easier to live by rules than by love. To live by love you have to really care about other people, to live by rules you don't have to. You can just follow the rules and be seen outwardly to do the right thing...

Maybe it's because people are naturally self centred that God gave Moses so many rules, rules that would make them do the right thing. Rules were the next best thing, but they are not the replacement for caring and loving in practice. If we really cared about others, we wouldn't need to be told to leave the gleaning for the poor etc... but because mankind is not naturally like this, God gave Moses many rules so people would do the right thing. Of course God *wanted it* to be from the heart, not just obedience to rules.

When Jesus came, he tried to show that it's what God had always intended. He wants us to love one another as he has loved us- hence he described his command to love each other *as he loved us* as "A new commandment I give to you". Great men such as David understood this, he was called a "man after God's heart". But just as it was under the law of Moses, so it can be today... you can obey rules, keep Church traditions, be seen to be outwardly righteous as the Pharisees, but without love, without really caring for others, it's shallow. This is why Jesus said "by their fruits you shall know them". It becomes evident by what we do whether we really care about others. None of us is perfect, but if we try our best to be more thoughtful and caring and genuinely loving to other people, then it really shows and is a witness of itself. The reverse is also true. If we don't really care about others, if we hang on to grudges, if we don't forgive, our time is spent trying to tear down instead of building up. It's even possible to kid ourselves that we find justification from scripture to do it in the name of God, yet what it really shows is that we do not really love the other person. So much harm has been done in the name of God, yet God has made it clear that he wants us to love others as He has loved us, and gave His Son to die for us while we were still sinners.

Love must be the motivating factor for everything we do, it must be behind every action and thought. We could learn the whole Bible off by heart, but without love our actions are meaningless and we can't view all the other advice from God in the right way. The second letter of John places so much emphasis on love and the humanity of Jesus, and warns that those who don't understand these things should be avoided. So it's vitally important that we understand that love should be behind our every thought and action and dealings with others, and it will affect how we understand God's word to us. It will open up a whole new way of seeing and living.

BEING BORN AGAIN

The life of true love is a new life. Reading the word of God can cause God's Spirit to dwell in us. This is such an important aspect of our lives that Jesus said to Nicodemus that we must be born again! And He also said that we must be "born of water and the spirit" (Jn. 3:3-5). All too often people are 'born of water and the doctrines of men'. The Pharisees even asked John the Baptist for baptism, i.e. to be born of water; but he basically told them that they must be born of the spirit. The Jews of Jesus' day had a rigid set of doctrines- and Jesus even endorsed what they taught by saying to His disciples: "do as they say but not as they do". But they just didn't have God's spirit dwelling in them. They had head knowledge but did not bring forth the fruits of repentance. We are told by Paul what the fruits of the spirit are in Gal. 5:22. They are (*firstly!*) love, then joy, patience, peace, kindness, gentleness, forgiveness. Being born of the spirit produces these attributes in us. It's not only reading God's word that changes our hearts to become "spirit filled", but also being encouraged by other faithful believers. Heb. 10:24 speaks of how we should "stir one another up to love and good works". Another way we can be "born of the spirit" is by talking to God in prayer, in fact we are told that prayer is not just something we recite to God at meals, but a way of life (Rom. 12:12).

Being born of the spirit does not mean possessing special gifts that the early apostles had to perform miraculous healings. It is having God's spirit dwelling in us. We can have all the head knowledge in the world but if we don't have God's spirit of genuine love for others then it wont do us any good. If we say we love God but hate our brother, it makes a mockery of all we profess to believe. We must be "born again" in that we have a new way of seeing others, a compassion and sympathy for them that God feels for us. Without this we can study the "doctrines" of the Bible all our lives yet end our days as the Pharisees did- who thought they were so righteous when actually they were still in sin, for they had not known the God who *is* love.

1.3   God's Name And Character

If there is a God, it is reasonable to think that He will have devised some means of telling us about Himself. We believe that the Bible is God's revelation to man, and that in it we see the character of God revealed. If we allow this word of God to fill our mind, a new creature is formed within us which has the characteristics of God (James 1:18; 2 Cor. 5:17). Therefore the more we apply ourselves to God's word and take the lessons to ourselves, the more we will become "conformed to the image of His Son" (Rom. 8:29) who was in character the perfect image of God (Col. 1:15). In this lies the value of studying the historical parts of the Bible; they are full of lessons telling us how God has dealt with men and nations, always displaying the same basic characteristics.

In Hebrew and Greek a person's name often reflected their character and/or information about them. Some clear examples:

- 'Jesus' = 'Saviour' - because "He will save His people from their sins" (Mt. 1:21).
- 'Abraham' = 'Father of a great multitude' - "for I have made you a father of many nations" (Gen. 17:5)
- 'Eve' = 'Living' - "because she was the mother of all living" (Gen. 3:20).
- 'Simeon' = 'hearing' - "Because the LORD has heard that I am unloved, He has therefore given me this son" (Gen. 29:33).

In Jer. 48:17, knowing the people of Moab is paralleled with knowing the name of Moab. The Psalms often parallel God Himself with His name, His word and actions (Ps. 103:1; 105:1; 106:1,2,12,13).

It is therefore to be expected that God's name and titles will give us much information about Himself. A detailed study of the Name of God is advisable after baptism; further appreciation of God's character as expressed in His name is something which should go on during all our life in the Lord. What follows is therefore very much an introduction.

When Moses wanted a deeper knowledge of God to strengthen his faith during a very traumatic period of his life, an angel proclaimed the Name of the Lord. ""The LORD, the LORD God, merciful and gracious, longsuffering, and abounding in goodness and truth, keeping mercy for thousands, forgiving iniquity and transgression and sin, by no means clearing the guilty" (Ex. 34:5-7).

This is clear proof that the Name of God entails His characteristics. His possession of them is proof that God is a personal being.

God has chosen one particular Name by which He would like to be known and remembered by His people; it is a summary, an epitome, of His purpose with men.

The Israelites were slaves in Egypt, and needed to be reminded of God's purpose with them. Moses was told to tell them God's name, so that this would help motivate them to leave Egypt and start the journey towards the promised land (cf. 1 Cor. 10:1). We too need to understand the basic principles concerning God's Name before we are baptised and start our journey towards God's Kingdom.

God told Israel that His Name was YAHWEH, meaning "I am that I am" or, perhaps, "I will be who I will be" (Ex. 3:13-15). This name was then slightly extended. "God said moreover (i.e. in addition) unto Moses. This is what you shall say unto the children of Israel, the LORD (Yahweh) God of your fathers, the God of Abraham, the God of Isaac and the God of Jacob...this is My name for ever, and my memorial to all generations" (Ex. 3:15). God's full Name is therefore "The LORD God".

The Old Testament was written mostly in Hebrew, and our English translation inevitably misses out a lot of detail when it comes to translating the Hebrew words for 'God'. One of the common Hebrew words translated 'God' is 'Elohim', meaning 'mighty ones'. God's "memorial", the name by which He wants us to remember Him, is therefore

YAHWEH ELOHIM

Implying

HE WHO WILL BE REVEALED IN A GROUP OF MIGHTY ONES

It is therefore God's purpose to reveal His character and His essential being in a large group of people. By obedience to His word we can develop some of God's characteristics in ourselves now, so that in a very limited sense God reveals Himself now in true believers in this life. But God's name is a prophecy of the time to come when the earth will be filled with people who are like Him, both in character and by nature (cf. 2 Pet. 1:4). If we wish to be associated with the purpose of God and to become like God. If we wish to die no more, living for ever in complete moral perfection, then we must associate ourselves with His name. The way to do this is to be baptised into the name - i.e. Yahweh Elohim (Mt. 28:19). This also makes us the descendants of Abraham (Gal. 3:27-29) who were promised the eternal inheritance of the earth (Gen. 17:8; Rom. 4:13) - the group of 'mighty ones' ('Elohim') in whom the prophecy of God's name will be fulfilled. This is explained in more detail in Study 3.4.

Belief In Practice 3:

The Grace Of God

John Parkes

"However , I consider my life worth nothing to me, if only I may finish the race and complete the task the Lord Jesus has given me - the task of testifying to the good news of God's grace" (Acts 20:24, NIV).

These are the sentiments about the gospel from the apostle Paul as he shares the things that are very deepest and dearest to his heart. The thing that he was so passionate about was the grace of God. He was so eager to tell people about it, and share it with everyone he came across, hoping that they too would respond to God's kindness, God's undeserved kindness to them, and share in a life of peace with their Creator, having been forgiven of their wrong, sinful, rebellious ways. For trying to pass on this amazing message he was beaten and outcast, by those who even used to be his friends; ultimately he was killed for trying to share this gospel of grace. Not only was forgiveness and reconciliation on offer, through grace, but also the hope of eternal life. God is prepared to forgive our wicked ways, which truly deserve death, according to the law, and give us the gift of eternal Life which we do not deserve (Rom 6:23). This is indeed grace. Not only do sinners not deserve life, but unfortunately no matter how hard we work at it there is really no way to escape from the fact that we will end up dead. Scientists are trying to dream up ways to stop us from dying, and many religious people have even come to the conclusion that death is really a release from some physical jail, (our bodies), and that on death, we are released to a life of bliss in eternity with God. Tragically they have made death equal life. Although there are a variety of thoughts and convictions on the matter we all really and truly end up as dust, dead, as the Bible so plainly describes in lots of places.

Being gracious is a part of God's character. Back in Exodus when the Name of our Heavenly Father was proclaimed to Moses in chapter 34 verse 6, it went like this: "The Lord, The Lord, the compassionate and *gracious* God, slow to anger abounding in love… In 2 Chron 30:9 we are told: "The Lord your God is graciousness and compassionate. He will not turn his face from you if you return to Him", and again in Neh. 9:17: "But you are a forgiving God, *gracious* and compassionate, slow to anger and abounding in love. Therefore you did not desert them."

You may notice at the end of the last quote it says "therefore you did not desert them". The point is, they very much deserved to be deserted. The context is in regard to the people that Moses brought out of Egypt; not far out of Egypt the people "became arrogant, stiff necked, and did not obey your commands. They refused to listen and failed to remember the miracles you performed among them". In fact they were so rebellious that they wanted to throw Moses out of the leadership and set a new leader over them to take them back to slavery in Egypt, but as it says, "you did not desert them", even though they deserved to be. That equals grace. Our God thankfully showed His love by being gracious beyond measure to them, as we are reminded in Ps. 103:10: "he does not treat us as our sins deserve, or repay us according to our iniquities. For as high as the heavens are above the earth, so great is his love for those who fear him; as far as the east is from the west, so far has he removed our transgressions from us. As a father has compassion on his children, so the Lord has compassion on those who fear him". Indeed, "The Lord is gracious and compassionate, slow to anger and rich in love. The Lord is good to all; he has compassion on all he has made" (Ps. 145:8,9).

God knew that we would find it hard to be convinced of how gracious and loving He is, He knew that from the moment we were created, but He was determined that he would not stop until the full measure of His grace was poured out to us. This grace of God was revealed through the Lord Jesus Christ. In John 1:17 we are told, "the law (justice) was given through Moses, grace and truth came through Jesus Christ".

And what a challenging revelation this grace that the demonstrated proved to be, and still proves to be up to this very day. In Lk. 1:40 we are told of Jesus: "the child grew and became strong; he was filled with wisdom and the *grace* of God was upon him". In Lk. 4:22 again: "All spoke well of him and were amazed at the *gracious* words that came from his lips".

Jesus came proclaiming a God that the people hadn't even imagined, having a heart of compassion and grace for those who were not acceptable by the religious or secular standards of the day, mixing with even the ones who were thought to be under the curse of God, and even touching the supremely unclean, the lepers, and allowing himself to be touched by the wicked in Lk. 7:37-50.

In his stories Jesus shared his insights of the forgiving, loving, compassionate, gracious and joyful God that our Heavenly Father is. One of the most challenging and memorable would surely have to be the parable of the merciful father in Luke 15. You can read the full story in Lk. 15:11 - 31, think about it and see where you fit into the picture.

It is a story about the truly gracious, loving heart of our Heavenly Father. Jesus tells the story of a son who wants to go his own way, leave the family home, and the family, take his share of the inheritance and go and do his own thing. The son ends up squandering all the inheritance in wild living, in the end not even being able to afford enough food to feed himself. Who wouldn't say 'Serves him right!'. I have certainly felt like that, and I can feel justified in harbouring this attitude. We can even find lots of Bible verses to support our attitude, e.g. Prov 5:23; Prov 10:4; and also the popular saying "A person will reap what they sow".

Not so with the Father. We don't find dad sitting down inside the house, sulking in his self righteousness, thinking up ideas of confession for the son to go through, making plans to ensure that this will never happen again, being ready to mete out justice, pouring over the thought of how much money the son has wasted and how it will have to be repaid for him to find favour with the family again. We find a dad who is not being reasonable at all. At the father's response I can imagine that many would be horrified: "What are you doing, don't you know what this wicked boy has done, he deserves to be punished, to pay for his wrongdoing!". Instead dad is up there pouring out grace and love on this undeserving, wayward lad. I love dad's response, in Lk 15:20 "While he was still a long way off, his father saw him (he had to be looking for him, surely) and was filled with compassion for him; he ran to his son, threw his arms around him and kissed him... The father said to the servants, Quick! Bring the best robe and put it on him. put a ring on his finger and sandals on his feet. Bring the fattened calf, let's have a feast and celebrate. For this son of mine was dead and is alive again: he was lost and is found". So they began to celebrate". I can imagine that the listeners were shocked and dumbfounded, Jesus was telling the listeners, and us, the readers, what God is like, a God of such love compassion and grace.

The reason I love the dad's response is because I too need our Heavenly Father and Jesus to respond to me, just like the father in Jesus' story responded to his son. In fact we all need the grace of God to reach out and touch us. We all have been like sheep that have strayed out of the way, our sins have separated us from our God. All have sinned and fallen short of the glory of God, we all have the heart that is described in Jeremiah as being deceitful and beyond cure, and it would seem that most of us have done things that we would not like everyone to know about. But God is there, He knows our lives inside out, there is nothing that is hidden from Him, He actually knows us better than we know ourselves, which is a very humbling awareness to have.

Although God knows us and our weaknesses and wickedness, our father is always wanting us to return to Him, ready to throw an incredible celebration, and have rejoicing (Lk. 15:6,10,32) in heaven when we repent of our ways, and determine in our hearts to follow Jesus.

That is typical of God's grace and love, he has taken the initiative in reaching out to us in a very clear and unmistakable way- by raising up for us his own special Holy one, his dear sinless Son, Jesus, to be our Saviour from sin and death. As has been quoted previously from Acts 24, it was the apostle Paul's life's labour, it was the thing that drove him, that he might complete his task of testifying to the gospel of God's grace. He had experienced the wonder of God's undeserved kindness, his grace, being richly poured out on him- and wanted to let everybody else know how great it was. In 1 Tim 1:13, 14 he tells us of the wonder of his conversion: "Even though I was once a blasphemer and a persecutor and a violent man, I was shown mercy because I acted in ignorance and unbelief. The grace of our Lord Jesus was poured out on me abundantly, along with the faith and the love that are in Christ Jesus". Under God's justice Paul was worthy of death, under God's grace, that is found only in Jesus, Paul was given a new start, and he knew that this new start, this freedom, this peace with God, is on offer to all, as is stated in Titus 3:7: "So that having been justified by his grace, we might become heirs having the hope of eternal life". In Romans 3:23 we are told: "for all have sinned and have fallen short of the glory of God... [we] are justified freely by his grace through the redemption that came by Christ Jesus ". In 1 Tim. 2:4 it says that God "wants all men saved and to come to a knowledge of the truth". The extent of God's desire to have us become part of his family and share in his grace and the blessings that flow from it is described in Rom. 5:8: "But God demonstrates his own love for us in this: While we were still sinners , Christ died for us".

"Amazing grace how sweet the sound that saved a wretch like me, I once was lost, but now am found, was blind but now I see". Such is the truth for all who come to understand the gospel, the good news of God's grace in all its' marvellous truth. For now we can but wait, but not be idle. We are encouraged by Peter in his first letter, "to prepare our minds for action; be self controlled; set our hope fully on the grace to be given you when Jesus Christ is revealed from heaven".

Belief In Practice 4:

The All Seeing God

That God sees and knows all things has a number of major implications for our lives in practice.

NO SECRET SINS

Job knew this, and therefore, he commented, it was impossible that, e.g., he would lust after a woman, if he really believed (as he claimed he did) that God was omniscient. 'Why then should I think upon a young girl [as the friends implied he had done]? ...does not he [God] see my ways, and count all my steps?' (Job 31:4). Proverbs 5:20,21 makes the same warning against being "embraced in the arms of a seductress", "For the ways of man are before the eyes of the Lord, and he ponders all his goings". Also in the context of sexual sin, David could say that his awareness of his sin was 'ever before him' (Ps. 51:3); and also that he sensed God 'ever before him' (Ps. 16:8). A sense of the real presence of God leads us to an awareness of our sins. Likewise God had to remind Israel: "Can any hide himself in secret places that I shall not see him? ...do not I fill heaven and earth?" (Jer. 23:24). The context is appealing to the people to quit their sins. We should labour to enter the Kingdom, *because* God knows absolutely every thought and action of ours and will ultimately judge them (Heb. 4:11-13). The Sermon on the Mount is really based around translating the knowledge that God sees and knows all things into practice. Our thoughts are equivalent to our actions; and yet often we think that the fact we are clever enough not to express them in action is somehow a lesser failure. And yet God sees our thought afar off. Realizing this will help us avoid the greatest danger in the religious life: to have an outward form of spirituality, when within we are dead. Note how the Lord Jesus begins each of His letters to the churches with the words: "I know..." ; His omniscience of His people ought to motivate them to appropriate behaviour. His criticisms of those ecclesias imply that they *didn't* appreciate the fact that He knew them and their ways. Hannah had reflected upon God's omniscience; and on this basis she tells Peninah not to be proud and not to use hard words against her, exactly because of this: "Talk no more so exceeding proudly; let not hardness [AVmg.] come out of your mouth: *for* the Lord is a God of knowledge, and by him actions are weighed" here and now, *because* He sees and knows all things (1 Sam. 2:3).

Fred Barling commented: "What God loves is the man who is genuine through and through; in whom the "without" and the "within" are really one; whose dominant persuasion is, "You God see me" " . The Hebrew language reflects certain realities about the nature of God's ways. The common Hebrew word for 'to see', especially when used about God's 'seeing', means also 'to provide'. Abraham comforted Isaac that " God will see for himself [AV 'provide'] the lamb" (Gen. 22:8 RVmg.); and thus the RVmg. interprets 'Jehovah-Jireh' as meaning 'the Lord will see, or provide' (Gen. 22:14). The same word is used when Saul asked his servants to " provide" him a man (1 Sam. 16:17). When Hagar said " You God see me" (Gen. 16:13), she was expressing her gratitude for His *provision* for her. What this means in practice is that the fact God sees and knows all things means that He can and will therefore and thereby provide for us in the circumstances of life; for He sees and knows all things.

FAITH IN PRAYER

If God really does see and know all things, then He surely hears prayer. We raise our eyebrows when we read David's desperate prayer: "Don't be deaf unto me" (Ps. 28:1). He who made the ear shall surely hear. God of course isn't deaf- and just as surely and obviously, He will likewise hear prayer.

Belief In Practice 5:

God Really Is Omnipotent

NO TRUST IN WEALTH

God has 'spoken twice', an idiom for Divine emphasis upon something, that all power belongs to Him, God is omnipotent- and exactly because of this, David says, we should not set our heart upon riches if they happen to increase (Ps. 62:10,11). As the world economy develops more and more wealth, increase in riches is a temptation which faces many believers, both relatively rich and relatively poor, in most countries of the world. I'd guess that well over 50% of Christians have experienced an increase in riches over the past 20 years. The temptation is of course to 'set our heart' upon them, and the illusion of freedom which increased wealth brings. This most insidious temptation, David says, can be overcome by a deep sense of how important it is to believe that *all* power is *of God alone*. This means that money is *not* equal to power; because all power is of God. Don't set your heart upon *money* because *power* is from God… these simple, inspired words dramatically torpedo this world's most crucial principle: that money = power. It doesn't. Quite simply, because all power is *of God.*

Belief In Practice 6:

Responding To The One God

A DEMAND FOR OUR ALL

That God is one is not just a numerical description. If there is only one God, He therefore demands our *all*. Because He is the One God, He demands all our worship; and because He is One, He therefore treats all His people the same, regardless, e.g., of their nationality (Rom. 3:30). All true worshippers of the one God, whether Jew or Gentile, are united in that the one God offers salvation to them on the same basis. The fact there is only one Lord Jesus implies the same for Him (Rom. 10:12). Paul saw these implications in the doctrine of the unity of God. But that doctrine needs reflecting on before we come to grasp these conclusions. Christ taught that the command that God was one and therefore we must love God *included* the second command: to love our neighbour as ourselves. The first and second commands were in fact one command; they were inseparably part of the first commandment (Mk. 12:29-31). This is why the 'two' commandments, to love God and neighbour, are spoken of in the singular in Lk. 10:27,28: " *this* do..." . If God is one, then our brother bears the one Name of God, and so to love God is to love our brother (cp. 1 Jn. 4:21). And because there is only one God, this demands *all* our spiritual energy. There is only one, the one God, who seeks glory for men and judges them (Jn. 8:50)- therefore the unity of God should mean we do not seek glory of men, neither do we judge our brother.

That God is one is a command, an imperative to action (Mk. 12:28,29). It underlies the whole law and prophets (Mt. 22:40)- it's that fundamental. If there were two Gods, Yahweh would only demand half our energies. Nothing can be given to anything else; for there is nothing else to give to. There's only one God. There can be no idolatry in our lives, because there is only one God (2 Kings 19:18,19). Because "there is none else, you shalt keep *therefore* his laws" (Dt. 4:39,40). The one God has only one people; not all religious systems can lead to the one Hope.

Dt. 6:4 is far more than a proof text. Indeed God is one; but consider the context. Moses has set the people up to expect him to deliver them a long list of detailed commands; he has told them that God told him to declare unto them "all the commandments...that they may do them...you shall observe to do therefore as the Lord your God has commanded you...you shall walk in all the ways which the Lord your God has commanded you...now these are the commandments...that you might do them...*hear therefore O Israel and observe to do it* [singular]..." . Now we expect him to reel off a long list of commands. But Moses mirrors that last phrase with simply: "*Hear, O Israel, the Lord our God is one*" (Dt. 5:31-6:4). And in this context he gives no other commandments. "Observe to do *it* " is matched with "The Lord our God is one" . This is the quintessence of all the commands of God. And he goes straight on to say: "And these words...shall be in your heart" and they were to talk of them to their children in the house and by the way, bind them upon their hands and on the posts of their homes. It was the unity of God and the imperative from it to love Him with all the heart which is what was to be programmatic for their daily living. This is why it was Jewish practice to recite the *shema* several times a day, and also on their deathbed.

Dt. 6:1 RV reads: "Now this is *the commandment* [singular], the statutes and the judgments...the Lord our God is one" . And then they are told to write the statutes on their door posts etc. It would have been hard to literally write all 613 of them there. Yet the whole way of life for Israel was epitomized in the single command...that God is one. It was and is a *command*; not a mere statement.

We do not have two masters; only one. Therefore, the more we grasp this, the more we will give ourselves solely to Him. And this leads on, in the thinking of Jesus, to having no anxious thought for tomorrow; for a life of total devotion to Him means that we need not worry about tomorrow (Mt. 6:24,25).

NO IDOLATRY

There is a religious impulse within all men, a desire to serve someone or something. Generally, men and women sink this in the worship of the many idols of this materialistic age. But for us, there is to be one God, one channel alone for our devotion; for God is one. When Israel rejected the fountain of Yahweh, they hewed out many other fountains, in the form of idols (Jer. 2:13). The urge to worship is there within all men and women. We are asked to concentrate and consecrate that passion solely for the one God- not to share it between the many things that demand it. Romans 1 goes so far as to condemn men because they worshipped the created things *besides* (Gk.) the Creator. *All* their adoration should have gone to the one God Himself. And there will come a day when all the world realizes that God is one (Is. 37:20 Heb.)- in that they will realize that He alone is God and all else is pure vanity. Because God alone is holy, only He will be worshipped then (Rev. 15:4). "The Lord alone shall be exalted in that day" (Is. 2:11,17).

Our worlds, our lives and hearts, are full of potential idols. And what, in the most fundamental essence, is wrong with idolatry? It seems to me that idolatry *trivializes* this wonderful God of whom we have spoken. It makes the Almighty God into a piece of wood or stone, or into a smart career or new house. And so *anything* that reduces the majesty, the surprise, the passion, the vitality in our relationship with God is an idol. Time and again in our lives, God is edged out by petty distractions- a car that needs repair, a leaking gutter, a broken window. One could almost weep for the frequency and the way in which all this occurs, so tragically often.

FAITH

The unity of God is related to His sovereign power in our lives: " He is one [and therefore] what his soul desires, even that he does. For he performs that which is appointed" (Job 23:13,14 RVmg.). The idea of truth is often linked with the fact there is only one God (Is. 45:5,6,14,18,21,22). This means that all He says is the total Truth; for there is no other God. Thus one God has given us only one faith, hope etc (Eph. 4:4-6). Other belief systems can't be acceptable with us. Such was the crucial importance of the unity of God; and likewise it should influence our lives, hourly.

David had to remind himself: " My soul, hope only upon God [one-ly upon the one God]; for my expectation is from him [i.e. Him alone]" (Ps. 62:5). There is only one God, one source of help and power- and thus the oneness of God inspires our faith in Him. This motivated Asa to cry unto Yahweh in faith: "LORD, there is none beside you to help...help us, O LORD...for we rely on you" (2 Chron. 14:11 RV). Summing up, James 2:14-18 speaks of the connection between *faith* (believing) and *works* (doing). It is no co-incidence that 2:19 then says in this context: " You *believe* that God is one; you *do* well" (RV). To have *faith* in the unity of God will lead to *works*, 'doing well'. God would not be inquired of by Israel, i.e. He would not answer their prayers, because they worshipped other gods, whereas God is one (Ez. 20:31). Prayer and wholeheartedly requesting things from the one God, relying on nothing and nobody else, is thus a form of worship of the one God. If we are truly believing in one God, then we shouldn't feel awkward about asking Him for things- it's a form of worshipping Him.

Paul, writing to those who thought they believed in the unity of God, had to remind them that this simple fact implies the need for unity amongst us His children, seeing He treats us all equally as a truly good Father: " If so be that God is one...he shall justify the circumcision by faith, and [likewise] the uncircumcision through faith" (Rom. 3:30 RV).

1.4 The Angels

All that we have considered so far in this study is brought together by a consideration of the angels:

- real, personal beings
- carrying God's Name
- beings in whom God's Spirit works to execute His will
- in accordance with His character and purpose
- and thereby manifesting Him.

We mentioned in Study 1.3 that one of the most common of the Hebrew words translated 'God' is 'Elohim', which strictly means 'mighty ones'. The word can frequently be shown to refer to the angels who, as God's 'mighty ones', carry this name and can effectively be called 'God' because they represent God.

The record of the creation of the world in Gen. 1 tells us that God spoke certain commands concerning creation, "and it was done". It was the angels who carried out these commands.

"Angels, that excel in strength, that do His commandments, hearkening unto the voice of His word" (Ps. 103:20).

It is therefore reasonable to assume that when we read of 'God' creating the world, this work was actually performed by the angels. Job 38:4-7 hints this way too. Now is a good time to summarise the events of the creation as recorded in Gen.1.

Day 1 "God said, Let there be light: and there was light" (v.3)

Day 2 "God said, Let there be an expanse in the midst of the waters, and let it divide the waters (on the earth) from the waters (in the clouds)...and it was so" (v.6,7)

Day 3 "God said, Let the waters under the heaven be gathered together (forming seas and oceans)...and let the dry land appear; and it was so" (v.9)

Day 4 "God said, Let there be lights...in heaven...and it was so" (v.14,15)

Day 5 "God said, Let the waters bring forth abundantly the moving creatures...and birds that may fly...and God *created* every living creature" (v.20,21) - i.e. "it was so"

Day 6 "God said, Let the earth bring forth the living creature...cattle, and creeping things ...and it was so" (v.24).

Man was created on that same sixth day. "God said, Let us make man in our image, after our likeness" (Gen. 1:26). We commented on this verse in Study 1.2. For the present, we want to note that "God" here is not just referring to God Himself in person - "Let *us* make man" shows that 'God' is referring to more than one person. The Hebrew word translated 'God' here is 'Elohim', meaning 'Mighty Ones', with reference to the angels. They are very real beings, sharing the same nature as God.

In the Bible there are two 'natures'; by the very meaning of the word it is not possible to have both these natures simultaneously.

GOD'S NATURE ('DIVINE NATURE')
- He cannot sin (perfect) (Rom. 9:14; 6:23 cf. Ps. 90:2; Mt. 5:48; James 1:13)
- He cannot die, i.e. immortal (1 Tim. 6:16)
- He is full of power and energy (Is. 40:28)

This is the nature of God and the angels, and was given to Jesus after his resurrection (Acts 13:34; Rev. 1:18; Heb. 1:3). This is the nature which we are promised (Lk. 20:35,36; 2 Pet. 1:4; Is. 40:28 cf. v 31).

HUMAN NATURE
- We are tempted to sin (James 1:13-15) by a corrupt natural mind (Jer. 17:9; Mk. 7:21-23)
- We are doomed to death, i.e. mortal (Rom. 5:12,17; 1 Cor. 15:22)
- We are of very limited strength, both physically (Is. 40:30) and mentally (Jer.10:23)

This is the nature which all men, good and bad, now possess. The end of that nature is death (Rom. 6:23). It was the nature which Jesus had during his mortal life (Heb. 2:14-18; Rom. 8:3; Jn. 2:25; Mk. 10:18).

It is unfortunate that the English word 'nature' is rather vague: we can use it in a sentence like 'John is of a generous nature - it just isn't in his nature to be mean; but he can be rather proud of his car, which is just human nature, I suppose'. This is not how we will be using the word 'nature' in these studies.

The angels who are of God's nature must therefore be sinless and unable to die - seeing that sin brings death (Rom. 6:23). Often when angels appeared on earth they looked like ordinary men.

- Angels came to Abraham to speak God's words to him; they are described as "three men", whom Abraham initially treated as human beings, since that was their appearance: "Let a little water, I beg you, be fetched, and wash your feet, and rest yourselves under the tree" (Gen. 18:4).

- Two of those angels then went to Lot in the city of Sodom. Again, they were recognised only as men by both Lot and the people of Sodom. "There came two angels to Sodom", whom Lot invited to spend the night with him. But the men of Sodom came to his house, asking in a threatening way: "Where are the men which came in to you this night?". Lot pleaded: "Unto these men do nothing". The inspired record also calls them 'men'. "The men (angels) put forth their hand" and rescued Lot; "And the men said unto Lot...The Lord has sent us to destroy" Sodom (Gen. 19:1,5,8,10,12,13).

- The New Testament comment on these incidents confirms that angels appear in the form of men: "Remember to entertain strangers; for some (e.g. Abraham and Lot) have entertained angels unawares" (Heb. 13:2).

- Jacob wrestled all night with a strange man (Gen. 32:24), which we are later told was an angel (Hos. 12:4).

- Two men in shining white clothes were present at the resurrection (Lk. 24:4) and ascension (Acts 1:10) of Jesus. These were clearly angels.

- Consider the implications of "the measure of a man, that is, of the angel" (Rev. 21:17).

ANGELS DO NOT SIN

As angels share God's nature they cannot die. Seeing that sin brings death, it follows therefore that they cannot sin. The original Greek and Hebrew words translated 'angel' mean 'messenger'; the angels are the messengers or servants of God, obedient to Him, therefore it is impossible to think of them as being sinful. Thus the Greek word 'aggelos' which is translated 'angels' is also translated 'messengers' when speaking of human beings - e.g. John the Baptist (Mt. 11:10) and his messengers (Lk. 7:24); the messengers of Jesus (Lk. 9:52) and the men who spied out Jericho (James 2:25). It is, of course, possible that 'angels' in the sense of *human* messengers can sin.

The following passages clearly show that all the angels (not just some of them!) are by nature obedient to God, and therefore cannot sin:

"The Lord has prepared His throne in the heavens; and his kingdom rules over all (i.e. there can be no rebellion against God in heaven). Praise the Lord, you His angels, that excel in strength, that do his commandments, hearkening unto the voice of His word. Praise the Lord, *all* you His hosts; you ministers of His, that do his pleasure" (Ps. 103:19-21).

"Praise him, *all* his angels...his hosts" (Ps. 148:2)

"The angels...are they not *all* ministering spirits, sent forth to minister for them (the believers) who shall be heirs of salvation?" (Heb. 1:13,14).

The repetition of the word "*all*" shows that the angels are not divided into two groups, one good and the other sinful. The importance of clearly understanding the nature of the angels is that the reward of the faithful is to share their nature: "They which shall be accounted worthy...neither marry...neither can they die any more: for they are equal unto the angels" (Lk. 20:35,36). This is a vital point to grasp. Angels cannot die: "Death...does not lay hold of angels" (Heb. 2:16 Diaglott margin). If angels could sin, then those who are found worthy of reward at Christ's return will also still be able to sin. And seeing that sin brings death (Rom. 6:23), they will therefore not have eternal life; if we have a possibility of sinning, we have the capability of dying. Thus to say angels can sin makes God's promise of eternal life meaningless, seeing that our reward is to share the nature of the angels. The reference to "*the* angels" (Lk. 20:35,36) shows that there is no categorisation of angels as good or sinful; there is only one category of angels. Dan. 12:3 says that the faithful will shine as the stars; and stars are associated with the Angels (Job 38:7). We will be made like Angels; and yet we will be given immortal, sinless nature. Therefore, Angels can't sin. Our hope is to enter into the wonderful freedom of nature which the "Sons of God", i.e. the Angels, now share (Rom. 8:19).

If angels could sin, then God is left impotent to act in our lives and the affairs of the world, seeing that He has declared that He works through His angels (Ps. 103:19-21). God achieves all things by His spirit power acting through the angels (Ps. 104:4). That they should be disobedient to Him is an impossibility. Christians should daily pray for God's kingdom to come on earth, that His will should be done here as it is now done in heaven (Mt. 6:10). If God's obedient angels had to compete with sinful angels in heaven, then His will could not be fully executed there, and therefore the same situation would obtain in God's future kingdom. To spend eternity in a world which would be a perpetual battlefield between sin and obedience is hardly an encouraging prospect, but that, of course, is not the case.

ANGELS AND BELIEVERS

There is good reason to believe that each true believer has angels - perhaps one special one - helping them in their lives.

- "The Angel of the Lord camps round about those that fear him, and delivers them" (Ps. 34:7).

- "...these little ones which believe in me (i.e. weak disciples - Zech. 13:7 cf. Mt. 26:31)...in heaven their angels do always behold the face of my Father" (Mt. 18:6,10).

- The early Christians clearly believed that Peter had a guardian angel (Acts 12:14,15).

- The people of Israel went through the Red Sea, and were led by an angel through the wilderness towards the promised land. Going through the Red Sea represents our baptism in water (1 Cor. 10:1), and so it isn't unreasonable to assume that afterwards we, too, are led and helped by an angel as we journey through the wilderness of life towards the promised land of God's Kingdom.

If the angels could be evil in the sense of being sinful, then such promises of angelic control and influence in our lives would become a curse instead of a blessing.

We have seen, then, that angels are beings...

- with God's eternal nature
- who cannot sin
- who always do God's commands
- and who are the beings through whom God's spirit-power speaks and works (Ps. 104:4).

BUT...?

Many churches have the idea that angels can sin, and that sinful angels now exist who are responsible for sin and problems on the earth. We will discuss this misconception more fully in Study 6. For the present we will make the following points.

- It has been suggested that there was a creation previous to our own, i.e. to that recorded in Gen. 1. It is also conceivable that the present angels came to have an awareness of "good and evil" (Gen. 3:5) through having been in a similar situation to what we are in this life. That some of the beings who lived in that age did sin is not to be ruled out; but all this is the kind of speculation which men love to indulge in. The Bible does not tell us of these things but tells us clearly what we need to know about the present situation, which is that there are no sinful angels; all angels are totally obedient to God.

- There can be no sinful beings in heaven, seeing that God is "of purer eyes than to behold evil" (Hab. 1:13). In similar vein, Ps. 5:4,5 explains: "Neither shall evil dwell with you. The foolish shall not stand" in God's heavenly dwelling place. The idea of there being rebellion against God in heaven by sinful angels quite contradicts the impression given by these passages.

- The Greek word translated "angel" means "messenger" and can refer to human beings, as we have shown. Such human "messengers" can, of course, sin.

- That there are evil, sinful beings upon whom all the negative aspects of life can be blamed is one of the most commonly held beliefs in paganism. In the same way that pagan ideas concerning Christmas have entered what passes for 'Christianity', so, too, have those pagan notions.

- There is only a handful of Biblical passages which can be misunderstood to support this idea of sinful angels now being in existence. These are considered in *The Real Devil*, available from the publishers. Such passages cannot be allowed to contradict the wealth of Bible teaching to the contrary which has been presented.

Belief In Practice 7:

God As Creator

The fact that we have been created by God means that life and existence around us has a purpose. Job was told that the very fact he had been created by God and his breath was in God's hand meant that his apparently inexplicable trials had indeed come from God and had a purpose (Job 12:10). If He created us in the first place, then we can expect that His hand will continue to mould our lives through trials in an ongoing, creative way.

RESPECT FOR GOD'S WORD AND HIS CREATION

Because of the work of God as Creator and the power of the Word that formed it all, we should likewise stand in awe of Him and recognize the power of His word (Ps. 33:6-9). Ps. 147:15-19 draws a parallel between the way God sends out His word to give snow like wool, and then again to melt it; and the way that this very same word works in our lives: " He sends out His word, and melts them...He shows His word unto Jacob, His statutes and His judgments unto Israel" . The word we have in our Bibles has the same creative power as the word through which the world was created and exists even now. Because we are created in God's image, the structure of our very bodies is an imperative to give ourselves totally to His cause (Mt. 22:19-21). Whatever bears God's image- i.e. our very bodies- must be given to Him. "It is he that has made us, and [therefore] we are his" (Ps. 100:3 RV). We must be His in practice *because* He is our Creator. So it is not that we merely believe in creation rather than evolution; more than this, such belief in creation must elicit a life given over to that Creator. God as creator created man in His own image; and therefore we shouldn't curse men (James 3:9). By reason of the image they bear, we are to act to all men as we would to God Himself; we are not to treat some men as we would animals, who are not in the image of God. Because we are made in God's image, we should therefore not kill other humans (Gen. 9:6). James says the same, in essence, in teaching that because we are in God's image, we shouldn't curse others. To curse a man is to kill him. That's the point of James' allusion to Genesis and to God as Creator. Quite simply, respect for the person of others is inculcated by sustained reflection on the way that they too are created in God's image.

PERCEIVING THE VALUE OF PERSONS

Only those who believe that we were created by God and have the possibility of eternal redemption can truly perceive the value of persons. Only they can grasp the worth of human beings, that we are not mere animals, but there is a wonder to human life which inspires us to seek to save humans through the preaching of the Gospel.

Digression 1: God Manifestation

What follows will not be easy to grasp fully at first reading, but the importance of the subject will become more evident as your studies proceed. We include it at this point so that you will leave this study having fully considered the Bible's basic revelation about God Himself.

The name of God can be carried by anyone through whom He chooses to 'manifest' or reveal Himself. So men and angels as well as Jesus can carry God's name. This is a vital principle which opens up so much of the Bible to us. A son especially may carry the name of his father; he has certain similarities with his father, he may have the same first name - but he is not one and the same person as the father. In the same way a representative of a company may speak on behalf of the company; he may telephone someone on business and say, 'Hello, this is Unilever here'; he is not Mr. Unilever, but he carries their name because he is working on their behalf. And so it was with Jesus.

ANGELS CARRYING GOD'S NAME

We are told in Ex. 23:20,21 that God told the people of Israel that an angel would go ahead of them; "My name is in Him", they were told. The personal name of God is 'Yahweh'. So the angel carried the name of Yahweh, and could thus be called 'Yahweh', or 'The LORD', in small capitals, as the word 'Yahweh' is translated in the NIV. and AV. We are told in Ex. 33:20 that no man can see the face of God and live; but in Ex. 33:11 we read that "The LORD (Yahweh) spoke to Moses face to face, as a man speaketh to his friend" - i.e. directly. It could not have been the LORD, Yahweh, Himself in person, who spoke to Moses face to face, because no man can see God Himself. It was the angel who carried God's name who did so; and so we read of the LORD speaking face to face with Moses when it was actually an angel who did so (Acts 7:30-33).

There are many other examples of the words 'God' and 'LORD' referring to the angels as opposed to God Himself. One clear example is Gen. 1:26: "And God (the angels) said, Let us make man in our image".

MEN WITH GOD'S NAME

One of the passages which is most helpful in demonstrating all this is John 10:34-36. Here the Jews made the mistake which many do today. They thought that Jesus was saying he was God Himself. Jesus corrected them by saying, "Is it not written in your law, I said, You are gods? If He called them 'gods'...why do you say of (me)...'You blaspheme!' because I said, I am the Son of God?'. Jesus is really saying 'In the Old Testament men are called 'gods'; I am saying I am the *Son* of God; so why are you getting so upset?' Jesus is actually quoting from Ps. 82, where the judges of Israel were called 'gods'.

As has been shown, the full name of God in Hebrew is 'Yahweh Elohim' - implying 'He who will be revealed in a group of mighty ones'. The true believers are those in whom God is revealed in a limited sense in this life. However, in the Kingdom, they will be 'mighty ones' in whom the LORD will be fully manifested. This is all beautifully shown by a comparison of Is. 64:4 and 1 Cor. 2:9. "Men have not heard, nor perceived by the ear, neither has the eye seen, O God, besides you, what He has prepared for him that waits for him". Paul quotes this in 1 Cor. 2:9,10: "It is written, Eye has not seen, nor ear heard, neither has entered into the heart of man, the things which God has prepared for them that love Him. But God has revealed them unto *us* by His Spirit". The passage in Is. 64 says that no one except God can understand the things He has prepared for the believers. However 1 Cor. 2:10 says that those things have been revealed to *us*.

The priests were God's representatives, and for a man to 'appear before the Lord' effectively referred to his appearance before the priest. When we read of "men going up to God at Bethel", the 'house of God' (1 Sam. 10:3), we aren't to think that God Himself lived in a house in Bethel. The reference is to the priests, his representative, being there.

JESUS AND THE NAME OF GOD

It is not surprising that Jesus, as the Son of God and His supreme manifestation to men, should also carry God's name. He could say "I am come in my Father's name" (Jn. 5:43). Because of his obedience, Jesus ascended to heaven and God "gave him a name which is above every name" - the name of Yahweh, of God Himself (Phil. 2:9). So this is why we read Jesus saying in Rev. 3:12: "I will write upon him (the believer) the name of my God...and I will write upon him my new name". At the judgment Jesus will give us God's name; we then will fully carry the name of God. He calls this name, "My new name". Remember, Jesus gave the book of Revelation some years after his ascension into heaven and after he had been given God's name, as explained in Phil. 2:9. So he can call God's name "My new name"; the name he had recently been given. We can now properly understand Is. 9:6, where concerning Jesus we are told, "His *name* (note that) shall be called, Wonderful, Counsellor, the mighty God, the everlasting Father...". This is a prophecy that Jesus would carry *all* the name of God - that he would be the total manifestation or revelation of God to us. It was in this sense that he was called 'Emmanuel', meaning, 'God is with us', although He personally was not God. Thus the prophecy of Joel 2 that men would call on the name of Yahweh was fulfilled by people being baptised into the name of Jesus Christ (Acts 2:21 cf. 38). This also explains why the command to baptize into the name of the Father was fulfilled, as detailed in the Acts record, by baptism into the name of Jesus.

Digression 2: Why The Trinity Was Accepted

In my opinion, the Biblical evidence against the trinity is compelling. And yet the majority of professing Christians are trinitarian; and moreover, they stigmatize non-trinitarians as non-Christian, many claiming that non-trinitarians are automatically a 'sect'. Clearly enough, neither the word 'trinity' nor the wording of the trinitarian formula were known to New Testament Christianity. In a sense, Jesus 'became' God to many Christians all because a group of bishops decided it was so. But *why* did this happen? And why was there so much angst to label those who didn't accept the trinity as heretics? Having read around the history of the early centuries of Christianity, the following are some suggested reasons:

1. There was a mixture of paganism and Christianity, to make the changeover from paganism to nominal Christianity less controversial and more painless.

2. There was an element of genuine misinterpretation. As you read through the New Testament chronologically, it becomes apparent that the Lord Jesus is spoken of in ever more exalted language. For example, the term "son of man" is a favourite of the Gospel writers to describe the Lord Jesus. But it occurs only once in the later New Testament. Mark, the first Gospel, never calls Jesus "Lord"- but "Lord" is Paul's most common title of Jesus some years later. John's Gospel, clearly written after the other three, uses much more exalted language about the Lord Jesus than the earlier Gospels. Presumably this trend continued after the death of the Gospel writers, as believers realized more and more that the carpenter from Nazareth had in fact been God's Son, and is now the exalted King of Heaven and earth. The penny dropped that in fact "we can never exalt Christ too highly", as Robert Roberts put it in the 19th century. But... and it's a big but. The language of exaltation can reach a point where Jesus is no longer Jesus, but somehow God Himself. Further, it's my observation that intellectual failure very often has an underlying psychological basis. To make Jesus God was one thing, but to accept the doctrine of three Gods in one, the trinity, was another. And I submit that this intellectual failure was rooted, even unconsciously, in a desire for an easier ride. It is after all extremely demanding to accept that a man, born into all our dysfunction, could be perfect; that from the larynx of a Palestinian Jew there could come forth the words of God Almighty. It's a challenge, because we too are human; and if this was how far one of us could rise, above all the things that hold us down, that retard our growth towards the image of God Himself... then He is setting us an example so challenging that it reaches into the very core of our being, uncomfortably, inconveniently and even worryingly. To have a Jesus who was in fact not truly human, but just acting out, a Jesus who was really God and not man... this removes so much of the challenge of the real, human Christ.

The human desire to believe in a god rather than a man is demonstrated in Israel's attitude to Moses. They complained about "this Moses, the *man* that brought us up out of the land of Egypt"; and therefore made the golden calf, proclaiming: "These be your *gods*, O Israel, which brought you up out of the land of Egypt" (Ex. 32:1,4). Note in passing how they created *one* calf, but worshipped it as *gods* plural. They committed the trinity fallacy of many centuries later. They couldn't handle a saviour who was human, like them, and so they decided that a god had been their saviour, who existed as a plurality, gods, within a unity, i.e. the golden calf.

3. Remember that the trinity was adopted at the Council of Nicea in AD325. This Council was called by Constantine after he decided he wished to turn the official religion of the Roman empire from paganism to Christianity. Not long before that Council, Christians had been cruelly persecuted. Some of the delegates at that Council even bore on their faces and in their bodies the marks of that persecution. The pagans had [falsely] accused the Christians of making Jesus into a God whom they worshipped. Pliny had reported how they "chant antiphonally a hymn to Christ as to a god". In the pagan Roman world, only the Jews refused to worship other gods on the basis that there was only one true God. The fact the Christians did the same led to the perception that they too thought that there was only one God, just that they called Him 'Christ'. The Jews likewise wrongly assumed that anyone claiming to be the Son of God was claiming to be God (Jn. 10:33-36; 19:7)- even though Jesus specifically corrected them over this! As often happens, the perceptions of a group by their enemies often come to define how the group perceive themselves. Constantine was a politician and a warrior. He wasn't a Bible student, nor a theologian, in fact he wasn't even a very serious Christian. Although he accepted Christianity, he said he didn't want to be baptized because he wanted to continue in sin. He seems to have figured that Christianity was the right thing for the empire. So, Christianity, here we come. Constantine, and many others who jumped on the 'Christian' bandwagon, shared the perception of Christ which had existed in the pagan world which they had grown up in. And the pagan perception, as Pliny and many others make clear, was that Jesus was a kind of God. And so when Constantine presided over the dispute amongst the bishops at Nicea about who Jesus was, he naturally assumed that the 'Jesus is God Himself' party were in fact traditional Christians.

4. The true Christian believer has ever been under pressure from the world. Paul wrote words of eternal relevance when he asked that we not allow the world to press us into its' mould, but rather allow Christ to transform us. The acceptance of the trinity was a result of the world pressurizing the church. The Roman and Jewish worlds which surrounded the Christians had a way of divinizing human figures. If you concluded a man had been a hero, then you applied Divine language to him- a form of what the Greeks had called apotheosis. This is why some of the Rabbinic commentary on men like Moses and Elijah use God-like language about them, although clearly the intention was not to make them equal to the one and only God of Israel whom they believed in. There's no lack of evidence that Christians did this with regards to Jesus, indeed there are examples of it in the New Testament. And it has also been observed that some of the exalted Jewish language used about Moses- e.g. "the one for and on account of whom the world was created"- was purposefully appropriated by Paul and applied to Jesus. Such glorified figures were also spoken of with the language of pre-existence, as if they had existed from the beginning of creation, even though that wasn't literally the case.

But as Christianity generally turned against the Jews, as Jewish Christians were thrown out of the church or returned to the synagogues, the actual human roots of Jesus were overlooked. The Jewish background to the language of exaltation used about Him was no longer appreciated. Instead, Christ remained in the minds of many Christians just with the Divine titles attached to Him; and so they ended up concluding that He was God Himself. Why? Because they overlooked the Jewish origins of Jesus, and the Old Testament background to Him; and because they preferred to stick with forms of wording which were comfortable and familiar to them, rather that searching out the meaning behind those words. And today, nothing much has changed. Still Christians remain almost wilfully ignorant of the basic principle of 'God manifestation' which is found throughout Scripture, whereby Divine language can be used of a person without making them God Himself.

5. The argument between Arius (non-trinitarian) and Athanasius (trinitarian) was more political than it was theological or Biblical. There was a power struggle between the two men. Once Christianity became the state religion of the Roman empire, power within the church became political power. These two Christian leaders both had significant followings; and they both wanted power. The followers of the two groups fought pitched battles with each other in the cities of the empire. There are numerous accounts of Athanasius' followers beating and murdering non-trinitarian Christians in the lead up to the Council of Nicea, torturing their victims and parading their dead bodies around. The trinitarian Athanasius was by far the more brutal. As in any power struggle, the opponents of both sides became vilified and demonized; the issue of how to formulate a creed about the nature of Jesus became a matter of polemics and politics, with the non-trinitarians being described in the most vitriolic of language. Non-trinitarians were accused of "rending the robe of Christ", crucifying Him afresh, and far worse. Sadly this spirit of

vilification of those who hold another view has continued to this day, with many trinitarians refusing to accept any non-trinitarian as a Christian. It would be wrong to think of the dispute as a matter of learned men of God disagreeing with each other over a matter of Biblical interpretation. Athanasius, who had the ear of Constantine more than Arius, was out for victory. He therefore emotionalized the issue and used every manner of politics and destruction of his opponents in order to get Constantine to come down on his side, exile Arius for heresy, and therefore leave him as the senior churchman of the Roman empire- which meant major political power, in an empire which had newly adopted Christianity and sought to enforce it as the empire's religion. Often I hear the comment 'Well this matter was all looked into long ago, and wise Christians weighed it up and came to a prayerful conclusion, which tradition Christians rightly follow and uphold'. The history of the matter is quite different. Athanasius compounded his physical attacks on Arius' supporters, his burning of their churches etc, with a series of personal slanders against the leading non-trinitarians, calling them seducers, rapists, frequenters of prostitutes, etc. If the argument was really just about the interpretation of Scripture, there needn't have been all this personal attacking and politicking and rioting. Clearly, the issue of accepting the trinity was all about power politics.

6. Constantine was a politician, not a Bible student. He realized that Christianity itself had to be united if it were to be the state religion, and so he wanted there to be only one view on this contentious issue of who Jesus was. It was intolerable for him that Christians were rioting against each other over it. The matter had to be resolved. One side had to be chosen as right, and the other side must be silenced. He came down on the side of Athanasius for political reasons- adopted the trinitarian creed for the church, and exiled Arius. And so, Jesus 'became' God because of that. In the same spirit of wanting a united church at all costs, Constantine agreed at Nicea a whole range of other measures which were likewise not Biblical- e.g. that anyone excommunicated by a Bishop in one province could never be accepted in another province, and the appointment of "superbishops" in Alexandria, Rome and Antioch who would decide all contentious issues in future. Personal conscience and understanding didn't matter; all Constantine wanted was a united church, as he believed it would result in a united empire. One empire, one religion- and therefore, that religion had to be united, and dissent had to quashed. Someone had to be made out as totally right, and someone as totally wrong. Sadly one sees today the very same mentality in so many churches and local congregations. It's all about power. The mess made in early Christianity remains our sober warning in these last days.

STUDY 1: Questions

1. What will most help develop our faith in God?
    - ☐ Going to church
    - ☐ Prayerful Bible study
    - ☐ Talking to Christians
    - ☐ Looking at nature.

2. Which of the following is the most correct definition of God?
    - ☐ Just an idea in our mind
    - ☐ A piece of Spirit in the atmosphere
    - ☐ There is no God
    - ☐ A real, material person

3. Is God
    - ☐ A unity
    - ☐ A trinity
    - ☐ Many gods in one
    - ☐ Impossible to define in any way?

4. What does God's Name 'Yahweh Elohim' mean?
    - ☐ He who will be
    - ☐ He who will be revealed in a group of mighty ones
    - ☐ A great one
    - ☐ Strength

5. What does the word 'Angel' mean?
    - ☐ Man-like
    - ☐ Wing covered
    - ☐ Messenger

6. Can Angels sin?
    - ☐ Yes
    - ☐ No

7. What most convinces you that there is a God?

STUDY 2

The Spirit Of God

2.1   God's Spirit

As God is a real, personal being with feelings and emotions, it is to be expected that He will have some way of sharing His desires and feelings with us, His children, and of acting in our lives in a way that will be consistent with His character. God does all of these things by His "spirit". If we wish to know God and have an active relationship with Him, we need to know what this "spirit of God" is, and how it operates.

It isn't easy to define exactly what the word "spirit" means. If you went to a wedding, for example, you might comment, "There was a really good spirit there!" By this you mean that the atmosphere was good, somehow everything about the wedding was good; everyone was smartly dressed, the food was nice, people spoke kindly to each other, the bride looked beautiful, etc. All those various things made up the "spirit" of the wedding. Likewise the spirit of God somehow summarises everything about Him. The Hebrew word translated "spirit" in the Old Testament strictly means "breath" or "power"; thus God's spirit is His "breathing", the very essence of God, reflecting His mind. We will give examples of how the word "spirit" is used about someone's mind or disposition in Study 4.3. That the spirit does not just refer to the naked power of God is evident from Rom. 15:19: "the power of the spirit of God".

It is a common Bible teaching that how a man thinks is expressed in his actions (Prov. 23:7; Mt. 12:34); a little reflection upon our own actions will confirm this. We think of something and then we do it. Our 'spirit' or mind may reflect upon the fact that we are hungry and desire food. We see a banana going spare in the kitchen; that desire of the 'spirit' is then translated into action - we reach out for the banana, peel it and eat. This simple example shows why the Hebrew word for 'spirit' means both the breath or mind, and also power. Our spirit, the essential us, refers to our thoughts and therefore also to the actions which we take to express those thoughts or disposition within us. On a far more glorious scale, God's spirit is the same; it is the power by which He displays His essential being, His disposition and purpose. God thinks and therefore does things. "As I have thought, so shall it come to pass; and as I have purposed, so shall it stand" (Is. 14:24).

THE POWER OF GOD

Many passages clearly identify God's spirit with His power. In order to create the earth, "the spirit of God moved upon the face of the waters. And God said, Let there be light: and there was light" (Gen. 1:2,3).

God's spirit was the power by which all things, e.g. light, were made. "By His spirit He has created the heavens; His hand has formed the crooked serpent" (Job 26:13). A comparison of Mt. 12:28 and Lk. 11:20 shows that "the finger of God" and "the spirit of God" are parallel - God in action is His spirit. "By the word of the Lord were the heavens made; and all the host of them by the breath of His mouth" (Ps. 33:6). God's spirit is therefore described as follows.

- His breath
- His word
- His finger
- His hand

It is therefore His power by which He achieves all things. For example, believers are born again by God's will (Jn. 1:13), which is by His spirit (Jn. 3:3-5). His will is put into operation by the spirit. Speaking of the entire natural creation, we read: "You send forth your spirit, they are created: and (thereby) you renew the face of the earth" (Ps. 104:30). This spirit/power is also the sustainer of all things, as well as the means of their creation. It is easy to think that this tragic life stumbles on without this active input of God's spirit. Job, a man who became weary of this life, was reminded of this by another prophet: "If he (God) gather unto himself his spirit and his breath; all flesh shall perish together, and man shall turn again unto dust" (Job 34:14,15). When pulling out of a similar trough of depression, David asked God to continue to uphold him with this spirit, i.e. to preserve his life (Ps. 51:12).

We shall see in Study 4.3 that the spirit given to us and all creation is what sustains our life. We have "the breath of the spirit of life" within us (Gen. 7:22 A.V. mg.) given to us by God at birth (Ps. 104:30; Gen. 2:7). This makes Him "the God of the spirits of all flesh" (Num. 27:16 cf. Heb. 12:9). Because God is the life force which sustains all creation, His spirit is present everywhere. David recognised that through His spirit God was constantly present with him wherever he went, and through that spirit/power He was able to know every corner of David's mind and thinking. Thus God's spirit is the means by which He is present everywhere, although He personally is located in heaven.

"You know my sitting down and standing up, you understand my thought far off... Where shall I go from your spirit? or where shall I flee from your presence? If I dwell in the uttermost parts of the sea; even there... your right hand (i.e. through the spirit) shall hold me" (Ps. 139:2,7,9,10).

A proper understanding of this subject reveals God to us as a powerful, active being. Many people have grown up with a vague 'belief' in God, but in reality 'God' is just a concept in their minds, a black box in part of the brain. An understanding of the true God and His very real presence all around us by His spirit can totally change our concept of life. We are surrounded by the spirit, constantly witnessing its actions, which reveal God to us. David found the encouragement of all this absolutely mind-blowing: "Such knowledge is too wonderful for me; it is high, I cannot attain unto it" (Ps. 139:6). Yet responsibilities come with such knowledge; we have to accept that our thinking and actions are totally open to God's view. As we examine our position before Him, especially when thinking about baptism, we need to bear this in mind. God's majestic words to Jeremiah apply to us, too: "Can any hide himself in secret places that I shall not see him? says the Lord. Do not I fill (by the spirit) heaven and earth?" (Jer. 23:24).

THE HOLY SPIRIT

We have seen that God's spirit is a vast concept to grasp; it is His mind and disposition, and also the power by which He puts His thoughts into operation. "As a man thinks in his heart, so is he" (Prov. 23:7); and so God is His thoughts, in that sense He is His spirit (Jn. 4:24), although this does not mean that God is not personal. To help us grapple with this vastness of God's spirit, we sometimes read of His "Holy Spirit".

The phrase "Holy Spirit" is to be found almost exclusively in the New Testament. In the A.V. the name "Holy Ghost" is often used, but it should always be translated as "Holy Spirit", as modern versions make clear. This is equivalent to the Old Testament phrases "the spirit of God" or "the spirit of the Lord". This is clear from passages such as Acts 2, which records the pouring out of the Holy Spirit upon the apostles on the day of Pentecost. Peter explained that this was a fulfilment of the prophecy of Joel, in which it is described as the pouring out of "my (God's) spirit" (Acts 2:17). The main fulfilment of this will be when Jesus returns (Is. 32:15,16). Again, Lk. 4:1 records that Jesus "being full of the Holy Spirit" returned from Jordan; later in the same chapter Jesus links this with Is. 61: "The spirit of the Lord God is upon me". In both cases (and in many others) the Holy Spirit is equated with the Old Testament term "the spirit of God".

Notice, too, how the Holy Spirit is paralleled with the power of God in the following passages.

- "The Holy Spirit shall come upon you (Mary), and the power of the Highest shall overshadow you" (Lk. 1:35)
- "The power of the Holy Spirit...mighty signs and wonders, by the power of the spirit of God" (Rom. 15:13,19)
- "Our gospel (preaching) came...in power, and in the Holy Spirit" (1 Thes. 1:5).
- The promise of the Holy Spirit to the disciples was spoken of as their being "endued with power from on high" (Lk. 24:49).
- Jesus himself had been "anointed...with the Holy Spirit and with power" (Acts 10:38).

- The "promise of the *Holy Spirit*" (Acts 1:5) is defined as "*power* from on high" in Lk. 24:49. Hence the disciples received *power* after the *Holy Spirit* came upon them (Acts 1:8).
- Paul could back up his preaching with undeniable displays of God's power: "My speech and my preaching was...in demonstration of the spirit and of power" (1 Cor. 2:4).

2.2 Inspiration

We have considered God's spirit as His power, thoughts and disposition, which He reveals through the actions which His spirit performs. We mentioned in the previous section how God's spirit was seen at work in the creation: "By his spirit he has created the heavens" (Job 26:13) - the spirit of God moving upon the face of the waters to bring about the present creation (Gen. 1:2). Yet we also read that "by the word of the Lord" the world was made (Ps. 33:6), as shown by the Genesis narrative recording that "God said" things were to be created, and it happened. God's spirit, therefore, is very much reflected in His word. Likewise our words express our inner thoughts and desires - the real 'us' - very accurately. Jesus wisely pointed out: "Out of the abundance of the heart (the mind) the mouth speaks" (Mt. 12:34). So if we would control our words, we must firstly work on our thoughts. God's Word, then, is a reflection of His spirit, or thoughts. It is such a blessing that in the Bible we have God's words written down so that we might understand God's spirit or mind. David spoke of how God's word and "own heart" are parallel (2 Sam. 7:21); God's mind/spirit is expressed in His Word. God achieved this miracle of expressing His spirit in written words by the process of *INSPIRATION*. This term is based around the word "spirit".

IN-SPIRIT-ATION

"Spirit" means "breath" or breathing, "Inspiration" means "in-breathing". This means that the words which men wrote while under "inspiration" from God were the words of God's spirit. Paul encouraged Timothy not to let his familiarity with the Bible lead him to forget the wonder of the fact that it is the words of God's spirit, and therefore provides all that we need in order to have a true knowledge of God.

"From a child you have known the holy Scriptures, which are able to make you wise unto salvation, through faith which is in Christ Jesus. All Scripture is given by inspiration of God, and is useful for doctrine, for reproof, for correction, for instruction in righteousness: that the man of God may be complete, thoroughly equipped unto all good works" (2 Tim. 3:15-17).

If the inspired Scriptures can provide such a totality of knowledge, then there is no need for some 'inner light' to show us the truth about God. But how many times do people speak of their personal feelings and experiences as being the source of their knowledge of God! If an acceptance in faith of God's inspired Word is enough to equip completely someone in the Christian life, there is no need for any other power of righteousness in our lives. If there is such a need, then God's Word has not completely equipped us, as Paul promises it will. To hold the Bible in our hands and believe that it really is the Word of God's spirit takes quite some faith. The Israelites were reasonably interested in what God's Word had to say, as are many today. We all need to carefully reflect on Heb. 4:2.

"Unto us was the gospel preached, as well as unto them (Israel in the wilderness): but the word preached did not profit them, not being mixed with faith in them that heard it".

This unwillingness to accept the huge spiritual power which is in God's word has led many to question whether all the Scriptures are fully inspired by God. They have suggested that much of what we read in the Bible was just the personal opinions of the writers. But Peter effectively disposes of such woolly reasoning:

"We have the word of the prophets made more certain, and you will do well to pay attention to it...above all, you must understand (this is vital!) that no prophecy of Scripture came about by the prophet's own interpretation. For prophecy never had its origin in the will of man, but men spoke from God as they were carried along by the Holy Spirit" (2 Pet. 1:19-21 N.I.V.).

We must "above all" believe that the Bible is inspired. The doctrine of inspiration is so often emphasised in the Bible text (e.g. Mt. 15:4; Mk. 12:36; Acts 1:16; 28:25; Heb. 3:7; 9:8; 10:15).

THE WRITERS OF THE BIBLE

A solid belief in the total inspiration of the Scriptures is therefore vital. The men who wrote the Bible were irresistibly carried along by the spirit which inspired them, so that their words were not their own. The Word of God being the truth (Jn. 17:17) and providing rebuke and correction (2 Tim. 3:16,17), it is not surprising that with many people it is unpopular - for truth hurts. The prophet Jeremiah suffered much opposition for speaking forth the words God inspired him with, and so he determined not to record or publicise the words which he was given. But because the writing of God's Word is a result of God's will rather than human desire, he was "carried along by the Holy Spirit" so that he had no choice in the matter. "I am in derision daily, every one mocks me...Then I said, I will not make mention of him, nor speak any more in his name. But his word was in my heart as a burning fire shut up in my bones, and I was weary with holding it back" (Jer. 20:7,9). Peter describes this idea of the Bible writers being 'carried along' with the same Greek word used in Acts 27:17,27 about a ship being 'driven' by the wind, out of control. Mic. 2:7 comments that truly inspired prophets can't be stopped from speaking forth God's word, because God's Spirit controlling them can't be constrained. Those men were truly 'carried along'.

Likewise when Balaam was determined to curse Israel, the spirit of God made him speak out a blessing on them instead (Num. 24:1-13 cf. Dt. 23:5). He could not 'escape from' God's word (Num. 22:12 Heb.). Jude says that he intended to write a letter about a totally different theme to the one he ended up writing about, because "I was constrained to write..." (Jude 3 RV)-by the Holy Spirit inspiring him.

A surprising number of the men whom God inspired to speak His word went through periods of reluctance to do so. The list is impressive.

- Moses (Ex. 4:10)
- Jeremiah (Jer. 1:6)
- Ezekiel (Ez. 3:14)
- Jonah (Jonah 1:2,3)
- Paul (Acts 18:9)
- Timothy (1 Tim. 4:6-14)
- Balaam (Num. 22-24)

This all confirms what we learnt in 2 Pet. 1:19-21 - that God's Word is not the personal opinion of men, but the result of men being inspired to write down what was revealed to them. The prophet Amos reflected: "The Lord God has spoken, who can but prophesy?" (Am. 3:8). At times Moses lost the sense of his own personality, so strong was his inspiration by God: "All these commandments, which the Lord has spoken unto Moses.." (Num. 15:22,23); these words were actually said by Moses (v. 17). Jeremiah spoke "from the mouth of the Lord" and yet the Lord spoke "by the mouth of Jeremiah" (2 Chron. 36:12,22) - this is how close was the relationship between God and the men He spoke through. Their mouth was His mouth. There are many times in the writings of the prophets where it is hard to determine whether the personal pronouns refer to God or the prophet (e.g. Jer. 17:13-15) - so close was the manifestation of God through them. "The beginning of the word of the Lord by Hosea" (Hos. 1:2) prefaces His command to tell Hosea to go and show God's love towards faithless Israel by marrying and living with a worthless woman. Hosea was God's Word to men, as supremely the Lord Jesus was "the word made flesh", and we likewise must put into practice the spirit which is in God's word.

Another strand of evidence for this is that the writers of the Bible realised that they did not fully understand the things which they wrote. They "searched" for the correct interpretation - "unto whom it was revealed, that not unto themselves, but unto us they did minister the things" which they wrote (1 Pet. 1:9-12). The actual words they recorded were not their own but God's and they wished to understand better the things they recorded for Him. The following provide obvious examples: Daniel (Dan. 12:8-10); Zechariah (Zech. 4:4-13); Peter (Acts 10:17). The child Samuel likewise didn't know Yahweh but still spoke His word (1 Sam. 3:7).

If these men were only partly inspired, we do not have access to the true Word of God. If what they wrote really was the Word of God, then it follows that they had to be completely taken over by God's spirit during the period of inspiration - otherwise the product would not have been God's Word in purity. An acceptance that God's Word is completely His, provides us with more motivation to read and obey it. "Your word is very pure: therefore your servant loves it" (Ps. 119:140).

The inspired writer of Psalm 45 says that his tongue is like the pen of a writer (Ps. 45:1). The writer is God. God was using the inspired person's words as His pen, with which to communicate to men. Ezra likewise saw himself as a "scribe of the law of the God of heaven" (Ezra 7:21). The God who is in Heaven wrote through a scribe here on earth. That's the idea of inspiration.

Thus the books of the Bible are the work of God through His spirit, rather than the literature of men. The truth of this is shown by considering how the New Testament refers to the Old Testament writings.

- Mt. 2:5 (R.V. mg.) speaks of how it was "written through the prophets" - God was writing through them. The R.V. margin always uses the word "through" when describing how God wrote by the prophets.
- Mt. 2:15 quotes from Micah, but says: "[that] which was spoken of the Lord by the prophet...". Likewise Heb. 2:6: "one [actually David] in a certain place testified...". The prophet is almost irrelevant compared to the fact that it is God's word which He spoke. There are other examples of where the name of the prophet is suppressed as if to show it is not so relevant (Mt. 1:22; 2:23; 21:4).
- "The Holy Spirit by the mouth of David spoke..." (Acts 1:16). This is how Peter quoted from the Psalms (cf. Heb. 3:7).

- "Well did the Holy Spirit speak by Isaiah" (Acts 28:25 - this was how Paul quoted Isaiah). Lk. 3:4 speaks of "the book of *the words of* Isaiah" rather than just, 'the book of Isaiah'.
- God "by the Holy Spirit, by the mouth of our father David...said..." (Acts 4:25 RV).

The human authors of the Bible were therefore relatively unimportant to the early Christians; it was the fact that their words had been inspired with the spirit of God which was important. We will conclude this section with a list of verses which show that God's spirit is revealed to us through His written word.

- Jesus plainly stated, "The words that I speak...are spirit" (Jn. 6:63); He spoke under inspiration from God (Jn. 17:8; 14:10). "It is the Spirit that gives life...the words that I speak unto you, they are spirit" (Jn. 6:63) must be connected with Rom. 8:11, which speaks of the Spirit which dwells within us quickening the believer. It is the word of Jesus within us which is the root of the Spirit that quickens.
- We are described as being re-born by both the spirit (Jn. 3:3-5) and the word of God (1 Pet. 1:23).
- "The words which the Lord of hosts has sent in his spirit by the...prophets" (Zech. 7:12).
- "I will pour out my spirit unto you, I will make known my words unto you" (Prov. 1:23) associates a true understanding of God's word with the action of His spirit upon us - reading the Book without understanding is of no avail, seeing that the spirit/mind of God is not being revealed to us.
- There are parallels between God's spirit and His word in many passages: "My spirit that is upon you, and my words which I have put in your mouth..." (Isa. 59:21); "For your word's sake, and according to your own heart (spirit)" (2 Sam. 7:21); "I will put my spirit within you (your heart - see context)..."; "I will put my law... in their hearts" (Ez. 36:27; Jer. 31:33).

There are clear parallels between Col. 3:16 and Gal. 5:18,19: "Let the **word of Christ** dwell in you richly in all wisdom; teaching and admonishing one another in psalms and hymns and spiritual songs, singing with grace in your hearts to the Lord... but be **filled with the Spirit**; Speaking to yourselves in psalms and hymns and spiritual songs, singing and making melody in your heart to the Lord; Giving thanks always for all things unto God and the Father in the name of our Lord Jesus Christ". Clearly the <u>Word of Christ</u> is equated with being "<u>filled with the Spirit</u>".

God is His spirit (Jn. 4:24), and God is His Word ("the word was God"); it evidently follows that His words therefore reflect His spirit. Our attitude to God's Word is our attitude to Him. Because that word is pure, therefore we love it (Ps. 119:140); when we break commandments, we are despising God's Word (Am. 2:4). This is where belief in inspiration has a powerful practical effect.

THE POWER OF GOD'S WORD

As God's spirit refers not only to His mind/disposition but also to the power by which He expresses those thoughts, it is to be expected that His spirit-word is not just a statement of His mind; there is also a dynamic power in that word.

A true appreciation of that power should make us eager to make use of it; any feelings of embarrassment associated with doing so should be overcome by our knowledge that obedience to God's word will give us the power which we need to accelerate out of the small things of this life, towards salvation. Out of much experience of this, Paul wrote:-

"I am not ashamed of the Gospel (the word) of Christ: for it is the power of God unto salvation" (Rom. 1:16).

Lk. 1:37 (R.V.) harps on the same theme: "No word of God shall be void of power (spirit)".

Bible study and applying it to our lives is therefore a dynamic process. It is quite unrelated to any spirit of cold, academic theology; and also to a 'feel-good Christianity', whereby a few passages are briefly quoted, but no effort made to understand or apply them. "The word of God is quick (living) and powerful"; "the word of His (God's) power" (Heb. 4:12; 1:3). "The word of God... dynamically works also in you that believe" (1 Thess. 2:13). Through the Word, God is actively at work in the minds of true believers, every hour of the day.

The Gospel which you are learning is therefore the true power of God; if you allow it to do so, it can work in your life to change you into a child of God, showing the spirit/mind of God to some degree in this life, preparing you for the change to God's spiritual nature which will come at Christ's return (2 Pet. 1:4). Paul's preaching was "in demonstration of the spirit and of power" (1 Cor. 2:4).

Our approach is mocked by the world ("You don't believe it like that, do you?!"), and so was that of Paul and his band of preachers: "The preaching of the cross is to them that perish foolishness; but unto us which are saved, it is the power of God" (1 Cor. 1:18).

Bearing all this in mind, can't we each hold the Bible in our hands with an ever greater measure of respect, and read it with ever more eagerness to understand and obey?

THE ATTITUDE OF GOD'S PEOPLE TO HIS WORD

A sensitive reading of the Biblical record indicates that the Bible writers not only recognised that they were inspired, but they also treated other Bible writers as inspired. The Lord Jesus is pre-eminent in this. When Jesus quoted from the Psalms of David, he prefaced this with the words, "David in spirit..." (Mt. 22:43), showing his recognition of the fact that David's words were inspired. Jesus also spoke of Moses' "writings" (Jn. 5:45-47), showing that he believed Moses to have literally written the Pentateuch. Some Bible critics have doubted whether Moses could write, but the attitude of Christ clearly contradicts their approach. He called Moses' writings "the commandment of God" (Mk. 7:8,9). It is also claimed that much of the Old Testament is myth, but Jesus and Paul never treat them as such. Jesus spoke of the Queen of Sheba as an accepted historical fact (Mt. 12:42); he did not say, 'As the story goes about the Queen of Sheba...'.

The attitude of the Apostles was identical to that of their Lord. It is epitomised by Peter who said that his personal experience of hearing Christ's words with his own ears was eclipsed by the "more sure word of prophecy" (2 Pet. 1:19-21). Peter believed that Paul's letters were "Scripture" as much as the "other Scriptures", a phrase normally used about the Old Testament writings. Thus Peter saw Paul's letters as being as authoritative as the Old Testament.

There are many allusions in Acts, the Epistles and Revelation to the Gospels (e.g. cf. Acts 13:51; Mt. 10:14), indicating not only that they were all inspired by the same spirit, but that the Gospel records were treated as inspired by the New Testament writers. Paul in 1 Tim. 5:18 quotes both Dt. 25:4 (in the Old Testament) and Lk. 10:7 as "Scripture". Paul hammers home the point that his message was from Christ, not himself (Gal. 1:11,12; 1 Cor. 2:13; 11:23; 15:3). This was recognised by the other apostles; thus James 4:5 quotes Paul's words of Gal. 5:17 as "Scripture".

God "has spoken" to us in Christ; there is therefore no need for any further revelation (Heb. 1:2). It can be observed that the Bible alludes to other writings which are now not available (e.g. the book of Jasher, the writings of Nathan, Elijah, Paul to Corinth), and John's third Epistle implies that John had written an unpreserved letter to the church which Diotrephes had refused to obey. Why have these writings not been preserved for us? Evidently because they were not relevant to us. We can therefore rest assured that God has preserved all that is relevant for us.

It is sometimes claimed that the New Testament books were gradually accepted as being inspired, but the fact that the Apostles treated each other's writings as inspired surely disproves this. There was a miraculous spirit gift available to test whether letters and words which claimed to be inspired really were so (1 Cor. 14:37; 1 Jn. 4:1; Rev. 2:2). This means that the inspired letters were immediately accepted as inspired. If there was any unguided human selection of what went into our Bible, then the book would have no authority.

2.3   Gifts Of The Holy Spirit

At various times in His dealings with men, God conferred the use of His power ("Holy Spirit") on men. However, this was never in the form of a "blank cheque", as it were, enabling them to do what they wished; always the use of this Holy Spirit was for a specific purpose. When it was accomplished, the gift of the Holy Spirit was withdrawn. We must remember that God's spirit acts in a way which fulfils the purpose which is in His mind. This purpose may allow short-term suffering in the lives of men in order to bring about His long-term purpose (see Study 6.1), so it is to be expected that His Holy Spirit would not necessarily be used to alleviate human suffering in this life. Any such relief it does achieve will be for the higher purpose of expressing God's mind to us.

This is in marked contrast to some attitudes to the Holy Spirit today; the impression is given that belief in Christ is worth it because of the immediate material benefit, e.g. healing from illness or the acquisition of money. This would explain why in poorer countries like Uganda there has been a marked outbreak of people claiming to possess spirit gifts of healing and, historically, such claims have often coincided with times of great human need. This in itself places present claims of spirit possession under some suspicion; if someone is looking for experience which transcends the present human plight, it is easy to claim to have found something which fills the bill.

God has always given His spirit to achieve specific, defined objectives. Because of this, those who truly possessed the gifts of the spirit knew exactly what they were to use them for, and therefore did not achieve only partial success in their use of them. This contrasts with the many failures and partial cures experienced by those who claim to have spirit gifts of healing today.

The following examples all indicate specific reasons and objectives being behind the granting of spirit gifts. In none of these cases was there any subjective element associated with possessing the gifts, nor were the possessors of the gifts able to use them just as they saw fit. Because we are talking of God's spirit, it is inconceivable that men could direct the use of it, seeing that it was given to them in order to perform certain specific desires of

God, rather than those of the men who had the temporary use of it (cf. Is. 40:13).

- Early in Israel's history, they were commanded to make an elaborate tent ("tabernacle") in which the altar and other holy items could be kept; detailed instructions were given concerning how to make all the items which would be necessary for the worship of God. To accomplish this, God gave His spirit to certain men. They were, "filled with the spirit of wisdom, *that* they may make Aaron's garments..." etc. (Ex. 28:3).

- One of these men, Bezaleel, was "filled with the spirit of God, in wisdom, and in understanding, and in knowledge, and in all manner of workmanship, *to*...work in gold and...in cutting of stones...in all manner of workmanship" (Ex. 31: 3-5).

- Num. 11:14-17 records how some of the spirit/power delegated to Moses was taken from him and given to the elders of Israel, for the purpose of enabling them to correctly judge the people's grievances so that there was less pressure on Moses. Just before Moses' death, the spirit gift was transferred from him to Joshua so that he, too, could properly lead God's people (Dt. 34:9).

- From the time that the people of Israel entered their land until their first king (Saul) they were governed by men called judges. During this period they were often oppressed by their enemies, but the book of Judges records how the spirit of God came upon some of the judges in order to deliver Israel miraculously from their invaders - Othniel (Jud. 3:10), Gideon (Jud. 6:34) and Jephthah (Jud. 11:29) exemplify this.

- Another judge, Samson, was given the spirit in order to kill a lion (Jud. 14:5,6); to kill 30 men (Jud. 14:19) and to break apart cords with which he had been tied up (Jud. 15: 14). Such "Holy Spirit" was therefore not possessed by Samson continually - it came upon him to achieve specific things and was then withdrawn.

- When God had a special message for His people, the spirit would inspire someone to speak out God's word. When the message was ended, the spirit gift of speaking directly on God's behalf was withdrawn, and that person's words would again be his own personal ones, rather than those of God. Of many examples:-
  o "The spirit of God came upon Zechariah...and said unto them (the people), Thus says God, Why do you transgress the commandments of the Lord...?" (2 Chron. 24:20)
  o See 2 Chron. 15:1,2 and Lk. 4:18,19 for other examples.

From this it should be evident that receiving the gift of the use of God's spirit for a particular purpose was not:
- A guarantee of ultimate salvation
- Something which endured all a person's life

It has to be said that there is much hazy reasoning about gifts of the Holy Spirit. People claim to have 'received the Holy Spirit', and in many a Gospel Hall the preacher dangles the carrot of 'receiving spirit gifts', wealth and health before those considering 'accepting Jesus'. But the question must be pressed, Which gifts? It is inconceivable that men do not know exactly which gift they possess. Samson was given a spirit gift to kill a lion (Jud. 14:5,6); as he faced the roaring animal he would have known exactly what the spirit had been given him for. There could have been no doubt in his mind. This stands in stark contrast to those today who claim to have received the Holy Spirit, but cannot perform any specific act; nor do they know which gift(s) they are supposed to have.

There is surely no alternative but to conclude that such people have had a dramatic emotional experience connected with Christianity, and the subsequent U-turn in their attitude to life has left them with a strange feeling of newness within themselves. Being aware of this, they have seized on the Bible passages concerning Holy Spirit gifts, and concluded, 'This must be what I'm experiencing!'.

As we struggle against the deceptiveness of our own feelings (Jer. 17:9), we must keep our feet on the solid rock of Bible principles. In nothing is this need more apparent than in a study of how God's spirit works. We all like to think that God's power is working with us in our lives. But how and why is He doing so? Do we really possess the spirit gifts as men did in the Bible record? If we wish to truly know God and have a living relationship with Him, we will recognise the urgency of properly understanding these things.

Having the Holy Spirit gifts was no guarantee of salvation. It is grace that saves, not Spirit gifts (Eph. 2:8). Men like Saul, Balaam (Num. 23:5,16), Judas (Mt. 10:1) and those of Mt. 7:21-23 all had the gifts; and yet they will not be saved. It's a scary thought- that God can use us to do His will, even empower us to do His work; and yet this of itself is irrelevant to our personal salvation.

REASONS FOR THE GIFTS IN THE FIRST CENTURY

Remembering the basic principles which we have already learnt about the gifts of God's spirit, we now come to the New Testament record of the spirit gifts which were possessed in the early church (i.e. the groups of believers who lived in the generation after the time of Jesus).

The Lord's last command was for the apostles to go throughout the world preaching the Gospel (Mk. 16:15,16). This they did, with the theme of Christ's death and resurrection foremost in their message. But remember that then there was no New Testament as we know it. As they stood in market places and synagogues speaking about this man Jesus of Nazareth, their story could have sounded bizarre - a carpenter from Israel who was perfect, who died and was then resurrected in accurate fulfilment of Old Testament prophecy, and who was now asking them to be baptised and follow His example.

In those days, other men were also trying to develop cult followings. There had to be some way of proving to the world that the message preached by the Christians was from God Himself, rather than being the philosophy of a band of fishermen from Northern Israel.

In our day we appeal to the New Testament records of the work and doctrine of Jesus in order to prove that our message is from God; but in those days, before it was written down and available, God allowed His preachers the use of His Holy Spirit in order to underline the truth of what they were saying. This was the specific reason for the use of the gifts in the sight of the world; the absence of the written New Testament would have also made it difficult for the new groups of believers to grow in their faith. The numerous practical problems which arose amongst them would have had no clear solution; there would have been little means of guidance for them to grow in their faith in Christ. So for these reasons the gifts of the Holy Spirit were made available for the guidance of the early believers through inspired messages, until the New Testament record of these messages and the teaching of Jesus was written and circulated. As ever, these reasons for the granting of the Holy Spirit were made abundantly plain.

- "When he (Jesus) ascended up on high (to heaven), he...gave (spirit) gifts unto men...for the perfecting of the saints, for the work of the (preaching) ministry, for the edifying of the body of Christ", i.e. the believers (Eph. 4:8,12).
- So Paul wrote to the believers at Rome, "I long to see you, that I may impart unto you some spiritual gift, to the end you may be established" (Rom. 1:11).
- Concerning the use of the gifts to confirm the preaching of the Gospel, we read:-
- "Our Gospel came not unto you in word only, but also in power, and in the Holy Spirit, and in much assurance" through the miracles wrought (1 Thess. 1:5 cf. 1 Cor. 1:5,6).
- Paul could speak of "those things which Christ has worked by me, to make the Gentiles obedient by word and (miraculous) deed, through mighty signs and wonders, by the power of the spirit of God" (Rom. 15:18,19).
- Concerning the preachers of the Gospel, we read, "God also bearing them witness, both with signs and wonders, and with various miracles...gifts of the Holy Spirit" (Heb. 2:4).

- A Gospel preaching campaign in Cyprus was backed up by miracles, so that "the deputy (governor), when he saw what was done, believed, being astonished at the doctrine" (Acts 13:12).

Thus the miracles led him to really respect the doctrines being taught. At Iconium also, "the Lord...gave testimony unto the word of his grace, and granted signs and wonders to be done" (Acts 14:3).

All this is summarised by the comment on the apostles' obedience to the command to preach: "They went forth, and preached every where, the Lord working with them, and confirming the word with signs following" (Mk. 16:20).

SPECIFIC THINGS AT SPECIFIC TIMES

These gifts of the spirit were therefore given in order to perform specific things at specific times. This shows the error of claiming that the miraculous possession of the gift is a permanent experience throughout a person's life. The apostles, including Peter, were "filled with the Holy Spirit" at the feast of Pentecost, soon after Jesus' ascension (Acts 2:4). They were therefore able to speak in foreign languages in order to launch the preaching of the Gospel in a spectacular way. When the authorities tried to clamp down on them, "Peter, filled with the Holy Spirit" was thereby able to convincingly answer them (Acts 4:8). On their release from prison they were enabled by the gifts to go on preaching - "they were all filled with the Holy Spirit, and they spake the word of God with boldness" (Acts 4:31).

The watchful reader will spot that it does not say that "they, being already full of the spirit", did those things. They were filled with spirit to perform certain things, but had to be re-filled to achieve the next objective in God's plan. Paul likewise was "filled with the Holy Spirit" at his baptism (Acts 9:17), but years later he was to again be "filled with the Holy Spirit" in order to punish a wicked man with blindness (Acts 13:9).

In speaking of the miraculous gifts, Paul wrote that the early believers possessed them "according to the measure of the gift of Christ" (Eph. 4:7). The Greek word for "measure" means "a limited portion or degree" (Strong's Concordance). Only Jesus had the gifts without measure, i.e. with total freedom to use them as He wished (Jn. 3:34).

We will now consider those spirit gifts which seem to have most mention as being possessed in the first century.

THE FIRST CENTURY SPIRIT GIFTS

- Prophecy

The Greek word for 'prophet' means someone who forth-tells God's Word - i.e. any person inspired to speak God's words, which at times included foretelling of future events (see 2 Pet. 1:19-21). Thus "prophets" - those with the gift of prophecy - came "from Jerusalem unto Antioch. And there stood up one of them named Agabus, and signified by the spirit that there should be a great famine throughout all the world: which came to pass in the days of Claudius Caesar. Then the disciples, every man according to his ability, determined to send relief unto the brethren" (Acts 11:27-29). This kind of highly specific prophecy, which had a clear fulfilment within a few years, is quite lacking amongst those who now claim to possess the gift of prophecy; indeed, so sure were the early church that this gift really was possessed amongst them, that they gave their time and money to relieving the hardship which had been prophesied. Few examples of this kind of thing can be found amongst those who claim the gift of prophecy today. Indeed, if the gift of prophecy is possessed, we ought to be able to write down the words 'prophesied' and treat them with the same respect as we do the Bible.

- Healing

Seeing that the apostles were preaching the good news (Gospel) of God's coming Kingdom of perfection on the earth, it was fitting that they should confirm their message by doing miracles which gave a foretaste of what that time would be like, when "the eyes of the blind shall be opened, and the ears of the deaf shall be unstopped. Then shall the lame man leap..." (Is. 35:5,6). For more about conditions in God's Kingdom, see Study 5. When God's Kingdom is established on earth, such promises as these will not be fulfilled in half measure, nor will there be ambiguity over whether the Kingdom is here or not. Therefore God's miraculous confirmation of the message of that Kingdom was in a conclusive, definite form which could not be denied; for this reason many of the miraculous healings performed by the early believers were in the sight of the general public.

A classic example is found in Peter's healing of the lame beggar who was laid each morning at the temple gate. Acts 3:2 mentions that they laid him there daily - so he would have been a familiar sight. Having been healed by Peter's use of the spirit gift, "he leaping up stood, and walked, and entered with them into the temple, walking and leaping...And all the people saw him walking and praising God: and they knew that it was he which sat for alms at the Beautiful gate of the temple: and they were filled with wonder and amazement at that which had happened unto him. And as the lame man which was healed held Peter...all the people ran together unto them in the porch...greatly wondering" (Acts 3:7-11).

Peter then immediately launched into an open-air talk about the resurrection of Christ. Having the unquestionable, irrefutable evidence before them in the form of that healed beggar, we can be sure that they would have taken Peter's words to be those of God. The temple gate at "the hour of prayer" (Acts 3:1) would have been thronged with people, like a shopping mall on a Saturday morning. It was in a place like this that God chose to confirm the preaching of His word by such a clear miracle. Likewise in Acts 5:12 we read that "by the hands of the apostles were many signs and wonders wrought among the people". The usual claims made by 'faith healers' today seem to revolve around things which have happened in some back-street hall rather than on the streets, and in the audience of 'believers' hyped up into a spirit of expectancy for a 'miracle' to occur, rather than before the hard-hearted general public.

Let it be said that the present writer has had considerable experience of discussing these issues with present claimants of spirit possession, and also of witnessing many claims of spirit possession. Yet my 'personal testimony' of seeing many inconclusive 'healings', and at best partial cures, need not be specifically elaborated; any honest member of these churches will admit that a lot of this goes on. On many occasions I have put it to my well-meaning Christian friends of this persuasion: "I'm not unwilling to believe that you might have these great powers. But God has always clearly shown who has His power and who hasn't; so it isn't unreasonable for me to ask you to demonstrate the fact to me - and then I might be more inclined to accept your doctrinal position, which at present I just can't reconcile with Scripture". Never has a clear "demonstration of the spirit and of power" been given me.

By contrast to my attitude, the orthodox Jews of the first century had closed minds to the possibility that Christians possessed God's miraculous spirit gifts. Yet even they had to admit, "This man does many miracles" (Jn. 11:47) and, "For that indeed a notable miracle has been done...is obvious to all them that dwell in Jerusalem; and we cannot deny it" (Acts 4:16). Likewise those who heard the Apostles speaking in tongues were "confounded" (Acts 2:6). The crowds who saw Christ's miracles commented: "We never saw it like this" (Mk. 2:12), as if they had seen plenty of pseudo-miracles of the kind claimed today, but those of the Lord Jesus were in an evidently different category. The same awed response from the unbelieving general public does not occur today in response to those claiming to speak with tongues. If just one miracle hit the headlines throughout Jerusalem, is it not reasonable to suggest that if a true miracle were done in London's Trafalgar Square or Nairobi's Nyaharuru Park or Moscow's Red Square, there would then be world-wide recognition that God's miraculous spirit gifts are possessed today? Instead, Christians of this persuasion expect the world to seize upon the following sorts of 'evidence' as reasons for their faith in this.

- Being cured (eventually) of stomach ulcers; the process of curing is supposed to have begun after a prayer meeting.
- Deformed limbs growing straight.
- Sight or hearing being improved, although frequently returning to its previous state.
- Depression being lifted.

To these examples must be added the fact that ambulances brought hospital patients to the T.O. Osborn healing crusades in Nairobi, Kenya; the drivers, faced with the ethical dilemma of whether to stay or return, remained - and just as well, for the sufferers received no cure.

Yet the challenge calls out from many publicity posters for such meetings: "Come expecting a miracle!" Psychologically the stage is set for all manner of autosuggestion and the like. Nowhere in the New Testament is there the slightest hint that such a massive psychological softening-up was needed before a miracle occurred. It is evident that some of those healed in the first century did not have faith - one did not know who Jesus was (Jn. 5:13; 9:36; Lk. 13:10-17; 7:11-17; 22:50; Mt. 8:14; Mk. 1:32; 5:1-20).

A similar bombardment of the psyche is achieved by the mind warping of repetitive prayers, the rhythm of drums and rousing music. There can be no doubt that any rational awareness of God - and anything else - is blanked out by all this. The writer can recall attending several such meetings in various places, and each time experiencing a cracking headache from the struggle to retain a rational, balanced, Biblical awareness in the face of the temptation to get lost in the rhythm of drums and hand-clapping. That all of this appears to be the necessary prelude for a 'miracle' is proof enough that the 'healings' are a result of emotional and psychological conditioning, rather than the direct operation of God's spirit. By contrast, Peter was able to use the true gift of miracles to heal people as they lay in the streets (Acts 5:15); Paul's use of the miraculous gifts was personally witnessed by an unbelieving Government minister (Acts 13:12,13), as well as by many of the pagans living in the city of Lystra (Acts 14:8-13). As was required by the very purpose and nature of the spirit gifts, these things were done publicly, and could in no way be shrugged off with any other explanation than to admit that here was God's power being openly displayed by His servants.

The effect of one of Christ's healing miracles was similar: "They were all amazed (those who saw it), and glorified God, saying, We never saw anything like this" (Mk. 2:12).

- Tongues

The apostles, rough fishermen that some of them were, received the great commission to go out into all the world, preaching the Gospel (Mk. 16:15,16). Perhaps their very first reaction was, "But I don't know the languages!" For them it wasn't even a case of, "I was no good at languages at school", for they had had no schooling. It was written all over them "that they were uneducated and ignorant men" (Acts 4:13) when it came to that kind of thing. And even for the more educated preachers (e.g. Paul), the language barrier was still formidable. When converts were made, the reliance which they would need to have on each other for edification (in the absence of the written New Testament) meant that not understanding each other's language was a sizeable problem.

To overcome this, the gift of speaking in foreign languages ("tongues") and being able to understand them, was granted. The N.I.V margin renders "tongues" as "languages". Obviously there is stark opposition between this view of "tongues" and that of many 'born again' Christians, who describe their ecstatic utterances of unintelligible sounds as ''tongues'. This confusion can be cleared up by showing that the Biblical definition of "tongues" is "foreign languages".

On the Jewish feast of Pentecost, soon after Christ's ascension to heaven, the apostles "were all filled with the Holy Spirit, and began to speak with other tongues...The crowds came together (again, a public display of the gifts!) and were confounded, because that every man heard them speak in his own language. And they were all amazed and marvelled, saying one to another, Behold, are not all these which speak Galilaeans? And how hear we every man in our own tongue (the same Greek word translated 'languages') wherein we were born? Parthians and Medes...we hear them speak in our tongues...And they were all amazed" (Acts 2:4-12). It is unlikely that the double emphasis on the people's amazement and their marvelling would have been necessary if they had heard only the mumbo-jumbo spoken by those who claim to have the gift today; that gives rise to petty sarcasm or indifference, rather than the amazement and conviction from understanding the words being spoken, which was experienced in Acts 2.

Apart from the clear parallel between "tongues" and "languages" in Acts 2:4-11, "tongues" is very evidently used to mean "languages" in other parts of the New Testament; the phrase "peoples, and nations, and tongues" is used five times in Revelation to speak of all the peoples of planet earth (Rev. 7:9; 10:11; 11:9; 13:7; 17:15). The Greek word for "tongues" occurs in the Greek version of the Old Testament (called the 'Septuagint') in the sense of languages (see Gen. 10:5; Dt. 28:49; Dan. 1:4).

1 Cor. 14 is a list of commands concerning the use of the gift of tongues; v. 21 quotes Is. 28:11 concerning how this gift would be used to witness against the Jews: "In the law it is written, With men of other tongues and other lips will I speak unto this people...". Is. 28:11 primarily refers to Israel's invaders speaking to the Jews in languages ("tongues") they would not have known. The parallel between "tongues" and "lips" indicates that "tongues" were foreign languages. There are many other indications in 1 Cor. 14 that "tongues" refers to foreign languages. This chapter is Paul's inspired criticism of the abuses of the gifts which were taking place in the early church, and as such it gives many insights into the nature of the gifts of tongues and prophecy. We will now attempt a brief commentary upon it. Verse 37 is a key verse.

"If any man thinks himself to be a prophet, or spiritually gifted, let him acknowledge that the things that I write unto you are the commandments of the Lord."

If anyone claims to be spiritually gifted, he must therefore accept that the preceding commands about the use of the gifts are inspired by God. Any who today disobey those commands are therefore openly admitting that they see fit to despise God's inspired words.

Verses 11-17:-

"Therefore if I know not the meaning of the voice, I shall be unto him that speaks like a barbarian, and he that speaks shall be like a barbarian unto me.

Even so you, as much as you are zealous of spiritual gifts, seek that you may excel to the edifying of the church.

Let him that speaks in an unknown tongue pray that he may interpret.

For if I pray in an unknown tongue, my spirit prays, but my understanding is unfruitful.

What is it then? I will pray with the spirit, and I will pray with the understanding also: I will sing with the spirit, and I will sing with the understanding also.

Else when you shall bless with the spirit, how shall he that is unlearned say Amen at your giving of thanks, seeing he understands not what you say?

For you truly give thanks well, but the other is not edified."

To speak in a language which those present at the service do not understand is therefore pointless. The use of unintelligible speaking is ruled out - for how can a truthful "Amen" be said at the end of a "prayer" composed of gibberish which cannot be understood? Remember that "Amen" means "So be it', i.e. 'I totally agree with what has been said in this prayer'. Speaking in language which is not understood by your brethren does not edify them, Paul says.

I remember meeting a very sincere Christian woman outside a major revival meeting. She sought to persuade me that my position on various issues was "devil-led" - by talking at me in "tongues" for 10 minutes. In no way could I be "edified" by that; surely this is exactly what Paul is commanding not to do.

Verse 18:-

"I thank my God, I speak with tongues more than you all."

Because of his wide travels in the preaching of Christ, Paul needed the gift of languages ("tongues") more than most.

Verse 19:-

"Yet in the church I had rather speak five words with my understanding, that by my voice I might teach others also, than ten thousand words in an unknown tongue."

This is quite plain. A brief sentence about Christ in English will do me more good than hours of preaching to me in a foreign language - or unintelligible speech.

Verse 22:-

"Wherefore tongues are for a sign, not to them that believe, but to them that believe not: but prophesying serves not for unbelievers, but for them which believe."

The use of tongues was therefore mainly to be used for outgoing preaching of the Gospel. Yet today most claims of 'tongues' possession occur among groups of believers or (apparently) in their individual, personal experience, while alone. There is a chronic dearth of examples of such people being able to speak miraculously in foreign languages in order to spread the Gospel. In the early 1990's the door of opportunity opened to preach Christ in Eastern Europe, but the 'evangelical' churches had to distribute their literature in English because of the language barriers! Surely the gift of tongues should have been used if it were possessed? And the great mass evangelist Reinhardt Bonke, whilst claiming phenomenal possession of the spirit, still had to speak to the crowds in Kampala, Uganda, through a translator.

Verse 23:-

"If therefore the whole church be come together into one place, and all speak with tongues, and there come in those that are ignorant, or unbelievers, will they not say that you are mad?"

This is exactly what has happened. In my experience, Muslims and pagans alike have mocked the bizarre behaviour of those claiming the gift of tongues throughout West Africa.

Verse 27:-

"If any man speak in an unknown tongue, let it be by two, or at the most by three, and that in order; and let one interpret."

Only two or three people were needed to speak in tongues during any service. It is unlikely that there would be more than three different languages spoken by any audience. A service would soon lose all coherence if each sentence of the speaker had to be translated more than twice. If the gift of tongues were possessed at a meeting in Central London, attended by English people, with some French and German tourists present, the speakers might begin:-

Pastor: *Good evening.*

First-tongue speaker: *Bon soir* (French)

Second-tongue speaker: *Guten abend* (German).

But naturally they must speak "in order", one after another. Confusion would result from them speaking simultaneously; yet, because of the fundamentally emotional nature of present 'speaking in tongues', the phenomena does occur from the mouths of many people simultaneously. I have observed that once one person starts, others are quickly influenced to do likewise. It would seem that the ecclesia in Corinth had some who were doing just what some Christians do today - they induced themselves to ecstatic behaviour. And Paul is roundly criticising this.

The gift of tongues would often have been used in conjunction with that of prophecy, so that an inspired message from God could be spoken forth (by the prophecy gift) in a language foreign to the speaker (by the gift of tongues). An example of such use of the two gifts can be found in Acts 19:6.

However, if at a meeting in London attended by English people and many French visitors, the speaker spoke in French, the English people present would "not be edified". Therefore the gift of interpreting tongues (or languages) would have to be present, so that everyone could understand - in our example, to translate from French to English. Likewise if a question were asked by one of the French speakers, the speaker would not be able to understand him unaided, even though he had the gift of speaking in French without personally knowing it. The gift of interpretation would therefore be present to help in this.

Without the presence of one with the gift of interpretation when it was needed, the tongue gift would not be used: "...let one interpret. But if there be no interpreter, let him keep silence in the church" (1 Cor. 14:27,28). The fact that many modern claimants of 'tongues' speak in 'language' which cannot be understood by anyone, and without an interpreter, is surely a case of flat disobedience to these commands.

Verses 32,33:-

"And the spirits of the prophets are subject to the prophets. For God is not the author of confusion, but of peace, as in all churches of the saints."

Possession of Holy Spirit gifts is not therefore to be associated with an experience which takes a person out of the realms of normal consciousness; the spirit is subject to the control of the user, rather than a force which takes them over so that they act involuntarily. It is often wrongly claimed that demons or 'evil spirits' possess the 'unsaved' (see Study 6.3), but that the Holy Spirit fills the believers. But the spirit power referred to in 1 Cor. 14:32 was subject to the possessor's control for specific ends; it was not an animating force of good in contrast to the force of evil which is in human nature. Besides, we have shown earlier that these powers of the Holy Spirit came on the apostles at certain times to perform specific things, rather than being present with them permanently.

The plea for possessors of the gifts to use them in a way befitting God's love of peace and hate of disorder (v. 33), seems to fall on deaf ears in parts of the Christian church today.

Verse 34:-

"Let your women keep silence in the churches: for it is not permitted unto them to speak; but they are commanded to be under obedience, as also says the law."

In this context of using the spirit gifts, it is undeniably laid down that a woman should not use them during a church service. The wholesale disregard for this is to be expected if the present phenomena of speaking in unintelligible language is explicable in terms of emotional excitation, passing from one person to another in an audience. Woman, children - indeed anyone present with a willing mind - can be affected by such stimulus, and therefore make the ecstatic utterances, which are passed off as 'tongues'.

The prominence of women in alleged 'tongue speaking' and 'prophecy' in modern churches just cannot be reconciled with the clear command of this verse. The desperate argument that Paul was a woman-hater is quashed a few verses later: "If any man think himself to be a prophet, or spiritually gifted, let him acknowledge that the things that I write unto you are the commandments of the Lord" (1 Cor. 14:37) - not Paul personally.

Any believer in an inspired Bible must therefore accept that these commands of 1 Cor. 14 must be taken seriously; to flout them openly can only indicate a lack of belief in the full inspiration of Scripture - or a self-declaration that one is not spiritually gifted, seeing that someone who lacks the gifts will deny that the commands of 1 Cor. 14 are the Lord's commands for us. The logic of this argument is telling, indeed devastating.

As a footnote to this section, it is highly significant that those sects which claim to speak in tongues have been scientifically proven to have higher levels of depression compared to people from other backgrounds. Keith Meador, Professor of Psychiatry at Vanderbilt University, U.S.A., undertook a major study analysing the relationship between depression and religious background. He found that "the rate of serious depression ...among Pentecostal Christians was 5.4% compared to 1.7% for the entire survey group". The results of his work are written up in the journal 'Hospital and Community Psychiatry', Dec., 1992.

An interesting article, reaching the same conclusion, appeared in the International Herald Tribune, Feb. 11, 1993; the title speaks for itself: "Pentecostals top charts when it comes to the blues". Why is this? Surely it must be related to the fact that the 'experience' of spirit-possession, which Pentecostals (and others) claim, is no more than a painful psychological illusion. It would seem that the Pentecostal movement cannot accept that faith is believing in what cannot be seen. They want to have God once again speaking to man directly, guaranteeing health, being visible on earth. But such a view of Him can only lead to disappointment with God [just consider the millions of sick and needy Christians alive at this moment]. Faith comes from hearing God's word and living it out in all the difficulty of a relationship with an invisible God, and a Lord and Master whom having not seen we love. It can also be that a constant emphasis on God's *power* can lead to a kind of fatalism; we need do nothing, because God's Spirit will work everything out regardless.

Felicitas Goodman made a study of the phenomena of 'tongue-speaking' world-wide, across cultures. She found that there is a consistent pattern of behaviour and speech even in persons of different language families and from different religious backgrounds. She concludes that the consistency is because the phenomena "has a neurophysiological basis", i.e. the mind controls the body and speech in a certain way, regardless of the religious beliefs held. Tongue speaking as practiced today is therefore a phenomena, not something inspired by the Truth and Spirit of God (*Speaking In Tongues: A Cross-Cultural Study Of Glossolalia*, Chicago: University Of Chicago Press, 1972).

Photo: A young man waits for healing in his wheelchair at a Pentecostal meeting. He was wheeled away unhealed.

2.4   The Withdrawal Of The Gifts

The miraculous gifts of God's spirit will be used again by the believers in order to change this present world into God's Kingdom, after the return of Christ. The gifts are therefore called "the powers of the world (age) to come" (Heb. 6:4,5); and Joel 2:26-29 describes a great outpouring of the spirit gifts after the repentance of Israel. The very fact that these gifts will be given to the believers on Christ's return is proof enough that they are not possessed now - seeing that to any Christian with eyes open to both Scripture and world events, the Lord's return must surely be soon. Mic. 3:6 prophesied that there would come a day when 'the sun would go down over the prophets', i.e. the Spirit gift of prophecy would be taken away. Jesus appears to have alluded to this idea when He said that He had to do miracles whilst He had the opportunity, "while it is day: the night comes, when no man can work" miracles (Jn. 9:4). It was as if Jesus foresaw that soon there would be no more open manifestation of the Spirit gifts- until the dawning of the glorious day of His Kingdom at His second coming.

From all the Biblical records of the use of spirit gifts, it is clear that they were given at particular times for particular purposes and were withdrawn by God when His purpose was accomplished.

"If there be prophecies, they shall fail; if there be tongues, they shall cease; if there be (the gift of) knowledge, it shall vanish away. For we know in part, and we prophesy in part. But when that which is perfect [complete] is come, then that which is in part shall be done away" (1 Cor. 13:8-10).

The gifts "are temporary" (G.N.B.).

Eph. 4:8-14 helps us understand this further.

"When he (Jesus) ascended up on high (to heaven), he...gave (spirit) gifts unto men...for the building up of the body of Christ: until we all come in (unto) the unity of the faith (i.e. the one faith), and of the knowledge of the Son of God, unto a perfect man...That we henceforth be no more children, tossed to and fro, and thrown about with every wind of doctrine."

The gifts of the first century were to be given until the perfect, or mature, man was reached. Note how Eph. 4:14 likens being under the ministry of the miraculous gifts, to spiritual childhood; and, in the context of prophesying, how the miraculous gifts were to be taken away. 1 Cor. 13:11 says the same. Making the claim of possessing the miraculous spirit gifts is therefore not a sign of spiritual maturity. The progress each reader of these words should now make is towards a deeper appreciation of the written Word of God, to rejoice in the completeness of God's basic revelation of Himself to us through it, and to respond to it in humble obedience. 2 Tim. 3:16,17 teach that response to "all scripture" enables the man of God to be "perfect", complete, mature. So once all scripture was inspired, the gifts were no longer needed; they had achieved their purpose, of guiding the early church up to the point where God's written revelation had been completed. The gifts were to enable the church to become "fully equipped" (Eph. 4:8 Weymouth). When the Bible was completed, they were.

Closer study of 1 Cor. 13 suggests that the time of the withdrawal of the gifts was in fact at the time when the Mosaic sacrifices ceased to be offered. There was an interim period between the death of the Lord Jesus and the destruction of the temple in AD70. During this time, various concessions were made to the Jewish believers; they were permitted to obey Mosaic regulations for the time being, even though the Spirit through Paul made it clear that they were unable to give salvation, and were in comparison to Christ "the weak and beggarly elements". The early believers were guided through this period by the presence of the miraculous Holy Spirit gifts amongst them, pronouncing, prophesying, enabling preaching in new areas through the gift of languages, organizing the ecclesias etc. But once the ecclesia came to maturity, the written word replaced the gifts. Most if not all the New Testament was completed by AD70, and this was around the time the gifts were withdrawn. Paul uses the same Greek word several times in 1 Cor. 13, even though it is somewhat masked in the translations. The following words in italics all translate the same Greek word: "Prophecies...shall *fail*...[the gift of] knowledge shall *vanish away*...that which is in part shall *be done away*...when I became a man, I *put away* childish things" (:8,10,11). Paul is predicting how the gifts of the Spirit would be withdrawn once the church reached the point of maturity; but he says that he himself has already matured, and he has "put away" the things of his immaturity- i.e. he no longer exercised the gifts for himself. He presents himself, as he often does, as the pattern for the church to follow. Thus the gifts "shall be done away" in the future for the church as a whole when they are perfect / mature, but for him, he has already 'done them away' as he has himself reached maturity. In the same language as Ephesians 4, he is no longer a child, tossed to and fro and needing the support of the Spirit gifts. He laments that the believers were still children (1 Cor. 3:1; Heb. 5:13)- yet, using the same Greek word, he says that he is no longer a child, but is mature. In Gal. 4:3, Paul speaks about how he had once been a child in the sense that he was under the Mosaic Law. But now, he has put that behind him. He is mature; and yet here in 1 Cor. 13:10 he associates being mature with putting away the gifts of the Spirit.

The same Greek word translated "fail...be done away....vanish away" is used in many other places concerning the passing away of the Mosaic Law:

- "We are *delivered* from the law" (Rom. 7:6). We are like a woman *loosed* from her husband, i.e. the Law of Moses (Rom. 7:2).

- The glory of the Law was to be *done away* (2 Cor. 3:7)

- The Law *is being done away* at the time Paul was writing (2 Cor. 3:11 Gk.). It was *abolished, done away* in Christ (:13,14)

- Christ *abolished* the law of commandments (Eph. 2:15)

- Likewise, the prophecy that "tongues shall *cease*" (1 Cor. 13:8) uses the same word as in Heb. 10:2, concerning how the sacrifices *cease* to be offered. The "perfect man" state of the church, at which the Spirit gifts were to be withdrawn (1 Cor. 13:10; Eph. 4:13) is to be connected with how the Lord Jesus is the "greater and more *perfect* tabernacle" compared to the Mosaic one (Heb. 9:11). The conclusion seems to be that the ending of the Spirit gifts was related to the ending of the Mosaic system in AD70. The "perfect" or mature state was something which the early church was clearly expected to achieve in their generation:

- Heb. 5:12-14 laments that the early believers were not yet 'perfect' [AV "of full age", the same Greek word translated "perfect" in 1 Cor. 13]- when, by implication, they ought to have been, so that they could benefit from the "strong meat" which the writer wished to feed them with.

- Some in Philippi, along with Paul, had reached this 'perfect' / mature state: "Let us therefore, as many of us as be perfect..." (Phil. 3:15). Likewise "we speak wisdom among them that are perfect" (1 Cor. 2:6).

- "In understanding be *men*", be perfect / mature (1 Cor. 14:20), Paul urges the church. And he prays earnestly that they may indeed become perfect / mature (Col. 1:28; 4:12).

Summing up, the Spirit gifts were given until the church became "perfect" or mature. This cannot refer to the second coming of Christ because the word is repeatedly used about how the believers in the first century ought to be become "mature". The 'passing away' of the gifts is related to the 'passing away' of the Jewish and Mosaic system in AD70. This was in any case moving into the second generation after Christ; and it seems that the miraculous gifts were largely obtained by the laying on of hands of the Apostles. As that generation died out, and the more mature ones like Paul stopped using the gifts widely, then the possession of the gifts would have declined in any case. The Spirit gifts were to be withdrawn, according to 1 Cor. 13:10. Yet Joel 2 says that they will be poured out around the time of the Lord's return. It therefore follows that they would not have been possessed in the church for a certain period of time.

PRESENT CLAIMS OF SPIRIT POSSESSION

A number of other points have to be made concerning the repeated claims of those who think they now possess the miraculous gifts. Whatever one makes of the above arguments for the withdrawal of the gifts, the reality is that the present claims to Spirit gift possession are sadly in conflict with the nature of the gifts as recorded in the New Testament. Whatever is being done today is different to that which happened in the early church.

Present "speaking in tongues" tends to repeat the same short syllables over and over again, e.g. "Lala, lala, lala, shama, shama. Jesus, Jesus...". This is not in the syntax associated with any language; when one hears someone speak in a foreign tongue, it is usually possible to discern that they are communicating something by the pattern of words they use, although we may not understand those words. Yet modern tongue-speaking does not feature this, underlining the fact that it is not providing edification, which was the purpose of the first century gifts.

Some Pentecostals claim that speaking in tongues is a sign of being "saved" and will therefore accompany every true conversion. This claim runs into serious difficulty with the description of the early churches as a body, in which those possessing different gifts were like the different parts. Not everyone was an arm or leg, and so likewise not everyone possessed any one gift, e.g. tongues. 1 Cor. 12:17, 27-30 makes this clear.

"If the whole body were an eye, where would the hearing be? If the whole were hearing, where would be the smelling?... Now you are the body of Christ, and members comprising many parts. And God has set some in the church, first apostles, secondarily prophets, thirdly teachers, after that miracles, then gifts of healings, helps, governments, various kinds of tongues. Are all apostles? are all prophets? are all teachers? are all workers of miracles? Have all the gifts of healing? do all speak with tongues? do all interpret?"

The same point was made earlier in that chapter:

"For to one is given by the spirit the word of wisdom; to another the word of knowledge by the same spirit; to another faith by the same spirit; to another the gifts of healing by the same spirit; to another the working of miracles; to another prophecy; to another discerning of spirits; to another various kinds of tongues; to another the interpretation of tongues: But through all these works that one and the same spirit, dividing to every man individually as he wills. For as the body is one, and has many members, and all the members of that one body, being many, are one body; so also is Christ" (1 Cor. 12:8-12).

Such emphasis cannot just be disregarded. We can't say that every New Testament passage has equal application to every believer (consider Mt. 10:9,10; Mk. 16:17; Lk. 10:4; Acts 15:23-29); so it is surely reasonable to place the references to the fact that *some* spoke in tongues in the early church in this same category.

Another problem for the Pentecostal argument is that Philip converted many people in Samaria - i.e. they were baptised in water after understanding the Gospel, but they did not receive the spirit gifts; because after this, Peter and John came to them: "Who, when they were come down, prayed for them, that they might receive the Holy Spirit...then laid they their hands on them, and they received the Holy Spirit...Simon saw that through the laying on of the apostles' hands the Holy Spirit was given" (Acts 8:4-18). It is possible that the passing on of the Spirit gifts was only by this laying on of hands, which is not frequently practised by modern claimants. Thus Paul wanted to visit the Romans in order to give them the gifts of the Holy Spirit (Rom. 1:11 cf. Eph. 4:12). It would therefore follow that once the generation who had this power passed away, there was no way of continuing the gifts. If indeed they are obtainable purely by prayer, it is difficult to understand why Paul had to visit Rome to transfer the gifts to them there, or why "through the laying on of the apostles' hands the Holy Spirit was given".

Other Pentecostals say that tongue-speaking is not a proof of having been saved. This highlights the fact that there are major doctrinal differences between those claiming to possess the gifts. Thus some 'charismatics' believe that God's Kingdom will be on earth, while others say it is in heaven. Catholic 'charismatics' claim that the Holy Spirit tells them to worship Mary and the Pope, whilst some Pentecostal 'charismatics' say that their possession of the Holy Spirit orders them to denounce the Pope as antichrist, and to condemn Catholic doctrine. Yet Jesus stated beyond doubt that those possessing the Comforter, "which is the Holy Spirit", would be guided "into all truth...in that day you shall (need to) ask me nothing...the Comforter...shall teach you all things, and bring all things to your remembrance, whatever I have said unto you" (Jn. 16:13,23; 14:26).

There should not be any split in fundamental doctrine amongst those who possess the Comforter - the fact that there is, indicates that those claiming its possession just cannot be taken seriously. The marked inability of some of these claimants to Biblically justify their beliefs indicates that they have not been guided into all truth and total knowledge by the Comforter.

The great importance attached by some to speaking in tongues is mismatched with the Biblical record. The list of spirit gifts in Eph. 4:11 does not even mention it, and it occurs at the bottom of a similar list in 1 Cor. 12:28-30. Indeed, there are only three occasions recorded in the New Testament where the gift was used (Acts 2:4; 10:46; 19:6).

The claims of tongue-speaking and miracles being achieved by modern charismatic Christians must be weighed against the considerable information which we have presented in this study concerning the work of God's spirit. The fundamental point to make is that whatever such people claim to achieve, it cannot be as a result of their possession of the Holy Spirit. Whoever argues that they do possess the gifts, has a hefty homework to do in answering the Biblical arguments which we have presented.

However, it is reasonable to expect some explanation of why the phenomena of partial healings and 'tongues' (in the sense of unintelligible speaking) occur.

It has been realised that human beings only use a fraction of their brain-power - as low as 1%, according to some estimates. It is also recognised that the mind can have an almost 'physical' control over the body; thus through psyching themselves to believe that fire cannot burn, Hindus have walked on fire barefoot without being burnt. In times of stimulus, it is possible for us to use a far greater percentage of our brain-power than usual, and therefore to have the capacity to achieve physical effects with, and upon, our body which are outside of normal experience. Thus, in the excitement of battle, a soldier may be quite unaware that he has been injured until afterwards.

In conditions of fervent religious belief and the stimulation of certain music, with the influence of a charismatic leader, it is quite possible that things outside the realm of normal human experience will occur. The 'miracles' claimed by Christians of today are of the same order of exceptionality as the paranormal experiences of other religions; thus voodoo worshippers experience the same phenomena of 'mumbo-jumbo' speaking, and Muslims can also testify to 'miracles' of a similar order to those claimed by some Christians today. Yet the whole point of the spirit gifts being possessed in the first century was to show the obvious supremacy of true Christianity over all other religions; the fact that the 'miracles' claimed today are of a similar order to those of other religions, shows that the Holy Spirit gifts of the first century are not now possessed.

Much significant information in this area is presented in William Campbell's 'Pentecostalism' (*The Churches of Christ*, 1967). He shows that many pagan religions have this same feature of 'tongue' speaking. Thus in Kawaii, the priests of the god Oro supposedly reveal his will with indistinct sounds which are interpreted by other priests. Exactly the same occurs in Pentecostal meetings. In the first century, the pagan priests seem to have had frenzies during which they proclaimed Christ as accursed. Paul uses this in criticising how some in the Corinth ecclesia were only imitating the frenzy of pagans in their use of the spirit gifts - is there a clearer proof that ecstasy doesn't mean we have spirit possession? It must also be remembered that possession of the gifts doesn't mean that we are acceptable with God, and they are therefore not a sign of salvation being presently possessed (Ps. 68:18 cf. Eph. 4:8, and consider how Saul of Israel possessed the gifts but wasn't saved). Even answered prayer, much gloried in by our Pentecostal friends, is no proof of itself that we have a relationship with God, in that He can answer the prayers of some in order to answer a man according to his folly and thus confirm him in the wrong way he has chosen (Ez. 14:4).

The continuing triumph of Islam over Christianity in much of Africa would surely not be seen if popular 'Christianity' were doing real miracles of the scale and convicting power of those in the first century. And those who truly possess the "Comforter" of the Holy Spirit gifts will do even "greater works" than those Jesus did (Jn. 14:12,16). The excuse that Christians could do such miracles if they had more faith, meets big problems here. Either they possess the miraculous gifts of the Comforter, or they do not, and if they claim that they do - "greater works than these *shall* you do" (Jn. 14:12) - not 'you *might* do'!

First century use of the gifts didn't require physical contact with the one who was healed - miracles could be done from a distance. Moreover, they didn't always require the faith of those who were healed (Lk. 22:51). There were no failed attempts at performing miracles in the first century - whereas there are many today. Also, it was possible to predict the miracles accurately - which simply cannot be done today. We leave this subject with a question: Who are those false teachers who do false miracles, posing as Christians (Mt. 7:22,23; 24:24; 2 Thess. 2:9,10)?

2.5   The Bible The Only Authority

From what we have seen so far in this study, God's spirit refers to His mind and purpose, and to the power by which He puts those things into operation. We have emphasised that that spirit is expressly revealed to us in the pages of God's Word. The many problems of contemporary Christianity all come down to a dire lack of appreciation of this. Because it

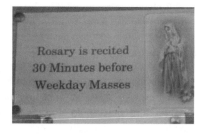

Rosary is recited 30 Minutes before Weekday Masses

is hard to believe that such great power is vested in one book, parts of which we find hard to understand, it is tempting to feel that there is some other form of God's revelation to men, other than the Bible. Because our fundamentally faulty human condition (Jer. 17:9) finds the pure truth of God's Word (Jn. 17:17) so hard to stomach, many have given in to this temptation by claiming other forms of revelation which are more attractive to the natural mind. A few examples are now given.

Religion	Other form of revelation claimed	Human advantage/attraction of this
Jehovah's Witnesses	Publications of the Watchtower Society, which are treated as inspired	No personal effort required to think out the correct interpretation of the Bible; an answer for everything
Roman Catholicism	The pronouncements by the Pope and opinions of priests, which they claim	No need for personal Bible reading - in the past, Catholicism has discouraged and even forbidden this.

	are automatically the true reflection of God's mind	Trusting in men rather than having to make the effort to verify things for oneself
Mormons	The book of Mormon	Takes away the need to believe in Biblical doctrines which are hard to accept – the Book of Mormon offers a chance of universal salvation, whilst the Bible says that there are many people who live and die with no hope through not being called to a knowledge of the Gospel

All this underlines the need for a fundamental acceptance of the Bible as God's Word, and to search its pages for the true message. The question, "One Bible, many churches - why?" is largely answered when it is appreciated how many churches have, to some degree, claimed another form of revelation of God's spirit, i.e. His will, doctrine and thinking, in addition to that of the Bible.

If you wish to find the one true church, the one true faith and the one true baptism (Eph. 4:4-6), the call must be coming to you loud and clear - "Back to the *Bible!*". It's not my purpose to recommend a mere denomination to you. For now, read through the early chapters of Acts some time; it is evident that it was Peter's logical, Bible-based reasoning that really touched the hearts of men and converted them, rather than the miracles he did.

All this said, it must be conceded that many Pentecostal churches exhibit a tremendous vitality and assurance when one enters them. Why is this? My own observation is that many join these groups and then leave them. Therefore those one meets within them tend to be relatively recent converts, who are full of the verve of having found a new church, a new understanding. And so the churches tend to exude energy, rather like the Jehovah's Witness organization does. But what one doesn't immediately perceive are the millions of disillusioned folks worldwide, who have been there, seen it all, and quit. If true miracles were being done, would so many become disillusioned with them?

Belief In Practice 8:

The Implications Of Biblical Inspiration

USE THE WORD WITH OTHERS

If we accept the Bible to be inspired by God, we will read, preach and study it with a zest no other piece of writing can command. The wonder of the fact that this book really is the words of God Himself needs repeated meditation. Out of Heaven, Israel heard the voice of God Himself (Dt. 4:36)- a God so infinitely far away, spoke to men. And those words have been recorded. When we read His word, we hear His voice. 1 Kings 13:21 speaks of us hearing " the *mouth* of God" . Jeremiah spoke " from the mouth of the Lord" (2 Chron. 36:12). His word brings Him that near to us, if we will perceive it for what it is. Our attitude to God is our attitude to His word. Because the word is so pure, *therefore* we love it (Ps. 119:140). John Carter rightly observed: " Upon our understanding of what the Bible is, our attitude to it will be determined".

A comparison of 2 Tim. 3:16 with 4:2,3 makes it clear that because the inspired word is profitable:

for doctrine *therefore*
preach the word; be instant in season, out of season (i.e. whether you naturally feel in the preaching mood or not)
for reproof *therefore*
reprove
for correction *therefore*
rebuke
for instruction in righteousness *therefore*
exhort with all patience and doctrine.

OBEDIENCE

" You have seen that I have talked with you from heaven [therefore] you shall not make with me gods of silver" (Ex. 20:22,23). Because of the wonder of having heard God's voice, therefore idolatry of any form will be meaningless for us. One can sense how much Paul felt the passion of God's word. It wasn't just black print on white paper to him. Thus he speaks of how " Isaiah is very bold, and says...Isaiah also *cries* concerning Israel..." (Rom. 9:27; 10:20). Paul had meditated deeply upon Isaiah's words, even to the point of considering the tone of voice in which he first spoke them. It was because the rulers of Israel " knew not...the *voices* of the prophets which are read every sabbath day" (Acts 13:27) that they crucified the Lord. He speaks of their " voices" rather than merely their words. They had heard the words, but not felt and perceived that these were the actual voices of men who being dead yet speak. They didn't *feel* the wonder of inspiration in their attitude to Bible study- even though they would have devoutly upheld the position that the Bible texts were inspired. And here we have a lesson for ourselves. The Lord brought this out in Jn. 5:39, in saying that " You search the Scriptures, because you think that in them you have eternal life…and you will not come to *me*, that you may have life" (RV). Their Bible study did not lead them to Him. And it is just as possible that we too can be Bible-centred and not Christ-centred. For to academically study a document and perceive its connections and intellectual purity does not require the living, transforming, demanding relationship which knowing Jesus does.

There is a power in the inspired word, whereby one mind- God's- can penetrate another with no intermediary but a piece of flattened wood pulp, black print on white paper. It's an amazing phenomena to be part of. Leo Tolstoy in his spiritual autobiography *A Confession* tells in gripping manner how he read the words of Jesus "Sell everything you have and give to the poor" and then finally overcame all the restraints of his nature to do just that. He freed his serfs, gave away the copyrights to his writings and began to dispose of his huge estate. Words on paper must likewise lead to action in us. The more familiar we become with the text of Scripture by daily reading, the stronger is the temptation to become blasé, and not read the word expecting to be taught something new, nor expecting to be challenged to change.

Speaking of the witness of Jesus to the words of God Himself, John comments: "He that has received his witness has set his seal to this, that God is true" (Jn. 3:33). By accepting words to be Divinely inspired, we set or affix our seal to them- we undertake to have them as binding upon us in daily life. Accepting the proposition that the Bible is inspired is therefore not a merely academic thing, assenting to a true proposition. It has to affect our lives. And note the humility of God here- that human beings can affix the seal of validation to the truth of God's word. This works out in the way in which lives of obedience to God's word are actually an affixed seal and testament to the truth of those words. Thus it becomes our lives which are the greatest proof of Biblical inspiration.

PERSONAL RESPONSE TO THE WORD: FEELING THE WORD SPEAKING TO US

Although we would all agree that the Bible is the inspired word of God, it is quite possible that we fail to *feel* this as we might when we read it. The people "verily held John to be a prophet" (Mk. 11:32 RV) but they rejoiced only for a short time in the light of his words. They rejected his most essential message- whilst still believing he was an inspired prophet. Or, thinking they believed he was. Moses trembled and Sinai shook and the people fled when they heard God's word. To quote John Carter again: "God's voice was heard at Sinai: the same voice spoke in the Psalmist's words. But the appeal stands written in Scripture and therefore Paul can say that "Today" is a time with limits, but it was yet "today" when the Hebrews was written and Paul repeats the word of the Psalmist as God's voice to the Hebrews of his day. It is significant that Paul immediately adds that "the word of God is living and powerful" . The words he quoted were no dead message but God's living voice... The exhortation "My son, despise not the chastening of the Lord" was God speaking " unto you" , says Paul to the Hebrews. Is it less so to sons of any generation?". Heb. 12:5 alludes to this idea of a living word by speaking of an Old Testament passage as 'reasoning' (R.V.) with us.

Abel, through the account of him in Scripture, "is yet spoken of" (Heb. 11:4 AVmg.). Isaiah was prophesying directly to the hypocrites of the first century, according to the Lord in Mk. 7:6 RV. The passage in the scrolls that said " I am the God of Abraham" was " spoken unto *you* by God" , Jesus told first century Israel (Mt. 22:31). Note in passing how demanding He was-expecting them to figure from that statement and usage of the present tense that God considered Abraham effectively still alive, although he was dead, and He would therefore resurrect him. Although God spoke to Moses alone in the mount, Moses stresses that actually God "spake unto *you* in the mount out of the midst of the fire" . The word of God to His scribes really is, to the same gripping, terrifying degree, His direct word to us (Dt. 4:36; 5:45; 10:4). This explains why David repeatedly refers to the miracle at the Red Sea as if this had affected him personally, to the extent that he could ecstatically rejoice because of it. When Dt. 11:4 speaks of how " the Lord has destroyed [the Egyptians] unto this day", it sounds as if we are to understand each victory and achievement of God as somehow ongoing right down to our own day and our own lives and experience. Thus Ps. 114:5,6 RV describes the Red Sea as even now fleeing before God's people. And thus because of the records of God's past activities, we should be motivated in our decisions now. Josh. 24:13,14 reminds Israel of the record of their past history with God, and then on this basis exhorts them: "Now therefore fear the Lord and serve him..." .

Personal Relationship With God

"Therefore have I hewed them by the prophets; I have slain them by the words of my mouth" (Hos. 6:5). This was and is the power behind the black print on white pages in our Bibles. Yet we can fail to perceive that God's word is His voice to us personally. Like David hearing Nathan's parable, we can get so caught up in the Bible story that we fail to perceive the message for us personally.

Our Speech

The majority of words we hear lack power. We have got used to not paying deep attention to words. The Christian who hears a Sunday morning sermon every week for 40 years will have heard about 9 million words. 50,000 new books will appear this year alone. Those words, as my words, are coloured by the dysfunctions, background, experience, limited perception of the writer or speaker. And so we skim read, we listen with only half an ear to conversations. Rarely are we transfixed by a speaker or writer. And sadly we can tend to feed this attitude back into the words of God. We aren't used to reading inspired words. Words which have meaning and relevance and power. If we truly believe the Bible to be inspired, we will come to it in quite a different frame of mind to that which we normally have. But we need to click into this; a moment's silence and a prayer before we begin our daily reading are surely good disciplines. We should speak "as oracles of God" ; not in that we are infallible, but in that our words should have real weight and intention. As God's word signals to the world that He is both real and credible, so should ours. We should be putting meaning into our words. And yet the confessions of one-time journalist Malcolm Muggeridge surely resonate with our own consciences: "It is painful to me now to reflect, the ease with which I got into the way of using this non-language; these drooling non-sentences conveying non-thoughts, propounding non-fears and offering non-hopes". Our words are so easily empty and meaningless and pointless. All this is why we simply must read the word of God daily; for it is designed for "the reformation of manners" (2 Tim. 3:16 NEB), it is able to change habits and reconstruct our daily human personality.

MATERIALISM

The Bible has so much to say against this, the pervading evil of human societies down the ages. Ezekiel's audiences loved to come and hear God's words at his mouth- and in response to them, " with their mouth they shew much love, but their heart goes after their gain" (Ez. 33:31 RV). Materialism stopped them from really accepting those words, even though they theoretically assented to their inspiration. Only in their condemnation would they know "that a prophet *has* been among them" (:33). And so there is a chilling choice: to *really* accept the power of inspiration now; or have to learn it through the process of condemnation when judgment comes.

TRUE SENSITIVITY

I suspect we all tend to read the Bible subconsciously searching for more evidence for our own pre-conceived ideas, be they doctrinal issues or practical. Yet if the words of the Bible are truly God's words, and we feel this, than we can actually be nothing other than truly sensitive and open hearted to whatever He is going to teach us through them. We will not seek, therefore, to induce our own conclusions from Scripture, but will rather come seeking to simply be taught, whatever the cost, whatever the surprise. Much of the knowledge which we have about life is merely the reflection of our own ideas. Imagine looking at the Mona Lisa painting in the Louvre art gallery in Paris, protected as it is behind glass casing. You look into her eyes, asking the usual questions as to what that look of hers is really saying, or whether it's just your own worldview which suggests to you what meaning there might be in her eyes. But then you see that your own eyes, and those of the other viewers, are being reflected back to you from the glass casing. To come to true knowledge is so hard. We need to clear our minds as far as we can before we begin our Bible reading, and pray earnestly that what we read there will be for us " *the* truth" ; that we will not read those words to just find our own preconceived ideas there. We are up against this problem continually, when we ask, e.g., a Catholic to read the Biblical record about Mary with a clean, child-like mind, with no expectations as to what we expect to find there. And actually it's still just as hard for us to read Scripture with that same pure mind, as the years pass by after our baptism. Israel 'heard' the word, and yet they did not "hearken" to it (Rom. 10:16,18)- we can hear but not hear. Yet if we *really* believed that Scripture is inspired, we wouldn't be like this. It is awesome to reflect how those Hebrew letters, those Greek ciphers written on parchment 1950 years ago, were actually the very words of God Almighty. But this is the real import of our understanding of inspiration. Israel literally 'heard' the words of Ezekiel, knowing that a prophet had been among them- but they weren't obedient. We too can pay such lip service to the doctrine of inspiration- and yet not be truly obedient to the word we know to be inspired.

SELF EXAMINATION

James 1:24,25 parallel looking at ourselves, and looking into the perfect law of liberty. To read Scripture as God really intended, not as mere words on paper, is to find ourselves engaged in an inevitable self-examination. Reflect a while on two consecutive verses in Ez. 8:18; 9:1: "Though they [Israel] *cry in my ears with a loud voice* [when they are under judgment for their actions, which I now ask them to repent of], yet will I not hear them. He [God] *cried also in my* [Ezekiel's] *ears with a loud voice*, saying…". Do you see the connection? As we read and hear God's word today, He is passionately crying in our ears with a loud voice. Just imagine someone literally doing this to you! If we refuse to hear it, then we will cry in *His* ears with a loud voice in the last and final day of condemnation. The intensity of *His* appeal to us now will be the intensity with which the rejected plead for Him to change His verdict upon them; and God, like them in this life, will refuse to hear. What arises from this is a simple fact: as we read and hear the pages of Scripture, as we turn the leaves in our Bibles, God is crying in our ears with a loud voice. Our response to Him is a foretaste of our acceptance or rejection at the day of judgment.

Knowing that the Bible is God's inspired word means that of course we will read it in a way that we do not read any other literature. This may seem obvious, but we need to consciously reflect upon the reality of inspiration before we settle down to any protracted Bible reading or study. Here we have the very word of God. " Recent research has indicated that the average individual listens for only seventeen seconds before interrupting and interjecting his own ideas". This happens, of course, when we read the Bible, and hear God's voice. 'Our' voice is there in conflict with God's; but the reality of inspiration should mean that we bring ourselves back to *His* voice, the words of God rather than those of men or ourselves.

Digression 3: Is The Holy Spirit A Person?

Studies 2.1 and 2.2 have given ample evidence that God's spirit refers to His power, which reflects His "mind" in a very broad way. Because the way God's spirit acts is such an accurate reflector of the essence and personality of God, some have argued that God's spirit is a person who is also God. A careful re-reading of the previous sections will show that God's spirit is His mind and power. Electricity is an unseen power that can produce results for the person controlling it, but it cannot be a person. Love is a part of someone's character, but it cannot be a person. God's spirit includes His love, as part of His character, and also refers to His power, but in no way can it refer to a person who is separate from Him.

It is a tragedy to me that this mistaken view (of the spirit being a person) is believed by the majority of Christians, seeing that they believe in the doctrine of the 'trinity'. This effectively states that there are three gods who are somehow also the same - God the Father, the Holy Spirit and Jesus.

There is good reason to believe that the 'trinity' was fundamentally a pagan idea imported into Christianity - hence the word does not occur in the Bible. If we accept this idea that God is a trinity, we are then driven to reach the conclusion that somehow God's power/spirit is a person, who is also God, although not God the Father. When confronted with the illogicality of their position, the most popular escape route is for such people to claim that God is a mystery, and that we should accept such things in faith without requiring a logical explanation.

This pointedly overlooks the references in the New Testament to the mystery of God being revealed through the word and work of Christ.

- "I would not, brothers, that you should be ignorant of this mystery" (Rom. 11:25).
- "The preaching of Jesus...the revelation of the mystery" (Rom. 16:25).
- "I shew (explain to) you a mystery..." (1 Cor. 15:51).
- "Having made known unto us the mystery of his will" (Eph. 1:9; 3:3).
- Paul's preaching was "to make known the mystery of the Gospel" (Eph. 6:19; Col. 4:3).
- "The mystery...now is made manifest to his saints" (Col. 1:26,27).

With all this emphasis - and it is that - on there not now being any mystery attached to fundamental doctrines, it will only be someone still in darkness who will claim that there is. And does such a person not worry that the Bible's name for "Babylon", the system of false religion described in Revelation, is "Mystery" (Rev. 17:5)? The obvious implication is that this system proclaims that its beliefs are a mystery; but the true believers understand the mystery of that woman (Rev. 17:7).

Such hazy reasoning arises from having an understanding of God which is based upon subjective things like human experience, or the sense we have of church traditions. If we are expected to be truly humble to the teaching of God's Word, it follows that we are also required to use basic powers of reasoning and deduction in order to discover its message.

Never did any preacher of the Gospel recorded in the Bible resort to saying, 'This is a complete mystery, you cannot begin to understand it'. Instead, we read of them appealing to people through reason and drawing logical conclusions from Scripture.

In his preaching of the type of Gospel fundamentals which we are considering in these Studies, Paul "reasoned with them out of the Scriptures, ... that Christ needed to have suffered, and risen again" (Acts 17:2,3). Here was systematic, logical Bible reasoning par excellence; and the record prefaces this sentence with, "Paul, as his manner was...reasoned...". This was, therefore, his usual style (see also Acts 18:19). In keeping with this, during the great campaign at Corinth, Paul "*reasoned* in the synagogue every sabbath, and persuaded the Jews...(but) when they opposed themselves..." (Acts 18:4-6). Those who were converted went through a process of persuasion by Paul's Bible-based reasoning.

Notice, too, that the inspired record makes an appeal to logic and rationality, by pointing out that they "opposed themselves". Likewise at Antioch, Paul and Barnabas "speaking (the word) to them, persuaded them..." (Acts 13:43). Their next stop was Iconium, where they "so spake, that a great multitude...believed" (Acts 14:1).

As he stood trial for his life a while later, the same glorious logic continued to inspire Paul's sure hope for the future: "He *reasoned* of righteousness, temperance and judgment to come" with such penetrating clarity that even his cynical, laid-back judge "trembled" (Acts 24:25).

Because our conversion should be based on such a process of reasoning, we should be able to give a logical Biblical account of our hope and doctrine.

"Be ready always to give an answer to every man who asks you a reason of the hope that is in you" (1 Pet. 3:15).

To talk in a sober voice about one's personal experiences, valid testimony as this can be, is not the same as the Gospel. We must be ever giving a reason of the Gospel hope. Such personal anecdotes must not be allowed to conflict with the words of Paul: "We preach not ourselves, but Christ" (2 Cor. 4:5) - and that from a man who 'had a personal relationship with Jesus' more than most.

The logical, Biblically reasonable manner of our conversion should set the pattern for our wider relationship with God through the rest of our days. Our examples, as always, are the first Christians who used "reason" to figure out the solutions to their problems of administration (Acts 6:2). The New Testament letters also assume their readers' acceptance of using Biblical logic. Thus "by reason of" what the High Priests were like under the Law of Moses, we can understand details about the work of Christ (Heb. 5:3). Having spoken of the surpassing love of God in Christ, Paul urges that it is "your reasonable (Greek 'logikos' - i.e. logical) service" to totally dedicate ourselves to Him in response (Rom. 12:1). The word ''logikos' is derived from the Greek 'logos', which is the word normally translated "the word" with reference to God's Word. Our "logical" response in Biblical terms is therefore one which is derived from God's Word.

If we cannot draw logical conclusions from the Scriptures, then all Bible study is vain, and there is no need for the Bible, which can be treated just as sweet platitudes or a piece of fascinating literature. This is all it seems to be on many bookshelves.

However, to their credit, there are many earnest Christians who believe that the spirit of God is a person, and they do try to give Biblical reasons. The verses quoted are those which speak of God's spirit in personal language, e.g. as "the comforter" in Jn. 14-16, or reference to the spirit being "grieved".

We demonstrate in Study 4.3 that a man's "spirit" can be stirred up (Acts 17:16), made troubled (Gen. 41:8) or happy (Lk. 10:21). His "spirit", i.e. his very essence, his mind and purpose, which gives rise to his actions, is therefore spoken of as a separate person, but, of course, this is not literally so. God's spirit, too, can be spoken of in the same way.

It must also be understood that the Bible often uses the language of personification when talking about abstract things, e.g. wisdom is referred to as a woman in Prov. 9:1. This is to demonstrate to us what a person who has wisdom would be like in practice; 'wisdom' cannot exist except in someone's mind, and so this device of personification is used. For more on this, see Digression 4, "The Principle of Personification".

Paul's letters contain opening salutations which refer to God and Jesus, but not to the Holy Spirit (Rom. 1:7; 1 Cor. 1:3; 2 Cor. 1:2; Gal. 1:3; Eph. 1:2; Phil. 1:2; Col. 1:2; 1 Thess. 1:1; 2 Thess. 1:2; 1 Tim. 1:2; 2 Tim. 1:2; Tit. 1:4; Philemon 3). This is strange if he considered the Holy Spirit to be part of a godhead, as the 'trinity' doctrine wrongly supposes. *Some* of the Holy Spirit was poured out on men (Acts 2:17,18; the same Greek construction is found in Mk. 12:2; Lk. 6:13; Jn. 21:10 and Acts 5:2). How can we receive part of a person? We are given "of His [God's] spirit" (1 Jn. 4:13). This is nonsense if the Holy Spirit is a person. Another serious nail in the coffin of the proposition that the Holy Spirit is a person is the fact that the Holy Spirit is described in the Greek text with a neuter gender (as reflected in the AV of 1 Jn. 2:27, where it is called "it"). This means that when we read passages which speak of the Holy Spirit as "he", we are definitely seeing a personification of a power, not a reference to an actual person.

Digression 4:   The Principle Of Personification

Some may find it difficult to accept the explanation of the personification of the devil, because the devil is so often referred to in the Bible as if it were a person and perhaps this confuses some people. This is easily explained by pointing out that it is a recognised feature of the Bible that inanimate or non-living things such as wisdom, riches, sin, the church are personified, but only in the case of the devil is some fantastic theory woven around it. The following examples will illustrate the point.

WISDOM IS PERSONIFIED

"Happy is the man who finds wisdom, and the man that gets understanding. For the merchandise of it is better than the merchandise of silver, and the profit thereof than fine gold. *She* is more precious than rubies: and all the things you could desire are not to be compared unto *her*" (Prov. 3:13-15). "Wisdom has builded *her* house, *she* has hewn out *her* seven pillars" (Prov. 9:1).

These verses, and indeed the rest of the chapters in which they appear, show that wisdom is personified as a woman, but because of this, no-one has the idea that wisdom is a literal beautiful woman who roams around the earth; all recognise that it is a very desirable characteristic which all people should try to acquire.

RICHES ARE PERSONIFIED

"No man can serve two *masters*: for either he will hate the one, and love the other: or else he will hold to the one, and despise the other. You cannot serve God and mammon [riches]" (Mt. 6:24).

Here, riches are likened to a *master*. Many people strive very hard to gain riches and in this way they become their master. Jesus is here telling us that we cannot do that and serve God acceptably at the same time. The teaching is simple and effective, but no-one assumes from this that riches is a man named Mammon.

SIN IS PERSONIFIED

"...Whoever commits sin is the servant of sin" (Jn. 8:34). "Sin has *reigned* unto death" (Rom. 5:21). "Don't you know, that to whom you yield yourselves servants to obey, *his* servants you are to whom you obey; whether of sin unto death, or of obedience unto righteousness?" (Rom. 6:16).

As in the case of riches, sin is likened here to a master and those who commit sin are its servants. No reasonable reading of the passage justifies assuming that Paul is teaching that sin is a person.

THE SPIRIT IS PERSONIFIED

"When *he*, the spirit of truth, is come, *he* will guide you into all truth: for *he* shall not speak of *himself*..." (Jn. 16:13).

Jesus is here telling His disciples that they would receive the power of the Holy Spirit, and this was fulfilled on the day of Pentecost, as recorded in Acts 2:3-4, where it is stated that "there appeared unto them cloven tongues like as of fire, and it sat upon each of them. And they were all filled with the Holy Spirit", which gave them remarkable power to do wonderful things to prove that their authority was from God. The Holy Spirit was not a person, it was a power, but when Jesus was speaking of it He used the personal pronoun "he".

DEATH IS PERSONIFIED

"Behold a pale horse: and his name that sat on him was Death" (Rev. 6:8).

THE NATION OF ISRAEL IS PERSONIFIED

"Again I will build you, and you shalt be built, *O virgin of Israel*; you shall again be adorned..." (Jer. 31:4). "I have surely heard Ephraim bemoaning *himself* thus; You have chastised me, and I was chastised, as a bullock unaccustomed to the yoke: turn me, and I shall be turned; for you are the Lord my God" (Jer. 31:18).

Adapted from *"Christendom Astray"* by Robert Roberts.

STUDY 2: Questions

1. What does the word 'Spirit' mean?
   - ☐ Power
   - ☐ Holy
   - ☐ Breath
   - ☐ Dust

2. What is the Holy Spirit?
   - ☐ A person
   - ☐ God's power
   - ☐ Part of a trinity.

3. How was the Bible written?
   - ☐ Men wrote down their own ideas
   - ☐ Men wrote what they thought God meant
   - ☐ Through the inspiration of men, by God's Spirit
   - ☐ Some of it was inspired, other parts were not.

4. Which of the following are reasons why the miraculous gifts of the Spirit were given?
   - ☐ To back up the verbal preaching of the Gospel
   - ☐ To develop the early church
   - ☐ To force people to be righteous
   - ☐ To save the apostles from personal difficulties.

5. From where can we learn God's truth?
   - ☐ Partly from the Bible, partly from our own thinking
   - ☐ From the Holy Spirit telling us things directly
   - ☐ From the Bible alone
   - ☐ From religious ministers / priests.

6. Name spirit gifts possessed in the first century.

7. When were they withdrawn? Can we have them now?

8. How can the Holy Spirit work in our lives today?

STUDY 3

The Promises Of God

3.1 The Promises Of God: Introduction

At this point in our studies we have reached a broad understanding of who God is and how He works. In doing so we have cleared up a number of common misunderstandings about these things. Now we want to look more positively at the things which God has "promised to them that love him" (James 1:12; 2:5) by keeping His commandments (Jn. 14:15). If we open the New Testament, the first book we read is a transcript of the Gospel message as preached by Matthew. He starts off in the very first verse by introducing Jesus Christ as the son of David and the son of Abraham, and then gives a genealogy to prove this (Luke does similarly). This may seem odd at first reading. The point is, these early believers recognised that the fulfilment of the promises to Abraham and David through Jesus Christ is the basis of the Christian message. Paul preached likewise- the Gospel is centred in the promises (Gal. 3:8). Paul taught "the good tidings [Gospel] of the promise made unto the [Jewish] fathers" (Acts 13:32 RV).

The promises of God in the Old Testament comprise the true Christian hope. When on trial for his life, Paul spoke of the future reward for which he was prepared to lose all things. "Now I stand and am judged for the hope of the promise made of God unto our fathers...the hope of Israel...for which hope's sake...I am accused" (Acts 26:6,7). He had spent much of his life preaching "glad tidings (the Gospel), how that the promise which was made unto the fathers, God has fulfilled...in that he has raised up Jesus"(Acts 13:32,33). Paul explained that belief in those promises gave hope of resurrection from the dead (Acts 26:6-8 cf. 23:8), a knowledge of the second coming of Jesus in judgment and of the coming Kingdom of God (Acts 24:25; 28:20,31). It must be understood at the outset that the true Christian hope is "the hope of Israel". God sent His Son to save the Jews first and foremost (Gal. 4:4,5); yet God is not willing that any should perish and by His grace the Gentiles may share in the promise of salvation also.

All this sinks the myth that the Old Testament is merely a rambling history of Israel which does not speak of eternal life. To understand the promises of salvation explained there is to understand the Christian Gospel. God did not suddenly decide 2,000 years ago that He would offer us eternal life through Jesus. That purpose was with Him from the beginning.

"(The) hope of eternal life, which God, that cannot lie, promised before the world began; but has in due times manifested his word (concerning it) through preaching" (Tit. 1:2,3).

"That eternal life, which was with the Father, and was manifested unto us" (1 Jn. 1:2).

Seeing that God's purpose of giving His people eternal life was with Him from the beginning, it is unlikely that He would remain silent about it during the 4,000 years of His dealings with men recorded in the Old Testament. In fact, the Old Testament is full of prophecies and promises which give more detail of this hope which God has prepared for His people. It is because of this that an understanding of God's promises to the Jewish fathers is vital for our salvation. Paul reminded the believers in Ephesus that before they knew these things, they "were without Christ, being aliens from the commonwealth of Israel, and strangers from the covenants of promise, having no hope, and without God in the world" (Eph. 2:12) - although doubtless they had thought that their previous pagan beliefs did give them some hope and knowledge of God. But this is the seriousness of not knowing the promises of God - in reality "having no hope, and without God in the world". Remember how Paul defined the Christian hope as "the hope of the promise made of God unto our (Jewish) fathers" (Acts 26:6).

It is a sad fact that few place the emphasis on these parts of the Old Testament that they should. Some parts of Christianity have degenerated into a solely New Testament religion. Jesus clearly put the emphasis the right way round:

"If they hear not Moses (i.e. the first five books of the Bible which he wrote) and the prophets, neither will they be persuaded, though one rose from the dead" (Lk. 16:31).

The natural mind might reason that believing in the resurrection of Jesus is enough (cf. Lk. 16:30), but Jesus said that without a solid understanding of the wider issues surrounding it, this would not be fully possible.

The disciples' collapse of faith after the crucifixion was traced by Jesus to their lack of careful attention to the Old Testament.

"He said unto them, O fools, and slow of heart to believe (properly) all that the prophets have spoken: ought not Christ to have suffered these things, and to enter into his glory? And beginning at Moses and *all* the prophets, he expounded unto them in *all* the Scriptures the things concerning himself" (Lk. 24:25-27).

Note his emphasis on how the *entire* Old Testament spoke of him. It was not that the disciples had never read or heard the words of the Old Testament, but they had not properly understood them, and therefore they could not truly believe them. So a correct understanding of God's Word, rather than just reading it, is necessary to develop a true faith. The Jews were fanatical in their reading of the Old Testament (Acts 15:21), but because they did not understand its reference to the things of Jesus and his Gospel, they did not really believe it, and so Jesus told them.

"Had you believed Moses, you would have believed me: for he wrote of me. But if you believe not his writings, how shall you believe my words?" (Jn. 5:46,47).

Despite all their Bible reading, they were just not seeing the real message about Jesus, although they liked to think they were assured of salvation. Jesus had to tell them.

"You search the Scriptures for in them you think (are confident) you have eternal life: and they are they which testify of me" (Jn. 5:39 R.V.).

And so it can be with many people who have an outline knowledge of some of the incidents and teachings of the Old Testament: it is just knowledge which they have picked up incidentally. The wonderful message of Christ and the Gospel of God's Kingdom still eludes them. It is the purpose of this study to take you out of that position by demonstrating the real meaning of the main promises of the Old Testament.

- In the Garden of Eden
- To Noah
- To Abraham
- To David

Information about them is found in the first five books of the Bible (Genesis-Deuteronomy) which were written by Moses, and in the Old Testament prophets. All the elements of the Christian Gospel are found here. Paul explained that his preaching of this Gospel said "none other things than those which the prophets and Moses did say should come: that Christ should suffer, and that he should be the first that should rise from the dead, and should shew light unto the people" (Acts 26:22,23).

The hope of Paul, that supreme Christian, should be the hope which motivates us also; as it was the glorious light at the end of the tunnel of his life, so it should be for every serious Christian. Fired with this motivation, we can now "search the Scriptures".

3.2   The Promise in Eden

The story of humanity's fall is related in Genesis chapter 3. The serpent was cursed for misquoting God's word and tempting Eve to disobey it. The man and woman were punished for their disobedience. But a ray of hope comes into this dark picture when God says to the serpent:

"I will put enmity (hatred, opposition) between you and the woman, and between your descendant and her (special, notable) descendant; it (the woman's descendant) shall bruise your head, and you shall bruise his heel" (Gen. 3:15).

This verse is highly concentrated; we need to carefully define the various things involved. We will see later that Abraham's special descendant was Jesus (Gal. 3:16), but that if we are in Jesus by baptism, then we also are the "descendant" (Gal. 3:27-29). This word "descendant" is translated "seed" in some versions, as it also refers to the idea of sperm (1 Pet. 1:23); so a true 'seed' will have the characteristics of its father.

The seed or descendant of the serpent must therefore refer to that which has the family likeness of the serpent:

- distorting God's Word
- lying
- leading others into sin.

We will see in Study 6 that there is not a literal person doing this, but that within us there is:
- "our old man" of the flesh (Rom. 6:6)
- "the natural man" (1 Cor. 2:14)
- "the old man, which is corrupt according to the deceitful lusts" (Eph. 4:22)
- "the old man with his deeds" (Col. 3:9).

This "man" of sin within us is the Biblical "devil", the serpent.

The descendant of the woman was to be a specific individual - "you (the serpent) shalt bruise *his* heel" (Gen. 3:15). This person was to crush permanently the serpent, i.e. sin - "it shall bruise your head". Hitting a snake on the head is a deathblow - its brain is in its head. The only person who is a candidate for the descendant of the woman must be the Lord Jesus.

- "Jesus Christ, who has (by the cross) abolished death (and therefore the power of sin - Rom. 6:23), and has brought life and immortality to light through the Gospel" (2 Tim. 1:10).

- "God sending His own Son in the likeness of sinful flesh, and for sin, condemned sin, in the flesh", i.e. the Biblical devil, the serpent (Rom. 8:3).

- Jesus "was manifested to take away our sins" (1 Jn. 3:5).

- On the cross, it was by His being 'bruised' [an allusion to Gen. 3:15] that we find forgiveness (Is. 53:5 AVmg.).

- "You shalt call his name Jesus (meaning "Saviour"): for he shall save his people from their sins" (Mt. 1:21).

Jesus was literally "made of a woman" (Gal. 4:4). He was the son of Mary, although God was his Father. Thus in this sense he was the descendant of the woman but not the descendant of a man as he had no human father. This descendant of the woman was to be temporarily wounded by sin, the serpent - "you shalt bruise his heel" (Gen. 3:15). A snakebite on the heel is normally a temporary wound, compared to the permanence of hitting the snake on the head. Many figures of speech have Biblical roots: "knock it on the head" (i.e. completely stop or end something) is probably based on this prophecy of Jesus hitting the snake on the head.

The condemnation of sin, the serpent, was through Christ's sacrifice on the cross - notice how the verses quoted above speak of Christ's victory over sin in the past tense. The temporary wound to the heel suffered by Jesus is therefore a reference to his death for three days. His resurrection proved that this was only a temporary wound, compared to the deathblow that he gave sin. It is interesting that non-Biblical historical records indicate that victims of crucifixion were nailed through their heel to the stake of wood. Thus Jesus was "wounded in the heel" through his death. Is. 53:4,5 describes Christ as being 'bruised' by God through his death on the cross. This plainly alludes to the prophecy of Gen. 3:15 that the serpent would bruise Christ. However, ultimately God worked through the evil which Christ faced, *He* is described here as doing the bruising (Is. 53:10), through controlling the forces of evil which bruised His Son. And so God also works through the evil experiences of each of His children.

THE CONFLICT TODAY

But the question may have arisen in your mind: 'If Jesus destroyed sin and death (the serpent), why are those things still present today?'. The answer is that on the cross Jesus destroyed the power of sin in himself: the prophecy of Gen. 3:15 is primarily about the conflict between Jesus and sin. Now this means that because he has invited us to share in his victory, eventually we, too, can conquer sin and death. Those who are not invited to share in his victory, or decline the offer, will, of course, still experience sin and death. Although sin and death are also experienced by true believers, through their association with the descendant of the woman by being baptised into Christ (Gal. 3:27-29), they can have forgiveness of their sins and therefore eventually be saved from death, which is the result of sin. Thus in prospect Jesus "abolished death" on the cross (2 Tim. 1:10), although it is not until God's purpose with the earth is completed at the end of the Millennium that death will never again be witnessed upon earth. "For he must reign (in the first part of God's Kingdom) till he has put all enemies under his feet. The last enemy that shall be destroyed is death" (1 Cor. 15:25,26).

If we are "baptised *into* Christ" then promises about Jesus, like that in Gen. 3:15, become personal to ourselves; no longer are they just interesting parts of the Bible, they are prophecies and promises which involve us also! Those who are properly baptised into Christ by dipping under water, associate themselves with his death and resurrection - symbolised by the rising up from the water (see Rom. 6:3-5).

If we are truly in Christ, then our lives will reflect the words of Gen. 3:15 - there will be a constant sense of conflict ("enmity") within us, between right and wrong. The great apostle Paul described an almost schizophrenic conflict between sin and his real self that raged within him (Rom. 7:14-25).

After baptism into Christ, this conflict with the sin that is naturally within us should increase - and continue to do so all our days. In a sense it is difficult, because the power of sin is strong. But in another sense it is not, seeing that we are *in* Christ, who has already fought and won the conflict.

The very first descendant of the serpent was Cain. Unlike the serpent who had no understanding of morality, Cain did understand what was truth and what was lies, and he understood what God required of him, yet he chose to follow the thinking of the serpent which led him into murder and lying.

As the Jews were the people who actually put Jesus to death - i.e. bruised the descendant of the woman in the heel - it is to be expected that they were prime examples of the serpent's descendant. John the Baptist and Jesus confirm this.

"When he (John) saw many of the Pharisees and Sadducees (the group of Jews who condemned Jesus) come to his baptism, he said unto them, O generation of (i.e. gendered by, created by) vipers (snakes), who has warned you to flee from the wrath to come?" (Mt. 3:7).

"Jesus knew their (the Pharisees') thoughts, and said...O generation of vipers, how can you, being evil, speak good things?" (Mt. 12:25,34).

The world has these same serpent characteristics. How Jesus treated the people who were the serpent's descendant or family must be our example.

- He preached to them in a spirit of love and true concern, yet
- He did not let their ways and thinking influence Him, and
- He showed them the loving character of God by the way in which He lived.

Yet for all this they hated him. His own effort to be obedient to God made them jealous. Even his family (Jn. 7:5; Mk. 3:21) and close friends (Jn. 6:66) put up barriers and some even went away from him physically. Paul experienced the same thing when he lamented to those who had once stood with him through thick and thin:

"Am I therefore become your enemy, because I tell you the truth?" (Gal. 4:14-16).

The truth is never popular; knowing it and living it as we should will always create some form of problem for us, even resulting in persecution:

"As then he that was born after the flesh persecuted him that was born after the Spirit (by true knowledge of God's Word – 1 Pet. 1:23), even so it is now" (Gal. 4:29).

"An unjust man is an abomination to the just: and he that is upright in the way is an abomination to the wicked" (Prov. 29:27). There is a mutual antagonism between the believer and the world.

If we are truly united with Christ we must experience some of his sufferings, so that we may also share in his glorious reward. Again Paul sets us a matchless example in this:

"It is a faithful saying: For if we be dead with him (Christ), we shall also live with Him: if we suffer (with Him), we shall also reign with him...therefore I endure all things (2 Tim. 2:10-12).

"If they have persecuted me (Jesus), they will also persecute you...all these things will they do unto you for my name's sake" (Jn. 15:20,21).

Faced with verses like these, it is tempting to reason, "If that's what being associated with Jesus, the woman's descendant, is all about, I'd rather not". But of course we will never be expected to undergo anything which we cannot cope with. Whilst self-sacrifice is definitely required in order to unite ourselves fully with Christ, our association with him will result in such a glorious reward "that the sufferings of this present time are not worthy to be compared with the glory which shall be revealed in us". And even now, his sacrifice enables our prayers for help through the traumas of life to be especially powerful with God. And add to this the following glorious assurance:

"God is faithful, who will not suffer you to be tempted above that you are able; but will with the temptation also make a way to escape, that you may be able to bear it" (1 Cor. 10:13).

"These things I have spoken unto you, that in me you might have peace. In the world you shall have tribulation: but be of good hope: I have overcome the world" (Jn. 16:33).

"What shall we then say to these things? If God be for us, who can be against us?" (Rom. 8:31).

3.3   The Promise To Noah

As human history progressed after the time of Adam and Eve, man became increasingly wicked. Things reached the stage when civilisation was so morally corrupt that God decided to destroy that system of things, with the exception of Noah and his family (Gen. 6:5-8). He was told to make an ark in which he and representatives of all the animals would live during the time when the world was being destroyed by flooding. In passing, there is scientific reason to believe that this huge flood did literally occur, apart from the clear statements of Scripture! Notice that the earth (i.e. this literal planet) was not destroyed, just the wicked human set-up which was upon it: "all flesh died that moved upon the earth" (Gen. 7:21). Jesus (Mt. 24:37) and Peter (2 Pet. 3:6-12) both saw the judgment on Noah's world as having similarities with what will occur at Christ's second coming. Thus the desperate wickedness of man in Noah's time is matched by our present world, which is about to be punished at Christ's return.

Because of the gross sinfulness of man and the programme of self-destruction this planet has embarked upon, there has arisen a belief, even among Christians, that this earth will be destroyed. This idea clearly demonstrates a misunderstanding of the fact that God is *actively* concerned with the affairs of this planet, and that soon Jesus Christ will return to establish God's Kingdom here on the earth. If man is to be allowed to destroy this planet then these promises just cannot be kept. Considerable evidence that God's Kingdom *will* be on the earth is found in **Study 4.7** and **Study 5**. Meanwhile, the following should be proof enough that the earth and solar system will not be destroyed.

- "The earth which he has established for ever" (Ps. 78:69).
- "The earth abides for ever" (Ecc. 1:4).

- "Sun and moon...stars...heavens...he has also established them for ever and ever: he has made a decree which shall not pass" (Ps. 148:3-6).
- "The earth shall be full of the knowledge of the Lord as the waters cover the sea" (Is. 11:9; Num. 14:21) - difficult, if God lets the earth destroy itself. This promise has not yet been fulfilled.
- "God himself that formed the earth and made it; he has established it; he created it not in vain, he formed it to be inhabited" (Is. 45:18). If God made earth only to see it destroyed, then His work was in vain.

But right back in Genesis God had promised all this to Noah. As he began to live again in the new world created by the flood, perhaps Noah feared that there could be another wholesale destruction. Whenever it started raining after the flood, this thought must have come to his mind. And so God made a covenant (a series of promises) that this would never happen again.

"I, behold, I establish my covenant with you...I will establish my covenant with you (notice the emphasis on "I" - the *wonder* of God choosing to make promises to mortal man!); neither shall all flesh be cut off any more by the waters of a flood; neither shall there any more be a flood to destroy the earth" (Gen. 9:9-12).

This covenant was confirmed by the rainbow.

"When I bring a cloud (of rain) over the earth, the bow shall be seen in the cloud: and I will remember my covenant...between me and you...the everlasting covenant between God and every living creature of all flesh that is upon the earth...This (rainbow) is the token of the covenant" (Gen. 9:13-17).

Because it is an eternal covenant between God and the people and animals of the earth, it follows that the earth must have people and animals living on it forever. This in itself is proof that God's Kingdom will be on earth rather than in heaven.

Thus the promise to Noah speaks of the Gospel of the Kingdom; it demonstrates how God's attention is focused on this planet, and how He has an eternal purpose with it. Even in wrath He remembers mercy (Hab. 3:2), and such is His love that He even cares for His animal creation (1 Cor. 9:9 cf. Jonah 4:11).

3.4   The Promise To Abraham

There's a connection between the promise in Eden and the promises to Abraham. Abraham was promised the very things which were lost in Eden.

A land flowing with milk and honey (cp. the garden of Eden); a nation without number (cp. "be fruitful and multiply"), and kingship (cp. "subdue it and rule…", Gen. 1:28). We can see here the golden thread of God's purpose developing a link further- His intention, revealed through the promises, was to enable His people to have again what had been lost in Eden.

The Gospel taught by Jesus and the apostles was not fundamentally different from that understood by Abraham. God, through the Scriptures, "preached before the gospel unto Abraham" (Gal. 3:8). So crucial are these promises that Peter started and ended his public proclamation of the Gospel with reference to them (Acts 3:13,25). If we can understand what was taught to Abraham, we will then have a very basic picture of the Christian Gospel. There are other indications that "the gospel" is not something which just began at the time of Jesus.

- "We declare unto you glad tidings (the Gospel), how that the promise which was made unto the (Jewish) fathers, God has fulfilled" (Acts 13:32,33).

- "The gospel of God, which he had promised afore by his prophets (e.g. Abraham, Gen. 20:7) in the holy scriptures" (Rom. 1:1,2).

- "For this cause was the gospel preached also to them that are dead" (1 Pet. 4:6) - i.e. believers who had lived and died before the first century.

- "For unto us was the gospel preached, as well as unto them" (Heb. 4:2) - i.e. Israel in the wilderness.

The promises to Abraham have two basic themes.

(1) things about Abraham's special descendant and

(2) things about the land which was promised to Abraham.

These promises are commented on in the New Testament, and, in keeping with our policy of letting the Bible explain itself, we will combine the teachings of both Testaments to give us a complete picture of the covenant made with Abraham.

Abraham originally lived in Ur, a prosperous city in what is now Iraq. Modern archaeology reveals the high level of civilisation that had been reached by the time of Abraham. There was a banking system, civil service and related infrastructure. Somehow Abraham was aware of the Lord and of His Word, but he was the only faithful one in Ur (Is. 51:2; Nehemiah. 9:8).

Then the extraordinary call of God came to him - to leave that sophisticated life and embark on a journey to a promised land. Exactly where and exactly what was not made completely clear. All told, it turned out to be a 1,500 mile journey. The land was Canaan - modern Israel.

Occasionally during his life, God appeared to Abraham and repeated and expanded His promises to him. Those promises are the basis of Christ's Gospel, so as true Christians that same call comes to us as it did to Abraham, to leave the transient things of this life, and go forward in a life of faith, taking God's promises at face value, living by His Word. We can well imagine how Abraham would have mulled over the promises on his journeys. "By faith Abraham, when he was called to go out (from Ur) into a place (Canaan) which he should after receive for an inheritance, obeyed; and he went out, not knowing whither he went" (Heb. 11:8).

As we consider God's promises for the first time, we, too, can feel that we do not know exactly what the promised land of God's Kingdom will be like. But our faith in God's Word should be such that we also eagerly obey.

Abraham was no wandering nomad with nothing better to do than take a chance on these promises. He was from a background which, in fundamental terms, has much similarity with our own. The difficult decisions he faced were similar to those we may also have to face as we consider whether to accept and act on God's promises - the strange looks from business colleagues, the sly look in the eye from the neighbours ("He's got religion!") ...Abraham would have known these things. The motivation which Abraham needed to go through with it all must have been tremendous. The only thing that provided that motivation throughout his long travelling years was the word of promise. He must have memorised those words and daily meditated upon what they really meant to him.

By showing a similar faith and acting upon it, we can have the same honour as Abraham - to be called the friends of God (Is. 41:8), to find the knowledge of God (Gen. 18:17) and to have the sure hope of eternal life in the Kingdom. Again we emphasise that the Gospel of Christ is based on these promises to Abraham. To believe truly in the Christian message, we too must believe firmly the things promised to Abraham. Without them our faith is not faith. With eager eyes we should therefore read and re-read the dialogue between God and Abraham.

THE LAND

1. "Get out of your country...unto a land that I will show you" (Gen. 12:1).

2. Abraham "went on his journeys...to Bethel (in Central Israel). And the Lord said unto Abram...Lift up now your eyes, and look from the place where

you are northward, and southward, and eastward, and westward: for all the land which you see, to you will I give it, and to your descendant for ever...walk through the land...for I will give it unto you" (Gen. 13:3,14-17).

3. "The Lord made a covenant with Abraham, saying, Unto your descendant [singular- i.e. one special descendant] have I given this land, from the river of Egypt unto the great river, the river Euphrates" (Gen. 15:18).

4. "I will give unto you, and to your descendant [singular- i.e. one special descendant] after you, the land wherein you are a stranger, all the land of Canaan, for an everlasting possession" (Gen. 17:8).

5. "The promise that he (Abraham) should be the heir of the world" (Rom. 4:13).

We see here a progressive revelation to Abraham.

1. 'There is a land which I would like you to go to'.

2. 'You have now arrived in the area. You and your children will live here forever'. Note how this promise of eternal life is recorded without glamour or emphasis; a human author would no doubt have jazzed it up.

3. The area of the promised land was more specifically defined.

4. Abraham was not to expect to receive the promise in this life - he was to be a "stranger" in the land, although he would later live there forever. The implication of this is that he would die and then later be resurrected to enable him to receive this promise.

5. Paul, under inspiration, evidently saw the promises to Abraham as meaning his inheritance of the whole earth.

Scripture goes out of its way to remind us that Abraham did not receive the fulfilment of the promises in his lifetime.

"By faith he sojourned (implying a temporary way of life) in the land of promise, as in a strange country, living in tents" (Heb. 11:9).

He lived as a foreigner in the land, perhaps with the same furtive sense of insecurity and mismatch which a refugee feels. He was hardly living with his descendant in his own land. Along with his descendants, Isaac and Jacob, (to whom the promises were repeated), he "died in faith, not having received the promises, but having seen them afar off, and (they) were persuaded of them, and embraced them, and confessed that they were strangers and pilgrims on the earth" (Heb. 11:13). Notice the four stages.

- Knowing the promises - as we are doing through this study.

- Being "persuaded of them" - if it took a process of persuasion with Abraham, how much more so with us?

- Embracing them - by being baptised into Christ (Gal. 3:27-29).

- Confessing to the world by our way of life that this world is not our real home, but we are living in hope of that future age to come upon the earth.

Abraham becomes our great hero and example if we appreciate these things. The ultimate recognition that the fulfilment of the promises lay in the future came for the tired old man when his wife died; he actually had to buy part of the promised land in which to bury her (Acts 7:16). Truly God "gave him none inheritance in it, no, not so much as to set his foot on: yet he promised that he would give it to him for a possession" (Acts 7:5). The present spiritual children / descendants of Abraham may feel the same incongruity as they buy or rent property - on an earth which has been promised to them for their personal, eternal inheritance!

But God keeps His promises. There must come a day when Abraham and all who have those promises made to them will be rewarded. Heb. 11:13,39,40 drives home the point.

"These all died in faith, not having received the promises; God having provided some better thing for us, that they without us should not be made perfect".

All true believers will therefore be rewarded at the same point in time, i.e. at the judgment seat at the last day (2 Tim. 4:1,8; Mt. 25:31-34; 1 Pet. 5:4). It follows that to be in existence in order to be judged, Abraham and others who knew those promises must be resurrected just before the judgment. If they have not now received the promises and will only do so after their resurrection and judgment at Christ's return, there is no alternative but to accept that the likes of Abraham are now unconscious, awaiting the coming of Christ. Yet stained glass mosaics in churches throughout the world have been known to depict Abraham as now in heaven, experiencing the promised reward for a life of faith. Thousands of people for hundreds of years have filed past those pictures, religiously accepting such ideas. Will you have the Bible-based courage to step out of line?

THE DESCENDANT

As explained in Study 3:2, the promise of a descendant applies primarily to Jesus and, secondarily, to those who are "in Christ" and therefore are also counted as the descendant of Abraham..

1. "I will make of you a great nation, and I will bless you...and in you shall all families of the earth be blessed" (Gen. 12:2,3).

2. "I will make your descendant as the dust of the earth: so that if a man can number the dust of the earth, then shall your descendant also be numbered...all the land which you see, to you will I give it, and to your descendant for ever" (Gen. 13:15,16).

3. "Look now toward heaven, and count the stars, if you be able to number them...So shall your descendant be...Unto your descendant have I given this land" (Gen. 15:5,18).

4. "I will give unto...your descendant[s] after you...the land of Canaan, for an everlasting possession; and I will be their God" (Gen. 17:8).

5. "I will multiply your descendant as the stars of the heaven, and as the sand which is upon the sea shore; and your descendant shall possess the gate of his enemies; and in your descendant shall all the nations of the earth be blessed" (Gen. 22:17,18).

Again, Abraham's understanding of the "descendant" was progressively extended.

1. Firstly he was just told that somehow he would have an extraordinary number of descendants, and that through his "descendant" the whole earth would be blessed.

2. He was later told that he would have a descendant who would come to include many people. These people would spend eternal life, along with himself, in the land at which he had arrived, i.e. Canaan.

3. He was told that his descendant would become as many as the stars in the sky. This may have suggested to him that he would have many spiritual descendants (stars in heaven) as well as many natural ones (as "the dust of the earth").

4. The previous promises were underlined with the additional assurance that the many people who would become part of the descendant could have a personal relationship with God.

5. The descendant would have victory against his enemies.

Notice that the descendant was to bring "blessings" to be available to people from all over the earth. In the Bible the idea of blessing is often connected with forgiveness of sins. After all, this is the greatest blessing a lover of God could ever want. So we read things like: "Blessed is he whose transgression is forgiven" (Ps. 32:1); "The cup of blessing" (1 Cor. 10:16), describing the cup of wine which represents Christ's blood, through which forgiveness is possible.

The only descendant of Abraham who has brought forgiveness of sins to the world is, of course, Jesus, and the New Testament commentary on the promises to Abraham provides solid support:

"He (God) doesn't say, 'And to descendants', in the plural, but in the singular, 'And to your descendant', which is Christ" (Gal. 3:16).

"...the covenant which God made with our fathers, saying unto Abraham, And in your descendant shall all the tribes of the earth be blessed. Unto you first God, having raised up his Son Jesus (i.e. the descendant), sent him to bless you, in turning away every one of you from his iniquities" (Acts 3:25,26).

Notice here how Peter quotes and interprets Gen. 22:18.

The descendant = Jesus

The blessing = forgiveness of sins.

The promise that Jesus, the descendant, would have victory over his enemies now slots more neatly into place if this is read with reference to his victory over sin - the greatest enemy of God's people, and therefore of Jesus, too.

BECOMING PART OF THE DESCENDANT

By now it should be clear that Abraham understood the basic elements of the Christian Gospel. But these vital promises were to Abraham and his descendant, Jesus. What about anyone else? Even physical descent from Abraham would not automatically make someone part of that one specific descendant (Jn. 8:39; Rom. 9:7). Somehow we have to become intimately part of Jesus, so that the promises to the descendant are shared with us as well. This is by baptism into Jesus (Rom. 6:3-5); frequently we read of baptism *into* his name (Acts 2:38; 8:16; 10:48; 19:5). Gal. 3:27-29 could not make the point any clearer:

"As many of you (i.e. only as many!) as have been baptised into Christ have put on Christ. There is neither Jew nor Greek (Gentile), there is neither slave nor free man, there is neither male nor female: for you are all one (through being) in Christ Jesus (by baptism). And if you be Christ's (by baptism into him), then are you Abraham's descendants, and heirs according to the promise".

The promise is of eternal life on earth, through receiving the "blessing" of forgiveness through Jesus. It is by being baptised into Christ, the descendant, that we share the promises made to him; and so Rom. 8:17 calls us "joint heirs with Christ". People from all nations "bless themselves" by becoming part of that descendant through baptism into Him- they thus appropriate to themselves the promised blessings (Gen. 22:18 RVmg.).

Remember that the blessing was to come on people from all parts of the earth, through the descendant; and the descendant was to become a worldwide group of people, like the sand of the shores and the stars of the sky. It follows that this is due to their first receiving the blessing so that they can become the descendant. Thus the (singular) descendant "shall be accounted to the Lord for a generation" (i.e. many people; Ps. 22:30).

We can summarise the two strands of the promises given to Abraham.

1. THE LAND

Abraham and his descendant, Jesus, and those in him would inherit the land of Canaan and by extension the whole earth, and live there forever. In this life they would not receive it, but would do so at the last day, when Jesus returns.

2. THE DESCENDANT

This was primarily Jesus. Through Him the sins ("enemies") of mankind would be overcome, so that the blessings of forgiveness would be made available world-wide.

By baptism into the name of Jesus we become part of the descendant promised to Abraham.

These same two threads occur in New Testament preaching, and, not surprisingly, it is often recorded that when people heard them taught, they were then baptised. This was, and is, the way through which these promises can be made to us. We can now understand why, as an old man faced with death, Paul could define his hope as "the hope of Israel" (Acts 28:20): the true Christian hope is the original Jewish hope. Christ's comment that "salvation is of the Jews" (Jn. 4:22) must also refer to the need to become spiritual Jews, so that we can benefit from the promises of salvation through Christ which were made to the Jewish fathers.

We read that the early Christians preached:-

1. "The things concerning the Kingdom of God

and

2. the name of Jesus Christ" (Acts 8:12).

These were the very two things explained to Abraham under slightly different headings.

1. Promises about the land

and

2. Promises about the descendant.

Note in passing that "the things" (plural) about the Kingdom and Jesus are summarised as "preaching Christ" (Acts 8:5 cf. v. 12). At times, this has taken to mean "Jesus loves you! Just say you believe he died for you and you're a saved man!". All of which is valid in some sense. But the phrase "Christ" clearly summarises the teaching of a number of things about him and his coming Kingdom. The good news about this Kingdom which was preached to Abraham played a big part in the early preaching of the Gospel.

In Ephesus, Paul was "three months, disputing and persuading the things concerning the Kingdom of God" (Acts 19:8; 20:25); and his swansong in Rome was the same, "He expounded and testified the Kingdom of God, persuading them concerning Jesus...out of the law...and out of the prophets" (Acts 28:23,31). That there was so much to talk about shows that the basic Gospel message about the Kingdom and Jesus was not simply and only a matter of saying "Believe on Jesus". God's revelation to Abraham was more detailed than that, and the things promised to him are the basis of the true Christian Gospel.

We have shown that baptism into Jesus makes us part of the promised descendant and therefore able to inherit the promises (Gal. 3:27-29), but baptism alone is not enough to gain us the salvation promised. We must remain in the descendant, in Christ, if we are to receive the promises made to the descendant. Baptism is therefore just a beginning; we have entered a race which we then need to run. Don't forget that just physically being Abraham's descendant does not mean that we are acceptable to God. The Israelis are Abraham's descendants but this does not mean that they will be saved without being baptised and conforming their lives to Christ and the example of Abraham (Rom. 9:7,8; 4:13,14). Jesus told the Jews: "I know that you are Abraham's descendants; but you seek to kill me...If you were Abraham's children, you would do the works of Abraham" (Jn. 8:37,39), which was to live a life of faith in God and Christ, the promised descendant (Jn. 6:29).

The descendant or "seed" must have the characteristics of its ancestor. If we are to be the true descendant of Abraham we must therefore not only be baptised but also have a very real faith in God's promises, just as he had. He is therefore called "the father of all them that believe...who also walk in the steps of that faith of our father Abraham, which he had" (Rom. 4:11,12). "Know therefore (i.e. really take it to heart!) that they which are of faith, the same are the children of Abraham" (Gal. 3:7). Paul is alluding here to the practice of Gentile converts to Judaism ["proselytes"] taking the name *ben Avraham*, son of Abraham. The real conversion to the hope of Israel, Paul is saying, is not through joining Judiasm but through faith and baptism (Gal. 3:27-29).

Real faith must show itself in some sort of action, otherwise, in God's eyes, it isn't faith (James 2:17). We demonstrate our belief in these promises that we have studied by first being baptised, so that they come to apply to us personally (Gal. 3:27-29). This is even an Old Testament idea- for David says that the true believer will share the promise to Abraham that "his descendant shall inherit the land", and thus God will make us know personally His covenant with us (Ps. 25:13,14 RVmg.). So do you really believe God's promises? This is a question we must continually ask ourselves all our lives long.

THE OLD AND NEW COVENANT

It should be evident by now that the promises to Abraham summarise the Gospel of Christ. The other major set of promises which God made were with the Jews in the context of the law of Moses. These stated that if the Jews were obedient to this law, then they would be physically blessed in this life (Dt. 28). There was no direct promise of eternal life in this series of promises, or "covenant". So we see that there have been two "covenants" made.

1. To Abraham and his descendant, promising forgiveness and eternal life in God's Kingdom when Christ returns. This promise was also made in Eden and to David. This is the "new covenant". When this "new covenant" is made with Israel when Christ returns, it will include the promise to Abraham that "I will be their God" (Jer. 31:33 cf. Gen. 17:8).

2. To the Jewish people at the time of Moses, promising them peace and happiness in this present life if they obeyed the law which God gave to Moses.

God promised Abraham forgiveness and eternal life in the Kingdom, but this was only possible through the sacrifice of Jesus. For this reason we read that Christ's death on the cross confirmed the promises to Abraham (Gal. 3:17; Rom. 15:8; Dan. 9:27; 2 Cor. 1:20), therefore his blood is called the "blood of the new testament" (covenant, Mt. 26:28). It is to remember this that Jesus told us to regularly take the cup of wine, symbolising his blood, to remind us of these things (see 1 Cor. 11:25): "This cup is the new testament (covenant) in my blood" (Lk. 22:20). There is no point in "breaking bread" in memory of Jesus and his work unless we understand these things.

The sacrifice of Jesus made forgiveness and eternal life in God's Kingdom possible; he therefore made the promises to Abraham sure; he was "a surety of a better testament" (Heb. 7:22). Heb. 10:9 speaks of Jesus taking "away the first (covenant), that he may establish the second". This shows that when Jesus confirmed the promises to Abraham, he did away with another covenant, i.e. the covenant given through Moses. The verses already quoted about Jesus confirming a new covenant by his death, imply that there was an old covenant which he did away with (Heb. 8:13).

This means that although the covenant concerning Christ was made first, it did not come into operation until his death, therefore it is called the "new" covenant. The purpose of the "old" covenant made through Moses was to point forward to the work of Jesus, and to highlight the importance of faith in the promises concerning Christ (Gal. 3:19,21). Conversely, faith in Christ confirms the truth of the law given to Moses (Rom. 3:31). Paul sums it up: "The law was our schoolmaster to bring us unto Christ, that we might be justified by faith" (Gal. 3:24). It is for this purpose that the law through Moses has been preserved, and is still beneficial for us to study.

These things are not easy to understand at first reading; we can summarise as follows:

- Promises concerning Christ made to Abraham - New Covenant.

- Promises to Israel associated with the law given to Moses - Old Covenant.

- Death of Christ - Old Covenant ended (Col. 2:14-17); New Covenant came into operation.

For this reason things like tithing, Sabbath-keeping etc., which were part of the Old Covenant, are not now necessary - see Study 9.4. The New Covenant will be made with natural Israel when they repent and accept Christ (Jer. 31:31,32; Rom. 9:26,27; Ez. 16:62; 37:26). Of course any Jew who does that now and is baptised into Jesus, can immediately enter the New Covenant (in which there is no Jew/Gentile distinction - Gal. 3:27-29).

Truly appreciating these things makes us realise the certainty of God's promises. Sceptics unfairly accused the early Christian preachers of not giving a positive message. Paul replied by saying that because of God's confirmation of His promises on account of the death of Christ, the hope they spoke of was not a touch-and-go affair, but a totally certain offer: "As God is true, our word (of preaching) toward you was not Yes and No. For the Son of God, Jesus Christ, who was preached among you by us...was not Yes and No, but in him was Yes. For all the promises of God in him are Yes, and in him, Amen" (2 Cor. 1:17-20).

Surely this torpedoes the attitude of, 'Well, I suppose there *might* be some truth in all that...'?

"I WILL BE WITH YOU"

There are two other things promised to Abraham and his descendants: "I will be their God...I will be with you" (Gen. 17:8; 26:3; 28:15 cf. Ex. 6:7). The Lord Jesus Christ is 'God with us' (Emmanuel, Is. 7:14). For those of us who have part in these promises concerning Jesus Christ and the Kingdom of God, God will be with us and guide us to that happy end. Time and again God's people in their times of desperation have come back to these promises to Abraham, in their realisation that truly God *is* with us (e.g. 2 Chron. 32:7,8). Covenant relationship with God means that He will give us foretastes of His future salvation by being our God *now* and going with us in salvation *now* (Ps. 111:9). And we will respond to this, and fulfil the truth of 2 Cor. 1:20, which says that the sure outworking of God's promises to us results in us glorifying Him.

3.5   The Promise To David

David, like Abraham and many other recipients of God's promises, did not have an easy life. He grew up as the youngest son in a large family which, in the Israel of 1000 B.C., meant looking after the sheep and running errands for his older brothers (1 Sam. 15-17). During this time he learnt a level of faith in God which few men have since approached.

The day came when Israel were faced with the ultimate challenge from their aggressive neighbours, the Philistines; they were challenged to let one of their men fight the giant Goliath, the Philistine champion, on the understanding that whoever won that fight would rule over the losers. With God's help David defeated Goliath by using a sling, which earned him even greater popularity than their king (Saul). "Jealousy is cruel as the grave" (Song 8:6), words which were proved true by Saul's persecution of David chasing him around the wilderness of southern Israel.

Eventually David became king, and to show his appreciation of God's love toward him during the wilderness of his life, he decided to build God a temple. The reply from God was that David's son, Solomon, would build the temple and that God wanted to build *David* a house (2 Sam. 7:4-13). Then followed a detailed promise which repeats much of what was told Abraham, and which also filled in some other details.

"And when your days are fulfilled, and you shall sleep with your fathers, I will set up your descendant after you, which shall proceed out of your body, and I will establish his kingdom. He shall build an house for my name, and I will establish the throne of his kingdom forever. I will be his father, and he shall be my son. If he commit iniquity, I will chasten him with the rod of men, and with the stripes of the children of men: But my mercy shall not depart away from him, as I took it from Saul, whom I put away before you. And your house and your kingdom shall be established forever before you: your throne shall be established forever" (v.12-16).

From our previous studies we would expect the "descendant" to be Jesus. His description as the Son of God (2 Sam. 7:14) confirms this, as do many other references in other parts of the Bible.

- "I am the...offspring of David", Jesus said (Rev. 22:16).

- "(Jesus), made of the family [AV "seed"] of David according to the flesh" (Rom. 1:3).

- "Of this man's descendants (David's) has God, according to His promise, raised unto Israel a saviour, Jesus" (Acts 13:23).

- The angel told the virgin Mary concerning her son, Jesus: "The Lord God shall give unto him the throne of his father (ancestor) David...and of his Kingdom there shall be no end" (Lk. 1:32,33). This is applying the promise of David's descendant, in 2 Sam. 7:13, to Jesus.

With the descendant firmly identified as Jesus, a number of details now become significant.

1. THE DESCENDANT

"Your descendant...which shall proceed out of your body...I will be his father, and he shall be my son." "...of the fruit of your body will I set upon your throne" (2 Sam. 7:12,14; Ps. 132:10,11). Jesus, the descendant, was to be a literal, bodily descendant of David, and yet have God as his Father. This could only be achieved by the virgin birth as described in the New Testament; Jesus' mother was Mary, a descendant of David (Lk. 1:32), but he had no human father. God acted miraculously upon Mary's womb by the Holy Spirit in order to make her conceive Jesus, and so the Angel commented: "Therefore also that holy thing which shall be born of you shall be called the Son of God" (Lk. 1:35). The "virgin birth" was the only way in which this promise to David could be properly fulfilled.

2. THE HOUSE

"He shall build an house for my name" (2 Sam. 7:13) shows that Jesus will build a temple for God. God's "house" is where He is willing to live, and Is. 66:1,2 tells us that He will come to live in the hearts of men who are humble to His word. Jesus is therefore building a spiritual temple for God to dwell in, made up of the true believers. Descriptions of Jesus as the foundation stone of God's temple (1 Pet. 2:4-8) and of Christians as the temple stones (1 Pet. 2:5) now slot into place.

3. THE THRONE

"I will establish the throne of his (Christ's) kingdom for ever... your (David's) house and your kingdom... your throne shall be established for ever" (2 Sam. 7:13,16 cf. Is. 9:6,7). Christ's kingdom will therefore be based on David's kingdom of Israel; this means that the coming kingdom of God will be a re-establishment of the kingdom of Israel - see Study 5.3 for more on this. To fulfil this promise, Christ must reign on David's "throne", or place of rulership. This was literally in Jerusalem. This is another proof that the kingdom must be established here on earth in order to fulfil these promises.

4. THE KINGDOM

"Your house and your kingdom shall be established for ever before you" (2 Sam. 7:16) suggests that David would witness the establishment of Christ's eternal kingdom. This was therefore an indirect promise that he would be resurrected at Christ's return so that he could see with his own eyes the kingdom being set up world-wide, with Jesus reigning from Jerusalem.

These things which were promised to David are absolutely vital to understand. David joyfully spoke of these things as "an everlasting covenant... this is all my salvation and all my desire" (2 Sam. 23:5). These things relate to our salvation too; rejoicing in them should likewise be all our desire. As with the promises to Abraham, if we are in Christ, all that is true of the promised descendant of David is in some way true of us if we are in Christ (Is. 55:3 cf. Acts 13:34). So again the point is made that these doctrines are so important. It is a tragedy that parts of Christendom have adopted doctrines which flatly contradict these marvellous truths.

- If Jesus physically "pre-existed", i.e. he existed as a person before he was born, then this makes nonsense of these promises that Jesus would be David's descendant.

- If the kingdom of God will be in heaven, then Jesus cannot re-establish David's kingdom of Israel, nor can he reign from David's "throne" or place of rulership. These things were literally on the earth, and so their re-establishment must be in the same place.

FULFILMENT IN SOLOMON?

David's son, Solomon, fulfilled some part of the promises to David. He built a temple for God (1 Kings 5-8), and he had a very prosperous kingdom. Nations from all around sent representatives to pay respect to Solomon (1 Kings 10), and there was great spiritual blessing from the use of the temple. Solomon's reign therefore pointed forward to the much greater fulfilment of the promises to David which will be seen in the kingdom of Christ.

Some have claimed that the promises to David were completely fulfilled in Solomon, but this is disallowed by the following.

- Abundant New Testament evidence shows that the "descendant" was Christ, not Solomon.

- David seems to have connected the promises God made to him with those to Abraham (1 Chron. 17:27 = Gen. 22:17,18).

- The kingdom of the "descendant" was to be everlasting - which Solomon's was not.

- David recognised that the promises were concerning eternal life, which precluded any reference to his immediate family: "Although my house be not so with God; yet he hath made with me an everlasting covenant" (2 Sam. 23:5).

- The descendant of David is the Messiah, the Saviour from sin (Is. 9:6,7; 22:22; Jer. 33:5,6,15; Jn. 7:42). But Solomon later turned away from God (1 Kings 11:1-13; Neh. 13:26) due to his marriage with those outside the hope of Israel.

Belief In Practice 9:

Covenant Relationship With God

The real import of the covenant-relationship with God which we have is brought out by David in 1 Chron. 16:15-18: "Be you mindful always of his covenant; the word which he commanded to a thousand generations; even of the covenant which he made with Abraham, and of his oath unto Isaac; and has confirmed the same to Jacob for a law, and to Israel for an everlasting covenant, Saying, Unto you will I give the land of Canaan, the lot of your inheritance". The covenant, the promise that God's people really will inherit the land, becomes a law, a "word which he commanded", something which should be thought about all the time. The sure promise of entering the Kingdom, the knowledge that by grace, according to the covenant, 'we will be there', cannot be accepted passively. The covenant-certainty of that great salvation becomes a command to action. We'll now look at some of those actions in practice. Reflect a moment upon the sheer power and import of the fact that the Father *promised* things to us, who are Abraham's children by faith and baptism. The Law of Moses was a conditional promise, because there were two parties; but the promises to us are in some sense unconditional, as God is the only "one" party (Gal. 3:19,20). And as if God's own unconditional promise isn't enough, He confirmed those promises to us with the blood of His very own son. Bearing this in mind, it's not surprising that Ps. 111:5 states that God "will *ever* be mindful of His covenant". This means that He's thinking about the covenant made with us *all* the time! And yet how often in daily life do we reflect upon the fact that we really are in covenant relationship with God... how often do we recollect the part we share in the promises to Abraham, how frequently do we feel that we really are in a personal covenant with God Almighty?

JOY

Abraham rejoiced to see the day of Christ (Jn. 8:56)- and this is surely an allusion to how he laughed [for joy] at the promise of Isaac. He " gladly received the promises" (Heb. 11:17 RV). And realizing that through baptism the promises are made to us ought to inspire a deep seated joy too. Yet we will only achieve this if we firmly grasp the  real, pointed relevance of the promises to us; that we who are baptized are each one truly and absolutely in Christ, and the promises apply to *me* personally.

STUDY 3: Questions

1. Which of God's promises predicts a constant struggle between sin and the righteous?
- ☐ The promise to Noah
- ☐ The promise in Eden
- ☐ The promise to David
- ☐ The promise to Abraham

2. Which of the following statements are true concerning the promise in Eden?

- ☐ The seed of the serpent is Lucifer
- ☐ Christ and the righteous are the woman's seed
- ☐ The seed of the serpent was temporarily wounded by Christ
- ☐ The seed of the woman was bruised by Christ's death.

3. Where would Abraham's seed live for ever?
- ☐ In Heaven
- ☐ In the city of Jerusalem
- ☐ On the earth
- ☐ Some in Heaven and some on earth.

4. Which of the following were promised to David?
- ☐ That his great descendant would reign for ever
- ☐ That his 'seed' would have a Kingdom in Heaven
- ☐ That the seed would be God's son
- ☐ That his seed, Jesus, would live in Heaven before birth on earth.

5. How can we become the seed of Abraham?

6. Will the earth ever be destroyed?
- ☐ Yes
- ☐ No

7. How do God's promises prove your answer to question 6?

8. Explain the promise in Eden in Genesis 3:15.

STUDY 4
God and Death

4.1   The Nature Of Man

The majority of people seem to spend little time thinking about death, or about their own nature. Such lack of self-examination leads to a lack of self-knowledge, and therefore people drift along through life, making their decisions according to the dictates of their own natural desires. There is a refusal - albeit heavily masked - to take on board the fact that life is so short that all too soon the finality of death will be upon us. "For what is your life? It is even a vapour, that appears for a little time, and then vanishes away". "We will surely die and become like water spilled on the ground, which cannot be gathered up again". "Like grass which grows up; in the morning it flourishes and grows up; in the evening it is cut down and withers" (James 4:14; 2 Sam. 14:14; Ps. 90:5,6). Moses, a truly thoughtful man, recognised this, and pleaded to God: "So teach us to number our days, that we may gain a heart of wisdom." (Ps. 90:12) Therefore, in view of life's brevity, we should make our acquisition of true wisdom a number one priority.

Human response to the finality of death is varied. Some cultures have tried to make death and funerals part of life, to lessen the sense of loss and finality. The majority of those bearing the name Christian have concluded that man has an 'immortal soul' or some element of immortality within him which survives death, going on to some place of reward or punishment afterwards. Death being the most fundamental problem and tragedy of human experience, it is to be expected that the human mind has been much exercised to lessen its mental impact; therefore a whole range of false theories have arisen concerning death and the very nature of man. As always, these must be tested against the Bible in order to find the real truth about this vital topic. It should be remembered that the very first lie recorded in the Bible is that of the serpent in the garden of Eden. Contrary to God's plain statement that man would "surely die" if he sinned (Gen. 2:17), the serpent asserted, "You will not surely die" (Gen. 3:4). This attempt to negate the finality and totality of death has become a characteristic of all false religions. It is evident that in this area especially, one false doctrine leads to another, and another, and another. Conversely, one piece of truth leads to another, as shown by 1 Cor. 15:13-17. Here Paul jumps from one truth to another (notice "if...if...if...").

To understand our true nature, we need to consider what the Bible says about the creation of man. The record is in plain language, which, if taken literally, leaves us in no doubt about exactly what we are by nature (see Digression 18 concerning the literality of Genesis). "The Lord God formed man of the dust of the ground...out of it (the ground) you (Adam) were taken; for dust you are, and to dust you shall return" (Gen. 2:7; 3:19). There is absolutely no hint here that man has any inherent immortality; there is no part of him that will live on after death.

There is a marked Biblical emphasis on the fact that man is fundamentally composed of mere dust: "We are the clay" (Is. 64:8); "man is of the earth, made of dust;" (1 Cor. 15:47); man's "foundation is in the dust" (Job 4:19); "and man would return to dust" (Job 34:14,15). Abraham admitted that he was "but dust and ashes" (Gen. 18:27). Immediately after disobeying God's command in Eden, God "drove out the man...lest he put out his hand, and take also of the tree of life, and eat, and live for ever" (Gen. 3:24,22). If man had an immortal element within him naturally, this would have been unnecessary.

CONDITIONAL IMMORTALITY

The constantly repeated message of the Gospel is that man can find a way to gain eternal life and immortality through the work of Christ. This is the only type of immortality that the Bible speaks about and it follows that the idea of an eternity of conscious suffering for wrongdoing is without any Biblical support. The only way to gain immortality is through obedience to God's commands, and those who are so obedient will spend immortality in a state of perfection - the reward for righteousness.

The following passages should be proof enough that this immortality is conditional, and is not something that we naturally possess.

- "Christ...has brought life and immortality to light through the gospel" (2 Tim. 1:10; 1Jn. 1:2). He is the "author" or "cause" of "eternal salvation" (Heb. 2:10; 5:9 RVmg.).

- "Unless you eat the flesh of the Son of man and drink his blood, you have no life in you (i.e. 'inherent in you'). Whoever eats My flesh, and drinks My blood has eternal life, and I will raise him up at the last day" - to give him this "eternal life" (Jn. 6:53,54). Christ's reasoning throughout Jn. ch. 6 is that he is the "bread of life", and that only through correct response to him can there be any hope of immortality (Jn. 6:47,50,51,57,58).

- "God has given us (believers) eternal life, and this life is in His Son" (1 Jn. 5:11). There can be no hope of immortality for those not "in Christ". Only through Christ has immortality been made possible; He is the "Prince of (eternal) life" (Acts 3:15) - "the author of eternal salvation to all who obey him" (Heb. 5:9). Immortality for men was therefore originated through the work of Christ.

- The true believer seeks for immortality, and will be rewarded for this by the gift of eternal life - something he does not naturally possess (Rom. 2:7; 6:23; Jn. 10:28). Our mortal body "must put on immortality" at the return of Christ (1 Cor. 15:53); thus immortality is something promised, not now possessed (1 Jn. 2:25).

- If it should be that Christ did not rise from the dead, then those who have died in Him would perish (1 Cor. 15:18). It follows therefore that they did not have 'immortal souls' that went to reward in Heaven on death.

- God alone has inherent immortality (1 Tim. 6:16).

4.2   The Soul

In the light of the foregoing it ought to be inconceivable that man has an 'immortal soul' or any immortal element within him naturally. We will now attempt to clear up the confusion surrounding the word 'soul'.

The Hebrew and Greek words which are translated 'soul' in the Bible ('Nephesh' and 'Psuche' respectively) are also translated in the following ways:

Body, Breath, Creature, Heart, Mind,
Person, Himself, Life

The 'soul' therefore refers to the person, body or self. The famous 'Save Our Souls' (SOS) clearly means 'Save us from death!' The 'soul' is therefore 'you', or the summation of all the things that make up a person. It is understandable, therefore, that many modern versions of the Bible (e.g. the N.I.V.) rarely use the word 'soul', translating it instead as 'you' or 'the person'. The animals which God created are called "living creatures...every living thing that moves" (Gen. 1:20,21). The Hebrew word translated "creatures" and "living thing" here is 'nephesh', which is also translated 'being'; for example in Gen. 2:7: "...and man became a living being". Thus man is a 'soul' or 'living being', just as the animals are 'souls' or 'living beings'. The only difference between mankind and animals is that man is mentally superior to them; he is created in the image of God (Gen. 1:26; see **Study 1.2**), and some men are called to know the Gospel through which the hope of immortality is opened up to them (2 Tim. 1:10). As regards our fundamental nature and the nature of our death, there is no difference between man and animals.

"What happens to the sons of men also happens to beasts; one thing befalls them: (note the double emphasis): as one dies, so dies the other... man has no advantage over beasts...All (i.e. man and animals) go to one place (the grave); all are from the dust, and all return to dust" (Ecc. 3:19,20). The inspired writer of Ecclesiastes prayed that God would help men to appreciate this hard fact, "that (men) may see that they themselves are like beasts" (Ecc. 3:18). It is therefore to be expected that many people will find this fact hard to accept; indeed, it can be humiliating to realise that by nature we are just animals, living out the same instincts of self-preservation, survival of the fittest and procreation. The N.I.V. translation of Ecc. 3:18 says that God 'tests' man by making him see that he is just an animal; i.e. those who are humble enough to be His true people will realise the truth of this, but those who are not will fail this 'test'. The philosophy of humanism - the idea that human beings are of such supreme importance and value - has quietly spread throughout the world during the twentieth century. It is a considerable task to clear our thinking of the influence of humanism. The plain words of Ps. 39:5 are a help: "Man at his best state is but vapour". "It is not for man to direct his steps" (Jer. 10:23 N.I.V.).

One of the most basic things that we know is that all human bodies - indeed all "living creatures" - eventually die. The 'soul', therefore, dies; it is the exact opposite of something that is immortal. Indeed, 652 of the 754 times the Hebrew word *nephesh* occurs, it is used about the soul or creature dying. It is not surprising that about a third of all uses of this word in the Bible are associated with the death and destruction of the 'soul'. The very fact that the word 'soul' is used in this way shows that it cannot be something which is indestructible and immortal.

- "The soul who sins shall die" (Ez. 18:4).
- God can destroy the soul (Mt. 10:28). Other references to souls being destroyed are: Ez. 22:27 (people = *nephesh*); Prov. 6:32; Lev. 23:30 (person = *nephesh*).
- All the "people" (*nephesh*) that were within the city of Hazor were killed by the sword (Josh. 11:11; cf. Josh. 10:30-39).
- "...every living creature (*psuche*). died" (Rev. 16:3; cf. Ps. 78:50).

- The Hebrew word *nephesh* translated "soul" is also translated "dead body" in Num. 9:6. "No man can deliver his life (*nephesh*) from the power of the grave" (Ps. 89:48).
- Frequently the Law of Moses commanded that any "person" (*nephesh*) which disobeyed certain laws should be killed (e.g. Num. 15:27-31).
- References to the soul being strangled or snared can only make sense if it is understood that the soul can die (Prov. 18:7; 22:25; Job 7:15).
- None can "keep himself (*nephesh*) alive" (Ps. 22:29).
- Christ "poured out his soul unto death" so that his "soul", or life, was made an offering for sin (Is. 53:10,12).
- That the 'soul' refers to the person or body rather than some immortal spark within us is shown by the majority of verses in which the word occurs, here are some obvious examples.
- "The blood of the lives (*nephesh*) of ... " (Jer. 2:34).
- "If a person (*nephesh*) sins in hearing ... an oath ...if he does not tell it...if he (*nephesh*) touches human uncleanness ...if a person (*nephesh*) swears, speaking thoughtlessly with his lips" (Lev. 5:1-4).
- "O my soul...all that is within me...Bless the Lord, O my soul...Who satisfies your mouth with good things" (Ps. 103:1,2,5).
- Num. 21:4 shows that a group of people can have one "soul". The "soul" therefore cannot refer to a spark of personal immortality within each of us.

"Whosoever will save his life ('soul') shall lose it; but whosoever shall lose his life ('soul') for my sake...shall save it" (Mk. 8:35). This is proof enough that the soul does not refer to any spiritual element within man; here, 'soul' (Greek 'psuche') just means one's physical life, which is how it is translated here. We must give our lives/souls after the pattern of the Lord Jesus on the cross, who "poured out his soul unto death" (Is. 53:12).

Not that it makes any difference to Bible truth, but it's worth mentioning that many eminent Bible students and theologians have come to the same conclusions as we've reached here - the soul isn't immortal. One of the clearest evidences for this is in the following quote: "Contrary to what is usually supposed, the doctrine of the immortality of the soul finds no place in the Old Testament or the New" John Robinson, Bishop of Woolwich, *On Being The Church In The World* (Harmondsworth, UK: Penguin, 1960) p. 18.

4.3   The Spirit Of Man

There is an unfortunate confusion in many people's minds between the soul and the spirit. This is aggravated by the fact that in some languages and Bible translations, the English words 'soul' and 'spirit' have only one equivalent. The 'soul' fundamentally referring to all the constituents of a person can sometimes refer to the spirit as well. However, normally there is a difference in meaning between 'soul' and 'spirit' as used in the Bible; soul and spirit can be 'divided ' (Heb. 4:12).

The Hebrew and Greek words for 'spirit' ('Ruach' and 'Pneuma' respectively) are also translated in the following ways.

Life, Spirit, Mind, Wind, Breath

We have studied the idea of 'spirit' in Study 2.1. God uses His spirit to preserve the natural creation, including man. The spirit of God which is within man is therefore the life force within him. "The body without the spirit is dead" (James 2:26). "God breathed into (Adam's nostrils) the breath (spirit) of life; and man became a living being" (Gen. 2:7). Job speaks of "the breath of God" as being "in my nostrils" (Job 27:3 cf. Is. 2:22). The spirit of life within us is therefore given to us at birth, and remains as long as our body is alive. When God's spirit is withdrawn from anything, it immediately perishes - the spirit is the life force. If God "gather to Himself His spirit and His breath, all flesh would perish together, and man would return to dust. If you have understanding, hear this" (Job 34:14-16). The last sentence again hints that man finds this exposure of his real nature very hard to come to terms with.

When God takes away His spirit from us at death, not only does our body die, but our entire consciousness ceases. David's appreciation of this led him to trust in God rather than in creatures as weak as man. Ps. 146:3-5 is a tough counter to the claims of humanism: "Do not put your trust in princes, nor in a son of man, in whom there is no help. His spirit departs, he returns to his earth (the dust from which we are made); in that very day his plans perish. Happy is he who has the God of Jacob for his help".

At death, "the dust will return to the earth as it was, and the spirit will return to God who gave it" (Ecc. 12:7). We have shown earlier that God is present everywhere through His spirit. In this sense "God is Spirit" (Jn. 4:24). When we die we 'breathe our last' in the sense that God's spirit within us departs from us. That spirit is absorbed into God's spirit which is all around us; so at death "the spirit will return to God".

Because God's spirit sustains all of creation, this same process of death occurs to animals. Men and animals have the same spirit, or life force, within them. "What happens to the sons of men also happens to beasts; one thing befalls them: as one dies, so dies the other. Surely, they all have one (i.e. the same) breath (spirit); man has no advantage over beasts" (Ecc. 3:19). The writer goes on to say that there is no discernible difference between where the spirit of men and animals goes (Ecc. 3:21). This description of men and animals having the same spirit and dying the same death, appears to allude back to the description of how both men and animals, who both had the spirit of life from God (Gen. 2:7; 7:15), were destroyed with the same death at the flood: "All flesh died that moved on the earth: birds and cattle and beasts and every creeping thing that creeps on the earth, and every man. All in whose nostrils was the breath of the spirit of life...died... all living things were destroyed" (Gen. 7:21-23). Note in passing how Ps. 90:5 likens death to the flood. The record in Genesis 7 clearly shows that in fundamental terms, man is in the same category as "all flesh... all living things". This is due to his having the same spirit of life within him as they do.

Some have argued that the fact God breathed His Spirit into man means that by nature we have immortality within us. This is not so. The fact that God breathed into Adam the spirit/power of life meant that he became a living soul; but this fact is quoted in 1 Cor. 15:45 as proof that Adam was *mortal*; he was only a living soul, a living creature, but was mortal compared to the *immortality* of the Lord Jesus.

4.4   Death Is Unconsciousness

From what we have learnt so far about the soul and spirit, it should follow that while dead, a person is totally unconscious. Whilst the actions of those responsible to God will be remembered by Him (Mal. 3:16; Rev. 20:12; Heb. 6:10), there is nothing in the Bible to suggest that we have any consciousness during the death state. It is hard to argue with the following clear statements concerning this.

- "(Man's) spirit (breath K.J.V.) departs, he returns to his earth; in that very day (moment) his plans perish" (Ps. 146:4).
- "The dead know nothing...their love, their hatred, and their envy is now perished" (Ecc. 9:5,6). There is no "wisdom in the grave" (Ecc. 9:10) - no thinking and therefore no consciousness.

- Job says that on death, he would be "as though he had not been" (Job 10:18-19); he saw death as the oblivion, unconsciousness and total lack of existence which we had before we were born.
- Man dies as the animals do (Ecc. 3:19); if man consciously survives death somewhere, so must they, yet both Scripture and science are silent about this.
- God "remembers that we are dust. As for man, his days are like grass; as a flower of the field, so he flourishes...it is gone, and its place remembers it no more" (Ps. 103:14-16).

That death is truly unconsciousness, even for the righteous, is demonstrated by the repeated pleas of God's servants to allow their lives to be lengthened, because they knew that after death they would be unable to praise and glorify God, seeing that death was a state of unconsciousness. Hezekiah (Is. 38:17-19) and David (Ps. 6:4,5; 30:9; 39:13; 115:17) are good examples of this. Death is repeatedly referred to as a sleep or rest, both for the righteous and the wicked (Job 3:11,13,17; Dan. 12:13).

Sufficient evidence has now been produced for us to state bluntly that the popular idea of the righteous going to a state of bliss and reward in heaven straight after their death, is simply not found in the Bible. The true doctrine of death and man's nature provides a great sense of peace. After all the traumas and pains of a man's life, the grave is a place of total oblivion. For those who have not known the requirements of God, this oblivion will last forever. Never again will the old scores of this tragic and unfulfilled natural life be raised; the futile hopes and fears of the natural human mind will not be realised or threaten.

In Bible study, there is a system of truth to be discovered; yet, sadly, there is also a system of error in man's religious thinking, due to inattention to the Bible. Man's desperate efforts to soften the finality of death have led him to believe that he has an 'immortal soul'. Once it is accepted that such an immortal element exists within man, it becomes necessary to think that it must go somewhere after death. This has led to the thought that at death there must be some difference between the fates of the righteous and the wicked. To accommodate this, it has been concluded that there must be a place for 'good immortal souls' to go, called Heaven, and another place for 'bad immortal souls' to go, called hell. We have shown earlier that an 'immortal soul' is a Biblical impossibility. The other false ideas inherent in the popular reasoning will now be analysed.

1. That the reward for our lives is given at death in the form of our 'immortal soul' being assigned to a certain place.

2. That the separation between righteous and wicked occurs at death.

3. That the reward for the righteous is to go to heaven.

4. That if everyone has an 'immortal soul', then everyone must go to either heaven or hell.

5. That the wicked 'souls' will go to a place of punishment called hell.

The purpose of our analysis is not just negative; by considering these points in detail, we believe that we will express many elements of Bible truth which are vital parts of the true picture concerning man's nature. And again, we're not alone in these conclusions:

"The Bible nowhere says that we go to heaven when we die, nor does it ever describe death in terms of going to heaven. In the Old Testament, you went to *sheol* when you died". John Robinson, Bishop of Woolwich, *On Being The Church In The World* (Harmondsworth, UK: Penguin, 1960) p. 156.

4.5   The Resurrection

The Bible emphasises that the reward of the righteous will be at the resurrection, at the coming of Christ (1 Thes. 4:16). The resurrection of the responsible dead (see Study 4.8) will be the first thing Christ will do; this will be followed by the judgment. If the 'soul' went to heaven at death there would be no need for the resurrection. Paul said that if there is no resurrection, then all effort to be obedient to God is pointless (1 Cor. 15:32). Surely he would not have reasoned like this if he believed that he would also be rewarded with his 'soul' going to heaven at death? The implication is that he believed the resurrection of the body to be the only form of reward. Christ encouraged us with the expectation that the recompense for faithful living now would be at "the resurrection" (Lk. 14:14).

At his return, Christ "will transform our lowly body, that it may be conformed to his glorious body" (Phil. 3:20,21). As he now has a literal bodily form, energised purely by Spirit rather than blood, so we will share a similar reward. Those who have died and decomposed to dust will "awake and sing" (Is. 26:19). At the judgment we will receive a recompense for how we have lived this life in a bodily form (2 Cor. 5:10). Those who have lived an unspiritual life will be left with their present mortal body, which will then rot back to dust; whilst those who in their lives have tried to overcome the unspiritual mind with that of the Spirit "will reap from it a harvest of eternal life" (Gal. 6:8 R.E.B.) in the form of a Spirit-filled body.

There is ample further evidence that the reward of the righteous will be in a bodily form. Once this is accepted, the vital importance of the resurrection should be apparent. Our present body clearly ceases to exist at death; if we can only experience eternal life and immortality in a bodily form, it follows that death must be a state of unconsciousness, until such time as our body is re-created and then given God's nature.

The whole of 1 Cor. 15 speaks in detail of the resurrection; it will always repay careful reading. 1 Cor. 15:35-44 explains how that as a seed is sown and then emerges from the ground to be given a body by God, so the dead will likewise rise, to be rewarded with a body. As Christ rose from the grave and had his mortal body changed to an immortalised body, so the true believer will share his reward (Phil. 3:21). Through baptism we associate ourselves with Christ's death and resurrection, showing our belief that we too will share the reward which he received through his resurrection (Rom. 6:3-5). Through sharing in his sufferings now, we will also share his reward: "carrying about (now) in the body the dying of the Lord Jesus, that the life of Jesus also may be manifested in our body" (2 Cor. 4:10). "He who raised Christ from the dead will also give life to your mortal bodies through his Spirit" (Rom. 8:11). With this hope, we therefore wait for "the redemption of our body" (Rom. 8:23), through that body being immortalised.

This hope of a literal bodily reward has been understood by God's people from earliest times. Abraham was promised that he, personally, would inherit the land of Canaan forever, as surely as he had walked up and down in it (Gen. 13:17; see Study 3.4). His faith in those promises would have necessitated his belief that his body would somehow, at a future date, be revived and made immortal, so that this would be possible.

Job clearly expressed his understanding of how, despite his body being eaten by worms in the grave, he would, in a bodily form, receive his reward: "My redeemer lives, and...shall stand at last on the earth: and after my skin is destroyed, ... in my flesh (or bodily form) I shall see God, whom I shall see for myself, and my eyes shall behold, and not another. How my heart yearns within me!" (Job 19:25-27). Isaiah's hope was identical: "My dead body shall...arise" (Is. 26:19).

Very similar words are found in the account of the death of Lazarus, a personal friend of Jesus. Instead of comforting the man's sisters by saying that his soul had gone to heaven, the Lord Jesus spoke of the day of resurrection: "Your brother will rise again". The immediate response of Lazarus' sister Martha shows how much this was appreciated by the early Christians: "Martha said to him, I know that he will rise again in the resurrection at the last day" (Jn. 11:23,24). Like Job, she did not understand death to be the gateway to a life of bliss in heaven, but, instead, looked forward to a resurrection "at the last day" (cf. Job's "at last"). The Lord promises: "Everyone who has heard and learned from the Father...I will raise him up at the last day" (Jn. 6:44,45).

4.6   The Judgment

Bible teaching concerning the judgment is one of the basic principles of the one faith (Acts 24:25; Heb. 6:2). Frequently the Scriptures speak of "the day of judgment" (e.g. 2 Pet. 2:9; 3:7; 1 Jn. 4:17; Jude 6), a time when those who have been given the knowledge of God will receive their reward. All these must "stand before the judgment seat of Christ" (Rom. 14:10); we "must all have our lives laid open before the tribunal of Christ" (2 Cor. 5:10) to "receive what is due to him for his conduct in the body, good or bad." (R.E.B.)

Daniel's visions concerning Christ's second coming, included one of this judgment seat in the form of a throne (Dan. 7:9-14). The parables help to flesh out the details somewhat. That of the talents likens it to the return of a master, who calls his servants and assesses how well they have used the money which he had left them (Mt. 25:14-29). The parable of the fishermen likens the call of the gospel to a fishing net, gathering all kinds of people; the men then sat down (cf. the judgment sitting) and divided the good fish from the bad (Mt. 13:47-49). The interpretation is clear: "At the end of the age. The angels will come forth, (and) separate the wicked from among the just".

From what we have seen so far, it is fair to assume that after the Lord's return and the resurrection, there will be a gathering together of all who have been called to the Gospel to a certain place at a specific time, when they will meet Christ. An account will have to be given by them, and he will indicate whether or not they are acceptable to receive the reward of entering the Kingdom. It is only at this point that the righteous receive their reward. All this is brought together by the parable of the sheep and goats: "The Son of man comes in his glory, and all the holy angels with him, then he will sit on the throne of his glory (David's throne in Jerusalem, Lk. 1:32,33). All the nations (i.e. people from all nations, cf. Mt. 28:19) will be gathered before him, and he will separate them one from another, as a shepherd divides his sheep from the goats. And he will set the sheep on his right hand, but the goats on the left. Then the King will say to those on his right hand, 'Come, you blessed of my Father, inherit the Kingdom prepared for you ...'" (Mt. 25:31-34).

Inheriting the Kingdom of God, receiving the promises to Abraham concerning it, is the reward (by grace) of the righteous. Yet this will only be after the judgment, which will be at Christ's return. It is therefore impossible to receive the promised reward of an immortalised body before Christ's return; we therefore have to conclude that from the time of death until the resurrection, the believer has no conscious existence at all.

It is a repeated Biblical principle that *when* Christ returns, *then* the gracious reward will be given - and not before.

- "*When* the chief Shepherd (Jesus) shall appears, you will receive the crown of glory" (1 Pet. 5:4 cf. 1:13).

- "Jesus Christ...will judge the living and the dead at his appearing and his kingdom...the crown of righteousness, which the Lord, the righteous judge, will give to me *on that day*" (2 Tim. 4:1,8).

- At Messiah's return in the last days, "many of those who sleep in the dust of the earth (cf. Gen. 3:19) shall awake, some to everlasting life, and some to shame" (Dan. 12:2).

- When Christ comes in judgment, those "in the graves...will...come forth - those who have done good, to the resurrection of life, and those who have done evil, to the resurrection of condemnation" (Jn. 5:25-29).

- "I (Jesus) am coming quickly, and my reward is with me, to give to every one according to his work." (Rev. 22:12). We do not go to heaven to get the reward - Christ brings it from heaven to us.

Jesus bringing our reward with him implies that it has been prepared for us in heaven, but will be brought to us on the earth at the second coming; our "inheritance" of the land promised to Abraham is in this sense "reserved in heaven for you, who are kept by the power of God through faith for salvation ready to be revealed in the last time" of Christ's coming (1 Pet. 1:4,5). So sure is our reward that it is as if we have been given it; so sure are God's promises that He speaks of things which don't exist as if they do (Rom. 4:17).

As the reward will only be given at the judgment on Christ's return, it follows that the righteous and wicked go to the same place when they die, i.e. the grave. There is no differentiation made between them in their deaths. The following is proof positive for this.

- Jonathan was righteous but Saul wicked, yet "in their death they were not divided" (2 Sam. 1:23).
- Saul, Jonathan and Samuel all went to the same place at death (1 Sam. 28:19).
- Righteous Abraham was "gathered to his people", (or ancestors), on death; they were idolaters (Gen. 25:8; Josh. 24:2).
- The spiritually wise and foolish experience the same death (Ecc. 2:15,16).

All this is in sharp contrast to the claims of popular Christianity. Their teaching that the righteous immediately go to heaven at death destroys the need for a resurrection and judgment. Yet we have seen that these are vital events in God's plan of salvation, and therefore in the Gospel message. The popular idea suggests that one righteous person dies and is rewarded by going to heaven, to be followed the next day, the next month, the next year, by others. This is in sharp contrast to the Bible's teaching that *all* the righteous will be rewarded *together*, at the same time.

- The sheep are divided from the goats at the judgment, one by one. Once the judgment has finished, Christ will say to *all* the sheep assembled on his right hand:

- "Come, you blessed of my Father, inherit the Kingdom prepared for you" (Mt. 25:34). Thus all the sheep inherit the Kingdom at the same time (cf. 1 Cor. 15:51).

- At "the harvest" of Christ's return and judgment, all those who have laboured in the Gospel will "rejoice *together*" (Jn. 4:35,36 cf. Mt. 13:39).

- Rev. 11:18 defines "the time of the dead, that they should be judged" as the time when God will "reward Your servants...the prophets and the saints...those who fear Your name" - i.e. all believers together.

- Heb. 11 is a chapter listing many of the righteous men of the Old Testament. Verse 13 comments: "These all died in faith, not having received the promises" made to Abraham about salvation through entering God's Kingdom (Heb. 11:8-12). It follows that at their death, these people did not, one by one, go off to heaven to receive a reward. The reason for this is given in vs. 39,40: They "did not receive the promise, God having provided something better for us, that they should not be made perfect apart from us". The delay in granting their promised reward was because it was God's plan that all the faithful should "be made perfect" together, at the same moment. This will be at the judgment, at Christ's return.

4.7 The Place Of Reward: Heaven Or Earth?

Apart from the above reasons, any who still feel that heaven rather than earth will be the location of God's Kingdom, i.e. the promised reward by grace, need to also explain away the following points.

- The 'Lord's Prayer' asks for God's Kingdom to come (i.e. praying for the return of Christ), whereby God's desires will be done on earth as they are now done in heaven (Mt. 6:10). We are therefore praying for God's Kingdom to come on the earth. It is a tragedy that thousands of people thoughtlessly pray these words each day whilst still believing that God's Kingdom is now already fully established in heaven, and that the earth will be destroyed.

- "Blessed are the meek, for they shall inherit the earth" (Mt. 5:5) - not '...for their souls shall go to heaven'. This is alluding to Ps. 37, the whole of which emphasises that the final reward of the righteous will be upon the earth. In the very same location that the wicked had enjoyed their temporary supremacy, the righteous will be recompensed with eternal life, and possess this same earth that the wicked once dominated (Ps. 37:34,35). "The meek shall inherit the earth...those who are blessed by him shall inherit the earth...The righteous shall inherit the land, and dwell in it for ever" (Ps. 37:11,22,29).

- "David...is both dead and buried...David did not ascend into the heavens" (Acts 2:29,34). Instead, Peter explained that his hope was the resurrection from the dead at Christ's return (Acts 2:22-36).

- Earth is the arena of God's operations with mankind: "Heaven, even the heavens, are the Lord's, but the earth He has given to the children of men" (Ps. 115:16).

- Rev. 5:9,10 relates a vision of what the righteous will say when they are accepted at the judgment seat: (Christ) has "made us kings and priests to our God; and we shall reign on the earth". This picture of ruling in God's Kingdom on earth is quite removed from the vague conception that we will enjoy 'bliss' somewhere in heaven.

- The prophecies of Daniel chapters 2 and 7 outline a succession of political powers, which would finally be superseded by the Kingdom of God at Christ's return. The dominion of this Kingdom would be *under* the whole heaven", and would fill "the whole *earth*" (Dan. 7:27; 2:35 cf. v. 44). This everlasting Kingdom "shall be given to the people, the saints of the Most High" (Dan. 7:27); their reward is therefore eternal life in this Kingdom which is to be located on earth, *under* the heavens.

4.8   Responsibility To God

If humanity had an 'immortal soul' naturally, logically he would have an eternal destiny somewhere - either in a place of reward or of punishment. This implies that everyone is responsible to God. By contrast, we have shown how the Bible teaches that by nature man is like the animals, without any inherent immortality. However, some men have been offered the prospect of eternal life in God's Kingdom. It should be apparent that not everyone who has ever lived will be raised; like the animals, man lives and dies, to decompose into dust. Yet because there will be a judgment, with some being condemned and others rewarded with eternal life, we have to conclude that there will be a certain category amongst mankind who will be raised in order to be judged and rewarded.

Whether or not someone will be raised depends on whether they are responsible to the judgment. The basis of our judgment will be how we have responded to our knowledge of God's word. Christ explained: "He who rejects Me, and does not receive My words, has that which judges him - the word that I have spoken will judge him in the last day" (Jn. 12:48). Those who have not known or understood the word of Christ, and therefore had no opportunity to accept or reject him, will not be accountable to the judgment. "As many as have sinned without (knowing God's) law, will also perish without law, and as many as have sinned in the law (i.e. knowing it), will be judged by the law" (Rom. 2:12). Thus those who have not known God's requirements will perish like the animals; whilst those who knowingly break God's law need to be judged, and therefore raised to face that judgment.

In God's sight "sin is not imputed when there is no law"; "by the law is the knowledge of sin" (Rom. 5:13; Rom. 3:20). Without being aware of God's laws as revealed in His Word, "sin is not imputed" to a person, and therefore they will not be raised or judged. Those who do not know God's Word will therefore remain dead, as will animals and plants, seeing they are in the same position. "Man who...does not understand, is like the beasts that perish" (Ps. 49:20). "Like sheep they are laid in the grave" (Ps. 49:14).

It is the knowledge of God's ways that makes us responsible to Him for our actions and therefore necessitates our resurrection and appearance at the judgment seat. It should therefore be understood that it is not only the righteous or those baptised who will be raised, but also all who are responsible to God by reason of their knowledge of Him. This is an oft-repeated Scriptural theme.

- Jn. 15:22 shows that knowledge of the Word brings responsibility: "If I (Jesus) had not come and spoken to them, they have no sin, but now they have no excuse for their sin". Rom. 1:20,21 likewise says that knowing God leaves men "without excuse".

- "Therefore everyone who has heard and learned from the Father...I (Christ) will raise him up at the last day" (Jn. 6:44,45).

- The Lord's attitude at the judgment seat to those who rejected Him in the first century will be: "Bring here those enemies of mine (out of the grave), and slay them before me" (Lk. 19:27).

- "Whoever will not hear (i.e. obey) my words…I will require it of him" (Dt. 18:19).

- God only "overlooked" the actions of those who are genuinely ignorant of His ways. Those who know His ways, He watches and expects a response (Acts 17:30).

- In the final judgment of the world, it will be "the nations that did not obey" who are condemned (Mic. 5:15 NRSV). Their hearing but not obeying God's word will be the basis of their punishment.

- Because Belshazzar *knew* he ought to submit to God's superiority, but refused, *therefore* he was punished (Dan. 5:22).

- "That servant who knew his master's will, and did not prepare himself or do according to his will, shall be beaten with many stripes. But he who did not know, yet committed things worthy of stripes, shall be beaten with few. (e.g. by remaining dead). For everyone to whom much is given, from him much will be required; and to whom much has been committed, of him they will ask the more" (Lk. 12:47,48) - so how much more *God*?

- "Therefore, to him who *knows* to do good and does not do it, to him it is sin" (James 4:17).

- Israel's special responsibility to God was on account of His revelations to them concerning Himself (Am. 3:2). "Therefore I will punish you for all your iniquities …" "and you shall all bow down to the slaughter; because, when I called, you did not answer; when I spoke, you did not hear, but did evil" (Is. 65:12).

- Because of this doctrine of responsibility, "it would have been better for them (who later turn back from God) not to have known the way of righteousness, than having known it, to turn from the holy commandment delivered to them" (2 Pet. 2:21). Other relevant passages include: Jn. 9:41; 3:19; 1 Tim. 1:13; Hos. 4:14; Deut. 1:39.

Knowledge of God making us responsible to the judgment seat, it follows that those without this knowledge will not be raised, seeing that they do not need to be judged, and that their lack of knowledge makes them "like the beasts that perish" (Ps. 49:20). There are ample indications that not all who have ever lived will be raised.

The people of the ancient nation of Babylon "will ... sleep a perpetual sleep and not awake" after their death because they were ignorant of the true God (Jer. 51:39; Is. 43:17).

Isaiah encouraged himself: "O Lord our (Israel's) God, other masters besides You have had dominion over us (e.g. the Philistines and Babylonians)...They are dead, they will not live (again); they are deceased, they will not rise...all their memory to perish" (Is. 26:13,14). Note the triple emphasis here on their not being raised: "will not live (again)...will not rise...all their memory to perish". By contrast, Israel had the prospect of resurrection on account of their knowledge of the true God: "Your (Israel's) dead shall live; together with my dead body they shall arise" (Is. 26:19).

Speaking about God's people Israel, we are told that at Christ's return, "many of those who sleep in the dust of the earth shall awake, some to everlasting life, and some to shame and everlasting contempt" (Dan. 12:2). Thus "many", but not all, of the Jews will be raised, due to their responsibility to God as His chosen people. Those of them who are totally ignorant of their true God "shall fall, and never rise again", seeing they are unable to find "the word of the Lord" (Am. 8:12,14).

We have now learnt that

1. Knowledge of God's Word brings responsibility to Him

2. Only the responsible will be raised and judged

3. Those adults who do not know the true God will therefore remain dead like the animals

The implications of these conclusions make a hard hit on human pride and what we would naturally prefer to believe. Our questioning of God's ways in these matters is grossly out of order: "O man, who are you to reply against God?" (Rom. 9:20). We may admit incomprehension, but never must we accuse God of injustice or unrighteousness. The implication that God can be in any way unloving or in error opens up the horrific prospect of an all-powerful God, Father and Creator who treats His creatures in an unreasonable and unjust way.

Finally, it has to be said that many people, on grasping this principle of responsibility to God, feel that they do not wish to gain any more knowledge of Him in case they become responsible to Him and the judgment. Yet to some degree it is likely that such people are already responsible to

God, seeing their knowledge of God's Word has made them aware of the fact that God is working in their lives, offering them a real relationship with Him. It must ever be remembered that "God IS love", He is "not willing that any should perish", and "gave His only begotten Son, that whoever believes in him should not perish, but have everlasting life" (1 Jn. 4:8; 2 Pet. 3:9; Jn. 3:16). God wants us to be in His Kingdom.

Such an honour and privilege inevitably bring responsibilities. Yet these are not designed to be too heavy or onerous for us; if we truly love God, we will appreciate that His offer of salvation is not an automatic reward for certain works, but a loving desire on His part to do all that He can for His children, to grant them an eternal life of happiness, through their appreciation of His marvellous character.

As we come to appreciate and hear the call of God to us through His Word, we will realise that as we walk through the crowds, God is watching us with a special intensity, eagerly seeking signs of our response to His love, rather than waiting for us to fail to live up to our responsibilities. Never is that loving eye off us; never can we forget or undo our knowledge of Him in order to indulge the flesh, free of responsibility to God. Instead, we can and should rejoice in the special closeness we have to God, and so trust in the greatness of His love, that we ever seek to know more of Him rather than less. Our love of God's ways and desire to know them, so that we might more accurately copy Him, should outweigh our natural fear of His supreme holiness.

4.9   Hell

The popular conception of hell is of a place of punishment for wicked 'immortal souls' straight after death, or the place of torment for those who are rejected at the judgment. It is our conviction that the Bible teaches that hell is the grave, where all men go at death.

As a word, the original Hebrew word 'sheol', translated 'hell', means 'a covered place'. 'Hell' is the anglicised version of 'sheol'; thus when we read of 'hell' we are not reading a word which has been fully translated. A 'helmet' is literally a 'hell-met', meaning a covering for the head. Biblically, this 'covered place', or 'hell', is the grave. There are many examples where the original word 'sheol' is translated 'grave'. Indeed, some modern Bible versions scarcely use the word 'hell', translating it more properly as 'grave'. A few examples of where this word 'sheol' is translated 'grave' should torpedo the popular conception of hell as a place of fire and torment for the wicked.

- "Let the wicked...be silent in the grave" (sheol [Ps. 31:17]) - they will not be screaming in agony.

- "God will redeem my soul from the power of the grave" (sheol [Ps. 49:15]) - i.e. David's soul or body would be raised from the grave, or 'hell'.

The belief that hell is a place of punishment for the wicked from which they cannot escape just cannot be squared with this; a righteous man can go to hell (the grave) and come out again. Hos. 13:14 confirms this: "I will ransom them (God's people) from the power of the grave (sheol); I will redeem them from death". This is quoted in 1 Cor. 15:55 and applied to the resurrection at Christ's return. Likewise in the vision of the second resurrection (see Study 5.5), "Death and Hades (Greek for 'hell') delivered up the dead who were in them" (Rev. 20:13). Note the parallel between death, i.e. the grave, and Hades (see also Ps. 6:5).

Hannah's words in 1 Sam. 2:6 are very clear: "The Lord kills and makes alive (through resurrection); he brings down to the grave (sheol), and brings up".

Seeing that 'hell' is the grave, it is to be expected that the righteous will be saved from it through their resurrection to eternal life. Thus it is quite possible to enter 'hell', or the grave, and later to leave it through resurrection. The supreme example is that of Jesus, whose "soul was not left in Hades (hell), nor did his flesh see corruption" (Acts 2:31) because he was raised. Note the parallel between Christ's 'soul' and his 'flesh' or body. That his body "was not *left* in Hades" implies that it was there for a period, i.e. the three days in which his body was in the grave. That Christ went to 'hell' should be proof enough that it is not just a place where the wicked go.

Both good and bad people go to 'hell', i.e. the grave. Thus Jesus "made his grave with the wicked" (Is. 53:9). In line with this, there are other examples of righteous men going to hell, i.e. the grave. Jacob said that he would "go down into the grave (hell)...mourning" for his son Joseph (Gen. 37:35).

It is one of God's principles that the punishment for sin is death (Rom. 6:23; 8:13; James 1:15). We have previously shown death to be a state of complete unconsciousness. Sin results in total destruction, not eternal torment (Mt. 21:41; 22:7; Mk. 12:9; James 4:12), as surely as people were destroyed by the Flood (Lk. 17:27,29), and as the Israelites died in the wilderness (1 Cor. 10:10). On both these occasions the sinners *died* rather than being eternally tormented. It is therefore impossible that the wicked are punished with an eternity of conscious torment and suffering.

We have also seen that God does not impute sin - or count it to our record - if we are ignorant of His word (Rom. 5:13). Those in this position will remain dead. Those who have known God's requirements will be raised and judged at Christ's return. If wicked, the punishment they receive will be death, because this is the judgment for sin. Therefore after coming before the judgment seat of Christ, they will be punished and then die again, to stay dead for ever. This will be "the *second* death", spoken of in Rev. 2:11; 20:6. These people will have died once, a death of total unconsciousness. They will be raised and judged at Christ's return, and then punished with a second death, which, like their first death, will be total unconsciousness. This will last forever.

It is in this sense that the punishment for sin is 'everlasting', in that there will be no end to their death. To remain dead for ever is an everlasting punishment. An example of the Bible using this kind of expression is found in Dt. 11:4. This describes God's one-off destruction of Pharaoh's army in the Red Sea as an eternal, on-going destruction in that this actual army never again troubled Israel: "He made the waters of the Red sea overflow them... the Lord has destroyed them to this day".

One of the parables about Christ's return and the judgment speaks of the wicked being 'slain' in his presence (Lk. 19:27). This hardly fits into the idea that the wicked exist forever in a conscious state, constantly receiving torture. In any case, this would be a somewhat unreasonable punishment - *eternal* torture for deeds of 70 years. God has no pleasure in punishing wicked people; it is therefore to be expected that He will not inflict punishment on them for eternity (Ez. 18:23,32; 33:11 cf. 2 Pet. 3:9).

A misbelieving Christendom often associates 'hell' with the idea of fire and torment. This is in sharp contrast to Bible teaching about hell (the grave). "Like sheep they are laid in the grave (hell); death shall feed on them" (Ps. 49:14) implies that the grave is a place of peaceful oblivion. Despite Christ's soul, or body, being in hell for three days, it did not suffer corruption (Acts 2:31). This would have been impossible if hell were a place of fire. Ez. 32:26-30 gives a picture of the mighty warriors of the nations around, lying in their graves: "the mighty who are fallen (in battle)...who have gone down to hell with their weapons of war; they have laid their swords under their heads...they shall lie...with those who go down to the Pit". This refers to the custom of burying warriors with their weapons, and resting the head of the corpse upon its sword. Yet this is a description of "hell" - the grave. These mighty men lying still in hell (i.e. their graves), hardly supports the idea that hell is a place of fire. Physical things (e.g. swords) go to the same "hell" as people, showing that hell is not an arena of spiritual torment. Thus Peter told a wicked man, "Your money perish with you" (Acts 8:20).

The record of Jonah's experiences also contradicts this. Having been swallowed alive by a huge fish, "Jonah prayed unto the Lord his God from the fish's belly. And he said: 'I cried...to the Lord...out of the belly of Sheol (hell) I cried" (Jonah 2:1,2). This parallels "the belly of Sheol" with that of the fish. The fish's belly was truly a 'covered place', which is the fundamental meaning of the word 'sheol'. Obviously, it was not a place of fire, and Jonah came out of "the belly of Sheol" when the fish vomited him out. This pointed forward to the resurrection of Christ from 'hell' (the grave) - see Mt. 12:40.

FIGURATIVE FIRE

However, the Bible does frequently use the image of eternal fire in order to represent God's anger with sin, which will result in the total destruction of the sinner in the grave. Sodom was punished with "eternal fire" (Jude v. 7), i.e. it was totally destroyed due to the wickedness of the inhabitants. Today that city is in ruins, submerged beneath the waters of the Dead Sea; in no way is it now on fire, which is necessary if we are to understand 'eternal fire' literally. Likewise Jerusalem was threatened with the eternal fire of God's anger, due to the sins of Israel: "Then I will kindle a fire in its gates, and it shall devour the palaces of Jerusalem, and it shall not be quenched" (Jer. 17:27). Jerusalem being the prophesied capital of the future Kingdom (Is. 2:2-4; Ps. 48:2), God did not mean us to read this literally. The houses of the great men in Jerusalem were burnt down with fire (2 Kings 25:9), but that fire did not continue eternally. Fire represents the anger/punishment of God against sin, but His anger is not eternal (Jer. 3:12). Fire turns what it burns to dust; and we know that the ultimate wages of sin is death, a turning back to dust. This perhaps is why fire is used as a figure for punishment for sin.

Similarly, God punished the land of Idumea with fire that would "not be quenched night nor day; its smoke shall ascend for ever. From generation to generation it shall lie waste...the owl and the raven shall dwell in it...thorns shall come up in its palaces" (Is. 34:9-15). Seeing that animals and plants were to exist in the ruined land of Idumea, the language of eternal fire must refer to God's anger and His total destruction of the place, rather than being taken literally.

The Hebrew and Greek phrases which are translated "for ever" mean strictly, "for the age". Sometimes this refers to literal infinity, for example the age of the kingdom, but not always. Is. 32:14,15 is an example: "The forts and towers will become lairs for ever...until the spirit is poured upon us". This is one way of understanding the 'eternity' of 'eternal fire'.

Time and again God's anger with the sins of Jerusalem and Israel is likened to fire: "My anger and My fury will be poured out on this place -

(Jerusalem)...it will burn, and not be quenched" (Jer. 7:20; other examples include Lam. 4:11 and 2 Kings 22:17).

Fire is also associated with God's judgment of sin, especially at the return of Christ: "For behold, the day is coming, burning like an oven, and all the proud, yes, all who do wickedly will be stubble. And the day which is coming shall burn them up" (Mal. 4:1). When stubble, or even a human body, is burnt by fire, it returns to dust. It is impossible for any substance, especially human flesh, to literally burn forever. The language of 'eternal fire' therefore cannot refer to literal eternal torment. A fire cannot last forever if there is nothing to burn. It should be noted that "Hades" is "cast into the lake of fire" (Rev. 20:14). This indicates that Hades is not the same as "the lake of fire"; this represents complete destruction. In the symbolic manner of the book of Revelation, we are being told that the grave is to be totally destroyed, because at the end of the Millennium there will be no more death.

GEHENNA

In the New Testament there are two Greek words translated 'hell'. 'Hades' is the equivalent of the Hebrew 'sheol' which we have discussed earlier. 'Gehenna' is the name of the rubbish tip which was just outside Jerusalem, where the refuse from the city was burnt. Such rubbish tips are typical of many developing cities today (e.g. 'Smoky Mountain' outside Manila in the Philippines.) As a proper noun - i.e. the name of an actual place - it should have been left untranslated as 'Gehenna' rather than be translated as 'hell'. 'Gehenna' is the Aramaic equivalent of the Hebrew 'Ge-ben-Hinnon'. This was located near Jerusalem (Josh. 15:8), and at the time of Christ it was the city rubbish dump. Dead bodies of criminals were thrown onto the fires which were always burning there, so that Gehenna became symbolic of total destruction and rejection.

Again the point has to be driven home that what was thrown onto those fires did not remain there forever - the bodies decomposed into dust. "Our God (will be) a *consuming* fire" (Heb. 12:29) at the day of judgment; the fire of His anger with sin will consume sinners to destruction rather than leave them in a state of only being singed by it and still surviving. At the time of God's previous judgments of His people Israel at the hand of the Babylonians, Gehenna was filled with dead bodies of the sinners among God's people (Jer. 7:32,33).

In his masterly way, the Lord Jesus brought together all these Old Testament ideas in his use of the word 'Gehenna'. He often said that those who were rejected at the judgment seat at His return would go "to hell (i.e. Gehenna), into the fire that shall never be quenched ... where their worm does not die" (Mk. 9:43,44). Gehenna would have conjured up in the Jewish mind the ideas of rejection and destruction of the body, and we have seen that eternal fire is an idiom representing the anger of God against sin, and the eternal destruction of sinners through death.

The reference to "where their worm does not die", is evidently part of this same idiom for total destruction - it is inconceivable that there could be literal worms which will never die. The fact that Gehenna was the location of previous punishments of the wicked amongst God's people, further shows the aptness of Christ's use of this figure of Gehenna.

Joachim Jeremias explains how the literal valley of Gehenna came to be misinterpreted as a symbol of a 'hell' that is supposed to be a place of fire: "[*Gehenna*]…since ancient times has been the name of the valley west and south of Jerusalem…from the woes pronounced by the prophets on the valley (Jer. 7:32 = 19:6; cf. Is. 31:9; 66:24) because sacrifices to Moloch took place there (2 Kings 16:3; 21:6), there developed in the second century BC the idea that the valley of Hinnom would be the place of a fiery hell (Eth. Enoch 26; 90.26)…it is distinguished from *sheol*" *(New Testament Theology*, London: SCM, 1972 p. 129).

Photo: The smouldering rubbish dump outside the city of Antananarivo, Madagascar

Belief In Practice 10:

The Motivational Power Of Understanding Death

The neo-Platonists showed the moral danger of believing in an immortal soul. They reasoned that since body and soul are totally different from each other, therefore immoral conduct by the body doesn't affect the inner man. Yet once we realize that the same Hebrew word *nephesh* is translated both 'soul' and 'body', it becomes apparent that the actions of our body cannot be separated from our 'soul' or essential being. The Bible faces us up to the death issue. To consider the reality of one's own death, and that death is truly total unconsciousness, marvellously focuses the mind. It cuts through the chatter and noise and distraction of our mind, refocusing us upon the things that ultimately matter. Many religions, wrong and confused as they may be on many other issues, have correctly discerned that contemplation of one's own death is a vital part on personal transformation. What would happen if you were to die today...? What would your gravestone look like... These are the sorts of questions we can profitably meditate upon, once we grasp true Bible teaching about the death state and the hope of resurrection.

RESPONSIBILITY

As in our own day, literature and thought of Bible times tried to minimize death. Yet in both Old and New Testaments, death is faced for what it is. Job 18:14 calls it "the king of terrors"; Paul speaks of death as the last and greatest enemy (1 Cor. 15:26). Humanity lives all their lives "in fear of death" (Heb. 2:17). Facing death for what it is imparts a seriousness and intensity to human life and endeavour, keeps our sense of responsibility to God paramount, and the correct functioning of conscience all important. We see this in people facing death; but those who've grasped Bible truth about death ought to live like this all the time, rejoicing too that we have been delivered from it. Because we do not have an immortal soul that is somehow recycled into us through reincarnation, our soul / life is given to us by God. In the parable of the rich fool, the Lord says that in the day of his death, his soul was "required" of him (Lk. 12:20). The Greek word for 'required' means 'to ask back, to request to be given again'. The fact we have life [a 'soul'] makes us responsible to God; and at the judgment we will be asked to give that life back to Him with an account. And, as the parable shows, this utterly precludes a focus upon material acquisition. The Lord goes on to say that therefore we should take no anxious thought about what our soul will eat or wear- because our soul / life is in fact God's soul / life, and He will care for it until He takes it back to Himself (Lk. 12:22). The soul is greater than food and clothes (Lk. 12:23 Gk.). The wonder that we are alive, with God's life in us, should be far greater to us than what we feed or clothe it with. Because we can't take that life out of ourselves until God does, nor can we give it to another person, nor can we make our body / soul grow taller, *therefore* we should not take anxious thought for the material things related to it, which are all peripheral compared to the wonder of the fact that we have life from God: "why take thought for the rest [Gk. 'the things that are left over / extraneous']?" (Lk. 12:26). And to drive the point home, we are bidden "consider" (s.w. 'discover') the birds and plants, who are simply content with the life God has given them. This was the Lord's way of doing what Solomon did in Ecc. 3:17-20- showing that man and plants and animals are all possessed of the same God-given spirit / life. As Gen. 2:7; Ecc. 12:7 make clear, the spirit / life is given by God to our bodies; it doesn't come from anywhere else. There is no reincarnation. And this is no painless Bible fact; it demands that we live lives that are *His*, and not lived out as if our spirit / life / soul is *ours*. The fact that God "holds our soul in life", a reference to Gen. 2:7, means that David wanted to "make the voice of his praise to be heard" (Ps. 66:8,9). This was the meaning of the basic facts of creation for David!

PRESERVATION OF OTHERS

The fact God has given us life and preserves our soul (the Hebrew word *nephesh*) means that we likewise should seek to save and preserve the life of others, through our preaching and spiritual care of them: "If you forbear to deliver them that are drawn unto death, and those that are ready to be slain; if you say, Behold, we knew it not; does not he that ponders the heart consider it? *and he that keeps your soul*, does not he know it? and shall not he render to every man according to his works?" (Prov. 24:11,12). The emphasis is surely upon God keeping *our* soul meaning that we must keep the soul of others. It could be said that the [false] doctrine of an immortal soul has resulted in a devaluing of the human person. The Christian salvation is "the salvation of the body"; our real, present person and body really matters; who we are and how we live, using the talents of our health and bodies, is of crucial importance. Sickness and death become positive, rather than negative, for the true believer. For they are all in the context of God's hand in our lives.

PREACHING

There was once a master butcher, working in Harrod's- one of the most prestigious butcheries in central London. He was an earnest Christian, and over the counter there was a simple hand-written notice: " Like sheep they are laid in the grave" . And many noticed that, and over the years, came to accept the Faith. Realizing the tragic brevity and ultimate vanity of the human experience " under the sun" will motivate us to bring this to the attention of the perishing millions with whom we rub shoulders daily. If we see the tragedy of life under the sun and realize we have been redeemed from it, we *must* say something to somebody! And on a personal level, the fact David knew that after death he would not go on praising God in Heaven, resulted in him wanting to live his mortal life only to utter forth God's praise. The only reason he wanted to stay alive was to praise God (Ps. 6:5; 115:17,18). And Hezekiah too had something of this spirit.

We shouldn't see the mortality of man and the true meaning of the Hebrew word *nephesh* as a negative thing that we unfortunately have to tell people who believe their loved ones are alive in Heaven. "The voice" tells Isaiah to cry. " And I said, What shall I cry?" (Is. 40:6 LXX; RVmg.). What was to be the message of Isaiah's Gospel? The voice addresses Isaiah as " O you who tells good tidings" , and tells him the good news he is to preach. It is that " All flesh is grass…the people is grass. The grass withers, the flower fades: but the word of our God shall stand for ever" . The reality of man's mortality is the backdrop against which we can see the eternity of God and the offer made to us through His abiding word that we really can escape from our condition. Christian preaching about " man is mortal" need not be bad news. The message can be turned into good news! For it was this message of mortality which prepared the way for men to accept Christ (Is. 40:3-5); the mountains of human pride are made low by this message so that we can accept salvation in Christ. 1 Pet. 1:24 RVmg. quotes these verses and concludes that we are being offered salvation through " the word of the God who lives for ever" - the Gospel that is prefaced by the message of human mortality. God's eternity and man's mortality are placed side by side- and thus the way is prepared for the wonder of the fact that through " the word" of Jesus, of the Gospel, we the mortal are invited to share in that immortality.

The fact that sin really does result in eternal death, and that death is really unconsciousness, there is no immortal soul, the Hebrew word *nephesh* doesn't mean that, leads us to preach the hope of resurrection which we have. It must do- for otherwise we would be plain selfish. And it makes us realize for ourselves the decisiveness and finality of this life's decisions for the determining of eternal destiny. The hope of resurrection is the first and most basic need of our fellows.

ZEAL

Perhaps the Lord was speaking in a kind of soliloquy when He mused that " the night cometh, when no man can work" , and therefore man should walk and work while he has the light (Jn. 9:4, quoting Ecc. 9:10). He was speaking, in the context, not only of His own zeal to 'work' while He had life, but also applying this to His followers.

It's only when faced with death that we realize the crucial and wonderful importance of every hour which we've been given to live. Facing death as he thought, Job reflected upon the tragic brevity and speed of passing of human life, and the true meaning of the Hebrew word *nephesh*: "My days sprint past me like runners; I will never see them again. They glide by me like sailboats…" (Job 9:25). Life is indeed racing by; time management, and freeing our real selves from all the myriad things which compete to take up our time, become of vital importance once we realize this. There is only one ultimate thing worth studying, striving after, labouring for, reading about, working towards… and grasping the mortality of man inspires us in living out this understanding. TV, novels, endless surfing of the internet, engagement in pointless communication and discussion in this communication-crazy world... all this beguiles us of life itself.

MATURITY IN BEHAVIOUR

The tragic brevity of life means that "childhood and youth are vanity" , we should quit the time wasting follies of youth or overgrown childhood (and the modern world is full of this), and therefore too " remove anger from your heart and put away evil from your flesh" (Ecc. 11:10 AVmg.). Ecclesiastes uses the mortality of man not only as an appeal to work for our Creator, but to simply have faith in His existence. Likewise: " We had the sentence of death in ourselves [" in our hearts we felt the sentence of death" , NIV], *that* we should not trust in ourselves, but in God who raises the dead" (2 Cor. 1:9). The fact we are going to die, relatively soon, and lie unconscious...drives the man who seriously believes it to faith in the God of resurrection. It seems that at a time of great physical distress, Paul was made to realize that in fact he had " the sentence of death" within him, he was under the curse of mortality, and this led him to a hopeful faith that God would preserve him from the ultimate " so great a death" as well as from the immediate problems. Death being like a sleep, it follows that judgment day is our next conscious experience after death. Because death is an ever more likely possibility for us, our judgment is effectively *almost upon us*. And we must live with and in that knowledge.

We know very well that sin brings death. But we sin. We can know that sin brings death as theory; and we can *really* know it. Ez. 18:14 RVmg speaks of the son who " sees all his father's sins, which he has done, and sees, and does not such like" . He sees the sins, and then he really sees them, and doesn't do them. This is how we must be in our registering of the fact that sin really brings death.

CARE FOR THE BODY

Nephesh is indeed translated both 'soul' and 'body'. The false dichotomy made between the two by believers in the wrong notion of an 'immortal soul' leads to a neglect of the body, even an abuse of it. And of course, if this life isn't so important, the body is merely a box in which the 'immortal soul' is stored- then the tendency will be to abuse or disregard the body. Recognition that we don't have an immortal soul heightens the wonder and importance of the human body.

FAITH IN GOD

Our faith in God is mitigated against by our misplaced faith in humanity. We would rather trust a doctor, a repair man, a kind neighbour, before throwing ourselves upon God as a last resort. "Cease from trusting man, whose breath is in his nostrils: for wherein is he to be accounted of" (Is.

2:22) compared to the great God of Israel? Job 27:9,10 seems to be saying [although the Hebrew text and use of the Hebrew word *nephesh* is rather obscure] that every man on his deathbed cries to God in some kind of prayer; but a belief in the mortality of man will result in the righteous man having lived a life of prayerful crying to the Father, which will be in context with his final cry to God in his time of dying. A true sense of our mortality will lead to our prayerful, urgent contact with the Father all our days. Thus destruction and death give insight into the true wisdom (Job 28:22). The spirit / life force is given by God and taken back by God. Hence man is unconscious after death. But this very basic fact is used by Elihu as reason to believe that the God who is so in control of men is therefore a just and righteous God, who means only good for us and not evil (Job 34:14,15,17). These conclusions and the comfort they contain are based by Elihu upon a simple understanding of the fact that it is God who gives the spirit / life-force, and it is God who takes it away again.

FREEDOM FROM FEAR

The Bible has so much to say about death, depicting us as having a "body of death" (Rom. 7:24). And yet humanity generally doesn't want to seriously consider death. Yet death is the moment of final truth, which makes all men and women ultimately equal, destroying all the categories into which we place people during our or their lives. If we regularly read and accept the Bible's message, death, with all its intensity and revelation of truth and the ultimate nature of human issues, is something which is constantly before us, something we realistically face and know, not only in sickness or at funerals. And the realness, the intensity, the truth... which comes from this will be apparent in our lives.

And yet the fear of death grips our society more than we like to admit. Psychologists note the huge number of people who dream that they are locked in, that everywhere they come up against iron-bound and padlocked doors, that they absolutely must escape, and yet there is no way out. This is the state of the nation, this is how we naturally are, this is the audience to which we preach. And we preach a freedom from that fear. Because the Lord Jesus was of our human nature- and here perhaps more than anywhere else we see the crucial practical importance of doctrine- we are freed from the ranks of all those who through fear of death live their lives in bondage (Heb. 2:15). For He died for us, as our representative. How true are those inspired words. "To release them who through fear / *phobos* of death were all their living-time subject to slavery" (Gk.). Nearly all the great psychologists concluded that the mystery of death obsesses humanity; and in the last analysis, all anxiety is reduced to anxiety about death. You can see it for yourself, in how death, or real, deep discussion of it, is a taboo subject; how people will make jokes about it in reflection of their fear of seriously discussing it. People, even doctors, don't quite know what to say to the dying. There can be floods of stories and chit-chat… all carefully avoiding any possible allusion to death. This fear of death, in which the unredeemed billions of humanity have been in bondage, explains the fear of old age, the unwillingness to accept our age for what it is, our bodies for how and what they are, or are becoming. I'm not saying of course that the emotion of fear or anxiety is totally removed from our lives by faith. The Lord Jesus in Gethsemane is proof enough that these emotions are an integral part of being human, and it's no sin to have them. I'm talking of fear in it's destructive sense, the fear of death which is rooted in a lack of hope. But the *phobos* of death which there is in this world generally is not for those who are secured in Christ and the sure hope of resurrection.

Digression 5: Ghosts and Reincarnation

The belief that man continues living in the form of another person or animal being possessed by his spirit, was one of the earliest ways in which man tried to convince himself that death was not as final as it appeared.

We have shown that the spirit of man refers to the breath/life force within him, which returns to God when he dies (Ecc. 12:7). This means that his spirit is not moving around as a 'ghost', nor is it free to possess another person or animal so that the man's personality is continued through them. We will each be judged for our own works (2 Cor. 5:10). If our actions and characteristics are a function of a previous person's character, then this concept of God judging and rewarding us according to our works (Rev. 22:12) is made a nonsense.

The spirit returns to God at death, and all consciousness ceases. Any attempt to contact the dead therefore shows a serious misunderstanding of the ample Bible teaching concerning this (see Is. 8:19,20; Lev. 19:31, 20:6). The Bible is quite plain that people do not return to their previous houses or towns in any way after they are dead; there can be no such thing as a 'spirit' or 'ghost' haunting such a place after the person has died. A humble acceptance of this will lead us to discount all claims to have seen the 'ghosts' of dead people, haunting their old houses. Such experiences must at best be tricks of the imagination.

Digression 6: The 'Rapture'

There is a widespread belief amongst the 'evangelical' churches that the righteous will be caught up into heaven at Christ's return (the rapture). This belief is often associated with the idea that the earth will then be destroyed. We see in Digression 9 that this is an impossibility. We have also shown in Study 4.7 that the place of reward is earth, not heaven. These erroneous beliefs are based around a mistaken interpretation of 1 Thes. 4:16,17: "The Lord himself will descend from heaven...and the dead in Christ will rise first. Then we who are alive and remain shall be caught up together with them in the clouds to meet the Lord in the air. And thus we shall always be with the Lord".

Apart from the evident danger of basing such a major belief on just one passage of Scripture, it should be noted that there is no mention here of the righteous being caught up to *Heaven*. Christ descends from heaven before the believers meet him. Christ will reign forever on David's throne in Jerusalem, and we will be with him, here on earth. It is therefore impossible that we should spend eternity with him suspended in mid-air. 'The air' extending only a few kilometres above the earth's surface means that it cannot refer to Heaven, the dwelling place of God.

The Greek phrase translated "caught up" really means to be snatched away; it does not carry the idea of any specific direction. It occurs in Lev. 6:4 and Dt. 28:31 in the Greek Old Testament (the Septuagint) to describe the 'snatching away' of goods in a robbery. It also occurs in Acts 8:39: "The Spirit of the Lord *caught away* Philip, so that the eunuch saw him no more...But Philip was found at Azotus". This records how Philip was miraculously transported from one place on earth to another.

When Christ comes, the responsible will be gathered together to the place of judgment; they will not be left to make their own way there. It is possible that our means of transportation to that place will be literally through the air.

Jesus said that "in the day when the Son of man is revealed...two men will be in the field: the one will be taken and the other left" (Lk. 17:30,36). This gives the same picture of a sudden snatching away. The disciples earnestly asked, "Where, Lord? So He said to them, 'Wherever the body is, there the eagles will be gathered together" (Lk. 17:37). As the eagles fly instinctively through the air and then land on earth where the carcase is, so the responsible will be brought to the place where they will meet their Lord in judgment.

We must again emphasise the importance of the doctrine of the judgment seat of Christ; the responsible must first appear there, before the righteous amongst them are rewarded. A superficial reading of 1 Thess. 4:16,17 could lead us to conclude that all the responsible will be snatched up into the air, and remain there with Christ forever. Instead, we know that the responsible will be gathered to the place of judgment, possibly by being transported through the air, and *then* receive their rewards.

STUDY 4: Questions

1. What happens after death?
   - ☐ The soul goes to Heaven
   - ☐ We are unconscious
   - ☐ The soul is stored somewhere until judgment
   - ☐ Wicked souls go to hell and the good ones to Heaven.

2. What is the soul?
   - ☐ An immortal part of our being
   - ☐ A word meaning 'body, person, creature'
   - ☐ Exactly the same as the spirit
   - ☐ Something which goes to Heaven or hell after death.

3. What is the spirit of man?

4. Briefly describe the nature of man.

5. List two Bible verses which prove that death is a state of unconsciousness.

6. What do you know about the judgment seat of Christ?

7. Who will be resurrected and judged?

8. What is hell?

9. What is Gehenna?

STUDY 5
The Kingdom Of God

5.1   Defining The Kingdom Of God

Our previous studies have shown that it is God's purpose to reward His faithful people with eternal life at the return of Christ. This eternal life will be spent on earth; God's repeated promises concerning this never imply that the faithful will go to heaven. Only Jesus went to Heaven, and He promised His followers that although they could not go *there* (Jn. 13:33), He would come back to earth and eternally be with them *here* (Jn. 14:3). Our salvation and eternal life will be experienced in a bodily form (Rom. 8:11,23), and the arena of this salvation will be the Kingdom of God, to be literally and physically established upon this earth. "The Gospel (good news) of the kingdom of God" (Matt. 4:23) was preached to Abraham in the form of God's promises concerning eternal life on earth (Gal. 3:8). The "kingdom of God" is therefore the time after Christ's return when these promises will be fulfilled. Whilst God is ultimately the King of His entire creation even now, He has given man freewill to rule the world and his own life as he wishes. Thus at present the world is comprised of "the kingdom of men" (Dan. 4:17).

At Christ's return, "the kingdoms of this world (will) become the kingdoms of our Lord, and of his Christ; and he shall reign for ever and ever" (Rev. 11:15). Then God's will and desires will be completely and openly performed in this earth. Hence Jesus' command for us to pray: "Your kingdom come (that) Your will be done in earth, as it is (now) in heaven" (Matt. 6:10). Because of this, the "kingdom of God" is a phrase interchangeable with "the kingdom of heaven" (Matt. 13:11 cp. Mark 4:11). "Heaven" is often put for 'God' (Mt. 21:25; Lk. 15:18; Jn. 3:27). Note that we never read of 'the kingdom *in* heaven'; it is the kingdom *of* heaven which will be established by Christ on earth at his return. "We are a colony of heaven" (Phil. 3:20 Moffatt). As God's will is completely obeyed by the angels in heaven (Ps. 103:19-21), so it will be in the future kingdom of God, when the earth will only be inhabited by the righteous, who will then be "equal unto the angels" (Luke 20:36).

Entering the kingdom of God at Christ's return is therefore the end result of all our Christian endeavour in this life (Matt. 25:34; Acts 14:22); as such, it is absolutely vital to have a correct understanding of it. It is a major theme of God's revelation; "all the counsel [will] of God" is paralleled with "the kingdom of God" (Acts 20:25 cp. 27). All that it stands for, and our being in it, is all God's will. Philip's preaching of "Christ" is defined as teaching "the things concerning the kingdom of God and the name of Jesus Christ" (Acts 8:5,12). Passage upon passage remind us of how "the kingdom of God" was the main burden of Paul's preaching (Acts 19:8; 20:25; 28:23,31). It is therefore of paramount importance that we fully understand the doctrine of the Kingdom of God, seeing that it forms a vital part of the Gospel message. "We must through much tribulation enter into the kingdom of God" (Acts 4:22); it is the light at the end of the tunnel of this life, and therefore the motivation to make the sacrifices which the true Christian life involves.

Nebuchadnezzar, king of Babylon, wanted to know the world's future (see Dan. 2). He was given a vision of a great statue, composed of different metals. Daniel interpreted the head of gold as representing the king of Babylon (Dan. 2:38). After him there was to come a succession of major empires in the area around Israel, to be concluded by a situation in which "as the toes of the feet were part of iron, and part of clay, so the kingdom shall be partly strong, and partly broken" (Dan. 2:42).

The present balance of power in the world is split between many nations, some strong and some weak. Daniel then saw a little stone hit the image on the feet, destroying it, and itself growing into a great mountain which filled the whole earth (Dan. 2:34,35). This stone represented Jesus (Matt. 21:42; Acts 4:11; Eph. 2:20; 1 Peter 2:4-8). The "mountain" which He will create all over the earth represents the everlasting Kingdom of God, which will be established at his second coming. This prophecy is in itself proof that the kingdom will be on earth, not in heaven.

That the kingdom will only be fully established in reality upon Christ's return is a theme of other passages. Paul speaks of Jesus judging the living and dead "at his appearing and his kingdom" (2 Tim. 4:1). Micah 4:1 picks up Daniel's idea of God's kingdom being like a huge mountain: "In the last days it shall come to pass, that the mountain of the house of the Lord shall be established"; there then follows a description of what this kingdom will be like on the earth (Mic. 4:1-4). God will give Jesus the throne of David in Jerusalem: "He shall reign...for ever, and of his kingdom there shall be no end" (Luke 1:32,33). This necessitates there being a certain point at which Jesus begins to reign on David's throne, and his kingdom begins. This will be at Christ's return. "Of his kingdom there shall be no end" connects with Dan. 2:44: "The God of heaven (shall) set up a kingdom which shall never be destroyed: (it) shall not be left to other people". Rev. 11:15 uses similar language in describing how that at the second coming, "The kingdoms of this world are become the kingdoms of our Lord and of his Christ; and he shall reign for *ever and ever*". Again, there must be a specific time when Christ's kingdom and reign begins on earth; this will be at His return.

5.2   The Kingdom Of God Is Not Now Established

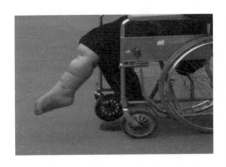

There is a widely held notion that God's Kingdom is now fully in existence, being comprised of present believers - 'the church'. Whilst in prospect the true believers have been 'saved' and given potential places in the Kingdom, there can be no doubt that we cannot now be fully in the Kingdom, seeing that Christ has not yet returned to establish it.

It should be obvious from what we have studied so far "that flesh and blood cannot *inherit* the kingdom of God" (1 Cor. 15:50). Our *inheritance* is our salvation which will be revealed "in the last time" (1 Pet. 1:4,5). We are "*heirs* of the kingdom which he has promised to them that love him" (James 2:5), seeing that baptism makes us heirs of the promises to Abraham - which promises comprise the basic Gospel of the Kingdom (Matt. 4:23; Gal. 3:8,27-29). It is therefore common to come across promises of *inheriting* the kingdom at Christ's return, when the promises to Abraham will be fulfilled (Matt. 25:34; 1 Cor. 6:9,10; 15:50; Gal. 5:21; Eph. 5:5). The very use of this language of future inheritance shows that the kingdom is not the believer's present possession.

Jesus told a parable to correct those who thought "that the kingdom of God should immediately appear. He said therefore, A certain nobleman went into a far country to receive for himself a Kingdom, and to return". In the meantime he left his servants with certain responsibilities. "When he was returned, having received the kingdom, then he commanded these servants to be called unto him", and judged them (Luke 19:11-27).

The nobleman represents Christ going away into the "far country" of heaven to receive the kingdom, with which he returns at the time of judgment, i.e. the second coming. It is therefore impossible that the "servants" should possess the kingdom now, during the time of their Lord's absence.

The following provide further proof of this:-

- "My kingdom is not of this world", Jesus plainly stated (John 18:36). However, even at that time He could say, "I am a king" (John 18:37), showing that Christ's present 'kingship' does not mean that His

Kingdom is now established. Even the faithful in the first century are described as WAITING "for the kingdom of God" (Mk.15:43).

- Christ told his disciples that he would never again drink wine "until I drink it new with you in my Father's kingdom" (Matt. 26:29). This clearly implies that the kingdom was to be in the future, which is how people understood Christ's preaching of "the glad tidings (i.e. advanced proclamation) of the kingdom of God" (Luke 8:1). "Blessed is he that *shall* (in the future) eat bread in the kingdom of God", was their comment (Luke 14:15).

- Luke 22:29,30 continues this theme: "I *appoint* unto you a kingdom, that *you may* eat and drink at my table in my kingdom".

- Jesus explained signs which would herald his second coming, and concluded with the comment, "When you see these things come to pass, know that the kingdom of God is near" (Luke 21:31). This is nonsense if the kingdom is now in existence before the second coming.

- "We must through much tribulation enter into the kingdom of God" (Acts 14:22). No wonder every suffering believer earnestly prays for the kingdom to *come* (Matt. 6:10).

- God has "called you unto his kingdom" (1 Thess. 2:12); in response, we must *seek* entrance to that kingdom through a spiritual life now (Matt. 6:33).

5.3   The Kingdom Of God In The Past

The Kingdom of God is the future reward for believers. As such, it is their motivation to live a life dedicated to imitating the example of Christ - something which will involve short term suffering and discomfort. It is therefore to be expected that all their days they will be consumed by an ever increasing desire to appreciate and understand the wonders of that future age. It will be the summation of all their spiritual strivings, and the full declaration of the God whom they have come to love as their Father.

The Scriptures abound with details of what the Kingdom will be like, and you will find it a lifetime's work to discover just a few of them. One way through which we can come to understand some of the basic principles of this future Kingdom is to appreciate that the Kingdom of God existed in the past in the form of the nation of Israel. This kingdom is to be re-established at Christ's return. Much of the Bible gives us information concerning the nation of Israel, in order that we can understand, in broad outline, how God's future Kingdom will be organized.

God is frequently described as "the king of Israel" (Isa. 44:6 cp. Isa. 41:27; 43:15; Ps. 48:2; 89:18; 149:2); it follows that the people of Israel were His kingdom. They began to be God's kingdom through entering into a covenant with Him at Mount Sinai, shortly after they had escaped from Egypt through the Red Sea. In response to their willingness to keep this covenant, they would "be unto (God) a kingdom...and an holy nation" (Ex. 19:5,6). Thus "When Israel went out of Egypt...Israel (was) His dominion" or kingdom (Ps. 114:1,2). After entering into this agreement, Israel travelled through the wilderness of Sinai and settled down in the promised land of Canaan. As God was their King, they were ruled over by "Judges" (e.g. Gideon and Samson) rather than kings. These judges were not kings, but Divinely guided administrators who governed certain parts of the country rather than ruling over the whole land. They were often raised up by God for specific purposes, e.g. to lead Israel to repentance and deliver them from their enemies. When the Israelites asked judge Gideon to be their king, he replied, "I will not rule over you...the Lord shall rule over you" (Jud. 8:23).

The last judge was Samuel. In his time the Israelites asked for a human king in order to be like the nations around them (1 Sam. 8:5,6). Throughout history, God's true people have been tempted to underestimate the closeness of their relationship to God, and to sacrifice this for an appearance of similarity to the world around them. These temptations are most acute in our present world. God lamented to Samuel: "They have rejected me, that I should not reign over them" (1 Sam. 8:7). However, God granted them kings, beginning with wicked Saul. After him came righteous David, and a whole line of kings descended from him. The more spiritually-minded kings realized that Israel were still God's kingdom, even though they had rejected His kingship. They therefore recognized that they were ruling Israel on God's behalf rather than in their own right.

Understanding this principle enables us to make sense of the description of Solomon, David's son, reigning on "(God's) throne, to be king for the Lord your God" (2 Chron. 9:8; 1 Chron. 28:5; 29:23). Solomon's reign of great peace and prosperity pointed forward to (or was 'typical' of) the future Kingdom of God. This is why it is emphasized that he was king over Israel on God's behalf, as Jesus will also sit on God's throne as King of Israel for God (Matt. 27:37,42; John 1:49; 12:13).

Many of the righteous kings recorded in the Old Testament enjoyed reigns which were typical of Christ's future Kingdom. Thus as Hezekiah and Solomon received presents and tribute from the surrounding nations (1 Kings 10:1-4; 2 Kings 20:12), and saw the land of Israel blessed with astounding fertility and prosperity (1 Kings 10:5-15; Isa. 37:30), so in Christ's world-wide Kingdom the same things will be seen on a far greater scale.

MARRIAGE

Despite Solomon's good start, whilst still quite young he made mistakes regarding his marital relationships which progressively sapped his spiritual strength as he grew older. "King Solomon loved many strange women...women of the Moabites, Ammonites, Edomites...of the nations concerning which the Lord said unto the children of Israel, You shall not go in to them, neither shall they come in unto you: for surely they will turn away your hearts after their gods: Solomon clave unto these in love...and his wives turned away his heart. For it came to pass, when Solomon was old, that his wives turned away his heart after other gods: and his heart was not perfect with the Lord...and Solomon did evil in the sight of the Lord, and went not fully after the Lord...and the Lord was angry with Solomon...Wherefore the Lord said...I will surely rend the kingdom from you" (1 Kings 11:1-11).

Solomon's slide into apostasy was a life-long process. His relationships with women who did not share his knowledge of Israel's God led him to have a sympathy towards their false gods. His love for his wives meant that he no longer saw these gods as the spiritual perversions of the true God which they were. As time went on, his heart was no longer in the worship of Israel's God. "His heart was not perfect", i.e. his conscience no longer pricked him at worshipping fake gods. His lack of wholehearted commitment to the true God was "evil in the sight of the Lord", resulting in God breaking off his relationship with Solomon. Israel were told time and again not to marry the women of the surrounding world (Ex. 34:12-16; Josh. 23:12,13; Deut. 7:3).

By baptism into Christ we become spiritual Israel. If we are single, we should only marry within spiritual Israel, "in the Lord" (1 Cor.7:39) - i.e. other baptized believers "in Christ". If we are already married at the time of our baptism, we should not separate from our partners; our marital relationship is sanctified by reason of our faith (1 Cor. 7:12-14). Consciously choosing to marry those who do not know the true God will, in the long term, lead to our apostasy. Solomon evidently failed to appreciate the strength of God's warning about such wives: "*Surely* they will turn away your heart" (1 Kings 11:2; Ex. 34:16). Only an extraordinary level of self-control and intensity of repentance can make us exceptions to this rule.

THE JUDGMENT OF GOD

As a result of Solomon's apostasy, the kingdom of Israel was divided into two; Solomon's son, Rehoboam, ruled over the tribes of Judah, Benjamin and half the tribe of Manasseh, whilst Jeroboam ruled over the other ten tribes. This ten-tribe kingdom was called Israel, or Ephraim, whilst the two-tribes were called Judah. The people of all these tribes, for the most part, followed Solomon's bad example - they claimed to believe in the true God, whilst at the same time worshipping the idols of the surrounding nations. Time and again God pleaded with them, through the prophets, to repent, but to no avail. Because of this, He punished them by driving them out of the kingdom of Israel into the lands of their enemies. This was through the Assyrians and Babylonians invading Israel and taking them away captive: "Many years did you (God) forbear them, and testified against them by your spirit (word) in your prophets: yet would they not give ear: therefore you gave them into the hand of the people of the (surrounding) lands" (Neh. 9:30).

The ten-tribe kingdom of Israel had no good kings at all. Jeroboam, Ahab, Jehoahaz etc. are all recorded in the book of Kings as idol-worshippers. Their last king was Hoshea, during whose reign Israel was defeated by Assyria, and the ten tribes carried into captivity (2 Kings 17). From this they never returned.

The two-tribe kingdom of Judah had some good kings (e.g. Hezekiah and Josiah), although the majority were evil. Due to the people's repeated sins, God overturned Judah as His kingdom in the reign of their last king, Zedekiah. This was caused by their being invaded by the Babylonians, who took them captive to Babylon (2 Kings 25). They remained in Babylon for 70 years, after which some returned to Israel under the leadership of Ezra and Nehemiah. They never again had their own king, being ruled by the Babylonians, Greeks and Romans. Jesus was born during the period of Roman rulership. Due to Israel's rejection of Jesus, the Romans invaded them in A.D. 70 and scattered them world-wide. Only in the past 100 years have they started to return, thus heralding the return of Christ.

Ezekiel 21:25-27 prophesied this ending of God's kingdom as seen in the nation of Israel: "You, profane, wicked prince of Israel (i.e. Zedekiah), whose day is come...Thus says the Lord God; Remove the diadem, and take off the crown (i.e. Zedekiah would cease to be king): this shall not be the same...I will overturn, overturn, overturn it: and it shall be no more, *until* he come whose right it is; and I will give it him". Passage after passage in the prophets laments the ending of God's kingdom (Hos. 10:3; Lam. 5:16; Jer. 14:21; Dan. 8:12-14).

The triple 'overturning' of Ez. 21:25-27 refers to the three invasions made by Nebuchadnezzar, king of Babylon. The watchful student will see in these verses another example of how the kingdom of God and its king can be treated as parallel; Zedekiah's overthrow was that of God's kingdom (see Section 5:2). Thus God's kingdom as it was in the nation of Israel ended: "I...will cause to cease the kingdom of the house of Israel" (Hos.1:4). "It shall be no more, *until*..." carries the implication that the kingdom would revive when "he come whose right it is; and (God) will give it him". God will "give (Jesus) the throne of his father David...and of his kingdom there shall be no end" (Luke 1:32,33) - at Christ's return. This, therefore, is when the promise of the kingdom's restoration will be fulfilled.

RESTORATION OF ISRAEL

There is a tremendous theme throughout the Old Testament prophets of the *restoration* of God's Kingdom on Messiah's return. Christ's disciples were well tuned in to this: "When they therefore were come together, they asked of him, saying, Lord, wilt you at this time *restore again the Kingdom to Israel?*" i.e. 'Will Ezekiel 21:27 be fulfilled now?' Jesus replied by saying that the exact time of his second coming they would never know, although the angels immediately afterwards assured them that he would, indeed, return at some point (Acts 1:6-11).

The restoration of the kingdom of God/Israel will therefore be at the second coming. Thus Peter preached that God would send "Jesus Christ...whom the heaven must receive (i.e. he must remain there) *until* the times of *restitution* of all things, which God has spoken by the mouth of all his holy prophets" (Acts 3:20,21). The second coming will bring about the re-establishment of God's kingdom as a restoration of the old kingdom of Israel.

The restoration of God's kingdom is truly the theme of "all (God's) holy prophets":-

- "In mercy shall the throne be established: and he (Jesus) shall sit upon it in truth in the tabernacle of David (at the second coming - Luke 1:32,33), judging... and hasting righteousness" (Is. 16:5).

- "In that day will I raise up the tabernacle of David (i.e. David's "throne" of Luke 1:32,33) that is fallen, and close up the breaches thereof; and I will raise up his ruins, and I will build it *as in the days of old*" (Amos 9:11). The last phrase is clearly the language of restoration.

- "Their (Israel's) children also shall be *as aforetime*, and their congregation shall be established before me" (Jer. 30:20).

- "The Lord shall choose Jerusalem *again*" (Zech. 2:12), making it the capital of His world-wide Kingdom (cp. Ps. 48:2; Is. 2:2-4).

- "The *former* dominion" or Kingdom is to return to Jerusalem (Mic. 4:8 RV).

- As God *was* in the land of Israel in their past, so when the Kingdom is re-established it will again be known that "The Lord is there" (Ez. 35:9 cp. 48:35).

- "I will cause the captivity of Judah and the captivity of Israel to return, and will build them, *as at the first...Again* there shall be heard in this place...the voice of joy...For I will cause to return the captivity of the land, *as at the first...again* in this place (Jerusalem)...shall be an habitation of shepherds...the flocks (shall) pass *again*" (Jer. 33:7-13).

The return of Christ to establish this Kingdom is truly "the hope of Israel", to which we must become related by baptism.

5.4   The Kingdom Of God In The Future

Sections 1 and 3 of this Study have yielded a fair amount of information concerning what this Kingdom will be like. We have seen that Abraham was promised that through his Seed people from all parts of the world will be blessed; Rom. 4:13 extends this to mean that the whole earth will be inherited by those people who are 'in' Abraham's Seed, i.e. Christ. The image prophecy of Dan. 2 explains how Christ will return as the little stone, and then the kingdom will gradually spread world-wide (cp. Ps. 72:8). This means that the Kingdom of God will not just be located in Jerusalem or the land of Israel, as some maintain, although these areas will certainly be its heartland.

Those who follow Christ in this life will be "kings and priests; and we shall reign on the earth" (Rev. 5:10). We will rule over settlements of various sizes and number; one will rule over ten cities, another over five (Luke 19:17). Christ will share his rulership over the earth with us (Rev. 2:27; 2 Tim. 2:12). "A king (Jesus) shall reign in righteousness, and princes (the believers) shall rule in judgment" (Is. 32:1; Ps. 45:16).

Christ is to reign for ever on David's re-established throne (Luke 1:32,33), i.e. he will have David's place and position of rulership, which was in Jerusalem. As Christ will reign from Jerusalem, this will be the capital of the future Kingdom. Nations "will go up from year to year to worship the King, the Lord of hosts" in Jerusalem (Zech. 14:16).

This annual pilgrimage to Jerusalem is also prophesied in Is. 2:2,3: "In the last days, the mountain (kingdom - Dan. 2:35,44) of the Lord's house shall be established in the top of the mountains (i.e. God's Kingdom will be exalted above the kingdoms of men)...and all nations shall flow unto it. And many people shall go and say, Come, and let us go up to the mountain of the Lord, to the house of the God of Jacob; and he will teach us of his ways...for out of Zion shall go forth the law, and the word of the Lord from Jerusalem". This appears to be a picture of the early days of the Kingdom, as people spread the knowledge of Christ's reign to others, and they go up to the "mountain" of God's Kingdom, which will be slowly spreading world-wide. Here we have a picture of real enthusiasm in religious worship.

One of the greatest human tragedies of our day is that most people 'worship' God for political, social, cultural or emotional reasons, rather than upon the basis of a true understanding of Him as their Father and Creator. In the Kingdom there will be world-wide enthusiasm to learn the ways of God; people will be so motivated by this desire that they will travel from all ends of the earth to Jerusalem in order to worship and learn of God.

Instead of the confusion and unfairness created by man's legal systems and administration of justice, there will be one universal legal code - "the law, and the word of the Lord", which will be pronounced by Christ from Jerusalem. "All nations shall *flow* unto" these teaching sessions, implying that this common desire to find the true knowledge of God will lessen the natural friction between nations, as it does between individuals who dedicate themselves to gaining such knowledge in this life.

This description of all the nations *flowing* unto Jerusalem is similar to the picture presented in Is. 60:5, where the Jews "flow together" along with the Gentiles (non-Jews) to worship God in Jerusalem. This connects perfectly with the Kingdom prophecy of Zech. 8:20-23:-

"There shall come people, and the inhabitants of many cities; and the inhabitants of one city shall go to another, saying, Let us go continually (A.V. mg. - cp. Zech. 14:16 'year by year') to pray before the Lord, and to seek the Lord of hosts: I will go also. Yes, many people and strong nations shall come to seek the Lord of hosts in Jerusalem...ten men shall take hold out of all languages of the nations, even shall take hold of the skirt of him that is a Jew, saying, We will go with you: for we have heard that God is with you".

This creates the picture of the Jewish people being made "the head, and not the tail" of the nations, due to their repentance and obedience (Deut. 28:13); the Jewish basis of God's plan of salvation will then be appreciated by everyone. The ignorance of this amongst contemporary Christianity will then be abruptly ended. People will then enthusiastically discuss these things, so that they can tell the Jews, "we have *heard* that God is with you". Conversation will then revolve around spiritual things, rather than the vain phantoms which fill the world's present thinking.

Given this greater commitment to godliness, it is not surprising that Christ "shall judge among the nations...they shall beat their swords into plowshares, and their spears into pruninghooks: nation shall not lift up sword against nation, neither shall they learn war any more" (Is. 2:4). The absolute authority of Christ and total justice of his arbitration in disputes will result in the nations willingly changing their military hardware into agricultural machinery, and abandoning all military training. "In his days shall the righteous flourish" (Ps. 72:7) - spirituality will then be exalted, and respect will be paid to those who reflect God's characteristics of love, mercy, justice etc. Contrast this with the present exaltation of the proud, self-assertive and selfishly ambitious.

The willing beating of "swords into plowshares" will be part of a much greater agricultural change which will come upon the earth. As a result of Adam's sin, the ground was cursed for his sake (Gen. 3:17-19), with the result that great effort is presently needed to get food from it. In the Kingdom "there shall be an handful of corn in the earth upon the top of the (once barren) mountains; the fruit thereof shall shake like (the crops of) Lebanon" (Ps. 72:16). "The plowman shall overtake the reaper, and the treader of grapes him that sows seed; and the mountains shall drop sweet wine" (Amos 9:13), such will be the improved fertility of the earth, and the reduction of the curse on the ground pronounced in Eden.

Such immense agricultural enterprise will involve many people. The Kingdom prophecies give the impression that people will return to a self-sufficient, agricultural lifestyle:-

- "They shall sit every man under his vine and under his fig tree;

- and none shall make them afraid" (Mic. 4:4).

- This self-sufficiency will overcome the abuses which are inherent in any system of employment of labour for cash. Spending a lifetime working to make others rich will then be a thing of the past.

- "They shall build houses, and inhabit them (themselves); and they shall plant vineyards and eat the fruit of them. They shall not build and another inhabit; they shall not plant and another eat...my elect shall long enjoy the work of their hands. They shall not labour in vain..." (Isa. 65:21-23).

Isaiah 35:1-7 contains a matchless prophecy of how infertile land will be changed, resulting in an aura of joy and happiness almost oozing from the land, due to the easier and more spiritual way of life of those who work it: "The wilderness...shall be glad...the desert shall rejoice, and blossom as the rose. It shall...rejoice even with joy and singing...for in the wilderness shall waters break out, and streams in the desert. And the parched ground shall become a pool". Even the natural aggression between the animals will be removed: "the wolf and the lamb shall feed together", and children will be able to play with snakes (Is. 65:25; 11:6-8).

In the same way as the curse which was placed upon the natural creation will be greatly reduced, so that which was placed on mankind will also be lessened. Thus Rev. 20:2,3 speaks in symbolic language of the devil (sin and its effects) being "bound", or restrained, during the Millennium. Life-spans will be increased, so that if someone dies at 100 years old, they will be considered but a child (Is. 65:20). Women will experience less sorrow in childbirth (Is. 65:23). "Then the eyes of the blind shall be opened, and the ears of the deaf shall be unstopped. Then shall the lame man leap as a deer, and the tongue of the dumb sing" (Is. 35:5,6). This will be due to the miraculous Spirit gifts again being possessed (cp. Heb. 6:5).

It cannot be too strongly emphasized that the Kingdom of God should not be seen as a tropical island paradise, which the righteous will enjoy in a similar way to which men enjoy sunbathing amidst the glories of nature. The fundamental purpose of the Kingdom of God is to give glory to God, until the earth is full of glory to Him "as the waters cover the sea" (Hab. 2:14). This is God's ultimate aim: "As truly as I live, all the earth shall be filled with the glory of the Lord" (Num. 14:21). Glory to God means that the inhabitants of the earth will appreciate, praise and copy His righteous attributes; because the world will be in this state, God will allow the physical earth to reflect this, too. Thus "the meek shall inherit the earth (in the Kingdom), and shall delight themselves in the abundance of (spiritual) peace" (Ps. 37:11), rather than in enjoying the easy life. Those "which do hunger and thirst after righteousness...shall be filled" with it in the Kingdom (Matt. 5:6).

Just the thought of possessing eternal life in the Kingdom is often used as a 'carrot' to induce people to an interest in Christianity. However, our possession of it then, will almost be incidental to the real reason for our being in the Kingdom - which is to glorify God. In what time may remain to us after our baptism, our appreciation of this should continually develop.

For me, just ten years of living in the joy of absolute perfection and good conscience with God would be worth all the trauma of this life. That this glorious state will last for ever simply blows the mind, taking us beyond the limits of human comprehension.

Even when viewed in slightly more physical terms, being in the Kingdom of God should be our supreme motivation to despise worldly advantages and materialism. Instead of taking excessive thought for the immediate future, Jesus advised, "Seek you first the Kingdom of God, and his righteousness; and all these things shall be added unto you" (Matt. 6:30-

34). Everything which we can now imagine and strive for is incomparable to the ultimate fulfilment of being in God's Kingdom.

We need to seek "(God's) righteousness", i.e. to try to develop a love of God's character, which means that we want to be in God's Kingdom because righteousness will be glorified there, because we want to be completely morally perfect rather than just because we, personally, want to escape death and live an easy life for eternity.

All too often the hope of the Gospel is presented in ways which appeal to human selfishness. Obviously our motivation for being in the Kingdom varies tremendously from day to day. What we are suggesting here is an ideal; our first priority is to learn the Gospel and show our submission to it in baptism from a motive of loving obedience to God. Our appreciation of the hope God is offering, and our exact reasons for wanting to be in the Kingdom, will grow and mature after our baptism.

5.5   The Millennium

At this point in our study of life in the Kingdom, the thoughtful reader will probably be asking, 'Doesn't this picture of the Kingdom of God all seem rather human?' People in the Kingdom will still be producing babies (Is. 65:23) and even dying (Is. 65:20). These people will still have disputes which Christ will settle (Is. 2:4), and will still need to work the ground in order to survive, even though this will be much easier than at present. This all seems a far cry from the promises that the righteous will receive eternal life, and a nature like God's, being made equal to the angels, who do not marry or reproduce (Luke 20:35,36) The answer lies in the fact that the first part of the Kingdom of God will last for 1,000 years - a 'Millennium' (see Rev. 20:2-7). During this Millennium there will be two groups of people on earth:-

1 The saints - those of us who have followed Christ acceptably in this life, who will have been given eternal life at the judgment seat. Note: a 'saint' means 'a called out' person, and refers to any true believer.

2 The ordinary, mortal people who did not know the Gospel at the time of Christ's return - i.e. they were not responsible to the judgment seat.

When Christ comes, two men will be in the field, one will be taken (to judgment), and the other left (Lk. 17:36); those who are "left" will be in this second group.

Having received God's nature at the judgment seat, the saints will be unable to die or produce children. The descriptions of people experiencing these things in the Kingdom must therefore apply to the second group - those who are alive at the time of Christ's return, but who did not know God's requirements. The reward of the righteous is to be "kings and priests: and we shall reign on the earth" (Rev. 5:10). Kings have to reign over somebody; those people who were ignorant of the Gospel at the time of the second coming will therefore be left alive, to be reigned over. Through being "in Christ" we will share His reward - which is to be the king of the world: "He that overcomes...to him will I give power over the nations: and he shall rule them with a rod of iron...even as *I* received of my Father" (Rev. 2:26,27).

Christ's parable of the pounds now falls into place - the faithful servants were rewarded with ten or five towns to rule over in the Kingdom (Luke 19:12-19). Knowledge of God's ways will not spread immediately Christ is declared King in Jerusalem; the people will travel to Jerusalem in order to find more knowledge about God (Is. 2:2,3). Recall, too, how the mountain of Dan. 2:35,44 (representing the Kingdom of God) gradually spreads over the earth. It will be the duty of the saints to spread the knowledge of God and therefore His Kingdom.

When Israel was the kingdom of God previously, the duty of the priests was to teach the knowledge of God (Mal. 2:5-7).For this purpose they were placed in various towns throughout Israel. In the more glorious re-establishment of the Kingdom, the saints will take over the role of the priests (Rev. 5:10).

Should Christ come today:

1. The responsible dead will be raised and, along with the responsible living, taken to the judgment seat.

2. The responsible wicked will be punished with death, and the righteous given eternal life. Judgment will also be given to the nations who resist Christ.

3. The righteous will then rule over those people who are then alive, but who are not responsible to God; they will teach them the Gospel as "kings and priests" (Rev. 5:10).

4. This will last for 1,000 years. During this time all the mortal people will hear the Gospel and therefore be responsible to God. These people will live much longer and happier lives.

5. At the end of the Millennium there will be a rebellion against Christ and the saints, which God will put down (Rev. 20:8,9).

6. At the end of the 1,000 years, all those who have died during that time will be resurrected and judged (Rev. 20:5,11-15).

7. The wicked amongst them will be destroyed, and the righteous will join us in having eternal life.

The purpose of God with the earth will then have been completed. It will be filled with immortal, righteous beings. God's Name 'Yahweh Elohim' (meaning 'He who will be revealed in a group of mighty ones') will then be fulfilled. Never again will sin, and therefore death, be experienced on earth; the promise that the seed of the serpent would be totally destroyed by being hit in the head, will then have been completely fulfilled (Gen. 3:15). During the Millennium, Christ will have reigned "till he has put all enemies under his feet. The last enemy that shall be destroyed is death...And when all things shall be subdued unto him (God), then shall the Son also himself be subject unto him (God) that put all things under him, that God may be all in all" (1 Cor. 15:25-28).

This is "the end, when he (Christ) shall have delivered up the kingdom to God, even the Father" (1 Cor. 15:24). What will follow in this period when God is "all in all" we are not told; all we know is that we will have eternal life, God's nature, and we will live to glorify and please God. It is presumption to even enquire further into what the state after the Millennium will be like.

An understanding of "the gospel of the kingdom of God" is vital for the salvation of every reader of these words. May we plead with you to re-read this study and look up the Bible passages quoted.

God wants us to be in His Kingdom. His whole purpose was designed for us to have a real part in, rather than just to express, His creative ability. Baptism relates us to the promises concerning this Kingdom. It is hard to believe that baptism, followed by a few years' humble obedience to God's word, can gain us entry to that glorious, eternal age. Yet our faith in God's vast love must be firm. Whatever our short-term problems, surely we have no sensible reason to resist the Gospel's call?

"If God be for us, who can be against us?" (Rom. 8:31).

"The sufferings of this present time are not worthy to be compared with the glory which shall be revealed in us" (Rom. 8:18).

"Our light affliction, which is but for a moment, works for us a far more exceeding and eternal weight of glory" (2 Cor. 4:17).

Belief In Practice 11:

What The Kingdom Of God Means For Us Today

It has been pointed out that "Your Kingdom come!" was violently in conflict with the Roman view that the lives of a subject people like Israel belonged to Caesar's kingdom. This is why the Roman authorities saw all talk of the coming Kingdom of Christ, and His Kingship, as subversive and not to be tolerated. And so with us, the seeking of the future Kingdom is a radical denial of the spirit of our age, which seeks its Kingdom now; it demands a separation from the world around us. The well known description of the Kingdom in Is. 2:1-4 is in the context of appealing to Israel to change their ways. Because they would *then* walk in the ways of the Lord, therefore " O house of Israel [therefore] Come [now] and walk in the ways of the Lord" (2:5). The hope of Israel ought to motivate Israel to live the Kingdom life here and now. If we will eternally walk in God's ways then, we ought to now too. "We labour and strive *because* we have our hope set on the living God, who is the Saviour of all men" (1 Tim. 4:10 RV).

Whilst the promise of immortal life is far from all that the Hope of the Kingdom is about, it is nonetheless wonderfully true that we are promised eternal, deathless life. The world in which we live has no such hope, nor even concept of a human being who now lives one day enjoying eternal life in a bodily form. Therefore they have come to value youth above all else. Sport and fitness have become national obsessions. Magazine covers present faces without wrinkles and gorgeous bodies. Old age is devalued; the elderly are disrespectfully ushered off into old folks homes, isolated from the general populace. Skin creams, cosmetic surgery, cures for baldness etc. are all the order of the day. Dieting and body building have become the equivalent of pagan rites. And thus the external rather than the internal features of personality have become emphasized. Compassion, self-sacrifice, humility etc. are all of little account. For the Christian, separation from the world of such superficiality is mandatory. Because there is no concept of judgment to come, no sense of the eternity we might miss, there is no moral constraint; enjoying ourselves in the here and now becomes the prevailing religion. And so it is tragic to see sisters worried sick about their weight increase, brethren spending hours each day on body building...caught up in the spirit of the age, in seeking to be conformed to the image of this passing world. The hope of life eternal in the Kingdom means that the attitude of this world to life should not be ours. May we die peaceful, slightly over-weight grandparents, joyfully anticipating the eternity to come!

MAKING SENSE OF THE WORLD NOW

There is a sense in all of us that the natural world around us somehow reflects something of the eternal, something of God; and yet we are not led by nature itself to the ultimate truth of God and the Gospel. This is why we have the Bible. Only an understanding of the Kingdom of God coming on earth can enable us to put all these hints and leads into some sort of framework and context, as from our position of separation from the world we observe it around us. We perceive that the whole of creation is groaning, not for nothing, but towards the coming of the day of the Kingdom.

Jeremiah lived the Kingdom life now, separate from the world, when on the eve of Judah's destruction, he bought a field and carefully had it witnessed- because Jeremiah knew that "Like as I have brought all this great evil upon this people, so will I bring upon them all the good that I have promised them. And fields shall be bought in this land, whereof you say, It is desolate, without man or beast; it is given into the hand of the Chaldeans. Men shall buy fields for money, and subscribe the deeds, and seal them, and call witnesses, in the land of Benjamin" (Jer. 32:42-44). And so as he saw his world falling apart, he could make sense of things because he sought to live in his day how, one day, in the restored Kingdom, he knew he would live.

WATCHING FOR THE RETURN

If we believe we really will be there, then we will look more earnestly for the day to come. We can never be truly enthusiastic about the Lord's return if we are unsure about our ultimate acceptance at His hand. Because we are *sure* that When Christ...shall be manifested, then shall you also with him be manifested in glory. Mortify *therefore* your members which are upon the earth; fornication..." etc. (Col. 3:4,5). We don't control ourselves because we think this will make us good enough to be accepted, but rather because we believe that we have already been accepted. By grace alone. That salvation is by grace enables us to look forward with eagerness rather than uncertainty to the second coming, and our lives are thereby changed. " The grace of God...teaches us that, denying ungodliness and worldly lusts...looking for that blessed hope, and the glorious appearing of the great God and our saviour Jesus Christ" (Tit. 2:11-13). In other words- separation from the world.

HUMILITY

And finally, the knowledge of the Kingdom should humble us. The wonderful good news of the coming Kingdom was explained to Belshazzar, but he had to be told that " you...have not humbled your heart, though you knew all this" (Dan. 5:22). Knowing all this as we do...who are *we* to be there, to have a part in it, to even have been told about it...? It ought to humble us.

And it humbles us in another way too. We all to some extent struggle with God. There is so much we simply don't understand. But if we firmly believe in the ultimate coming of the Kingdom, we have a perspective upon all the cancers, the deaths, the broken relationships...all the collected groanings of our savage planet will surely be taken away in the coming of the Kingdom. Without this ultimate perspective, the apparent injustices of present life and even God's dealings with us would leave us lost, angry and with no real basis for an ongoing relationship with the Father.

Digression 8: The Kingdom Of God Today

Graham Bacon

The sense in which the Kingdom of God has a meaning today is among true believers who follow Jesus, who make God their King. Paul wrote to the Ephesians describing their former pagan life as being "alien from the commonwealth of Israel" (Eph. 2:12). On the other hand, in Christ, we are in this "commonwealth". A commonwealth is groups of people who give their combined allegiance to a central governing body, in this case God. Over centuries these groups of people formed a spiritual kingdom with Jesus as king and God as Lord Almighty. The true believers of today form the latest of these groups. This kingdom is not a political kingdom but is bound together by the faith of the true believers and the present Lordship of Jesus and the acceptance of God's reign in their lives.

In the context of Jesus healing the blind, dumb and mentally disturbed man (Matthew 12) Jesus said, "If I cast out demons by the spirit of God surely the Kingdom of God has come upon you". The healing work of Jesus was a taste, a sample of the benefits of the coming kingdom. A little of the wonders of the kingdom had arrived, temporarily at least. The same thought recurs in Luke 10:9-11, again about miracle working by the seventy: "Heal the sick and say to them, 'The kingdom of God has come near to you'". When this message was rejected, "the very dust of your city that clings to us we wipe off against you. But nevertheless know this, the kingdom of God has come near to you". Tthe faithful disciples and true believers constitute a kingdom eminence clearly displayed among the people of the world. Again, this in no sense measures up to the future glories of the Kingdom of God on Earth, but is evidence of its future arrival. We are to live the Kingdom life now!

STUDY 5: Questions

1. Which of the following is the time for the establishment of God's Kingdom?
    ☐ It has always been established
    ☐ At Christ's return
    ☐ At the day of Pentecost in the first century
    ☐ In the hearts of believers at their conversion.

2. Did the Kingdom of God exist in the past? If so, in what form?

3. When did it end?

4. What is the Millennium?
    ☐ A reign of grace in our hearts
    ☐ A 1000 year reign of the believers in Heaven
    ☐ A 1000 year reign of Satan on the earth
    ☐ The first 1000 years of God's future Kingdom on earth.

5. What will the Kingdom be like?

6. What will the present believers do in the Millennium?
    ☐ Be rulers over the mortal people
    ☐ Be rulers in Heaven
    ☐ We do not know
    ☐ Live on another planet

7. Was the message about the Kingdom of God preached:
    ☐ Just in the New Testament
    ☐ Just by Jesus and the apostles
    ☐ In both Old and New Testaments
    ☐ Just in the Old Testament.

STUDY 6

God and Evil

6.1   God And Evil

Many Christians, along with many other religions, believe that there is a being or monster called the devil or satan who is the originator of the problems which are in the world and in our own lives, and who is responsible for the sin which we commit. The Bible clearly teaches that God is all-powerful. We have seen in Study 1.4 that the angels cannot sin. If we truly believe these things, then it is impossible that there is any supernatural being at work in

this universe that is opposed to Almighty God. If we believe that such a being *does* exist, then surely we are questioning the supremacy of God Almighty. This issue is so important that the correct understanding of the devil and satan must be considered a vital doctrine. We are told in Heb. 2:14 that Jesus destroyed the devil by his death; therefore unless we have a correct understanding of the devil, we are likely to misunderstand the work and nature of Jesus.

In the world generally, especially in the Christian world, there is the idea that the good things in life come from God and the bad things from the devil or satan. This is not a new idea; the Babylonians, for example, believed there were two gods, a god of good and light, and a god of evil and darkness, and that those two were locked in mortal combat. Cyrus, the great King of Persia, believed just this. Therefore God told him, "*I* am the Lord, and there is *no other;* there is no God besides me...I form the light, and create darkness, I make peace, and create calamity ('evil' KJV, 'disaster' NIV); I the Lord do all these things" (Is. 45:5-7,22). God creates peace and He creates evil, or disaster. In this sense there is a difference between evil and sin, which is man's fault; sin entered the world as a result of man, not God (Rom. 5:12).

God told Cyrus and the people of Babylon that "there is no (other) God besides me". The Hebrew word '*el*' translated 'God' fundamentally means 'strength, or source of power'. God was saying that there is no source of power in existence apart from Him. This is the reason why a true believer in God should not accept the idea of a supernatural devil or demons.

GOD: THE CREATOR OF DISASTER

The Bible abounds with examples of God bringing evil into people's lives and into this world. Am. 3:6 says that if there is calamity in a city, God has done it. If, for example, there is an earthquake in a city, it is often felt that 'the devil' had designs on that city, and had brought about the calamity. But the true believer must understand that it is *God* who is responsible for this. Thus Mic. 1:12 says that "disaster came down *from the Lord* to the gate of Jerusalem". In the book of Job we read how Job, a righteous man, lost the things which he had in this life. The book teaches that the experience of 'evil' in a person's life is not directly proportional to their obedience or disobedience to God. Job recognized that "The Lord gave, and the Lord has taken away" (Job 1:21). He does not say 'The Lord gave and satan took away'. He commented to his wife: "Shall we indeed accept good from God, and shall we not (also) accept adversity?" (Job 2:10). At the end of the book, Job's friends comforted him over "all the adversity that *the Lord* had brought upon him" (Job 42:11 cp. 19:21; 8:4).

Thus God, who is in control of all things, uses wicked people to bring evil as a chastisement or punishment on His people. "For whom the Lord loves he chastens...If you endure chastening ...afterward it yields the peaceable fruit of righteousness to those who have been trained by it" (Heb. 12:6-11). This shows that the trials which God gives us lead eventually to our spiritual growth. It is setting the Word of God against itself to say that the devil is a being which forces us to sin and be unrighteous, whilst at the same time he supposedly brings problems into our lives which lead to our developing "the peaceable fruit of righteousness". The orthodox idea of the devil runs into serious problems here. Especially serious for it are passages which speak of delivering a man to satan "that his spirit may be saved", or "that (they) may learn not to blaspheme" (1 Cor. 5:5; 1 Tim. 1:20). If satan is really a being bent on causing men to sin and having a *negative* spiritual effect upon people, why do these passages speak of 'satan' in a *positive* light? The answer lies in the fact that an adversary, a "satan" or difficulty in life, can often result in positive spiritual effects in a believer's life.

If we accept that evil comes from God, then we can pray to God to do something about the problems which we have, e.g. to take them away. If He doesn't, then we know that they are sent from God for our spiritual good. Now if we believe that there is some evil being called the devil or satan causing our problems, then there is no way of coming to terms with them. Disability, illness, sudden death or calamity have to be taken as just bad luck. If the devil is some powerful, sinful angel, then he will be much more powerful than us, and we will have no choice but to suffer at his hand. By contrast, we are comforted that under God's control, "all things (in life) work together for *good*" to the believers (Rom. 8:28). There is therefore no such thing as 'luck' in the life of a believer.

THE ORIGIN OF SIN

It must be stressed that *sin* comes from inside us. It is our fault that we sin. Of course, it would be nice to believe that it was not our fault that we sin. We could freely sin and then excuse ourselves with the thought that it was really the devil's fault, and that the blame for our sin should be completely laid upon him. It is not uncommon that in cases of grossly wicked behaviour, the guilty person has begged for mercy because he says that he was possessed by the devil at the time and was therefore not responsible for himself. But, quite rightly, such feeble excuses are judged to hold no water at all, and the person has sentence passed upon him.

We need to remember that "the wages of sin is death" (Rom. 6:23); sin leads to death. If it is not our fault that we sin, but that of the devil, then a just God ought to punish the devil rather than us. But the fact that we are judged for our own sins shows that we are responsible for our sins. The idea of the devil being a specific person outside of us rather than the principle of sin *within* us is an attempt to move the responsibility for our sins away from ourselves. This is yet another example of men refusing to come to terms with what the Bible teaches about man's nature.

"There is *nothing* that enters a man from outside which can defile him...For from within, out of the heart of men, proceed evil thoughts, adulteries, fornications, murders... pride, foolishness. All these evil things come from within and defile a man" (Mk. 7:15-23).

The idea that there *is* something sinful outside of us which enters us and causes us to sin is incompatible with the plain teaching of Jesus here. From *within*, out of the heart of man, come *all* these evil things. This is why, at the time of the flood, God considered that "the imagination of man's heart is evil from his youth" (Gen. 8:21). James 1:14 tells us how we are tempted: "each one (it is the same process for each human being) is tempted, when he is drawn away by his own desires and enticed". We are tempted by our *own* evil desires; not by anything outside of us. "Where do wars and fights come from among you?", James asks; "Do they not come from *your* desires for pleasure?" (James 4:1). Each of us has specific, personal temptations. They therefore have to be generated by our *own* evil desires, because they are personal to us. It has been truly said that we are our own worst enemies.

The book of Romans is largely concerned with sin, its origin, and how to overcome it. It is highly significant that there is no mention of the devil and just one of satan in the book; in the context of speaking about the origin of sin, Paul does not mention the devil or satan at all. In the same way, 'the devil' is a New Testament concept. If there is an external being who makes us sin, surely he would have been mentioned extensively in the Old Testament? But there is a very profound and significant silence about this. The record of the Judges period, or Israel in the wilderness, show that at those times Israel were sinning a great deal. But God did not warn them about some powerful supernatural being or force which could enter them and make them sin. Instead, He encouraged them to apply themselves to His word, so that they would not fall away to the ways of their own flesh (e.g. Dt. 27:9,10; Josh. 22:5).

Paul laments: "nothing good dwells in me – my unspiritual self, I mean - ...for though the will to do good is there, the ability to effect it is not...if what I do is against my will, clearly it is no longer I who am the agent, but sin that has its dwelling in me" (Rom. 7:18-21 REB). Now he does not blame his sin on an external being called the devil. He located his own evil nature as the real source of sin: it is not I that do it, "but *sin that has its dwelling in me.* I discover this principle, then; that when I want to do right, only wrong *is within my reach.*" So he says that the opposition to being spiritual comes from something that he calls "sin...dwelling in me". Sin is "the way of [man's] heart" (Is. 57:17). Every thoughtful, spiritually minded person will come to the same kind of self-knowledge. It should be noted that even a supreme Christian like Paul did not experience a change of nature after conversion, nor was he placed in a position whereby he did not and could not sin. Some elements of the Pentecostal movement claim that they are in such a position, and thereby place Paul well within the ranks of the 'unsaved' because of his statement here in Rom. 7:15-21. These verses have proved a major difficulty for their claims. David, another undoubtedly righteous man, likewise commented upon the constant sinfulness of his very nature: "I was brought forth in iniquity, and in sin my mother conceived me" (Ps. 51:5).

The Bible is quite explicit about the fundamentally wicked nature of man. If this is appreciated, there is no need to invent an imaginary person outside our human natures who is responsible for our sins. Jer. 17:9 says that the heart of man is so desperately wicked and deceitful that we cannot actually appreciate the gross extent of its sinfulness. Ecc. 9:3 could not be plainer: "The hearts of the sons of men are full of evil". Eph. 4:18 gives the reason for man's alienation from God as being "because of the ignorance that is *in* them, because of the hardening of their *heart*". It is because of our spiritually blind and ignorant hearts, our way of thinking that is within us, that we are distanced from God. In line with this, Gal. 5:19 speaks of our sins as "the works of the *flesh*"; it is our own flesh (unspiritual nature REB), which causes us to commit sin. None of these passages explain the origin of sin within us as being because the devil put it there; sinful tendencies are something which we all naturally have from birth; it is a fundamental part of the human make-up.

And yet although the heart is indeed a source of wickedness, we must seek to control it. We cannot blame our moral failures on the perversity of our nature. "A heart that devises wicked plans" is something God hates to see in men (Prov. 6:18). A reprobate Israel excused themselves by saying:

"That is hopeless! So we will walk according to our own plans, and we will every one do the imagination of his evil heart" (Jer. 18:12). The heart *is* evil, we are reminded in this very context (Jer. 17:9). But sin lies in assuming that therefore we have no need to strive for self-mastery, and that the weakness of our heart will excuse our committing of sin. We must recognize and even analyse the weakness of our natures [as this chapter seeks to] and in the strength of that knowledge, seek to do something to limit them. "Keep your heart with all diligence [Heb. 'above anything else'], for out of it spring the issues of life" (Prov. 4:23). Ananias could control whether or not 'satan' filled his heart, and was condemned for not doing so (Acts 5:3). If we think that a being called 'satan' irresistably influences us to sin, filling us with the desire to sin against our will, then we are making the same fatal mistake as Israel and Ananias.

6.2   The Devil And Satan

Sometimes the original words of the Bible text are left untranslated ("Mammon", in Mt. 6:24, is an Aramaic example of this). 'Satan' is an untranslated Hebrew word which means 'adversary', while 'devil' is a translation of the Greek word 'diabolos', meaning a liar, an enemy or false accuser. 'Satan' has been transferred from the Hebrew untranslated, just like 'Sabaoth' (James 5:4), 'Armageddon' (Rev. 16:16) and 'Hallelujah' (Rev. 19:1-6). If we are to believe that satan and the devil are some being outside of us which is responsible for sin, then whenever we come across these words in the Bible, we have to make them refer to this evil person. The Biblical usage of these words shows that they can be used as ordinary nouns, describing ordinary people. This fact makes it impossible to reason that the words devil and satan as used in the Bible do in themselves refer to a great wicked person or being outside of us.

THE WORD 'SATAN' IN THE BIBLE

1 Kings 11:14 records that "The Lord raised up an adversary (same Hebrew word elsewhere translated "satan") against Solomon, Hadad the Edomite". "And God raised up another adversary (another satan)...Rezon ...he was an adversary (a satan) of Israel" (1 Kings 11:23,25). This does not mean that God stirred up a supernatural person or an angel to be a

satan/adversary to Solomon; He stirred up ordinary men. Mt. 16:22,23 provides another example. Peter had been trying to dissuade Jesus from going up to Jerusalem to die on the cross. Jesus turned and said unto *Peter:* "Get behind me, Satan...you are not mindful of the things of God, but the things of men". Thus Peter was called a satan. The record is crystal clear that Christ was not talking to an angel or a monster when he spoke those words; he was talking to Peter.

Because the word 'satan' just means an adversary, a good person, even God Himself, can be termed a 'satan'. The word 'satan' does not therefore necessarily refer to sin. The sinful connotations which the word 'satan' has are partly due to the fact that our own sinful nature is our biggest 'satan' or adversary, and also due to the use of the word in the language of the world to refer to something associated with sin. God Himself can be a satan to us by means of bringing trials into our lives, or by standing in the way of a wrong course of action we may be embarking on. But the fact that God can be called a 'satan' does not mean that He Himself is sinful.

The books of Samuel and Chronicles are parallel accounts of the same incidents, as the four gospels are records of the same events but using different language. 2 Sam. 24:1 records: "The Lord...moved David against Israel" in order to make him take a census of Israel. The parallel account in 1 Chron. 21:1 says that "Satan stood up against Israel, and moved David" to take the census. In one passage God does the 'moving', in the other satan does it. The only conclusion is that God acted as a 'satan' or adversary to David. He did the same to Job by bringing trials into his life, so that Job said about God: "With the strength of Your hand You oppose me" (Job 30:21); 'You are acting as a satan against me', was what Job was basically saying. Or again, speaking of God: "I must appeal for mercy to my accuser (satan)" (Job 9:15 NRSV).

THE WORD 'DEVIL' IN THE BIBLE

The word 'devil' too is an ordinary word rather than a proper name. However, unlike 'satan', it is always used in a bad sense. Jesus said, "Did I not choose you, the twelve (disciples), and one of you is a devil? He spoke of Judas Iscariot..." (Jn. 6:70) who was an ordinary, mortal man. He was not speaking of a personal being with horns, or a so-called 'spirit being'. The word 'devil' here simply refers to a wicked man. 1 Tim. 3:11 provides another example. The wives of church elders were not to be 'slanderers'; the original Greek word here is 'diabolos', which is the same word translated 'devil' elsewhere. Thus Paul warns Titus that the aged women in the ecclesia should not be 'slanderers' or 'devils' (Tit. 2:3). And likewise he told Timothy (2 Tim. 3:1,3) that "In the last days...*men* will be...slanderers (devils)". This does not mean that human beings will turn into superhuman beings, but that they will be increasingly wicked. It ought to be quite clear from all this that the words 'devil' and 'satan' do not refer to a fallen angel or a sinful being outside of us.

SIN, SATAN AND THE DEVIL

The words 'satan' and 'devil' are used figuratively to describe the natural sinful tendencies within us which we spoke of in Study 6.1. These are our main 'satan' or adversary. Our lusts are deceitful (Eph. 4:22), and so the devil or 'deceiver' is an appropriate way of describing them. They are personified, and as such they can be spoken of as 'the devil' - our enemy, a slanderer of the truth. This is what our natural 'man' is like - the 'very devil'. The connection between the devil and our evil desires - sin within us - is made explicit in several passages: "Since the children (ourselves) have flesh and blood, he (Jesus) too shared in their humanity so that by his death he might destroy him who holds the power of death - that is, the devil" (Heb. 2:14 NIV). The devil is here described as being responsible for death. But "the wages of sin is death" (Rom. 6:23). Therefore sin and the devil must be parallel. Similarly James 1:14 says that our evil desires tempt us, leading us to sin and therefore to death; but Heb. 2:14 says that the devil brings death. The same verse says that Jesus had our nature in order to destroy the devil. Contrast this with Rom. 8:3: "God ... by sending his own Son in the likeness of sinful man (that is, in our human nature) ... condemned sin in sinful man ". This shows that the devil and the sinful tendencies that are naturally within human nature are effectively the same. It is vitally important to understand that Jesus was tempted just like us. Misunderstanding the doctrine of the devil means that we cannot correctly appreciate the nature and work of Jesus. It was only because Jesus had our human nature - the 'devil' within him - that we can have the hope of salvation (Heb. 2:14-18; 4:15). By overcoming the desires of his own nature Jesus was able to destroy the devil on the cross (Heb. 2:14). If the devil *is* a personal being, then he should no longer exist. Heb. 9:26 says that Christ appeared "to put away sin by the sacrifice of himself". Heb. 2:14 matches this with the statement that through his death Christ destroyed the devil in himself. By His death Jesus in prospect destroyed "the body of sin" (Rom. 6:6), i.e. human nature with its potential to sin in our very bodies.

"He who sins is of the devil" (1 Jn. 3:8), because sin is the result of giving way to our own natural, evil desires (James 1:14,15), which the Bible calls 'the devil'. "For this purpose the Son of God was manifested, that he might destroy the works of the devil" (1 Jn. 3:8). If we are correct in saying that the devil is our evil desires, then the works of our evil desires, i.e. what they result in, are our sins. This is confirmed by 1 Jn. 3:5: "He (Jesus) was manifested to take away our sins". This confirms that "our sins" and "the works of the devil" are the same. Acts 5:3 provides another example of this connection between the devil and our sins. Peter says to Ananias: "Why has satan filled your heart?" Then in verse 4 Peter says "Why have you *conceived this thing in your heart?"* Conceiving something bad within our heart is the same as satan filling our heart. If we ourselves conceive something, e.g. a sinful plan, then it begins *inside us*. Is. 59:13 defines lying as "conceiving and uttering *from the heart* words of falsehood". If a woman conceives a child, it doesn't exist outside of her; it begins inside her. James 1:14,15 use the same figure in describing how our desires *conceive* and bring forth sin, which brings forth death. Ps. 109:6 parallels a sinful person with a 'satan': "Set a wicked man over him: and let an accuser (satan) stand at his right hand", i.e. in power over him (cp. Ps. 110:1).

All through the Old Testament there is the same basic message - that the human heart is the source of disobedience to God. The Proverbs especially stress the need to give serious attention to the state of the heart. The human mind is the arena of spiritual conflict. David speaks of how "transgression" speaks deep in the heart of the wicked, inciting them to sin (Ps. 36:1 NRSV). The New Testament develops this idea further by calling the unspiritual element in the "heart of man" our enemy / adversary / opponent. The English pop star Cliff Richard expressed this connection between the devil and the human mind in one of his well known songs: "She's a devil woman, with evil on her mind". I'd describe the 'devil' as the 'echo' which I observe going on in my mind, and I'm sure you've had the same experience. "I believe in God", we think, and there comes back an echo 'Yes, but... is He *really* out there? Maybe this is just living out the expectations of my upbringing...?'. Or, "OK, I should be generous to that cause. OK, I'll give them some money". And the echo comes back: 'Yes but what if they aren't sincere? Can you really afford it? You need to be careful with your money...'. It's this 'echo' that is the Biblical 'devil'.

PERSONIFICATION

However, you may reasonably reply: 'But it does talk as if the devil is a person!' That is quite correct; Heb. 2:14 speaks of "him who holds the power of death - that is, the devil". Even a small amount of Bible reading shows that it often uses personification - speaking of an abstract idea as if it is a person. Thus Prov. 9:1 speaks of a woman called 'Wisdom' building a house, Prov. 20:1 compares wine to "a mocker", and Rom. 6:23 likens sin to a paymaster giving wages of death. This feature is further discussed in Digression 4. Our devil, the 'diabolos', often represents our evil desires. Yet you cannot have abstract diabolism; the evil desires that are in a man's heart cannot exist separately from a man; therefore 'the devil' is personified. Sin is often personified as a ruler (e.g. Rom. 5:21; 6:6,17; 7:13-14). It is understandable, therefore, that the 'devil' is also personified, seeing that 'the devil' also refers to sin. In the same way, Paul speaks of us having two beings, as it were, within our flesh (Rom. 7:15-21): the man of the flesh, 'the devil', fights with the man of the spirit. Yet it is evident that there are not two literal, personal beings fighting within us. This sinful part of our nature is personified as "the evil one" (Mt. 6:13 R.V.) - the Biblical devil. The same Greek phrase translated "evil one" here is translated as "wicked person" in 1 Cor. 5:13, showing that when a person gives way to sin, his "evil one" - he himself - becomes an "evil one", or a 'devil'. Even in the Old Testament, sin was personified as 'Belial' (1 Sam. 2:12 mg.). It really has to be accepted that 'devil' and 'satan' are used to personify sin, because if we read these words as always meaning a literal being, then we have serious contradictions. Thus "the devil" is a lion (1 Pet. 5:8), a hunter (2 Tim. 2:26) and a snake (Rev. 12:9); it can't be all these things. Whatever the devil is (and we believe it to essentially refer to human sin), it is personified in various ways.

'DEVIL' AND 'SATAN' IN A POLITICAL CONTEXT

These words 'devil' and 'satan' are also used to describe the wicked, sinful world order in which we live. The social, political and pseudo-religious hierarchies of mankind can be spoken of in terms of 'the devil'. The devil and satan in the New Testament often refer to the political and social power of the Jewish or Roman systems. Thus we read of the devil throwing believers into prison (Rev. 2:10), referring to the Roman authorities imprisoning believers. In this same context we read of the church in Pergamos being situated where satan's throne, was - i.e. the place of governorship for a Roman colony in Pergamos, where there was also a group of believers. We cannot say that satan himself, if he exists, personally had a throne in Pergamos. Individual sin is defined as a transgression against God's law (1 Jn. 3:4). But sin expressed collectively as a political and social force opposed to God is a force more powerful than individuals; it is this collective power which is sometimes personified as a powerful being called the devil. In this sense Iran and other Islamic powers have called the United States, "the great satan" - i.e. the great adversary to their cause, in political and religious terms. This is how the words 'devil' and 'satan' are often used in the Bible.

In conclusion, it is probably true to say that in this subject more than any other, it is vital to base our understanding upon a balanced view of the whole Bible, rather than building doctrines on a few verses containing catch-phrases which appear to refer to the common beliefs concerning the devil. Study 6.1 and this section will repay careful, prayerful re-reading. It is submitted that the doctrinal position outlined there is the only way of being able to have a reasonable understanding of all the passages which refer to the devil and satan. Those words can be used as ordinary nouns, or in some places they refer to the sin which is found within our own human nature. Some of the most widely misunderstood passages which are quoted in support of the popular ideas are considered my book *The Real Devil*.

Those who have problems in accepting our conclusions need to ask themselves: (1) Is sin personified? Clearly it is. (2) Is it true that 'satan' can be used just as a noun? Yes, it is. What real problem, therefore, can there be in accepting that sin is personified as our enemy/satan? The world is often personified in John's letters and Gospel (see R.V.); what better title for this personification than 'satan' or 'the devil'?

6.3   Demons

The previous two sections have explained why we do not believe the devil or satan to be a personal being or a monster. If we accept that there is no such being, then it surely follows that demons, who are held to be the servants of the devil, also do not exist. Many people seem to think that God gives us all the good things of life, and the devil and his demons give us the bad things, and take away the good things which God gives us.

The Bible clearly teaches that God is the source of all power (see Study 6.1), and that He is responsible for both the good things *and* the bad things in our lives.

"I form the light, and create darkness, I make peace and create calamity; I, the Lord, do all these things" (Is. 45:7).

"... disaster came down from the Lord to the gate of Jerusalem" (Mic. 1:12).

"If a trumpet is blown in a city, will not the people be afraid?

If there is calamity in a city, will not the Lord have done it?" (Am. 3:6)

Therefore when we get trials, we should accept that they come from God, not blame them on a devil or demons. Job was a man who lost many of the good things which God blessed him with, but he did not say: "These demons have taken away all God gave me". No; listen to what he said.

"The Lord gave, and the Lord has taken away; blessed be the name of the Lord" (Job 1:21).

"Shall we indeed accept good from God, and shall we not accept adversity?" (Job 2:10)

Once we understand that all things are from God, when we have problems in life we can pray to God for Him to take them away, and if He does not we can be assured that He is giving them to us in order to develop our characters and for our good in the long run.

"My Son, do not despise the chastening of the Lord, nor be discouraged when you are rebuked by Him; for whom the Lord loves He (not demons!) chastens, and scourges every son whom He receives. If you endure chastening, God deals with you as with sons; for what son is there whom a Father does not chasten? But if you are without chastening, of which all have become partakers, then you are illegitimate and not sons" (Heb. 12:5-8).

GOD: SOURCE OF ALL POWER

God is the source of all power.

"I am the Lord, and there is no other; there is no God (the Hebrew word for 'god' really means 'power') besides Me" (Is. 45:5).

"Is there a God besides Me? Indeed there is no other Rock; I know not one", God says (Is. 44:8).

"The Lord Himself is God; there is none other besides Him" (Dt. 4:35).

Such verses occur time and again throughout the Bible. Because God is the source of all power and the only God, He is therefore a jealous God, as He often reminds us (e.g. Ex. 20:5; Dt. 4:24).

God gets jealous when His people start believing in other gods, if they say to Him, 'You are a great God, a powerful God, but actually I believe there are still some other gods beside you, even if they are not as powerful as you'. This is why we cannot believe that there are demons or a devil in existence as well as the true God. This is just the mistake Israel made. Much of the Old Testament is spent showing how Israel displeased God by believing in other gods as well as in Him. We will see from the Bible that the 'demons' people believe in today are just like those false gods Israel believed in.

DEMONS REFER TO IDOLS

In 1 Corinthians Paul explains why Christians should have nothing to do with idol worship or believing in such things. In Bible times people believed demons to be little gods who could be worshipped to stop problems coming into their lives. They therefore made models of demons, which were the same as idols, and worshipped them. This explains why Paul uses the words "demon" and "idol" interchangeably in his letter.

"The things which the Gentiles sacrifice they sacrifice to demons and not to God, and I do not want you to have fellowship with demons...if anyone says to you, 'This was offered to idols,' do not eat it for the sake of the one who told you..." (1 Cor. 10:20,28). So idols and demons are effectively the same. Notice how Paul says they sacrificed "to demons (idols) and not to God" - the demons were not God, and as there is only one God, it follows that demons have no real power at all, they are not gods. The point is really driven home in 1 Cor. 8:4.

"Therefore concerning the eating of things offered to idols, we know that an idol (equivalent to a demon) *is nothing in the world, and that there is no other God but one*". An idol, or a demon, has no existence at all. There is only one true God, or power, in the world. Paul goes on (vs.5,6).

"For even if there are *so-called* gods...(as there are many gods and many lords, [just as people believe in many types of demons today - one demon causing you to lose your job, another causing your wife to leave you, etc.]) yet for *us* (the true believers) there is only *one* God, the Father, of whom are *all* things" (both good and bad, as we have seen from the earlier references).

Further proof that people in New Testament times believed demons to be idols or 'gods' is found in Acts 17:16-18; this describes how Paul preached in Athens, which was a "city given over to idols", therefore worshipping many different idols. After hearing Paul preach the Gospel, the people said: "'He seems to be a proclaimer of foreign (i.e. new) gods (demons)' because he preached to them Jesus and the resurrection". So the people thought that Jesus and the resurrection were new demons or idols that were being explained to them. If you read the rest of the chapter, you will see how Paul goes on to teach the truth to these people, and in v. 22 he says, "You are very religious" (literally: devoted to demon worship), and he explains how God is not present in their demons, or idols. Remember that God is the only source of power. If He is not in demons, then demons do not have any power because there is no other source of power in this universe - i.e. they do not exist.

OLD TESTAMENT 'DEMONS' WERE IDOLS

Going back to the Old Testament, there is more proof that 'demons' are the same as idols. Dt. 28:14-28,59-61 predicted that mental disease would be one of the punishments for worshipping other gods/demons. "They sacrificed to demons, not to God ..." (Dt. 32:17, cp. Ps. 106:37) This explains the association of demons with mental illness in the New Testament. But let it be noted that the language of demons is associated with illness, not sin. We do not read of Christ casting out demons of envy, murder etc. It must also be noted that the Bible speaks of people *having* a demon/disease, rather than saying that demons *caused* the disease. It is significant that the Greek version of the Old Testament (the Septuagint) used the word 'daimonion' for "idol";

this is the word translated "demon" in the New Testament. Ps. 106:36-39 describes the errors of Israel and likens the idols of Canaan to demons.

"They (Israel) served their *idols,* which became a snare to them. They even sacrificed their sons and their daughters to *demons*, and shed innocent blood, even the blood of their sons and daughters, whom they sacrificed to the *idols* of Canaan...Thus they were defiled by their own works, and played the harlot by their own deeds".

Quite clearly demons are just another name for idols. Their worship of demons is described by God as worshipping their "own works...their own deeds" because their belief in demons was a result of human imagination; the idols they created were their "own works". So those who believe in demons today are believing in things which have been imagined by men, the creation of men, rather than what God has taught us. The word used for idols literally means 'no-things', stressing that they have no existence in the real world, only in the minds of people who believe in them.

Dt. 32:15-24 describes just how angry God gets when His people believe in demons: Israel "scornfully esteemed the Rock of his salvation. They provoked Him to jealousy with foreign gods; with abominations they provoked Him to anger. They sacrificed to demons, not to God, to gods they did not know ... that your fathers did not fear ... And He (God) said: 'I will hide My face from them...for they are a perverse generation, children in whom is no faith. They have provoked Me to jealousy by what is not God; they have moved Me to anger by their foolish idols ...I will heap disasters upon them ...".

So God describes demons as the same as foolish idols, abominations, - things which are folly to believe in, which have no existence. Believing in demons shows a lack of faith in God. It is not easy to have faith that God provides everything, both good and bad, in life. It is easier to think that the bad things come from someone else, because once we say they come from God, then we need to have faith that God will take them away or that ultimately they are going to be beneficial to us.

NEW TESTAMENT DEMONS

But, you may say, 'How about all the passages in the New Testament which clearly speak about demons?'

One thing we must get clear: the Bible cannot contradict itself, it is the Word of Almighty God. If we are clearly told that God brings our problems and that He is the source of all power, then the Bible cannot also tell us that demons - little gods in opposition to God - bring these things on us. It seems significant that the word "demons" only occurs four times in the Old Testament and always describes idol worship, but it occurs many times in the Gospel records. We suggest this is because, at the time the Gospels were written, it was the language of the day to say that any disease that could not be understood was the fault of demons. If demons really do exist and are responsible for our illnesses and problems, then we would read more about them in the Old Testament. But we do not read about them at all in this context there.

DEMONS IN THE NEW TESTAMENT

To say that demons were cast out of someone is to say that they were cured of a mental illness, or an illness which was not understood at the time. People living in the first century tended to blame everything which they couldn't understand on imaginary beings called 'demons'. Mental illness was hard to understand with their level of medical knowledge and the people spoke of those afflicted as 'demon possessed'. In Old Testament times, an evil or unclean spirit referred to a troubled mental state (Jud. 9:23; 1 Sam. 16:14; 18:10 KJV). In New Testament times, the language of evil spirit/demon possession had come to refer to those suffering mental illness. The association between demons and sickness is shown by the following: "They brought to him (Jesus) many who were demon-possessed. And He cast out the spirits with a word...that it might be fulfilled which was spoken by Isaiah the prophet (in the Old Testament), saying, 'He himself took our infirmities, and bore our sicknesses" (Mt. 8:16,17). So human infirmities and sicknesses are the same as being possessed by "demons" and "evil spirits".

People thought that Jesus was mad and said this must be because He had a demon - "He has a demon, and is mad" (Jn. 10:20; 7:19,20; 8:52). They therefore believed that demons caused madness.

HEALING THE SICK

When they were healed, people "demon-possessed" are said to return to their "right mind" (Mk. 5:15; Lk. 8:35). This implies that being "demon-possessed" was another way of saying someone was mentally unwell - i.e. not in their right mind.

Those "demon-possessed" are said to be "healed" or "cured" (Mt. 4:24; 12:22; 17:18) implying that demon possession is another way of describing illness.

In Lk. 10:9 Jesus told His 70 apostles to go out and "heal the sick", which they did. They returned and said (v. 17): "even the demons are subject to us in Your name" - again, demons and illness are equated. Sometimes the apostles cured people in the name of Jesus and here we have an example of this (see also Acts 3:6; 9:34).

THE LANGUAGE OF THE DAY

So we see that in the New Testament it was the language of the day to describe someone as being possessed with demons if they were mentally ill or had a disease which no one understood. The contemporary Roman and Greek cultural belief was that demons possessed people, thereby creating mental disease. Those Christians who believe in the existence of demons are effectively saying that the contemporary pagan beliefs in this area were perfectly correct. The Bible is written in language which people can understand. Because it uses the language of the day does not mean that Jesus believed in demons. In the same way in English we have the word "lunatic" to describe someone who is mentally ill. Literally it means someone who is "moon struck". Years ago people used to believe that if a person went out walking at night when there was a clear moon, they could get struck by the moon and become mentally ill. We use that word "lunatic" today to describe someone who is mad, but it does not mean that we believe madness is caused by the moon.

If these words were written down and re-read in 2,000 years' time - if Jesus had not returned - people might think we believed that the moon caused madness, but they would be wrong because we are just using the language of our day, as Jesus did 2,000 years ago. Similarly we describe a certain hereditary disorder as "St. Vitus' Dance" which is neither caused by "St. Vitus" nor "dancing", but in using the language of the day we call it "St. Vitus' Dance". It is evident that Jesus Christ was not born on December 25th; yet I still use the term 'Christmas day' when speaking of that day, although I do not believe that we should keep that day as a celebration of Christ's birth. The names of the days of the week are based upon pagan idol worship - e.g. 'Sunday' means 'the day devoted to worshipping the sun'; 'Saturday' was the day upon which the planet Saturn was to be worshipped, 'Monday' for the moon, etc. To use these names does not mean that we share the pagan beliefs of those who originally coined our present language. 'Influenza' is likewise a term in common use today; it strictly means 'influenced by demons'. When Daniel was renamed 'Belteshazzar', a name reflecting a pagan god, the inspired record in Dan. 4:19 calls him 'Belteshazzar' without pointing out that this word reflected false thinking. I speak about 'the Pope' as a means of identifying someone, even though I think it wrong to actually believe that he is a 'pope' or 'father' (Mt. 23:9).

There was a myth in Ezekiel's time that the land of Israel was responsible for the misfortunes of those in it. This was not true and yet God reasons with Israel, using the idea that was then popular: "Thus says the Lord God: 'Because they say to you, "You (the land) devour men, and bereave your nation of children," therefore you shall devour men no more...says the Lord God'" (Ez. 36:13,14). There was a common pagan notion that the sea was a great monster desiring to engulf the earth. Whilst this is evidently untrue, the Bible often uses this figure in order to help its initial readership to grasp the idea being presented: see Job 7:12 (Moffat's Translation); Am. 9:3 (Moffat); Jer. 5:22; Ps. 89:9; Hab. 3:10; Mt. 14:24 (Greek text); Mk. 4:37. Assyrian mythology called this rebellious sea monster 'Rahab'; and this is exactly the name given to the sea monster of Egypt in Is. 51:9.

Seeing that the Bible is inspired by God, it is impossible that the Bible is merely reflecting the pagan influences which were current at the time in which it was written. It must be that God is consciously alluding to contemporary beliefs, in order to show that *He* is the ultimate source of power; *He* is the one who controls the 'monster' of the sea, so that it does *His* will. God therefore corrected the fundamental error in these people's beliefs, which was that there were forces at work in the world which were not subject to God's control, and were therefore evil by implication. However, the Bible does not, in this instance, go out of its way to decry the folly of believing that there is a massive monster lurking in the sea, or that the sea is a monster.

Another example is in the description of lightning and storm clouds as a "fleeing (or twisted) serpent" (Job 26:13; Is. 27:1). This was evidently alluding to the contemporary pagan belief that lightning and frightening cloud formations were actually visions of a massive snake. These passages do not expose the folly of such an idea, or attempt scientific explanation. Instead they make the point that *God* controls these things. The attitude of Christ to the prevailing belief in demons is identical in this regard; his miracles clearly demonstrated that the power of God was absolute and complete, unbounded by the superstitions of men concerning so-called 'demons'. Those who believe that the New Testament records of 'demons' prove that such beings do actually exist are duty bound to accept that the sea is really a monster, and that lightning is actually a huge serpent. This is surely a powerful point; there *must* be a recognition that the Bible uses the language of the day in which it was written, without necessarily supporting the beliefs which form the basis of that language. We have shown our own use of language to be similar. The Bible does this in order to confirm the kind of basic truths which we considered in Studies 6.1 and 6.2 - that God is all powerful; He is responsible for our trials; sin comes from within us - all these things can be made sense of by appreciating the greatness of God's power to save. The so-called 'higher critics' are constantly unearthing links between the language of Scripture and the beliefs and conceptions of the surrounding cultures in which the Bible was inspired and recorded. These are understandable, once it is realized that the Bible uses language which may allude to local beliefs, but does so in order to make the point that Yahweh, the only true God, is far greater than the petty beliefs of men which would have been known to those who first read the inspired words, fresh from the prophet's mouth.

With this in mind, it is surprising how many examples can be found in the New Testament of technically incorrect language being used without that language being corrected. Here are some examples.

- The Pharisees accused Jesus of doing miracles by the power of a false god called Beelzebub. Jesus said: "if I cast out demons by Beelzebub, by whom do your sons cast them out?" (Mt. 12:27). 2 Kings 1:2 clearly tells us that Beelzebub was a false god of the Philistines. Jesus did not say, 'Now look, 2 Kings 1:2 says Beelzebub was a false god, so your accusation cannot be true'. No, he spoke as if Beelzebub existed, because he was interested in getting his message through to the people to whom he preached. So in the same way Jesus talked about casting out demons - he did not keep saying, 'actually, they do not exist', he just preached the Gospel in the language of the day.

- Acts 16:16-18 are the words of Luke, under inspiration: "a certain slave girl possessed with a spirit of divination (Python KJV mg.) met us". As explained in the footnote in the Diaglott version, Python was the name of a false god believed in during the first century, possibly the same as the god Apollo. So Python definitely did not exist, but Luke does not say the girl was 'possessed with a spirit of Python, who, by the way, is a false god who does not really exist...'. In the same way the Gospels do not say that Jesus 'cast out demons which, by the way, do not really exist, it is just the language of the day for illnesses'.

- Lk. 5:32 records Jesus saying to the wicked Jews: "I have not come to call the righteous...". He was inferring, 'I have not come to call those who believe they are righteous'. But Jesus spoke to them on their own terms, even though, technically, he was using language which was untrue. Lk. 19:20-23 shows Jesus using the untrue words of the one-talent man in the parable to reason with him, but he does not correct the wrong words the man used.

- The Bible often speaks of the sun 'rising' and 'going down'; this is a human way of putting it, but it is not scientifically correct. Likewise illness is spoken of in the technically 'incorrect' language of 'demons'. Acts 5:3 speaks of how Ananias deceived the Holy Spirit. This, actually, is an impossibility, yet what Ananias thought he was doing is spoken of as fact, even though it was not.

- There are many Biblical examples of language being used which was comprehensible at the time it was written, but is now unfamiliar to us; for example, "skin for skin" (Job 2:4) alluded to the ancient practice of trading skins of equivalent value; a male prostitute is called a "dog" in Dt. 23:18. The language of demons is another example.

- The Jews of Christ's day thought that they were righteous because they were the descendants of Abraham. Jesus therefore addressed them as "the righteous" (Mt. 9:12,13), and said: "I know that you are Abraham's descendants" (Jn. 8:37). But he did not believe that they were righteous, as he so often made clear; and he plainly showed by his reasoning in Jn. 8:39-44 that they were *not* Abraham's descendants. So Jesus took people's beliefs at face value, without immediately contradicting them, but demonstrated the truth instead. We have shown that this was God's approach in dealing with the pagan beliefs which were common in Old Testament times. Christ's attitude to demons in New Testament times was the same; his God-provided miracles made it abundantly plain that illnesses were caused by God, not any other force, seeing that it was God who had the mighty power to heal them.

- Paul quoted from Greek poets in order to confound those who believed what the poets taught (Tit. 1:12; Acts 17:28). What we are suggesting is epitomized by Paul's response to finding an altar dedicated to the worship of "The Unknown God", i.e. any pagan deity which might exist, but which the people of Athens had overlooked. Instead of rebuking them for their folly in believing in this, Paul took them from where they were to understand the one true God, who they did not know (Acts 17:22,23).

- Eph. 2:2 speaks of "the prince of the power of the air". This clearly alludes to the mythological concepts of Zoroaster - the kind of thing which Paul's readers once believed. Paul says that they once lived under "the prince of the power of the air". In the same verse, Paul defines this as "the spirit (attitude of mind) which...works" in the natural man. Previously they had believed in the pagan concept of a heavenly spirit-prince; now Paul makes the point that actually the power which they were formally subject to was that of their own evil mind. Thus the pagan idea is alluded to and spoken of, without specifically rebuking it, whilst showing the truth concerning sin.

- Acts 28:3-6 describes how a lethal snake attacked Paul, fastening onto his arm. The surrounding people decided Paul was a murderer, whom "justice does not allow to live". Their reading of the situation was totally wrong. But Paul did not explain this to them in detail; instead, he did a miracle - he shook the snake off without it biting him.

- The miracles of Jesus exposed the error of local views, e.g. of demons, without correcting them in so many words. Thus in Lk. 5:21 the Jews made two false statements: that Jesus was a blasphemer, and that God alone could forgive sins. Jesus did not verbally correct them; instead he did a miracle which proved the falsity of those statements.

- It was clearly the belief of Jesus that actions speak louder than words. He rarely denounced false ideas directly, thus he did not denounce the Mosaic law as being unable to offer salvation, but he showed by his actions, e.g. healing on the Sabbath, what the Truth was. When he was wrongly accused of being a Samaritan, Jesus did not deny it (Jn. 8:48,49 cp. 4:7-9) even though his Jewishness, as the seed of Abraham, was vital for God's plan of salvation (Jn. 4:22).

- Even when the Jews drew the wrong conclusion (wilfully!) that Jesus was "making himself equal with God" (Jn. 5:18), Jesus did not explicitly deny it; instead he powerfully argued that his miracles showed him to be a man acting on God's behalf, and therefore he was NOT equal with God. The miracles of Jesus likewise showed the error of believing in demons. Christ's miracle of healing the lame man at the pool was to show the folly of the Jewish myth that at Passover time an angel touched the water of the Bethesda pool, imparting healing properties to it. This myth is recorded without direct denial of its truth; the record of Christ's miracle is the exposure of its falsehood (Jn. 5:4).

- 2 Pet. 2:4 talks of wicked people going to Tartarus (translated "hell" in many versions). Tartarus was a mythical place in the underworld; yet Peter does not correct that notion, but rather uses it as a symbol of complete destruction and punishment for sin. Christ's use of the word Gehenna was similar (see Study 4.9).

DO DEMONS REALLY CAUSE ILLNESSES?

Everyone who believes demons exist has to ask themselves the question: "When I am ill, is it caused by demons?" If you think the New Testament references to demons are about little gods going round doing evil, then you have to say "yes". In that case, how can you explain the fact that many diseases blamed on demons can now be cured or controlled by drugs? Malaria is the classic example. Most people in Africa believed until recently that malaria was caused by demons, but we know that malaria can be cured by quinine and other drugs. Are you then saying that as the demons see the little yellow tablets going down your throat they become frightened and fly away? Some of the diseases which Jesus cured, which are described as being the result of demon possession, have been identified as tetanus or epilepsy - both of which can be relieved by drugs.

A friend of mine comes from a village just outside Kampala in Uganda. He told us that people used to believe malaria was caused by demons, but once they saw how the drugs controlled it so easily, they stopped blaming the demons. However, when someone had cerebral malaria (causing serious mental illness) they still blamed the demons. A doctor came from the nearby town and offered them strong anti-malarial drugs as a cure, but they refused because they said they needed something to fight demons, not malaria. The doctor returned later and said, "I have a drug which will chase away the demons"; the sick person eagerly took the drug, and became better. The second tablets were just the same as the first ones. The doctor did not believe in demons, but he used the language of the day to get through to the person - just like the "Great Physician", the Lord Jesus, of 2,000 years ago.

Belief In Practice 12:

Battle For The Mind

We have seen that the devil is a common figure for our own sinfulness; sin and temptation comes from within. The real arena of spiritual conflict is the human heart; there is no external devil in the commonly accepted sense. The fact that the Lord Jesus really conquered the devil should mean for us that in our struggles against sin, victory is ultimately certain.

BATTLE FOR THE MIND, NOT BLAMING OTHERS

If we grasp this, we will battle daily for control of the mind, we will strive to fill our mind with God's word, we will do our daily readings, we will be cynical of our motivations, we will examine ourselves, we will appreciate the latent liability to sin which we and all men have by nature. We won't take the weakness of others towards us so personally; we will see it is their 'devil'. Belief in a personal devil is so popular, because it takes the focus away from our own struggle with our innermost nature and thoughts. Yet whilst we don't believe in a personal devil, we can create the same thing in essence; we can create an external devil such as TV or Catholicism, and feel that our entire spiritual endeavour must be directed to doing battle with these things, rather than focusing on our own desperation. A lack of focus on personal sinfulness and the need for personal cleansing and growth, with the humility this will bring forth, can so easily give place to a focus instead upon something external to us as the real enemy. Realizing who 'the devil' really is inspires us to more concretely fight against him. Albert Camus in his novel *The Rebel* develops the theme that "man is never greater than when he is in revolt, when he commits himself totally to the struggle against an unjust power, ready to sacrifice his own life to liberate the oppressed". Once we have the enemy clearly defined, we can rise up to that same struggle and challenge. Truly, man is never greater when he's in the one and only true revolt worth making, and sacrificing life for the ultimate cause.

We should not blame our nature for our moral failures in the way that orthodox Christians blame an external devil. We must hang our head over every sin we commit and every act of righteousness which we omit. In this we will find the basis for a true appreciation of grace, a true motivation for works of humble response, a true flame of praise within us, a realistic basis for a genuine humility. It has been truly observed "that man is dominated by his psychological make-up, but only in the sense that an artist is dominated by his material". We really *can* achieve some measure of self control; it cannot be that God is angry with us simply because we are human. It cannot be that our nature forces us to sin in a way which we can never counteract. If this were true, the anger of God would have been against His own spotless Son, who fully shared our nature. The Lord shared our nature and yet didn't commit sin, and in this He is our ever beckoning example and inspiration. The question 'What would Jesus do...?' in this or that situation has all the more inspirational power once we accept that the Lord Jesus, tempted just as we are, managed to put the devil to death within Him, triumphing over it in the cross, even though He bore our nature. People parrot off phrases like 'I'm a sinner', 'going to heaven', 'satan', without the faintest idea what they are really saying. And we can do just the same- we can speak of 'Sin' with no real idea what we ought to feel and understand by this.

Within each person there is a huge battle between the right and the wrong, good and evil, temptation and resistance to temptation. This battle goes on constantly, over even the most insignificant things- e.g. the choice to take an instant dislike to another person, to get angry and aggressive because we feel a person in a restaurant is somehow laughing at us, etc. Most people on earth wouldn't agree with the religious / theological conclusions we have reached- that the devil refers not to a 'fallen Angel' or supernatural being but rather to our own internal temptations which battle with us, as Peter says, like a roaring lion. Yet in practice, a psychiatric analysis of human beings reveals that indeed, like it or not, the 'violence within' is not only very real, but a fundamental part of our moment by moment spiritual experience. I mean that our Biblical / theological conclusions about the devil are actually confirmed by psychotherapy and psychiatric analysis of people. Our conclusions are true in practical experience, even if people don't want to accept the way we express them Biblically because they have a tradition of believing that the real problem is the supposed violence from without, supposedly perpetrated by a supernatural 'devil'. And here doctrine comes to have a biting practical relevance- for if we truly perceive and believe that in fact 'the devil' and its power has been vanquished in Jesus, if we survey the wondrous cross and see there the power of the devil finally slaughtered in the perfect mind of the Lord Jesus as He hung there, and that ultimate victory of victories shared with us who are in Him... the source, the root cause, of so much neurosis and dysfunction, is revealed to us as powerless. For we who have given in and do give in to temptation, who submit to 'the violence within' all too often, who are at times beaten in the fight, have been saved from the power of that defeat by grace and forgiveness, and are counted by the God of all grace as being 'in Christ'. The Lord Jesus was the one who overcame that 'violence within' moment by moment, as well as in the more accentuated and obvious scenes of 'the violence within' which we see in the wilderness temptations and on the cross. And by grace, we are counted as in Him. No wonder that to achieve this He had to share human nature, to have 'the violence within', in order to overcome it. Perfectly and seamlessly, to my mind at least, one true aspect of Biblical interpretation thus leads to another, and becomes the basis for a transformed life in practice. In all this we see the matchless, surpassing beauty of how God works with humanity towards our salvation.

SELF-TALK

It would be fair to say that the Biblical devil refers to our self-talk-the very opposite of the external devil idea. Jesus pinpointed the crucial importance of self-talk in His parable of the rich fool, who said to himself that he had many goods, and discussed with his own "soul" the need for greater barns etc. (Lk. 12:17-19). If we at least realize that our self-talk is potentially our greatest adversary ['satan'], then we will find the strength to move towards genuine spiritual mindedness, bringing into captivity every thought to the obedience of Christ. Paul's wording here suggests that naturally our "every thought" is not obedient to Christ; and this is his way of speaking about 'the devil'.

Dt. 15:9 has Moses warning Israel: "Beware that there be not a thought in your wicked heart". The Hebrew for 'thought' really means 'word'- the idea is to ensure that you don't have a self-talk that says... that because the year of release was coming up soon, therefore you would not lend your brother anything, knowing that you had to forgive him the debt in the year of release. Here we have the Old Testament equivalent of the New Testament 'devil'. We *can* control our self-talk, but we must be aware that it takes place. Moses is basically saying: 'Beware of your own self talk; see how you speak to yourself in unfinished sentences like "The year of release is at hand...", resulting in you 'finishing the sentence' by unkind deeds'.

Perceiving the reality and power of our own self-talk is one outcome of truly comprehending who the devil is. Ps. 36:1 warns: " Sin speaks to the wicked man in his heart" (Heb.). The path of Cain involved reviling what he did not understand (Jude 10,11). He didn't understand, or didn't let himself understand, the principles of sacrifice, and so he reviled his brother and God's commands, he became a true child of the Biblical devil- because he didn't *understand*.

Our self-talk actually defines where we go in our relationships. If we have a certain 'self-talk' opinion of someone and yet speak and act nicely to them, sooner or later we won't be able to keep up the act any longer. It's been truly observed: "An unconscious relationship is more powerful than a conscious one". This says it all. What you say to yourself about your wife, how you analyze to yourself the actions of your child... this has the real power, far beyond any forms of words and outward behaviour we may show. Yet sadly, this world thinks that *how* you say things is all important; it's a running away from the importance and crucial value of the real self within. And it's yet another reason why self-talk is crucial to true, real living and spiritual development. And this is all an outflow from a clear grasp of the fact that the real satan is the adversary of our own internal thoughts.

Digression 9: Witchcraft

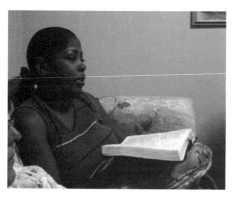

This digression is written largely to cater for the needs of those in Africa and other parts of the world where witchcraft is a common feature of daily life. It is recognized by all true Bible students that recourse to witches, African doctors and the like is incompatible with holding the truth. However, I do appreciate that witch doctors are cheaper and often more accessible than medical doctors, and that this, combined with their apparent success, makes them attractive. We need to look at this problem in a logical, Biblical way. This is the only way you will find the strength to resist the temptation to use these people.

THE CLAIMS OF WITCHCRAFT

Firstly, the claims of success that these witches make need to be analysed. We can be sure that a lot of exaggeration goes into the claims made for their success. Their cures are never done in the open, for all to see. If indeed they were successful then presumably they would be working in hospitals, and would be found world-wide. The exact condition of those they claim to heal is also never known - how much they really improve is not clear.

Those of you facing this temptation need to ask yourselves whether you have definite proof of their power - e.g. have you seen (not just heard about) a man with his arm sawn off in a saw mill go to a witch and return with a new arm working perfectly? This is the kind of evidence we need before we can give them any credibility at all. Dt. 13:1-3 is even more powerful: Israel were taught that if a witch did a sign or wonder which appeared to be a miracle, they were still not to believe that person unless they spoke true doctrine according to God's word. It is clear that witch doctors do not believe the truth as revealed in the Bible - therefore we should not be tempted to credit them as having real power, seeing that all power is from God (Rom. 13:1; 1 Cor. 8:4-6).

Secondly, the type of complaints they deal with is significant. It is now recognized that we use only about 1% of our brain power. The rest seems to be beyond our power to consciously harness (doubtless we will do so in the Kingdom). Without our realizing it, our minds can have an almost physical effect upon our bodies. Thus psychologists (those who study the mind) have been known to cure people of blood diseases by getting them to intensely imagine their blood being properly constituted and working normally. Doctors admit that occasionally such cures take place which are not dependent on orthodox medicine. Similarly, having a lot of stress in our mind can result in stomach ulcers and head pains. Relaxing the mind or exercising it in a certain way can cause these to go away. But if, for example, our arm is cut off in a saw mill, no amount of mental exercise can make it come back again. It is only ailments which are controlled by our minds which the witches seem able to affect. Because we do not fully understand how our minds work, this *appears* to be due to some physical power these witches have. But this is not so; it is through their influence on people's minds that they bring this effect about.

THE SOURCE OF POWER

However, all power is of God. Both good things and bad things such as sickness are brought by *Him* - not witches. This is a very common theme in Scripture: Is. 45:5-7; Mic. 1:12; Am. 3:6; Ex. 4:11; Dt. 32:39; Job 5:18. All of these passages will repay careful reading. It follows that it is to *Him* that we should turn in prayer if we are ill, whilst still doing all that is humanly possible through the use of conventional medicine to rectify the problem. If we turn to witch doctors, we are turning to people who claim that they have control over 'powers of darkness' which enables them to make us better. But we know that those powers which they believe in do not exist. God is the source of power. To turn to witches is to say that God is not all powerful and that other powers, with whom the witches claim to have influence, are bringing our sickness,

To think like that is very displeasing with God. Israel chose to believe in God but also believed there were other powers acting in their lives, which they had to deal with by worshipping idols made to those powers. This so angered God that He cast them off from being His people (Dt. 32:16-24). To God, unless we have complete faith in Him, we are not really believing in Him at all. To claim a belief in the true God of Israel but to also accept the existence of other powers separate from God, and to let a witch doctor try to influence those powers to leave us alone, is to act precisely as Israel did in the past. The long, sad history of Israel's idolatry is "written for our learning". We should have no fellowship at all with those who believe in these powers.

"What communion has light with darkness? ... what agreement has the temple of God with idols? For you are the temple of ...God...Therefore come out from among them and be separate, says the Lord... I will be a Father to you, and you shall be My sons and daughters" (2 Cor. 6:14-17).

If we really make the effort and sacrifice to separate from these things, then we have the glorious assurance that we really are the children of God Himself. A natural parent instinctively cares for his child when it is sick. Is it really that difficult to rally our faith to believe that our Heavenly Father will do so even more?

It is a fact that witches only have influence over those who believe in them. In a similar way, someone who has lost a loved one may go to a medium or witch and ask to see the dead person. The medium will tell them to close their eyes and imagine the face of the person very clearly. The client may fix his mind on a photograph of the person which they can clearly remember. The medium can then read the client's mind, and with a little exaggeration speak about the person in realistic terms, so that the client is persuaded that the medium has seen the dead person alive. Note that no solid proof is ever given that the person is alive. But if the client refuses to believe or obey the medium, then there is no result at all.

The magicians, i.e. 'witches' who normally told Pharaoh and Nebuchadnezzar their dreams would not have had their positions of responsibility unless they were reasonably successful. Doubtless they used this mind-reading technique a lot. However, when God was involved in the life of the person they were dealing with, as He intervened in the lives of Pharaoh and Nebuchadnezzar, then they lost this power. Similarly Balak trusted Balaam's powers of cursing people - he offered him huge financial rewards for his services, saying that he knew from past experience "that he whom you curse is cursed" (Num. 22:6). But Balaam, who was in some ways the equivalent of a witch doctor, found that his normal ability had left him when he was dealing with the people of Israel. Clearly, such people have no power at all when they are dealing with people who are associated with the true God, no matter what fame they may have gained for success when dealing with other people.

WITCHCRAFT IN THE BIBLE

The practical meaning of this is that if we are tempted to go to a witch doctor, then we have to have total faith in him. There is no point in using witches if we are just hoping for the best; and they themselves will probably make the same point. To put total faith in such people and in the existence of the powers they claim to control, means that we have a total lack of faith in the all-powerfulness of the true God. If we really believe the records of Pharaoh, Balak and Nebuchadnezzar mentioned above, then we will not be able to come to a witch with faith that they will have any effect upon us. The examples considered show that witches do not have power over God's people - which we know we are, by reason of our calling and baptism.

Witchcraft is clearly labelled by Paul as a work "of the flesh" (sinful nature), in the same category as "heresy" (false doctrine), adultery and pornography (Gal. 5:19-21). He comments: "I tell you... as I also told you in time past (i.e. this was a highly emphasized part of Paul's teaching), that those who practise such things will not inherit the Kingdom of God". The equivalent of this under the Law of Moses was the command that all mediums, sorcerers (another name for witches) and those who made their children pass through the fire were to be killed immediately (Dt. 18:10,11; Ex. 22:18). Those who put their children through fire were not the actual witches - the witches and leading idolaters taught that to secure protection against the forces of evil, the children of those who wanted protection had to be made to pass through fire. So we see that both witches and those who used them were to be killed; and under the new covenant the punishment for doing the same thing is exclusion from the Kingdom of God.

To use witchcraft as a means of personal betterment is something which God would not want us to do. In every decision we are faced with in our life in Christ, we have to seriously ask: 'Does God really want me to do this? Would I do this with Jesus standing next to me?' In view of God's clear condemnation of witchcraft I think the answer must be obvious - no, God does not want us to use it. Witchcraft is defined by Samuel as being related to "rebellion" (the Hebrew implies 'provocation') against the Word of God (1 Sam. 15:23). To provoke the Almighty, as Israel did by their belief in idols and witchcraft (Dt. 32:16-19), is surely unthinkable. God makes the point that He had commanded Israel to drive out the Canaanites because of their belief in witchcraft which was so abhorrent to Him; yet instead, they joined in the practice of it (Dt. 18:9-14). So for the new Israel of baptised believers, we must not do the things of this surrounding evil world, or else we will not be able to eternally inherit our promised land of the Kingdom. To reason that it is only the witch that is using it, not us, is irrelevant. If we hope that the effects of the witchcraft will be felt on us, then we are effectively using it.

May God bless us all as we walk through these closing days of the dark, Gentile world towards His Kingdom of light and truth and glory.

"Because they did not receive the love of the truth, that they might be saved...God will send them strong delusion, that they should believe the lie...But we are bound to give thanks to God always for you, brethren beloved by the Lord...Therefore, brethren, stand fast and hold the traditions which you were taught, whether by word or our epistle. Now may our Lord Jesus Christ Himself, and our God and Father, who has loved us and given us everlasting consolation and good hope by grace, comfort your hearts and establish you in every good word and work" (2 Thess. 2:10-17).

Digression 10: What Happened in Eden?

Gen. 3:4-5: "And the serpent said to the woman, 'You will not surely die. For God knows that in the day you eat of it your eyes will be opened, and you will be like God, knowing good and evil'".

POPULAR INTERPRETATION

It is wrongly assumed that the serpent here is an angel that had sinned, called "satan". Having been thrown out of heaven for his sin, he came to earth and tempted Eve to sin.

COMMENTS

1. The passage talks about "the serpent". The words 'satan' and 'devil' do not occur in the whole of the book of Genesis.

2. The serpent is never described as an angel.

3. Therefore it is not surprising that there is no reference in Genesis to anyone being thrown out of heaven.

4. Sin brings death (Rom. 6:23); angels cannot die (Lk. 20:35-36), therefore angels cannot sin. The reward of the righteous is to be made like the angels to die no more (Lk. 20:35-36). If angels could sin, then the righteous would also be able to sin and therefore would have the possibility of dying, which means they would not really have everlasting life.

5. The characters involved in the Genesis record of the fall of man are: God, Adam, Eve and the serpent. Nobody else is mentioned. There is no evidence that anything got inside the serpent to make it do what it did. Paul says the serpent "deceived Eve by his (own) craftiness" (2 Cor. 11,3). God told the serpent: "Because you have done this..." (Gen. 3:14). If 'satan' was using the serpent, why is he not mentioned and why was he not also punished?

6. Adam blamed Eve for his sin: "She gave me of the tree" (Gen. 3:12). Eve blamed the serpent: "The serpent deceived me, and I ate" (Gen. 3:13). The serpent did not blame the devil - he made no excuse.

7. If it is argued that snakes today do not have the power of speech or reasoning as the serpent in Eden had, remember that:

(a) A donkey was once made to speak and reason with a man (Balaam): "The (normally) dumb donkey speaking with a man's voice restrained the madness of the prophet" (2 Pet. 2:16).

(b) The serpent was one of the most intelligent of all the animals (Gen. 3:1). The curse upon it would have taken away the ability it had to speak with Adam and Eve.

8. God created the serpent (Gen. 3:1); another being called 'satan' did not turn into the serpent; if we believe this, we are effectively saying that one person can enter the life of someone else and control it. This is a pagan idea, not a Biblical one. If it is argued that God would not have created the serpent because of the great sin it enticed Adam and Eve to commit, remember that sin entered the world from man (Rom. 5:12); the serpent was therefore amoral, speaking from its own natural observations, and was not, as such, responsible to God and therefore did not commit sin.

Some suggest that the serpent of Gen. 3 is related to the seraphim. However, the normal Hebrew word for "serpent", which is used in Gen. 3, is totally unrelated to the word for "seraphim". The Hebrew word translated "seraphim" basically means "a fiery one" and is translated "fiery serpent" in Num. 21:8, but this is not the word translated "serpent" in Gen. 3.

Suggested Explanations

1. There seems no reason to doubt that what we are told about the creation and the fall in the early chapters of Genesis should be taken literally. "The serpent" was a literal serpent. The fact that we can see serpents today crawling on their bellies in fulfilment of the curse placed on the original serpent (Gen. 3:14), supports this. In the same way we see men and women suffering from the curses that were placed on them at the same time. We can appreciate that Adam and Eve were a literal man and woman as we know man and woman today, but enjoying a better form of existence, therefore the original serpent was a literal animal, although in a far more intelligent form than snakes we see today.

2. The following are further indications that the early chapters of Genesis should be read literally.

a)   Jesus referred to the record of Adam and Eve's creation as the basis of his teaching on marriage and divorce (Mt. 19:5-6); there is no hint that he read it figuratively.

b)   "For Adam was formed first, then Eve. And Adam was not deceived (by the serpent), but the woman being deceived, fell into transgression" (1 Tim. 2:13-14) - so Paul, too, read Genesis literally. And most importantly he wrote earlier about the way "the serpent deceived Eve by his craftiness" (2 Cor. 11:3) - notice that Paul doesn't mention the "devil" deceiving Eve.

3. Because the serpent was cursed with having to crawl on its belly (Gen. 3:14), this may imply that previously it had legs; coupled with its evident powers of reasoning, it was probably the form of animal life closest to man, although it was still an animal - another of the "beasts of the field which the Lord God had made" (Gen. 3:1,14).

Digression 11: Lucifer

Is. 14:12-14: "How you are fallen from heaven, O Lucifer, son of the morning! How you are cut down to the ground, you who weakened the nations! For you have said in your heart: 'I will ascend into heaven, I will exalt my throne above the stars of God; I will also sit on the mount of the congregation on the farthest sides of the north; I will ascend above the heights of the clouds, I will be like the Most High'".

POPULAR INTERPRETATION

It is assumed that Lucifer was once a powerful angel who sinned at the time of Adam and was therefore cast down to earth, where he is making trouble for God's people.

COMMENTS

1. The words "devil", "satan" and "angel" never occur in this chapter. This is the only place in Scripture where the word "Lucifer" occurs.

2. There is no evidence that Is. 14 is describing anything that happened in the garden of Eden; if it is, then why are we left 3,000 years from the time of Genesis before being told what really happened there?

3. Lucifer is described as being covered in worms (v. 11) and mocked by men (v. 16) because he no longer has any power after his casting out of heaven (vs. 5-8,12); so there is no justification for thinking that Lucifer is now on earth leading believers astray.

4. Why is Lucifer punished for saying, "I will ascend into heaven" (v. 13), if he was already there?

5. Lucifer is to rot in the grave: "Your pomp is brought down to Sheol (the grave),...and the worms cover you" (v. 11). Seeing angels cannot die (Lk. 20:35-36), Lucifer therefore cannot be an angel; the language is more suited to a man.

6. Verses 13 and 14 have connections with 2 Thess. 2:3-4, which is about the "man of sin" - thus Lucifer points forward to another man - not an angel.

SUGGESTED EXPLANATIONS.

1. The N.I.V. and other modern versions have set out the text of Isaiah chapters 13-23 as a series of "burdens" on various nations, e.g. Babylon, Tyre, Egypt. Is. 14:4 sets the context of the verses we are considering: "you will take up this proverb (parable) against the king of Babylon...". The prophecy is therefore about the human king of Babylon, who is described as "Lucifer". On his fall: "those who see you will...consider you, saying: 'Is this the man who made the earth tremble...?'" (v. 16). Thus Lucifer is clearly defined as a man.

2. Because Lucifer was a human king, "All the kings of the nations... shall speak and say to you: 'Have you also become weak as we? Have you become like us?" (vs. 9-10). Lucifer was therefore a king like any other king.

3. Verse 21 says that Lucifer's "children" will be destroyed. Verse 22 says that Babylon's "posterity" will be destroyed, thus equating them. 'Lucifer' desired to rise up to heaven, and so did Babylon (Jer. 51:53); "her judgment [i.e. her sin that warrants her judgment] reaches to heaven" (Jer. 51:9).

4. Remember that this is a "proverb (parable) against the king of Babylon" (v. 4). "Lucifer" means "the morning star", which is the brightest of the stars; it is in fact the planet Venus. In the parable, this star proudly decides to "ascend (higher) into heaven...exalt my throne above the (other) stars of God" (v. 13). Because of this, the star is cast down to the earth. The star represents the king of Babylon. Daniel chapter 4 explains how Nebuchadnezzar the king of Babylon proudly surveyed the great kingdom he had built up, thinking that he had conquered other nations in his own strength, rather than recognizing that God had given him success. "your greatness (pride) has grown and reaches to the heavens" (v. 22). Because of this "he was driven from men and ate grass like oxen; his body was wet with the dew of heaven till his hair had grown like eagles' feathers and his nails like birds' claws" (v. 33). This sudden humbling of one of the world's most powerful men to a deranged lunatic was such a dramatic event as to call for the parable about the falling of the morning star from heaven to earth. Stars are often symbolic of powerful people, e.g. Gen. 37:9; Is. 13:10 (concerning the leaders of Babylon); Ez. 32:7 (concerning the leader of Egypt); Dan. 8:10 cp. v.24. Ascending to heaven and falling from heaven are Biblical idioms often used for increasing in pride and being humbled respectively - see Job 20:6; Jer. 51:53 (about Babylon); Lam. 2:1; Mt. 11:23 (about Capernaum): "...you, Capernaum, who are exalted to heaven, will be brought down to Hades" (the grave).

5. Verse 17 accuses Lucifer of making the "world as a wilderness, (destroying) its cities... (not opening) the house of his prisoners... (filling) the face of the world with cities" (vs.21), "the exactress of gold" (vs.4 A.V. margin). These are all descriptions of Babylonian military policy - razing whole areas to the ground (as they did to Jerusalem), transporting captives to other areas and not letting them return to their homeland (as they did to the Jews), building new cities and taking tribute of gold from nations they oppressed. Thus there is emphasis on the fact that Lucifer was not even going to get the burial these other kings had had (vs. 18-19), implying that he was only a human king like them, seeing his body needed burying.

6. Verse 12 says that Lucifer was to be "cut down to the ground" - implying he was a tree. This provides a further link with Dan. 4:8-16, where Nebuchadnezzar and Babylon are likened to a tree being cut down.

7. Babylon and Assyria are often interchangeable phrases in the prophets; thus, having spoken of the demise of the king of Babylon, v 25 says, "I will break the Assyrian...". The prophecies about Babylon in Is. 47 are repeated concerning Assyria in Nah. 3:3-5,18 and Zeph. 2:13,15; and 2 Chron. 33:11 says that the king of Assyria took Manasseh captive to Babylon - showing the interchangeability of the terms. Am. 5:27 says that Israel were to go into captivity "beyond Damascus", i.e. in Assyria, but Stephen quotes this as "beyond Babylon" (Acts 7:43). Ezra 6:1 describes Darius the king of Babylon making a decree concerning the rebuilding of the temple. The Jews praised God for turning "the heart of the king of Assyria" (Ezra 6:22), again showing that they are interchangeable terms. The prophecy of Isaiah ch. 14, along with many others in Isaiah, fits in well to the context of the Assyrian invasion by Sennacherib in Hezekiah's time, hence v. 25 describes the breaking of the Assyrian. Verse 13 is easier to understand if it is talking about the blasphemous Assyrians besieging Jerusalem, wanting to enter Jerusalem and capture the temple for their gods. Earlier the Assyrian king, Tiglath-Pileser, had probably wanted to do the same (2 Chron. 28:20,21); Is. 14:13: "For you have said in your heart: 'I will ascend into heaven... (symbolic of the temple and ark - 1 Kings 8:30; 2 Chron. 30:27; Ps. 20: 2,6; 11:4; Heb. 7:26). I will also sit on the mount of the congregation (mount Zion where the temple was) on the farthest sides of the north" (Jerusalem - Ps. 48:1,2).

8. It is therefore necessary to understand "I will ascend to heaven" as hyperbole, as in 1 Sam. 5:12; 2 Chron. 28:9; Ezra 9:6; Ps. 107:26.

STUDY 6: Questions

1. Who is responsible for our problems and trials?
   - [ ] God
   - [ ] Chance
   - [ ] A sinful being called Satan

2. What is responsible for our temptation to sin?
   - [ ] Our own human nature
   - [ ] God
   - [ ] Evil spirits
   - [ ] A sinful being called satan.

3. What does 'devil' mean as a word?
   - [ ] Sin
   - [ ] False accuser/ slanderer
   - [ ] Lucifer

4. What does 'satan' mean as a word?
   - [ ] A sinner
   - [ ] An adversary
   - [ ] King of demons

5. Can the word 'satan' be applied to good people?
   - [ ] Yes
   - [ ] No

6. What can 'satan' and 'devil' refer to figuratively?

7. The word 'demons' in the New Testament refers to:
   - [ ] Sinful Angels
   - [ ] Sicknesses
   - [ ] The language of the day for sicknesses, which people thought were caused by 'demons'
   - [ ] Spirit beings

STUDY 7
The Origin Of Jesus

7.1   Old Testament Prophecies Of Jesus

Study 3 explained how God's purpose of salvation for men and women was centred in Jesus Christ. The promises which He made to Eve, Abraham and David all spoke of Jesus as their literal descendant. Indeed, the whole of the Old Testament points forward to, and prophesies about, Christ. The Law of Moses, which Israel had to obey before the time of Christ, constantly pointed forward to Jesus: "The law was our schoolmaster to bring us unto Christ" (Gal. 3:24). Thus at the feast of Passover, a lamb in perfect condition had to be killed (Ex. 12:3-6); this represented the sacrifice of Jesus, "the Lamb of God, which takes away the sin of the world" (Jn. 1:29; 1 Cor. 5:7). The spotless condition which was required for all the animal sacrifices pointed forward to the perfect character of Jesus (Ex. 12:5 cp. 1 Pet. 1:19).

Throughout the Psalms and prophets of the Old Testament there are countless prophecies about what Messiah would be like. They particularly focus on describing how he would die. Judaism's refusal to accept the idea of a Messiah who dies can only be due to their inattention to these prophecies, a few of which are now presented.

OLD TESTAMENT PROPHECY	FULFILMENT IN CHRIST
"My God, my God, why have you forsaken me?" (Ps. 22:1)	These were the very words of Jesus on the cross (Mt. 27:46)
"I am despised of the people. All they that see me laugh me to scorn: they shake the head, saying, He trusted on the Lord that he would deliver him: let him deliver him" (Ps. 22:6-8)	Israel despised Jesus and mocked him (Lk. 23:35; 8:53); they shook their heads (Mt. 27:39), and said this as He hung on the cross (Mt. 27:43)
"My tongue cleaves to my jaws...they pierced my hands and my feet" (Ps. 22:15,16)	This was fulfilled in Christ's thirst on the cross (Jn. 19:28). The piercing of hands and feet refers to the physical method of crucifixion used.

| "They parted my garments among them, and cast lots upon my clothing" (Ps. 22:18) | The precise fulfilment of this is found in Mt. 27:35. |

| Note that Ps. 22:22 is specifically quoted as applying to Jesus in Heb. 2:12 | |

| "I am become a stranger unto my brothers, and am an alien unto my mother's children. For the zeal of your house has eaten me up" (Ps. 69:8,9) | This well describes Christ's feeling of estrangement from his Jewish brethren and his own family (Jn. 7:3-5, Mt. 12:47-49). This is quoted in John 2:17. |

| "They gave me also gall for my meat; and in my thirst they gave me vinegar to drink" (Ps. 69:21) | This happened while Christ was on the cross (Matt. 27:34) |

| The whole of Isaiah 53 is a remarkable prophecy of Christ's death and resurrection, every verse of which had an unmistakable fulfilment. Just two examples will be given. | |

| "As a sheep before her shearers is dumb, so he opens not his mouth" (Is. 53:7) | Christ, the Lamb of God, remained silent during his trial (Mt. 27:12,14) |

| "He made his grave with the wicked, and with the rich in his death" (Is. 53:9) | Jesus was crucified along with wicked criminals (Mt. 27:38), but was buried in the tomb of a rich man (Mt. 27:57-60). |

It is little wonder that the New Testament reminds us that the "law and prophets" of the Old Testament is the basis of our understanding of Christ (Acts 26:22; 28:23; Rom. 1:2,3; 16:25,26). Jesus himself warned that if we do not properly understand "Moses and the prophets", we cannot understand him (Lk. 16:31; Jn. 5:46,47).

That the Law of Moses pointed forward to Christ, and the prophets prophesied of him, should be proof enough that Jesus did not exist physically before his birth. The false doctrine of the physical 'pre-existence' of Christ before birth makes a nonsense of the repeated promises that he would be the *descendant* of Eve, Abraham and David. The early preachers emphasized that Jesus was "of David's posterity" [Gk. *Spermatos*- Acts 2:29-31; 13:23; Rom. 1:3; 2 Tim. 2:8]. If he were already existing up in heaven at the time of these promises, God would have been incorrect in promising these people a descendant who *would be* Messiah. The genealogies of Jesus, recorded in Mt. 1 and Lk. 3, show how Jesus had a pedigree which stretched back to those people to whom God had made the promises.

The promise to David concerning Christ precludes his physical existence at the time the promise was made: "I *will* set up your descendant [singular] *after* you, which *shall* proceed out of your body...I *will be* his father, and he *shall be* my son" (2 Sam. 7:12,14). Notice the future tense used here. Seeing that God *would be* Christ's Father, it is impossible that the Son of God could have already existed at that point in time when the promise was made. That this seed *"shall proceed out of your body"* shows that he was to be a literal, physical descendant of David. "The Lord has sworn in truth unto David...Of the fruit of your body will I set upon your throne" (Ps. 132:11).

Solomon was the primary fulfilment of the promise, but as he was already physically in existence at the time of this promise (2 Sam. 5:14), the main fulfilment of this promise about David having a physical descendant who would be God's son, must refer to Christ (Lk. 1:31-33). "I *will* raise unto David a righteous Branch" (Jer. 23:5) - i.e. Messiah.

Similar future tenses are used in other prophecies concerning Christ. "I *will* raise (Israel) up a Prophet like unto (Moses)" (Dt. 18:18) is quoted in Acts 3:22,23, which defines the "Prophet" as Jesus. "A virgin (Mary) *shall* conceive, and bear a son, and *shall* call his name Immanuel" (Is. 7:14). This was clearly fulfilled in Christ's birth (Mt. 1:23).

7.2   The Virgin Birth

The record of Christ's conception and birth does not allow for the idea that he physically existed beforehand. Those who hold the false doctrine of the 'Trinity' are driven to the conclusion that at one moment there were three beings in heaven, and one of them then became the child in Mary's womb, leaving just two in heaven. We are therefore left to conclude from the 'pre-existence' belief that Christ somehow came down from heaven and entered into Mary's womb. All this complex theology is quite outside the teaching of Scripture. The record of Christ's beginning gives no reason whatsoever to think that he left heaven and entered into Mary. The lack of evidence for this is a big 'missing link' in trinitarian teaching.

The angel Gabriel appeared to Mary with the message that "you shall conceive in your womb, and bring forth a son, and shall call his name Jesus. He shall be great, and shall be called the Son of the Highest...Then said Mary unto the angel, How shall this be, seeing I know not a man? (i.e. she was a virgin). And the angel answered and said unto her, The Holy Spirit shall come upon you, and the power of the Highest shall overshadow you: therefore also that holy thing which shall be born of you shall be called the Son of God" (Lk. 1:31-35).

Twice it is emphasized that Jesus *would be* the Son of God on his birth; evidently the Son of God did not exist before his birth. Again, the many future tenses need to be noted - e.g. "he *shall be* great". If Jesus were already physically in existence as the angel spoke those words to Mary, he would already have been great. Jesus was the "offspring" of David (Rev. 22:16), the Greek 'genos' implying Jesus was 'generated from' David. He was born "of" Mary (Lk. 1:35).

THE CONCEPTION OF JESUS

Through the Holy Spirit (God's breath/power) acting upon her, Mary was able to conceive Jesus without having intercourse with a man. Thus Joseph was not the father of Jesus. It must be understood that the Holy Spirit is not a person (see Study 2); Jesus was the Son of God, not the Son of the Holy Spirit. Through God's use of His spirit upon Mary, "*therefore* also that holy thing" which was born of her was "called the Son of God" (Lk. 1:35). The use of the word "therefore" implies that without the Holy Spirit acting upon the womb of Mary, Jesus, the Son of God, could not have come into existence.

That Jesus was 'conceived' in Mary's womb (Lk. 1:31) is also proof that he could not have physically existed before this time. If we 'conceive' an idea, it begins within us. Likewise Jesus was conceived inside Mary's womb - he began there as a foetus, just like any other human being. Jn. 3:16, the Bible's most famous verse, records that Jesus was the "only *begotten* Son" of God. Millions of people who recite this verse fail to meditate upon what it implies. If Jesus was "begotten", he 'began' (a related word to "begotten") when he was conceived in Mary's womb. If Jesus was begotten by God as his Father, this is clear evidence that his Father is older than he - God has no beginning (Ps. 90:2) and therefore Jesus cannot be God Himself (Study 8 expands on this point).

It is significant that Jesus was "begotten" by God rather than being created, as Adam was originally. This explains the closeness of God's association with Jesus - "God was in Christ, reconciling the world unto Himself" (2 Cor. 5:19). Christ being *begotten* by God, rather than just created from dust, also helps explain his natural aptitude for the ways of God his Father.

Is. 49:5,6 contains a prophecy concerning Christ as the light of the world, which he fulfilled (Jn. 8:12). He is described as meditating on "the Lord that formed me from the womb to be his servant". Christ was therefore "formed" by God in Mary's womb, through the power of His Holy Spirit. Mary's womb was evidently the place of Christ's physical origin.

We have seen in Study 7.1 that Psalm 22 prophesies Christ's thoughts on the cross. He reflected that God "took me out of the womb...I was cast upon you from the womb: you are my God from my mother's belly" (Ps. 22:9,10). In his time of dying, Christ looked back to his origins - in the womb of his mother Mary, formed by the power of God. The very description of Mary in the Gospels as Christ's "*mother*" in itself destroys the idea that he existed before his birth of Mary.

Mary was an ordinary human being, with normal human parents. This is proved by the fact that she had a cousin, who gave birth to John the Baptist, an ordinary man (Lk. 1:36). The Roman Catholic idea that Mary was not of ordinary human nature would mean that Christ could not truly have been both "Son of man" and "Son of God". These are his frequent titles throughout the New Testament. He was "Son of man" by reason of having a totally human mother, and "Son of God" because of God's action on Mary through the Holy Spirit (Lk. 1:35), meaning that God was his Father. This beautiful arrangement is nullified if Mary was not an ordinary woman.

"Who can bring a clean thing out of an unclean? Not one...What is man, that he should be clean? and he which is born of a woman, that he should be righteous?...how can he be clean that is born of a woman?" (Job 14:4; 15:14; 25:4). This puts paid to any idea of an immaculate conception being possible, either of Mary or Jesus.

Mary being "born of a woman", with ordinary human parents, must have had our unclean, human nature, which she passed on to Jesus, who was "made of a woman" (Gal. 4:4). The language of his being "*made*" through Mary's agency is further evidence that he could not have physically existed without his birth by her. The Diaglott renders Gal. 4:4: "Having *been produced* from a woman". The Saviour was to be "the seed of the *woman*" (Gen. 3:15) - which promise occurs in the context of the record in Genesis of many *male-based* genealogies.

The Gospel records frequently indicate Mary's humanity. Christ had to rebuke her at least thrice for a lack of spiritual perception (Lk. 2:49; Jn. 2:4); she failed to understand all his sayings (Lk. 2:50). This is exactly what we would expect of a woman who was of human nature, whose son was the Son of God, and therefore more spiritually perceptive than herself, although he, too, shared human nature. Joseph had intercourse with Mary after Christ's birth (Mt. 1:25), and there is no reason to think that they did not have a normal marital relationship from then on.

The mention of Christ's "mother and his brethren" in Mt. 12:46,47 would therefore imply that Mary had other children after Jesus. Jesus was only "her *first* born". The Catholic teachings that Mary remained a virgin and then ascended to heaven therefore have absolutely no Biblical support. As a human being of mortal nature, Mary would have grown old and died; apart from this we read in Jn. 3:13, "no man has ascended up to heaven". The fact that Christ had human nature (see Heb. 2:14-18; Rom. 8:3) means that his mother must have had it too, seeing his Father did not have it. She saw herself as "the handmaid [female servant] of the Lord" (Lk. 1:38 cp. Ps. 86:16) - not 'the mother of God'.

The whole record of the virgin birth makes a nonsense of the claim that Jesus pre-existed as a person before His birth. This has even been recognized by theologians: "Jesus' virgin birth stands in an irreconcilable contradiction to the Christology of the incarnation of the pre-existent Son of God" (W. Pannenberg, *Jesus- God And Man*, Philadelphia: Westminster, 1968 p. 143). James Dunn likewise denies the literal pre-existence of Jesus: "There is no evidence that any NT writer thought of Jesus as actively present in Israel's past, either as the angel of the Lord, or as "the Lord" himself" (J.D.G. Dunn, *Christology In The* Making (London: SCM, 1980) p. 158). A pre-existent Jesus is merely a continuation of the old pagan idea that the gods came to earth and had relations with innocent women (cp. Acts 14:11).

7.3   Christ's Place In God's Plan

God does not decide on His plans on the spur of the moment, devising extra parts to His purpose as human history unfolds. God had a complete plan formulated right from the beginning of creation (Jn. 1:1). His desire to have a Son was therefore in His plan from the beginning. He loved that Son before he was born, just as parents may love a child still in the womb. The whole of the Old Testament reveals different aspects of God's plan of salvation in Christ.

We have frequently demonstrated that through the promises, the prophecies of the prophets, and the types of the Law of Moses, the Old Testament is constantly revealing God's purpose in Christ. It was on account of God's knowledge that He would have a Son that He brought creation into existence (Heb. 1:1,2, Greek text; "by" in the A.V. is better translated "on account of"). It was on account of Christ that the ages of human history were allowed by God (Heb. 1:2 (Greek). It follows that God's revelation to man down through the years, as recorded in the Old Testament, is full of references to Christ.

The supremacy of Christ and his fundamental importance to God is difficult for us to comprehend fully. It is therefore true to say that Christ existed in God's mind and purpose from the beginning, although he only came into existence physically through his birth of Mary. Heb. 1:4-7, 13,14, stress that Christ was not an angel; whilst in his mortal life he was less than angels (Heb. 2:7), he was exalted to a far greater honour than them seeing he was God's *"only begotten Son"* (Jn. 3:16). Christ did not exist as a 'spirit' before his birth. 1 Pet. 1:20 sums up the position: Christ "was foreordained before the foundation of the world but was manifest in these last times".

Jesus was the central pivot of the Gospel, which God "had promised afore by his prophets in the holy Scriptures, concerning his son, Jesus Christ our Lord, which was made (created by begettal) of the seed of David according to the flesh; and declared to be the Son of God with power, according to the spirit of holiness, by the resurrection from the dead" (Rom. 1:1-4).

This summarizes the history of Christ.

1. Promised in the Old Testament - i.e. in God's plan;

2. Created as a physical person through the virgin birth, as a seed of David;

3. Due to his perfect character ("the spirit of holiness"), shown during his mortal life

4. He was resurrected, and again publicly declared to be the Son of God by the apostles' spirit-gifted preaching.

THE FOREKNOWLEDGE OF GOD

We will be greatly helped in appreciating how fully Christ was in God's mind at the beginning, while not physically existing, if we can come to terms with the fact that God knows *all* things which will occur in the 'future'; He has complete 'foreknowledge'. God can therefore speak and think about things which do not exist, as though they do. Such is the totality of His knowledge of the future. There is strictly no Hebrew word for 'promise'- only a 'word'; so sure is God's word of promise of fulfilment. What He says is as if it has happened. Thus God "speaks of those things which be not as though they were" (Rom. 4:17). He can therefore declare "the end from the beginning, and from ancient times the things that are not yet done, saying, My counsel shall stand, and I will do all my pleasure" (Is. 46:10). Because of this, God can speak of the dead as if they are alive, and can speak of men as if they were alive before birth. He can speak of a day coming as if it has come (Is. 3:8; Ez. 7:10,12).

The "counsel", or word of God, had prophesied Christ from the beginning; he was always in God's purpose or "pleasure". It was therefore certain that at some time Christ would be physically born; God would fulfil His stated purpose in Christ. The certainty of God's foreknowledge is therefore reflected in the sureness of His word. Biblical Hebrew has a 'prophetic perfect' tense, which uses the past tense to describe future things which God has promised. Thus David said, "This *is* the house of the Lord God" (1 Chron. 22:1), when as yet the temple was only promised by God. Such was his faith in that word of promise that David used the present tense to describe future things. Scripture abounds with examples of God's foreknowledge. God was so certain that He would fulfil the promises to Abraham, that He told him: "Unto your seed *have* I *given* this land..." (Gen. 15:18) at a time when Abraham did not even have a seed. During this same period before the seed (Isaac/Christ) was born, God further promised: "A father of many nations *have I made you*" (Gen. 17:5). Truly, God "speaks of those things which be not as though they were".

Thus Christ spoke during his ministry of how God "*has given* all things into his (Christ's) hand" (Jn. 3:35), although this was not then the case. "You *have* put all things in subjection under (Christ's) feet...but now we see not yet all things put under him" (Heb. 2:8).

God spoke about His plan of salvation through Jesus "by the mouth of his holy prophets, which have been since the world began" (Lk. 1:70). The prophets "have been since the world began" (Acts 3:21 RV). Because they were so closely associated with God's plan, these men are spoken of as though they literally existed at the beginning, although this is evidently not the case. Instead, we can say that the prophets were in God's plan from the beginning. Jeremiah is a prime example. God told him: "Before I formed you in the belly I knew you; and before you came forth out of the womb I sanctified you, and I ordained you a prophet" (Jer. 1:5). Thus God knew everything about Jeremiah even before the creation. In like manner God could speak about the Persian king Cyrus before the time of his birth, using language which implies he was then in existence (Is. 45:1-5). Heb. 7:9,10 is another example of this language of existence being used about someone not then born.

In the same way as Jeremiah and the prophets are spoken of as existing even before creation, due to their part in God's plan, so the true believers are spoken of as existing then. It is evident that we did not physically exist then except in the mind of God. God "has saved us, and called us with an holy calling...according to his own purpose and grace, which was given us in Christ Jesus before the world began" (2 Tim. 1:9). God "has chosen us in (Christ) before the foundation of the world...having predestinated us...according to the good pleasure of His will" (Eph. 1:4,5). The whole idea of individuals being foreknown by God from the beginning, and being 'marked off' ('predestinated') to salvation, indicates that they existed in the mind of God at the beginning (Rom. 8:27; 9:23).

In the light of all this, it is not surprising that Christ, as the summation of God's purpose, should be spoken of as existing from the beginning in God's mind and plan, although physically he could not have done so. He was "the lamb slain from the foundation of the world" (Rev. 13:8). Jesus did not die then literally; he was the "Lamb of God" sacrificed about 4,000 years later on the cross (Jn. 1:29; 1 Cor. 5:7). In the same way as Jesus was chosen from the beginning (1 Pet. 1:20), so were the believers (Eph. 1:4; the same Greek word for "chosen" is used in these verses). Our difficulty in comprehending all this is because we cannot easily imagine how God operates outside of the concept of time. 'Faith' is the ability to look at things from God's viewpoint, without the constraints of time.

7.4   "In the beginning was the word" (Jn. 1:1-3)

"In the beginning was the Word, and the Word was with God, and the Word was God. The same was in the beginning with God. All things were made by him" (Jn. 1:1-3).

These verses, when properly understood, confirm and expand upon the conclusions reached in the last section. However, this passage is the one most widely misunderstood to teach that Jesus existed in heaven before his birth. A correct understanding of these verses hinges on appreciating what "the Word" means in this context. It cannot refer directly to a person, because a person cannot be "with God" and yet *be* God at the same time. The Greek word 'logos' which is translated "word" here, does not in itself mean 'Jesus'. It is usually translated as "word", but also as:-

Account, Cause, Communication, Doctrine, Intent, Preaching, Reason, Saying, Tidings

The "word" is only spoken of as "he" because 'logos' is masculine in Greek. But this does not mean that it refers to the man, Jesus. The German (Luther) version speaks of "das Wort" (neuter); the Russian likewise speaks of "slovo... ono bylo" in the neuter; the French (Segond) version speaks of "la parole" as feminine, showing that "the word" does not necessarily indicate a male person.

'Logos' can strictly refer to the inner thought which is expressed outwardly in words and other communication. In the beginning God had this 'logos'. This singular purpose was centred in Christ. All of creation came into existence on account of the purpose God had in Christ - the stars, planets etc. were all somehow created in connection with the birth and existence and victory of Christ [and behold therefore God's humility, in allowing the birth and death of His Son in the way He did]. We have shown how God's spirit puts His inner thoughts into operation, hence the connection between His spirit and His word (see Section 2.2). As God's spirit worked out His plan with men and inspired His written Word from the beginning, it thereby communicated the idea of Christ in its working and words. Christ was *the* 'logos' of God, and therefore God's spirit expressed God's plan of Christ in all its operations. This explains why so many Old Testament incidents are typical of Christ. However, it cannot be over-emphasized that Christ in person was not "the word"; it was God's plan of salvation through Christ which was "the word". 'Logos' ("the Word") is very often used concerning the Gospel about Christ - e.g. "the *word* of Christ" (Col. 3:16; cp. Mt. 13:19; Jn. 5:24; Acts 19:10; 1 Thess. 1:8 etc.). Notice that the 'logos' is *about* Christ, rather than him personally. When Christ was born, this "word" was turned into a flesh and blood form - "the word was made flesh" (Jn. 1:14). Jesus personally was 'the word made flesh' rather than "the word"; he personally became "the word" through his birth of Mary, rather than at any time previously.

The plan, or message, about Christ was with God in the beginning, but was openly revealed in the person of Christ, and the preaching of the Gospel about him in the first century. Thus God spoke His word to us through Christ (Heb. 1:1,2). Time and again it is emphasized that Christ spoke God's words and did miracles at God's word of command in order to reveal God to us (Jn. 2:22; 3:34; 7:16; 10:32,38; 14:10,24).

Paul obeyed Christ's command to preach the Gospel about him "to all nations": "The preaching of Jesus Christ, according to the revelation of the mystery, which was kept secret since the world began, but now is made manifest...made known to all nations" (Rom. 16:25,26 cp. 1 Cor. 2:7). Eternal life was only made possible for man through the work of Christ (Jn. 3:16; 6:53-54); yet in the beginning God had this plan to offer man eternal life, knowing as He did the sacrifice which Jesus would make. The full revelation of that offer only came after the birth and death of Jesus: "Eternal life, which God...promised before the world began; but has in due times manifested his word (of life) through preaching" (Tit. 1:2,3). We have seen how God's prophets are spoken of as always existing (Lk. 1:70) in the sense that "the word" which they spoke existed with God from the beginning.

The parables of Jesus revealed many of these things; he thereby fulfilled the prophecy concerning himself, "I will open my mouth in parables; I will utter things which have been kept secret from the foundation of the world" (Mt. 13:35). It was in this sense that "the word was with God...in the beginning", to be "made flesh" at Christ's birth.

"THE WORD WAS GOD"

We are now in a position to consider in what sense "the Word was God". Our plans and thoughts are fundamentally us. 'I am going to London' is a 'word' or communication which expresses my purpose, because it is my purpose. God's plan in Christ can be understood likewise. "As (a man) thinks in his heart, so is he" (Prov. 23:7), and as God thinks, so is He. Thus God's word or thinking *is* God: "the word was God". Because of this, there is a very close association between God and His word: parallelisms like Ps. 29:8 are common: "The voice of the Lord shakes the wilderness; the Lord shakes the wilderness" (cf. Ps. 56:4; 130:5). Statements like "You have not hearkened unto *Me*, saith the Lord" (Jer. 25:7) are common in the prophets. Effectively God means 'You have not listened to *My word* spoken by the prophets'. Indeed, sometimes 'Yahweh' is to be read as meaning 'the word of Yahweh' (e.g. 1 Sam. 3:8). And likewise "the scripture" is to be understood as meaning 'God' (Rom. 9:17 cp. Ex. 9:16; Gal. 3:8). David took the word of God as his lamp and light (Ps. 119:105), yet he also reflected: "*You* are my lamp, O Lord: and the Lord will lighten my darkness" (2 Sam. 22:29), showing the parallel between God and His word. It is understandable, therefore, that God's word is personified as He Himself, i.e. it is spoken of as though it is a person although it is not (see Digression 4 'The Principle of Personification').

God is truth itself (Jn. 3:33; 8:26; 1 Jn. 5:10), and therefore God's word is truth also (Jn. 17:17). In a similar way Jesus identifies himself with his words so closely that he personifies his word: "He that rejects me, and receives not my words, has one that judges him: the word that I have spoken, the same shall judge him in the last day" (Jn. 12:48). Jesus speaks of his word as if it is an actual person, i.e. himself. His words were personified, because they were so closely associated with Jesus.

God's word is likewise personified as a person, i.e. God Himself, in Jn. 1:1-3. Thus we are told concerning the Word, "All things were made by Him" (Jn. 1:3). However "*God* created" all things by His word of command (Gen. 1:1). Because of this, God's Word is spoken of as if it is God Himself. The devotional point to note from this is that through God's word being in our heart, God can come so close to us. God spoke of how Israel "profaned" the command to keep the Sabbath, and then of how they profaned *Him* (Ez. 22:26). He is His word, and to despise His commands is to despise Him. Our attitude to His word is our attitude to Him. Thus Saul sinned "against the

Lord, even against the word of the Lord, which he kept not" (1 Chron. 10:13).

It is evident from Gen. 1 that God was the Creator, through His word, rather than Christ personally. It was the *word* which is described as making all things, rather than Christ personally (Jn. 1:1-3). "By the word of the Lord were the heavens made; and all the host of them (i.e. the stars) by the breath of his mouth...he spake, and it was done" (Ps. 33:6,9). Even now it is by His word that the natural creation operates: "He sends forth his commandment upon earth: his word runs very swiftly. He gives snow like wool...He sends out his word...and the waters flow" (Ps. 147:15-18).

God's word being His creative power, He used it in the begettal of Jesus in Mary's womb. The Word, God's plan put into operation by His Holy Spirit (Lk. 1:35), brought about Christ's conception. Mary recognized this in her response to the news about her forthcoming conception of Christ: "Be it unto me according to your *word*" (Lk. 1:38).

We have seen that God's Word/spirit reflects His purpose, which had been stated throughout the Old Testament. The degree to which this is true is shown in Acts 13:27, where Jesus is spoken of as parallel to the words of the Old Testament prophets: "(The Jews) knew him not, nor yet the voices of the prophets". When Christ was born, all of God's Word/spirit was expressed in the person of Jesus Christ. Under inspiration, the apostle John exulted in how God's plan of eternal life had been expressed in Christ, whom the disciples had been able to physically handle and see. He now recognized that they had been handling the Word of God, His whole plan of salvation in Christ (1 Jn. 1:1-3). Whilst we cannot physically see Christ, we, too, can rejoice that through a true understanding of him, we can so intimately know God's purpose with us and thereby be assured of eternal life (1 Pet. 1:8,9). We must ask ourselves the question: 'Do I really *know* Christ?' Just accepting that a good man called Jesus once existed is not enough. Through continued, prayerful Bible study, it is possible to quickly understand him as your personal Saviour and relate yourself to him through baptism. He will judge men in the last day, but the word will also be their judge (Jn. 12:48). He was the perfect expression of the essence of God's word; He was that word in that sense, He was fully the Word/message which He preached.

Digression 12: Jesus The Son Of God (Hebrews 1:8)

Michael Gates

"But to the Son He says: "Your throne, O God, is forever and ever"" (Heb. 1:8). Here Christ Jesus is apparently addressed as 'God'.

"He who has seen Me has seen the Father .. do you not believe that I am in the Father, and the Father in Me? The words that I speak to you I do not speak on My own authority; but the Father who dwells in Me does the works. Believe Me that I am in the Father and the Father in Me. Or else believe Me for the very works' sake" John 14 :9-11. The Father is in Jesus and Jesus in the Father.

When Yahshua (Jesus) hung on the cross He called out, quoting Psalm 22 'My God, My God, why have You forsaken Me?'. Obviously the Son and the Father are two separate beings. When Yahshua was asked, "Good Teacher, what good thing shall I do that I may have eternal life?" Matthew 19:16,17; He replied "Why do you call Me good? No one is good but One, that is God." We learn from this that there is a difference between God and His Son.

Puzzling? This is where some knowledge of the original Hebrew or Greek is handy, which can usually be found in a concordance such as Strong's.

Let us examine the position. In the first quotation we have brought forward, viz. Hebrews 1 the writer is quoting Psalm 45:6 'Your throne, O God ...'. When we go to the concordance we find that the original Hebrew word used is 'Elohim'. Elohim can apply to many people, for example in Exodus 22:8,9 'Elohim' is translated "judges". Knowing this, it helps us to understand John 10:33-35: 'The Jews answered Him, saying, "For a good work we do not stone You, but for blasphemy, and because You, being a Man, make yourself God". Jesus answered them, "Is it not written in your law, 'I said, "You are gods"? "If He called them gods, to whom the word of God came ... do you say of Him whom the Father sanctified and sent into the world, 'You are blaspheming,' because I said, "I am the Son of God"? Some versions of the Bible in the margin refer us back to the Psalm 82:6, but the Psalms are not 'the law' that Jesus is referring to. He is referring to such passages as Exodus 21 and 22 where Elohim is translated 'Judges'.

In the second quotation "I am in the Father and the Father in Me", or in other words 'One with the Father', this is referring to the unity spoken of in John 17:20-23: "I do not pray for these alone, but also for those who will believe in Me ... that they all may be one, as You Father, are in Me, and I in You; that they also may be one in us ... that (believers) may be one just as We are one". In 1 John 5 verses 7-8 quoting the New King James a footnote informs us 'that from 'in heaven', v.7 to 'on earth', v. 8 only four or five **very late** manuscripts contain these words in Greek'. They are not to be found in the original texts. In the quotation of the words of Christ when He was on the cross, 'My God, My God why have you forsaken Me?;' The Father had not forsaken Him. Yahshua used the Hebrew 'El', the singular word of which Elohim is plural. El, Strong's concordance says, means 'strength'. His strength had temporally been removed. To sum up. Belief in the Trinity was not official Church doctrine until the 4th century. The words 'Trinity' or 'Triune God' are not found in the original manuscripts. The Scriptures teach, not 'One in Three' or 'Three in One', but many thousands in One and One in many thousands of believers, from righteous Abel, of Genesis 4 to all those referred to in John 20:29, when 'Jesus said to (Thomas), "Thomas, because you have seen Me, you have believed. **Blessed are those who have not seen and yet have believed.**"'

Belief In Practice 13:

Jesus Didn't Pre-Exist: And So What?

2 Jn. 11 speaks of how teaching that Jesus was not truly human is associated with " evil works" . Surely the implication is that good works are inspired by a true understanding of the Lord's humanity, and evil works by a refusal to accept this teaching. The tests of genuineness which John commanded centred around two simple things: Do those who come to you hold true understanding of the nature of Jesus; and do they love. The two things go together. And they are a fair test even today. For where there is no love, the true doctrine of Jesus is not truly believed, no matter how nicely it is expressed in words and writing.

BOLD PRAYER AND WITNESS

Therefore in the daily round of life, He will be a living reality, like David we will behold the Lord Jesus before our face all the day. We will really believe that forgiveness is possible through the work of such a representative; and the reality of his example will mean the more to us, as a living inspiration to rise above our lower nature. Appreciating the doctrines of the atonement enables us to pray acceptably; "we have boldness and access with confidence by *the* Faith" - not just 'by faith', but as a result of *the* Faith (Eph. 3:12). Hebrews so often uses the word "therefore" ; *because of* the facts of the atonement, we can *therefore* come boldly before God's throne in prayer, with a true heart and clear conscience (Heb. 4:16). This "boldness" which the atonement has enabled will be reflected in our being 'bold' in our witness (2 Cor. 3:12; 7:4); our experience of imputed righteousness will lead us to have a confidence exuding through our whole being. This is surely why 'boldness' was such a characteristic and watchword of the early church (Acts 4:13,29,31; Eph. 3:12; Phil. 1:20; 1 Tim. 3:13; Heb. 10:19; 1 Jn. 4:17). Stephen truly believed that the Lord Jesus stood as his representative and his advocate before the throne of grace. Although condemned by an earthly court, he confidently makes his appeal before the court of Heaven (Acts 7:56). Doubtless he was further inspired by the basic truth that whoever confesses the Lord Jesus before men, He will confess him before the angels in the court of Heaven (Lk. 12:8).

The connection between the atonement and faith in prayer is also brought out in 2 Cor. 1:20 RSV: " For all the promises of God in him are yea. That is why we utter the Amen through him" . The promises of God were confirmed through the Lord's death, and the fact that He died as the seed of Abraham, having taken upon Him Abraham's plural seed in representation (Rom. 15:8,9). Because of this, " we utter the Amen through [on account of being in] Him" . We can heartily say 'Amen', so be it, to our prayers on account of our faith and understanding of His atoning work.

LOVE

The fact the Lord Jesus didn't pre-exist as a person needs some meditation. The kind of thoughts that come to us as we stand alone at night, gazing into the sky. It seems evident that there must have been some kind of previous creation(s), e.g. for the creation of the Angels. God existed from infinity, and yet only 2,000 years ago did He have His only and His *begotten* Son. And that Son was a human being in order to save humans- only a few million of us (if that), who lived in a 6,000 year time span. In the spectre of infinite time and space, this is wondrous. That the Only Son of God should die for a very few of us here, we who crawled on the surface of this tiny planet for such a fleeting moment of time. He died so that God could work out our salvation; and the love of God for us is likened to a young man marrying a virgin (Is. 62:5). Almighty God, who existed from eternity, is likened to a first timer, with all the intensity and joyful expectation and lack of disillusion. And more than this. The Jesus who didn't pre-exist but was like me, died for *me*, in the shameful way that He did. Our hearts and minds, with all their powers, are in the boundless prospect lost. His pure *love* for us, His condescension, should mean that we also ought to reach out into the lives of all men, never thinking they are beneath us or too insignificant or distant from us. No wonder 1 Jn. 4:15,16 describes believing that Jesus is the Son of God as believing the love that God has to us.

True Christianity holds that personal relationships matter more than anything in this world, and that the truly human way to live is- in the last analysis- to lovingly, constantly, unreservedly give ourselves away to God and to others. And yet this is ultimately rooted in the fact that we are seeking above all else to follow after the example of Jesus. This example is only real and actual because of the total humanity of Jesus. As He taught these things, so He lived them. The word of love was made flesh in Him. At the deepest level of personhood, His was the one perfect human life which this world has seen. And exactly because of His humanity, exactly because He was not " very God" but " the man Christ Jesus" , because Jesus didn't pre-exist, we have the pattern for our lives and being. To claim Jesus was " God" is to depersonalize Him; it destroys the wonder of His character and all He really was and is and will ever be.

THE REALITY OF JUDGMENT

We will be judged in the man Christ Jesus (Acts 17:31 R.V. Mg.). This means that the very fact Jesus didn't pre-exist and was human makes Him our constant and insistent judge of all our human behaviour. And exactly because of this, Paul argues, we should right now repent. He is judge exactly because He is the Son of man.

CONCLUSION

John makes such a fuss about believing that Jesus came in the flesh because he wants his brethren to have the same Spirit that was in Jesus dwelling in *their* flesh (1 Jn. 4:2,4). He wants them to see that being human, being in the flesh, is no barrier for God to dwell in. As Jesus was in the world, so are we to be in the world (1 Jn. 4:17 Gk.). *This* is why it's so important to understand that the Lord Jesus was genuinely human.

STUDY 7: Questions

1. List two Old Testament prophecies concerning Jesus.

2. Did Jesus physically exist before his birth?
   - ☐ Yes
   - ☐ No

3. In what sense can Jesus be said to have existed before his birth?
   - ☐ As an Angel
   - ☐ As part of a trinity
   - ☐ As a spirit
   - ☐ Only in the mind and purpose of God.

4. Which of the following statements are true about Mary?
   - ☐ She was a perfect, sinless woman
   - ☐ She was an ordinary woman
   - ☐ She was made pregnant with Jesus by the Holy Spirit
   - ☐ She now offers our prayers to Jesus.

5. Did Jesus create the earth?
   - ☐ Yes
   - ☐ No

6. What do you understand by John 1:1-3 "In the beginning was the word?"

   What does it not mean?

7. Why do you think it is important to be certain about whether Jesus existed physically before his birth?

STUDY 8

The Nature Of Jesus

8.1   The Nature Of Jesus: Introduction

It is one of the greatest tragedies in Christian thinking that the Lord Jesus Christ has not received the respect and exaltation due to him for his victory over sin through the development of a perfect character. The widely held doctrine of the 'trinity' makes Jesus God Himself. Seeing that God cannot be tempted (James 1:13) and has no possibility of sinning, this means that Christ did not really have to battle against sin. His life on earth would therefore have been a sham, living out the human experience, but with no real feeling for the spiritual and physical dilemma of the human race, as he was not personally affected by it.

At the other extreme, groups like the Mormons and Jehovah's Witnesses fail to appreciate properly the wonder of Christ as the only begotten Son of God. As such, he could not have been an angel or the natural son of Joseph. It has been suggested by some that in his lifetime, Christ's nature was like that of Adam before the fall. There is no Biblical evidence for this view and it fails to appreciate that Adam was formed by God from dust, whilst Jesus was 'created' by being *begotten* of God in the womb of Mary. Thus, although Jesus did not have a human father, he was conceived and born like us. Many people cannot accept that a man with our sinful nature could have a perfect character. It is this fact which is an obstacle to a real faith in Christ.

To believe that Jesus was of our nature, but was sinless in his character, *always* overcoming his temptations, is not easy. It takes much reflection upon the Gospel records of his perfect life, coupled with the many Biblical passages which deny that he was God, to come to a firm understanding and faith in the real Christ. It is far easier to suppose that he was God Himself, and therefore automatically perfect. Yet this view demeans the greatness of the victory which Jesus won against sin and human nature.

He had human nature, by this is meant that he shared every one of our sinful tendencies (Heb. 4:15), yet he overcame them by his commitment to God's ways and seeking His help to overcome sin. This God willingly gave, to the extent that "God was in Christ, reconciling the world unto Himself" through His very own Son (2 Cor. 5:19). When Jesus bids us share his yoke, so that we might find rest (Mt. 11:29) the idea is that he was 'an ox' like us, of the same nature, and yet far stronger.

8.2   Differences Between God And Jesus

There is a fine balance to be drawn between those passages which emphasise the degree to which "God was in Christ", and those which highlight his humanity. The latter group of passages make it impossible to justify Biblically the idea that Jesus is God Himself, "very God of very God", as the doctrine of the Trinity wrongly states. (This phrase "very God of very God" was used at the Council of Nicea in 325 A.D., where the idea of God being a 'trinity' was first promulgated; it was unknown to the early Christians.) The word 'trinity' never occurs in the Bible. Study 9 will delve further into Christ's total victory over sin, and God's part in it. As we commence these studies, let us remember that salvation depends upon an acceptance of the real Jesus Christ (Jn. 3:36; 6:53;17:3). Once we have come to this true understanding of his conquest of sin and death, we can be baptised into him in order to share in this salvation.

One of the clearest summaries of the relationship between God and Jesus is found in 1 Tim. 2:5: "There is *one* God, *and* one *mediator* between God and men, the *man* Christ Jesus". Reflection upon the highlighted words leads to the following conclusions.

- As there is only *one* God, it is impossible that Jesus could be God; if the Father is God and Jesus is also God, then there are two Gods. "But to us there is but one God, the Father" (1 Cor. 8:6). 'God the Father' is therefore the only God. It is therefore impossible that there can be a separate being called 'God the Son', as the false doctrine of the trinity states. The Old Testament likewise portrays Yahweh, the one God, as the Father (e.g. Is. 63:16; 64:8).

- In addition to this one God, there is the mediator, the man Christ Jesus - "...*and* one mediator...". That word "and" indicates a difference between Christ and God.

- As Christ is the "mediator" it means that he is a go-between. A mediator between sinful man and sinless God cannot be sinless God Himself; it had to be a sinless man, of sinful human nature. "The *man* Christ Jesus" leaves us in no doubt as to the correctness of this explanation. Even though he was writing after the ascension of Jesus, Paul does not speak of "the God Christ Jesus".

Several times we are reminded that "God is not a man" (Num. 23:19; Hos. 11:9); yet Christ was clearly "the Son of man" or, as he is often called in the New Testament, "the *man* Christ Jesus". The Greek text calls him "son of *anthropos*", i.e. of mankind, rather than "son of *aner*" [husband, man]. In Hebrew thought, "the Son of man" meant an ordinary, mortal man

(Is. 51:12). "For since by man [Adam] came death, by man [Jesus] came also the resurrection of the dead" (1 Cor. 15:21). Yet He was also "the Son of the Highest" (Lk. 1:32). God being "*The* Highest" indicates that only He has ultimate highness; Jesus being "the *Son* of the Highest" shows that he cannot have been God Himself in person. The very language of Father and Son which is used about God and Jesus, makes it obvious that they are not the same. Whilst a son may have certain similarities to his father, he cannot be one and the same person, nor be as old as his father.

In line with this, there are a number of obvious differences between God and Jesus, which clearly show that Jesus was not God himself.

GOD	JESUS
"God cannot be tempted" (James 1:13).	Christ "was in all points tempted like as we are" (Heb. 4:15).
God cannot die - He is immortal by nature (Ps. 90:2; 1 Tim. 6:16).	Christ died and was in the grave for three days (Mt. 12:40; 16:21). He was once under the "dominion" of death (Rom. 6:9).
God cannot be seen by men (1 Tim. 6:16; Ex. 33:20).	Men saw Jesus and handled him (1 Jn. 1:1 emphasises this).

When we are tempted, we are forced to choose between sin and obedience to God. Often we choose to disobey God; Christ had the same choices, but always chose to be obedient. He therefore had the possibility of sinning, although he never actually did. It is unthinkable that God has any possibility of sinning. We have shown that the seed of David promised in 2 Sam. 7:12-16 was definitely Christ. Verse 14 speaks of Christ's possibility of sinning: "*If* he commit iniquity, I will chasten him".

The Centurion reasoned that because he was under authority, he therefore had authority over others; and he applies this very same logic to the abilities of the Lord Jesus. Because He was under *God's* authority, therefore and thereby He would have the power to have other things under His authority. And the Lord commended the Centurion for that perception. Clearly the Lord Jesus is to be understood as under the Father's authority; and it is only because He is in this subordinate position, that He has authority over all things now.

8.3   The Nature Of Jesus

The word 'nature' means 'fundamental, essential being'. We have shown in Study 1 that the Bible speaks of only two natures - that of God, and that of man. By nature God cannot die, be tempted etc. It is evident that Christ was not of God's nature during his life. He was therefore of human nature. From our definition of the word 'nature' it is evident that Christ could not have had two natures simultaneously. It was vital that Christ was tempted like us (Heb. 4:15), so that through his perfect overcoming of temptation he could gain forgiveness for us. "We have not an high priest which cannot be touched with the feeling of our infirmities; but was in all points tempted like us" (Heb. 4:15) expresses a truth negatively. It suggests that even in the first century there were those who thought that Jesus "cannot be touched with the feeling of our infirmities"; the writer is stressing that this is *not* the case; Jesus *can* be touched in this way. These incipient tendencies to wrong understanding of the nature of Jesus came to full fruit in the false doctrine of the trinity. The wrong desires which are the basis of our temptations come from within us (Mk. 7:15-23), from within our human nature (James 1:13-15). It was necessary, therefore, that Christ should be of human nature so that he could experience and overcome these temptations.

Heb. 2:14-18 puts all this in so many words.

"As the children (us) are partakers of flesh and blood (human nature), he (Christ) also himself likewise partook of the same (nature); that through death he might destroy...the devil...For truly he took not on him the nature of angels; but he took on him the (nature of the) seed of Abraham. Wherefore in all things it was appropriate that he be made like unto his brothers, that he might be a merciful and faithful high priest... to make reconciliation for the sins of the people. For in that he himself has suffered being tempted, he is able to help them that are tempted".

This passage places extraordinary emphasis upon the fact that Jesus had human nature: "He *also himself likewise*" partook of it (Heb. 2:14). This phrase uses three words all with the same meaning, just to drive the point home. He partook "of the *same*" nature; the record could have said 'he partook of IT too', but it stresses, "he partook of the *same*". Heb. 2:16 similarly labours the point that Christ did not have angels' nature, seeing that he was the seed of Abraham, who had come to bring salvation for the multitude of believers who would become Abraham's seed. Because of this, it was necessary for Christ to have human nature. In *every* way he had "to be made like unto his brothers" (Heb. 2:17) so that God could grant us forgiveness through Christ's sacrifice. To say that Jesus was not totally of human nature is therefore to be ignorant of the very basics of the good news of Christ.

Whenever baptised believers sin, they can come to God, confessing their sin in prayer through Christ (1 Jn. 1:9); God is aware that Christ was tempted to sin exactly as they are, but that he was perfect, overcoming that very temptation which they fail. Because of this, "God for Christ's sake" can forgive us (Eph. 4:32). It is therefore vital to appreciate how Christ was tempted just like us, and needed to have our nature for this to be possible. Heb. 2:14 clearly states that Christ had "flesh and blood" nature to make this possible. "God is spirit" (Jn. 4:24) by nature and as "spirit" He does not have flesh and blood. Christ having "flesh" nature means that in no way did he have God's nature during his mortal life.

Previous attempts by men to keep God's word, i.e. to overcome totally temptation, had all failed. Therefore "God sending his own Son in the likeness of sinful flesh, and by a sacrifice for sin, condemned sin, in the flesh" (Rom. 8:3).

"The wages of sin is death". To escape this predicament, man needed outside help. By himself he is incapable of perfection; it was and is not possible for us as fleshly creatures to redeem the flesh. God therefore intervened and gave us His own Son, who experienced our "sinful flesh", with all the temptation to sin which we have. Unlike every other man, Christ overcame every temptation, although he had the possibility of failure and sinning just as much as we do. Rom. 8:3 describes Christ's human nature as "sinful flesh". A few verses earlier, Paul spoke of how in the flesh "dwells no good thing", and how the flesh naturally militates against obedience to God (Rom. 7:18-23). In this context it is all the more marvellous to read that Christ had "sinful flesh" in Rom. 8:3. It was because of this, and his overcoming of that flesh, that we have a way of escape from our flesh; Jesus was intensely aware of the potential to sin within his own nature. He was once addressed as "Good master", with the implication that he was "good" and perfect by nature. He responded: "Why do you call me good? There is none good but one, that is, God" (Mk. 10:17,18). On another occasion, men started to testify of Christ's greatness due to a series of outstanding miracles which he had performed. Jesus did not capitalise on this "because he knew all, and needed not that any should testify of man: for he knew what was in man" (Jn. 2:23-25, Greek text). Because of his great knowledge of human nature ("he knew *all*" about this), Christ did not want men to praise him personally in his own right, he was aware of his own nature.

All this can seem almost impossible to believe; that a man with our weak nature could in fact be sinless by character. It requires less faith to believe that 'Jesus was God' and was therefore perfect. Hence the attraction of this false doctrine. Those who knew the half-sisters of Jesus in first century Palestine felt the same: "...his sisters, are they not all with us? Whence then has this man these things? And they were offended in him" (Mt. 13:56,57). And countless others have likewise stumbled in this way.

8.4   The Humanity Of Jesus

The Gospel records provide many examples of how completely Jesus had human nature. It is recorded that he was weary, and had to sit down to drink from a well (Jn 4:6). "Jesus wept" at the death of Lazarus (Jn. 11:35). Most supremely, the record of his final sufferings should be proof enough of his humanity: "Now is my soul troubled", he admitted as he prayed for God to save him from having to go through with his death on the cross (Jn. 12:27). He "prayed, saying, O my Father, if it be possible, let this cup (of suffering and death) pass from me; nevertheless not as I will, but as you will" (Mt. 26:39). This indicates that at times Christ's will / desires were different from those of God.

However, during his whole life Christ always submitted his own will to that of God in preparation for this final trial of the cross. "I can of mine own self do nothing: as I hear, I judge: and my judgment is just; because I seek not mine own will, but the will of the Father which has sent me" (Jn. 5:30). This difference between Christ's will and that of God is proof enough that Jesus was not God.

Throughout our lives we are expected to grow in our knowledge of God, learning from the trials which we experience in life. In this, Jesus was our great example. He did not have complete knowledge of God poured into him any more than we have. From childhood "Jesus increased in wisdom and stature (i.e. spiritual maturity, cp. Eph. 4:13), and in favour with God and man" (Lk. 2:52). "The child grew, and became strong in spirit" (Lk. 2:40). These two verses portray Christ's physical growth as parallel to his spiritual development; the growth process occurred in him both naturally and spiritually. If "The Son is God", as the Athanasian Creed states concerning the 'Trinity', this would not have been possible. Even at the end of his life, Christ admitted that he did not know the exact time of his second coming, although the Father did (Mk. 13:32). He asked questions of the teachers of the Law at age 12, eager to learn; and often He spoke of what He had *learnt* and *been taught* by His Father.

Obedience to God's will is something which we all have to learn over a period of time. Christ also had to go through this process of learning obedience to his Father, as any son has to. "Though he were a Son, yet learned he obedience (i.e. obedience to God) by the things which he suffered; and being *made* perfect (i.e. spiritually mature), he became the author of eternal salvation" as a result of his completed and total spiritual growth (Heb. 5:8,9). Phil. 2:7,8 records this same process of spiritual growth in Jesus, culminating in his death on the cross. He "*made* himself of no reputation, and *took upon him* the form (demeanour) of a servant...he *humbled himself* and *became* obedient unto...the death of the cross." The language used here illustrates how Jesus consciously grew spiritually, humbling himself completely, so that finally he "*became* obedient" to God's desire that he should die on the cross. Thus he was "*made* perfect" by the way he accepted his suffering.

It is evident from this that Jesus had to make a conscious, personal effort to be righteous; in no way was he automatically made so by God, which would have resulted in him being a mere puppet. Jesus truly loved us, and gave his life on the cross from this motive. The constant emphasis upon the love of Christ for us would be hollow if God compelled him to die on the cross (Eph. 5:2,25; Rev. 1:5; Gal. 2:20). If Jesus was God, then he would have had no option but to be perfect and then die on the cross. That Jesus *did* have these options, enables us to appreciate his love, and to form a personal relationship with him.

It was because of Christ's willingness to give his life voluntarily that God was so delighted with him: "Therefore does my Father love me, because I lay down my life...No man takes it from me, but I lay it down of myself" (Jn. 10:17,18). That God was so pleased with Christ's willing obedience is hard to understand if Jesus was God, living out a life in human form as some kind of tokenistic association with sinful man (Mt. 3:17; 12:18; 17:5). These records of the Father's delight in the Son's obedience, is proof enough that Christ had the possibility of disobedience, but consciously chose to be obedient.

CHRIST'S NEED OF SALVATION

Because of his human nature, Jesus was mortal as we are. In view of this, Jesus needed to be saved from death by God. Intensely recognising this, Jesus "offered up prayers and supplications with strong crying and tears unto him (God) that was able to save him from death, and was heard for his piety" (Heb. 5:7 A.V. mg.). The fact that Christ had to plead with God to save him from death rules out any possibility of him being God in person. After Christ's resurrection, death had "*no more* dominion over him" (Rom. 6:9), implying that beforehand it did.

Many of the Psalms are prophetic of Jesus; when some verses from a Psalm are quoted about Christ in the New Testament, it is reasonable to assume that many of the other verses in the Psalm are about him too. There are a number of occasions where Christ's need for salvation by God is emphasised.

- **Ps. 91:11,12** is quoted about Jesus in Mt. 4:6. Ps. 91:16 prophesies how God would give Jesus salvation: "With long life (i.e. eternal life) will I satisfy him, and shew him my salvation." Ps. 69:21 refers to Christ's crucifixion (Mt. 27:34); the whole Psalm describes Christ's thoughts on the cross: "Save me, O God...Draw nigh unto my soul, and redeem it...Let your salvation, O God, set me up on high" (vs. 1,18,29).

- **Ps. 89** is a commentary upon God's promise to David concerning Christ. Concerning Jesus, Ps. 89:26 prophesies: "He shall cry unto me (God), You are my father, my God, and the rock of my *salvation.*"

- Christ's prayers to God for salvation were heard; he was heard because of his personal spirituality, not because of his place in a 'trinity' (Heb. 5:7). That *God* resurrected Jesus and glorified him with immortality is a major New Testament theme.

- "*God*...raised up Jesus...Him has *God* exalted with his right hand to be a Prince and a Saviour" (Acts 5:30,31).

- "*God*...has glorified his Son Jesus...whom *God* has raised from the dead" (Acts 3:13,15).

- "This Jesus has *God* raised up" (Acts 2:24,32,33).

- Jesus himself recognised all this when he asked *God* to glorify him (Jn. 17:5 cp. 13:32; 8:54).

If Jesus was God Himself, then all this emphasis would be out of place, seeing that God cannot die. Jesus would not have needed saving if he were God. That it was God who exalted Jesus demonstrates God's superiority over him, and the separateness of God and Jesus. In no way could Christ have been "very and eternal God (with) two...natures...Godhead and manhood", as the first of the 39 Articles of the Church of England states. By the very meaning of the word, a being can only have one nature. We submit that the evidence is overwhelming that Christ was of our human nature.

8.5 The Relationship Of God With Jesus

Considering how God resurrected Jesus leads us on to think of the relationship between God and Jesus. If they are "co-equal...co-eternal", as the trinity doctrine states, then we would expect their relationship to be that of equals. We have already seen ample evidence that this is not the case. The relationship between God and Christ is similar to that between husband and wife: "The head of every man is Christ; and the head of the woman is the man; and the head of Christ is God" (1 Cor. 11:3). As the husband is the head of the wife, so God is the head of Christ, although they have the same unity of purpose as should exist between husband and wife. Thus "Christ is God's" (1 Cor. 3:23), as the wife belongs to the husband.

God the Father is often stated to be Christ's God. The fact that God is described as "the God and Father of our Lord Jesus Christ" (1 Pet. 1:3; Eph. 1:17) even after Christ's ascension to heaven, shows that this is *now* their relationship, as it was during Christ's mortal life. It is sometimes argued by trinitarians that Christ is only spoken of as less than God during his life on earth. The New Testament letters were written some years after Christ ascended to heaven, yet still God is spoken of as Christ's God and Father. Jesus still treats the Father as his God.

Revelation, the last book of the New Testament, was written many years after Christ's glorification and ascension, yet it speaks of God as "his (Christ's) God and Father" (Rev. 1:6 R.V.). In this book, the resurrected and glorified Christ gave messages to the believers. He speaks of "the temple of my God...the name of my God...the city of my God" (Rev. 3:12). This proves that Jesus even now thinks of the Father as his God - and therefore he (Jesus) is not God.

During his mortal life, Jesus related to his Father in a similar way. He spoke of ascending "unto my Father, and your Father; and to my God, and your God" (Jn. 20:17). On the cross, Jesus displayed his humanity to the full: "My God, my God, why have you forsaken me?" (Mt. 27:46). Such words are impossible to understand if spoken by God Himself. The very fact that Jesus prayed to God "with strong crying and tears" in itself indicates the true nature of their relationship (Heb. 5:7; Lk. 6:12). God evidently cannot pray to Himself. Even now, Christ prays to God on our behalf (Rom. 8:26,27 N.I.V. cp. 2 Cor. 3:18 R.V. mg.).

Belief In Practice 14:

The Real Christ

Non-trinitarians understand, quite correctly, that Jesus saved the world on account of being human- for all His Lordship and spiritual unity with the Father. If He had been of any other nature, salvation would not have been possible through Him. He in all ways is our pattern. It is our humanity that enables us to go into this world with a credible, convincing and saving message. We have to be enough of a man himself in order to save a man. We are not asking our hearers to be super-human. The way senior churchmen seem to lack a genuine, complete humanity has led so many to conclude that because they cannot rise up to such apparently austere and white-faced levels, therefore Christianity for them is not an authentically human possibility. Our message is tied to *us* as human people, just as the message of Jesus *was*

Him, the real, human Jesus. The word was made flesh in Him as it must be in us. This is why nowhere in the Gospels is Jesus described with a long list of virtues- His actions and relations to others are what are presented, and it is from them that we ourselves feel and perceive His righteousness. The teachings of Marxism, e.g., can be separated from Marx as a man. You can accept Marxism without ever having read a biography of Karl Marx. But real Christianity is tied in to the person of the real Christ. The biographies of Jesus which open the New Testament are in essence a précis of the Gospel of Jesus. His life was and is His message. We are to follow *Him*. This is His repeated teaching. A Marxist follows the ideas of Marx, not merely his personality. But a Christian follows Christ as a person, not just His abstract ideas.

If the message of Jesus is defined by us merely as ideas and principles, then we will inevitably find that ideas and principles lack the turbulence of real life- they are abstract. The principles of Bible Truth will be found to be colourless and remote from reality- unless they are tied in to the real, concrete person of Jesus. God forbid that our faith has given us just a bunch of ideas. The principles of the Truth, every doctrine of the Truth, is lived out in Jesus- and it is this fact, this image of Him, which appeals to us as live, passionate, flesh and blood beings. A person cannot be reduced to a formula. It is a living figure and not just dry theories that actually *draws* people, and in that sense is "attractive". The person of Jesus, as the person of each of us in Him, makes the ideas, the doctrines, the principles, real and visible; He "embodies" them. It is only a concrete, real person who can be felt to call and appeal to people. What I am saying is that if we present the principles of the Truth as they are in Jesus, then this will be far more powerful in its appeal than simply presenting dry theories. "The truth as it is in Jesus" is a Biblical phrase- surely saying that the doctrines of the one Faith are lived out in this Man. Because of this, the person hearing the Gospel will feel summoned, appealed to, called, by a *person*- the risen Jesus. And then later on in the life of the convert, it will become apparent to him or her that this same Jesus, by reason of His very person, makes demands, challenges, invitations to them, to yet greater commitment. And only a real, living person can be *encouraging* in life. Principles as mere abstractions cannot encourage much of themselves.

Jesus is our representative- a distinctive Bible doctrine. We are counted as being in Him. This means that His life is counted as being our life- and only because He was human and we now are human can this become true. The wonder of this is that so many people have acquired a new personal quality through their association with the risen Jesus- for all their human failures, humiliations, setbacks. No longer is it so important for them to ask 'Who am I? What have I achieved in this dumb life?'. Rather it is all important that we are in fact in Christ, and sharing in *His* life and being. Life has become so achievement and efficiency orientated that many of us feel failures. Only by achievement, it seems, can we justify ourselves in society. We have become caught up in a machine of life that robs us of our humanity. Our initiative, spontaneity, autonomy, our essential freedom- is lost. Yet if we are in Christ, secure in Him, part of His supreme personality, then our lives are totally different. We are no longer ashamed of our humanity. We are affirmed for who we are by God Himself, justified by Him- for we are in Christ. This is the real meaning, the wonderful implication, of being truly 'brethren-in-Christ'.

By losing our life, we gain it. But the life we gain is the life of Jesus. And therefore life has meaning and purpose, not only in successes but also in failures. Our lives then make sense; for we have and live the *true* life, even if we are destroyed by opponents and deserted by friends; if we supported the wrong side and came to grief; if our achievements slacken and are overtaken by others; if we are no use any more to anyone. The bankrupt businessman, the utterly lonely divorcee, the overthrown and forgotten politician, the unemployed middle aged man, the aged prostitute or criminal dying in prison...all these, even though their persons and lives are no longer recognized by this world, are all the same joyfully, gleefully, recognized by Him with whom there is no respect of persons; for they are in His beloved Son.

GENUINE HUMANITY

I remember the cold, Russian winter's day when it finally burst upon me that the Lord Jesus really was human. Because He was genuinely human, so genuinely so, I suddenly started thinking of all sorts of things which must have been true about Him, which I'd never dared think before. And in this, I believe I went up a level in knowing Him. He was the genuine product of the pregnancy process. He had all the pre-history of Mary in his genes. He had a genetic structure. He had a unique fingerprint, just as I have. He must have been either left-hand or right-handed (or ambidextrous!). Belonged to a particular blood group. Fitted into one psychological type more than another. He forgot things at times, didn't understand absolutely everything (e.g. the date of His return, or the mystery of spiritual growth, Mk. 4:27), made a mistake when working as a carpenter, cut His finger. But He was never frustrated with Himself; He was happy being human, comfortable with His humanity. And as I walked through that long Moscow subway from Rizhskaya Metro to Rizhsky Vokzal, the thoughts were coming thick and fast. Why did He look on the ground when the woman [presumably naked] caught in the act of adultery was brought before Him? Was it not perhaps from sheer embarrassment and male awkwardness? Why not ask these questions? If He was truly human, sexuality is at the core of personhood. He would have known sexuality, responding to stimuli in a natural heterosexual manner, "yet without sin". He was not a cardboard Christ, a sexless Jesus. He shared the same unconscious drives and libido which we do, with a temper, anxiety and 'anxious fear of death' (Heb. 5:7) as strong as ours. He was a real man, not free from the inner conflict, effort, temptation and doubt which are part of our human condition. No way can I subscribe to a Trinitarian position that "there was [not] even an infinitely small element of struggle involved" when the Lord faced temptation. He was tempted just as we are- and temptation surely involves feeling the pull of evil, and having part of you that feels it to be more attractive than the good.

I suspect I can see through that huge gap between writer and reader, to sense your discomfort and alarm, even anger, that I should talk about the Lord Jesus in such human terms. I can imagine the splutter and misunderstanding which will greet these suggestions. I am not seeking to diminish in any way from the Lord's greatness. I'm seeking to bring out His greatness; that there, in this genuinely human person, there was God manifest in flesh. The revulsion of some at what I'm saying is to me just another articulation of our basic dis-ease when faced with the fact the Lord Jesus really was our representative. I believe that in all of us, there's a desire to set some sort of break between our own humanity, and that of Jesus. But if He wasn't really like us, then I see the whole 'Christ-thing' as having little cash value in our world that seeks so desperately for authenticity and human salvation. The human, Son of God Jesus whom we preach is actually very attractive to people. There's something very compelling about a perfect hero, who nevertheless has a weak human side. You can see this expressed in novels and fine art very often. If He were really like us, then this demands an awful lot of us. It rids us of so many excuses for our unspirituality. And this, I'm bold enough to say, is likely the psychological reason for the growth of the Jesus=God ideology, and the 'trinity' concept. The idea of a personally pre-existent Jesus likewise arose out of the same psychological bind. The Jews wanted a Messiah whose origins they wouldn't know (Jn. 7:27), some inaccessible heavenly figure, of which their writings frequently speak- and when faced with the very human Jesus, whose mother and brothers they knew, they couldn't cope with it. I suggest those Jews had the same basic mindset as those who believe in a personal pre-existence of the Lord. The trinity and pre-existence doctrines place a respectable gap between us and the Son of God. His person and example aren't so much of an imperative to us, because He was God and not man. But if this perfect man was indeed one of us, a man amongst men, with our very same flesh, blood, sperm and plasma... we start to feel uncomfortable. It's perhaps why so many of us find prolonged contemplation of His crucifixion- where He was at His most naked and most human- something we find distinctly uncomfortable, and impossible to deeply sustain for long. But only if we properly have in balance the awesome reality of Christ's humanity, can we understand how one man's death 2,000 years ago can radically alter our lives today. We make excuses for ourselves: our parents were imperfect, society around us is so sinful. But the Lord Jesus was perfect- and dear Mary did her best, but all the same failed to give Him a perfect upbringing; she wasn't a perfect mother; and He didn't live in a perfect environment. And yet, He was perfect. And bids us quit our excuses and follow Him.

According to the Talmud, Mary was a hairdresser [*Shabbath* 104b], whose husband left her with the children because he thought she'd had an affair with a Roman soldier. True or not, she was all the same an ordinary woman, living a poor life in a tough time in a backward land. And the holy, harmless, undefiled Son of God and Son of Man... was, let's say, the son of a divorcee hairdresser from a dirt poor, peripheral village, got a job working construction when He was still a teenager. There's a wonder in all this. And an endless challenge. For none of us can now blame our lack of spiritual endeavour upon a tough background, family dysfunction, hard times, bad environment. We can rise above it, because in Him we are a new creation, the old has passed away, and in Him, all things have become new (2 Cor. 5:17). Precisely because He blazed the trail, blazed it out of all the limitations which normal human life appears to impress upon us, undeflected and undefeated by whatever distractions both His and our humanity placed in His path. And He's given us the power to follow Him.

He wasn't a God who came down to us and became human; rather is He the ordinary, very human guy who rose up to become the Man with the face of God, ascended the huge distance to Heaven, and received the very nature of God. It's actually the very opposite to what human theology has supposed, fearful as they were of what the pattern of this Man meant for them. The pre-existent view of Jesus makes Him some kind of Divine comet which came to earth, very briefly, and then sped off again, to return at the second coming. Instead we see a man from amongst men, arising to Divine status, and opening a way for us His brethren to share His victory; and coming back to establish His eternal Kingdom with us on this earth, His earth, where He came from and had His human roots. Take a passage must beloved of Trinitarians, Phil. 2. We read that Jesus was found (*heuretheis*) in fashion (*schemati*) as a man, and He humiliated Himself (*tapeinoseos*), and thereby was exalted. But in the next chapter, Paul speaks of *himself* in that very language. He speaks of how he, too, would be "found" (*heuretho*) conformed to the example of Jesus in His death, and would have his body of humiliation (*tapeinoseos*) changed into one like that of Jesus, "the body of his glory". We aren't asked to follow the pattern or *schema* of a supposed incarnation of a God as man. We're asked to follow in the path of the Lord Jesus, the Son of man, in His path to glory. Repeatedly, we are promised that *His* glory is what we will ultimately share, at the end of our path of humiliation and sharing in His cross (Rom. 8:17; 2 Cor. 3:18; Jn. 17:22,24).

THE CHALLENGE OF CHRIST'S HUMANITY

The undoubted need for doctrinal truth about the nature of Jesus can so easily lead us to overlooking the need for obedience to His most practical teaching. In this sense we need "to rescue Jesus from Christianity". We need to reconstruct in our own minds the person of Jesus and practical teaching of Jesus which so perfectly reflected His own life, free from the theology and creeds which have so often surrounded Him. As a result of this, our preaching of Christ so often ends up stressing those elements which the unbeliever or misbeliever finds most difficult to accept, rather than focusing on the Lord's humanity and His practical teachings, which they are more likely to accept because as humans they have a natural affinity with them. The Lord Jesus was not merely human, as a theologically correct statement. He passionately entered into human life to its' fullest extent.

There is an incredible challenge in the fact that the Lord Jesus had human nature and yet never sinned. He rose above sin in all its forms, and yet was absolutely human. It seems to me that many Christians feel that their calling is to rise above both sin, and also their own human nature. And this results in their belief that spirituality is in fact a denial of their humanity. In extreme forms, we have the white faced nun who has been led to believe that being spiritual equals being white faced, passionless, and somehow superhuman. In a more common expression of the same problem, there are many elders who believe it to be fatal to show any emotional conviction about anything, no chinks in their armour, no admission of their own human limitations or understanding. For this reason I see a similarity between the 'lives of the saints' as recorded in Catholic and Orthodox writings (replete with white faces and large holy eyes, hands ever folded in prayer, never making a slip)- and the glossy biographies of Evangelical leaders which jump out at you from the shelves of Protestant bookstores. They too, apparently, never set a foot wrong, but progressed from unlikely glory to unlikely glory. All this arises from an over-emphasis upon the Divine rather than the human side of the Lord Jesus. The character of the Lord Jesus shows us what it's like to be both human and sinless. It has been truly commented that "if we believe in the fact of his humanity, we must affirm our own". If we seek to rise above being human, we are aiming for something that doesn't exist. The Lord Jesus wasn't and isn't 'superhuman'; He was and is the image of God stamped upon humanity, and in this sense the New Testament still calls Him a "man" even now. We need not take false guilt about being human. We should be happy with who we are, made in the image of God.

Digression 13: How The Real Christ Was Lost

I feel I am obligated yet again to make the point that the real, genuinely human Son of God whom we have reconstructed from the pages of Scripture is at variance with the Trinitarian perspective. The trinity grew out of Gnosticism, which taught that life comes by leaving the world and the flesh. But John's Gospel especially emphasizes how the true life was and is revealed through the very flesh, the very worldly and human life, of the Lord

Jesus. True Christianity has correctly rejected the trinity and defined a Biblically correct view of the atonement. But we need to make something of this in practice; we must use it as a basis upon which to meet the real, personal Christ.

In the 2nd century, the urgent, compelling, radical, repentance-demanding Jesus was replaced by mere theology, by abstracting Him into effectively nothing, burying the real Jesus beneath theology and fiercely debated human definitions. And we can in essence make the same mistake. And I might add, it was this turning of Jesus into a mystical theological 'God' which made Him so unacceptable to the Jews. The preaching of the real, human Jesus to them ought to be the basis of our preaching. It must be realized that the growing pressure to make Jesus 'God' was matched by a growing anti-Judaism in the church. Some of the major proponents of the Trinitarian idea were raving anti-Judaists such as Chrysostom, Jerome and Luther. It was men like Adolf Hitler who pushed the idea that Jesus was not really a Jew, suggesting that the humanity of Jesus should be de-emphasized and the divinity stressed, so that the guilt of the Jews appeared the greater [1]. The point is, we have been greatly blessed with being able to return to the original, Biblical understanding of Jesus, which worldly theology and politics has clouded over for so many millions. But we must use this to build a Christ-centred life.

The humanity of Jesus was more radical for the early Christians than we perhaps realize. Against the first century background it must be remembered that it was felt impossible for God or His representative to be frightened, shocked, naked, degraded. And yet the Lord Jesus was all this, and is portrayed in the Gospels in this way. To believe that this Man was Son of God, and to be worshipped as God, was really hard for the first century mind; just as hard as it is for us today. It's not surprising that desperate theories arose to 'get around' the problem of the Lord's humanity.

We need to keep earnestly asking ourselves: 'Do I know Jesus Christ?'. The answers that come back to us within our minds may have orthodoxy ['I know He wasn't God, He had human nature....']. But do they have integrity, and the gripping practical significance which they should have for us? Too much emphasis, in my view, has been placed upon this word 'nature'. We're interested in knowing the essence of Jesus as a person, who He was in the very core of His manhood and personality. Not in theological debate about semantics. Athanasius, father of the Athanasian Creed that declared the 'trinity', claimed that "Christ... did not weigh two choices, preferring the one and rejecting another". This is total contrast to the real Christ whom we meet in the pages of the New Testament- assailed by temptation, sweating large concentrated blobs of moisture in that struggle, and coming through triumphant.

Trinitarians have ended up making ridiculous statements because they've separated the 'nature' of Jesus from the person of Jesus. "He permitted his own flesh to weep, although it was in its nature tearless and incapable of grief" (*Cyril of Alexandria, Commentary in John,* 7). "He felt pain for us, but not with our senses; he was found in fashion as a man, with a body which could feel pain, but his nature could not feel pain" (Hilary). "In the complete and perfect nature of very man, very God was born" (Leo, *Tome* 5). This is all ridiculous- because these theologians are talking about a nature as if it's somehow separate from Jesus as a person. And we non-trinitarians need to be careful we don't make the same mistake. Forget the theological terms, the talk about 'wearing a nature'; but focus upon the person of Jesus. The terms end up distracting people from focus upon Him as a person; and it's that focus which is the essence of true , Jesus-centred spirituality. The meaning and victory of the Lord Jesus depend upon far more than simply 'nature'. So much of the 'trinity' debate has totally missed this point. It was His personality, *Him,* not the words we use to define 'nature', that is so powerful.

Wading through all the empty, passionless theology about Jesus, it becomes apparent that the first error was to draw a distinction between the historical Jesus, i.e. the actual person who walked around Galilee, and what was known as "the post-Easter Jesus", "the Jesus of faith", the "kerygmatic [i.e. 'proclaimed'] Christ", i.e. the image of Jesus which was proclaimed by the church, and in which one was supposed to place their faith. Here we must give full weight to the Biblical statement that Jesus is the same yesterday, today and forever. Who He was then is essentially who He is now, and who He ever will be. This approach cuts right through all the waffle about the trinity, the countless councils of churches and churchmen. Who Jesus was then, in the essence of His teaching and personality, is who He is now. We place our faith in the same basic person as did the brave men and women who first followed Him around the paths over the Galilean hills and the uneven streets of Jerusalem, Capernaum and Bethany. Yes, His nature has now been changed; He is immortal. But the same basic person. The image we have of Him is that faithfully portrayed by the first apostles; and not that created by centuries and layers of later theological reflection. We place our faith in the Man who really was and is, not in a Jesus created by men who exists nowhere but in their own minds and theologies. This, perhaps above all, is the reason I am not a trinitarian; and why I think it's so important not to be.

Digression 14: The Divine Side Of Jesus

In many discussions with trinitarians, I came to observe how very often, a verse I would quote supporting the humanity of Jesus would be found very near passages which speak of His Divine side. For example, most 'proof texts' for both the 'Jesus=God' position and the 'Jesus was human' position-are all from the same Gospel of John. Instead of just trading proof texts, e.g. 'I and my father are one' versus 'the Father is greater than I', we need to understand them as speaking of one and the same Jesus. So many 'debates' about the nature of Jesus miss this point; the sheer wonder of this man, this more than man, was that He was so genuinely human, and yet perfectly manifested God. This was and is the compelling wonder of this Man. These two aspects of the Lord, the exaltation and the humanity, are spoken of together in the Old Testament too. A classic example would be Ps. 45:6,7: "Your throne, O God, is for ever [this is quoted in the New Testament about Jesus]...God, your God, has anointed you [made you Christ]".

The placing side by side of the Lord's humanity with His exaltation is what is so gripping about Bible teaching about Him. And it's what is so hard for people to accept, because it demands so much faith in a man, that He could be really so God-like. The juxtaposition [placing side by side] of ideas is seen in Hebrews so powerfully. Here alone in the New Testament is His simple, human name "Jesus" used so baldly- not 'Jesus Christ', 'the Lord Jesus', just plain 'Jesus' (Heb. 2:9; 3:1; 4:14; 6:20; 7:22; 10:19; 12:2,24; 13:12). And yet it's Hebrews that emphasizes how He can be called 'God', and is the full and express image of God Himself. I observe that in each of the ten places where Hebrews uses the name 'Jesus', it is as it were used as a climax of adoration and respect. For example: "... whither the forerunner is for us entered, even Jesus" (Heb. 6:20). "But you are come unto... unto... to... to... to... to... and to Jesus the mediator" (Heb. 12:22-24). The bald title 'Jesus', one of the most common male names in first century Palestine, as common as Dave or Steve or John in the UK today, speaking as it did of the Lord's utter humanity, is therefore used as a climax of honour for Him. The honour due to Him is exactly due to the fact of His humanity. John's Gospel uses exalted language to describe the person of Jesus- but actually, if one looks out for it, John uses the very same terms about all of humanity. Here are some examples:

ABOUT JESUS	ABOUT HUMANITY GENERALLY OR OTHER HUMAN BEINGS
Came into the world (9:39; 12:46; 16:28; 18:37)	1:9 [of "every man"]; 6:14. 'Came into the world' means 'to be born'

	in 16:21; 18:37
Sent from God (1:6; 3:28)	3:2,28; 8:29; 15:10
A man of God (9:16,33)	9:17,31
'What I saw in my Father's presence' (8:38)	The work of '*a man* who told you the truth as I heard it from God' (8:40)
God was His Father	8:41
He who has come from God (8:42)	8:47
The Father was in Him, and He was in the Father (10:37)	15:5-10; 17:21-23,26
Son of God (1:13)	All believers are 'the offspring of God Himself' (1:13; 1 Jn. 2:29-3:2,9; 4:7; 5:1-3,8)
Consecrated and sent into the world (17:17-19)	20:21
Jesus had to listen to the Father and be taught by Him (7:16; 8:26,28,40; 12:49; 14:10; 15:15; 17:8)	All God's children are the same (6:45)
Saw the Father (6:46)	The Jews should have been able to do this (5:37)
Not born of the flesh or will of a man, but the offspring of God Himself	True of all believers (1:13)

JUXTAPOSITION

This juxtaposition of the Lord's humanity and His exaltation is found all through Bible teaching about His death. It's been observed that the 'I am' sayings of Jesus, with their obvious allusion to the Divine Name, are in fact all found in contexts which speak of the subordination of Jesus to God. He was 'lifted up' in crucifixion and shame; and yet 'lifted up' in 'glory' in God's eyes through that act. We read in Is. 52:14 that His face was more marred, more brutally transmogrified, than that of any man. And yet reflecting upon 2 Cor. 4:4,6, we find that His face was the face of God; His glory was and is the Father's glory: "The glory of Christ, who is the image of God... the glory of God in the face of Jesus Christ". Who is the one who redeems His people? Isaiah calls him "the arm of the Lord": "to whom has *the arm of the Lord* been revealed?" (53:1; compare 52:10). Then he continues: "*He* grew up before Him like a tender shoot, and like a root out of dry ground" (v. 2). So, the *arm of the LORD* is a person -- a divine person! He is God's "right arm," His "right-hand Man"! He is also human: He grows up out of the earth like a root out of dry ground. The same sort of juxtaposition is to be found in the way the Lord healed the widow's son. He touched the coffin- so that the crowd would have gasped at how unclean Jesus was, and how He had identified Himself with the unclean to the point of Himself appearing unclean. It was surely shock that made the pallbearers stop in their tracks. But then the Lord raised the dead man- and the people perceived His greatness, convinced that in the person of Jesus "God has visited His people" (Lk. 7:14-16). His humanity and yet His greatness, His Divinity if you like, were artlessly juxtaposed together. Hence prophetic visions of the exalted Jesus in Daniel call Him "the Son of man".

Even after His resurrection, in His moment of glory and triumph, the Lord appeared in very ordinary working clothes, so that He appeared as a gardener. The disciples who met Him on the Emmaus road asked whether He 'lived alone' and therefore was ignorant of the news of the city about the death of Jesus (Lk. 24:18 RV). The only people who lived alone, outside of the extended family, were drop outs or weirdos. It was almost a rude thing for them to ask a stranger. The fact was, the Lord appeared so very ordinary, even like a lower class social outcast type. And this was the exalted Son of God. We gasp at His humility, but also at His earnest passion to remind His followers of their common bond with Him, even in His exaltation.

The Lord Jesus often stressed that He was the only way to the Father; that only through knowing and seeing / perceiving Him can men come to know God. And yet in Jn. 6:45 He puts it the other way around: "Every man therefore that hath heard, and hath learned of the Father, cometh unto me". And He says that only the Father can bring men to the Son (Jn. 6:44). Yet it is equally true that only the Son of God can lead men to God the Father. In this we see something exquisitely beautiful about these two persons, if I may use that word about the Father and Son. The more we know the Son, the more we come to know the Father; and the more we know the Father, the more we know the Son. This is how close they are to each other. And yet they are quite evidently distinctly different persons. But like any father and son, getting to know one leads us to know more of the other, which in turn reveals yet more to us about the other, which leads to more insight again into the other... and so the wondrous spiral of knowing the Father and Son continues. If Father and Son were one and the same person, the surpassing beauty of this is lost and spoilt and becomes impossible. The experience of any true Christian, one who has come to 'see' and know the

Father and Son, will bear out this truth. Which is why correct understanding about their nature and relationship is vital to knowing them. The wonder of it all is that the Son didn't automatically reflect the Father to us, as if He were just a piece of theological machinery; He made a supreme effort to do so, culminating in the cross. He explains that He didn't do *His* will, but that of the Father; He didn't do the works *He* wanted to do, but those which the Father wanted. He had many things to say and judge of the Jewish world, He could have given them 'a piece of His mind', but instead He commented: *"But*... I speak to the world those things which I have heard of [the Father]" (Jn. 8:26). I submit that this sort of language is impossible to adequately understand within the trinitarian paradigm. Yet the wonder of it all goes yet further. The Father is spoken of as 'getting to know' [note aorist tense] the Son, as the Son gets to know the Father; and the same verb form is used about the Good Shepherd 'getting to know' us His sheep. This wonderful, dynamic family relationship is what "the fellowship of the Holy Spirit", true walking and living with the Father and Son, is all about. It is into this family and wonderful nexus of relationships that trinitarians apparently choose not to enter.

THE PATH TO GLORY

The Lord's path to glory culminated in the Father 'making known unto Him the ways of life' (Acts 2:28). That statement, incidentally, is a major nail in the coffin of trinitarianism. But more significantly for us personally, in this the Lord was our pattern, who likewise are walking in the way to life (Mt. 7:14), seeking to 'know' the life eternal (Jn. 17:3). In being our realistic role model in this, we can comment with John: "The Son of God is come, and has given us an understanding, that we may know… the eternal life" (1 Jn. 5:20).

The New Testament implies that to accept Jesus as Lord is the essence of the Gospel. In this sense, whoever confesses Jesus as Lord will be saved (Rom. 10:9, 13)- but to confess Jesus as Lord means a radical surrender of every part of our lives. It doesn't merely refer to mouthing the words " Jesus is Lord" . Paul found that every hour of his life, he was motivated to endure by Christ's resurrection (1 Cor. 15:30); this was how deep was his practical awareness of the power of that most basic fact.

HOPE

The Lord's resurrection is the basis for ours. Despite the emotion and hardness of death itself, our belief in resurrection is rooted in our faith that our Lord died and rose. When comforting those who had lost loved ones in the Lord, Paul doesn't simply remind them of the doctrine of the resurrection at the Lord's coming. His focus instead is on the fact that " if we believe that Jesus died and rose again, even so them also which sleep in Jesus will God bring with him" (1 Thess. 4:14). The reality of the resurrection must mean something to us in the times of death which we face in life. Jesus and the New Testament writers seem to me to have a startling disregard of death. Paul says that Jesus has " abolished death" (2 Tim. 1:10) in that death as the world has to face it, final and total death, does not happen to us in Christ. This is why those who truly follow the Lord will never taste of death (Jn. 8:51,52); everyone who lives and believes in Him shall never die (Jn. 11:26). It really is but a sleep. I know the hard reality of the loss still hurts, still registers. But in the end, because He abolished death in Himself, so has He done already for all those in Him.

LIVING FOR OTHERS

The fact Jesus is Lord has vital practical import for us. In Rom. 14:7-9, Paul speaks of the need not to live unto ourselves, but to rather live in a way which is sensitive to the conscience and needs of others. Why? " For to this end Christ both died, and rose, and revived, that He [Jesus] might be Lord both of the dead and living" . Because He is our Lord we therefore don't live for ourselves, but for Christ our Lord and all those in Him. Jesus becomes an authority figure for us, because He is indeed Lord and Christ. This may sound obvious, but the blessings and implications of it become more apparent when we reflect how haphazard are the lives of those who have no such personal authority in their experience. They are so aimless, so easily distracted, so self-centred, because they have no sense of obligation to a Lord and Master as we have. Personal feelings of like and dislike are the only authority they have to recognize, and thus their hedonism is so haphazard in its nature. Yet for those who truly accept Jesus as personal Lord, there is a structure and purpose and order in human life which will essentially be continued in the eternal ages of the Kingdom.

QUITTING THE LIFE OF THE FLESH

When Paul exalts that Christ is King of Kings and Lord of Lords, dwelling in light which no man can approach unto, this isn't just some literary flourish. It is embedded within a context of telling the believers to quit materialism, indeed to flee from its snare. 1 Tim. 6:6-14 concern this; and then there is the passage about Christ's exaltation (:15,16), and then a continued plea to share riches rather than build them up (:17-19). Because He is Lord of all, we should quit our materialism and sense of self-ownership. For we are His, and all we have is for His service too. And the principle of His being Lord affects every aspect of our spirituality. Dennis Gillet truly observed: " Mastery is gained by crowning the Master as Lord and King" [1]. And Peter likewise says that those who reject the Lordship of Jesus (2 Pet. 2:10) indulge in sexual immorality. The height of His Lordship ought to mean self-control in our lives; because He, rather than our own passions, is the Lord and Master of our soul. Joseph's amazing exaltation in Egypt was clearly typical of that of the Lord after His resurrection. As a result of Joseph's exaltation, no man could lift up even his hand or foot except within the sphere of Joseph's power. And the Lord's exaltation has the same effect and imperative over us. Jude 4 parallels rejecting Jesus as Master and Lord with rejecting His moral demands. If He truly is Lord and Master, we simply won't live the immoral life which Jude criticizes.

HUMILITY

Because Jesus is Lord and Master, and because He is our representative in every way, therefore all that He did and was becomes an imperative for us to follow. Thus: "If I then, your Lord and Master, have washed your feet; you also ought to wash one another's feet" (Jn. 13:13,14). They called Him "Lord and Master", but *wouldn't* wash each other's feet. Like us so often, they had the right doctrinal knowledge, but it meant nothing to them in practice. To know Him as Lord is to wash each other's feet, naked but for a loincloth, with all the subtle anticipations of the cross which there are in this incident. "Wherefore [because of the exaltation of Jesus] [be obedient and] work out your own salvation with fear and trembling [i.e. in humility]" (Phil. 2:12). And so it is with appreciating God's greatness; the deeper our realization of it, the higher our response.

James 2:1 (Gk.) gives the Lord Jesus the title of "the glory" (as also in Lk. 2:32; Eph. 1:17). And James makes the point that we cannot believe that Jesus is Lord, in the Lord Jesus as the Lord of glory and have respect of persons. This may seem a strange connection at first sight. But perhaps the sense is that if we see the *height* and surpassing extent of *His* glory, all others will pale into insignificance, and therefore we will be biased for or against nobody and nothing because of the way they are all as nothing before the brightness of the glory of the Lord we follow. The RVmg. makes the point clearer: "Do ye, in accepting persons, hold the faith of the Lord of glory?". This explains why when Paul sat down to write to ecclesias troubled with worldliness, immorality and false doctrine, he takes as his repeated opening theme the greatness and exaltation of the Lord Jesus.

There's one more especially noteworthy thing which the sheer *height* of the Lord's exaltation leads us to. " Wherefore God also has highly exalted Him...that at the name of Jesus every knee should bow...and that every tongue should confess that Jesus Christ is Lord...wherefore...work out your own salvation with fear and trembling" (Phil. 2:9-12). These words are alluding to Is. 45:23,24: "...unto me every knee shall bow, every tongue shall swear. Surely, shall one say, in the Lord have I righteousness and strength" . We all find humility difficult. But before the height of His exaltation, a height which came as a result of the depth of the degradation of the cross, we should bow our knees in an unfeigned humility and realization of our sinfulness, and thankful recognition of the fact that through Him we are counted righteous. We will be prostrated in the day of judgment before Him, and yet will be made to stand. We therefore ought not to judge our brother who will likewise be made to stand in that day- to his Master he stands or falls, not to us.

SEPARATION FROM THE WORLD

As with many aspects of doctrine, it is often difficult for us to appreciate how radically revolutionary they were in the first century context; and in essence they should lose none of their radicalness with us. "Christ is Lord" was a radical challenge to the common dogma that "Caesar is Lord". It hurt, it cost, to recognize Him as Lord. And so it should with us. Men and women died for this; and we likewise give our lives in response to that very same knowledge. There is a tendency, which the Lord Himself brought to our attention, of calling Him Lord but not doing what He says. To know Him as Lord in truth is axiomatically to be obedient to Him (Lk. 6:46). The reality of the Lordship of Jesus is used in Revelation (19:12, 16) to encourage the brethren to continue fearless in their witness despite persecution. Jesus is Lord of the kings of the earth; He has control over the world; therefore, no human power can harm us without His express permission and purpose. The exhortation of Ps. 110 is powerful: because Jesus is now seated at the Father's right hand, His people offer themselves as freewill offerings in this, the day of His power.

Col. 2:8,9 reasons that because in Christ dwells all the fullness of God, so far is He exalted, that we therefore should not follow *men*. A man or woman who is truly awed by the height of the Lord's exaltation simply will not allow themselves to get caught up in personality cults based around individuals, even if they are within the brotherhood.

FAITH

Faith is also inculcated by an appreciation of the height of His exaltation. He now has all power in Heaven and in earth, and this in itself should inspire us with faith in prayer and hope in His coming salvation. On the basis of passages like Ex. 4:7; Num. 12:10-15; 2 Kings 5:7,8, leprosy was regarded as a " stroke" only to be removed God. The leper of Mk. 1:40 lived with this understanding, and yet he saw in Jesus nothing less than God manifest. Inspired by the height of the position which he gave Jesus in his heart, he could ask him in faith for a cure: " If you will, *you can* [as only God was understood to be able to] make me clean" .

LOVE FOR JESUS

We believe Jesus rose and ascended. We believe Jesus is Lord. Having not seen Him, we love Him. Because He is not now physically with us, our connection with Him is not through our physical senses. It is, therefore, through our inward application of Biblical material to our minds and hearts. We read the Gospel records and epistles, we study the Law, seeking to reconstruct who He really was and is, with a verve which is generated by the simple reality of the fact that He is not physically with us. And as we do this over the years, we will have the actual sense of being confronted, claimed, taught, restored, upheld and empowered by the Jesus of the Gospels.

PREACHING HIM

Because Christ is Lord of all, we must preach Him to all, even if like Peter we would rather not preach to them. This was the motivational power and reality of Christ's universal Lordship for Peter (Acts 10:36). The same link between Christ's Lordship and witness is found in Phil. 2:10 and 1 Pet. 3:15 (which alludes Is. 8:13- Yahweh of Hosts, of many ones, becomes manifest now in the Lord Jesus). The ascended Christ was highly exalted and given the Name above every Name, so that for those who believed this, they would bow in service at the Name of Jesus. Peter preached in and about the name of Jesus- this is emphasized (Acts 2:31,38; 3:6,16; 4:10,12,17,18,30; 5:28,40,41; 10:43). The excellence of knowing Him and His character and the wonder of the exalted Name given on His ascension (Phil. 2:9; Rev. 3:12) lead Peter to witness. Because of His exaltation, we confess Jesus as Lord to men, as we later will to God at judgment (Phil. 2:9). According as we confess Him before men, so our judgment will reflect this. Lifting up Jesus as Lord is to be the basis of giving a witness to every man of the hope that lies within us (1 Pet. 3:15 RSV). The knowledge and experience of His exaltation can only be witnessed to; it can't be kept quiet. 3 Jn. 7 refers to how the great preaching commission was obeyed: "For his name's sake they went forth, taking nothing (material help) from the Gentiles" (Gentile believers). For the excellence of knowing His Name they went forth in witness, and moreover were generous spirited, not taking material help to enable this. The knowledge of the Name of itself should inspire to active service: for the sake of the Lord's Name the Ephesians laboured (Rev. 2:3).

Because "all power is given unto me...go *therefore* and teach all nations" (Mt. 28:18,19). The great preaching commission is therefore not so much a commandment as an inevitable corollary of the Lord's exaltation. We will not be able to sit passively in the knowledge of the universal extent of His authority / power. We will have to spread the knowledge of it to all.

The greatness of Christ, the simple fact Jesus is Lord, clearly influenced Mark's witness; he began his preachings of the Gospel (of which his Gospel is but a transcript) by quoting Isaiah's words about how a highway was to be prepared " for our God" and applying them to the Lord Jesus, whom he saw as God manifest in flesh. Appreciating the height of who Jesus was and is, clearly motivated his preaching. And it should ours too. This is why Paul in the face of every discouragement could preach that " there *is* another king, one Jesus" (Acts 17:7). This was the core of his message; not only that there *will be* a coming King in Jerusalem, but that there *is* right now a King at God's right hand, who demands our total allegiance. The Acts record associates the height of Jesus with a call to repentance too. This is the message of Is. 55:6-9- *because* God's thoughts are so far higher than ours, *therefore* call upon the Lord whilst He is near, and let the wicked forsake his way. Because the Father and Son who are so high above us morally and physically are willing to deal with us, *therefore* we ought to seize upon their grace and repent.

OBEDIENCE

If we truly know Jesus is Lord, in reality rather than merely in words, then we will actually do the will of the Father (Mt. 7:21,22). To call Jesus 'Lord' and not do anything actual and concrete in response means that our words are empty. It's as simple as that.

NOT BEING MATERIALISTIC

If Jesus is Lord, He owns all. Nothing that we have is our own. The Old Testament stressed that God's ownership of all precludes our own petty materialism, our manic desire to 'own'. Abraham refused to take " from a thread even to a shoelatchet" of what he could justifiable have had for himself; because Yahweh " the most high God [is] possessor of heaven and earth" (Gen. 14:22,23). But now, all that power has been bestowed by the Father upon the Son. Our allegiance to the Lord Jesus demands the same resignation of worldly acquisition as Abraham showed.

CONTROL OF OUR WORDS

Those who do not accept the Lordship of God [or of Jesus] will have no reason to control their words: " Who have said, With our tongue will we prevail; our lips are our own: who is lord over us?" (Ps. 12:4). But the opposite is true; a realization of the tightness of Christ's Lordship over us results in a control of our words, knowing that our tongue and lips are not our own but His.

STUDY 8: Questions

1. Does the Bible teach that God is a trinity?

2. List three differences between God and Jesus.

3. Jesus was different from us because:
   ☐ He never sinned
   ☐ He was God's own begotten son
   ☐ He could never have sinned
   ☐ He was automatically made righteous by God

4. In which of the following ways was Jesus similar to   God?
   ☐ He had God's nature in his life on earth
   ☐ He had a perfect character like God
   ☐ He knew as much as God
   ☐ He was directly equal to God

5. In which of the following ways was Jesus like us?
   ☐ He had all of our temptations and human experiences
   ☐ He sinned while a young child
   ☐ He needed salvation
   ☐ He had human nature

6. Which of the following statements are true?
   ☐ Jesus was of a perfect nature and perfect character
   ☐ Jesus was of sinful nature but perfect character
   ☐ Jesus was both very God and very man
   ☐ Jesus had the nature of Adam before Adam sinned

7. Was it possible for Jesus to sin?

STUDY 9
The Work Of Jesus

9.1   The Victory Of Jesus

The previous Study has demonstrated how the Lord Jesus had our human nature and was tempted to sin just like us. The difference between him and us is that he completely overcame sin; whilst having our *nature*, he always exhibited a perfect *character*. The wonder of this should endlessly inspire us as we increasingly appreciate it. There is repeated New Testament emphasis upon Christ's perfect character:-

- He was "in all points tempted as we are, yet without sin" (Heb. 4:15).
- He "knew no sin". "In Him there is no sin" (2 Cor. 5:21; 1 John 3:5).
- "Who committed no sin, nor was guile found in His mouth" (1 Peter 2:22).
- "Holy, harmless, undefiled, separate from sinners" (Heb. 7:26).

The Gospel records demonstrate how his fellow men recognized the perfection oozing from his character, shown in his words and actions. Pilate's wife recognized that he was a "just man" (Matt. 27:19), undeserving of punishment; the Roman soldier who watched Christ's demeanour whilst hanging on the cross had to comment, "Certainly this was a righteous man" (Luke 23:47). Earlier in his life, Jesus challenged the Jews with the question: "Which of you convicts Me of sin?" (John 8:46). To this there was no reply.

As a result of His victorious perfection in every way, Jesus of Nazareth was *raised above* the Angels (Heb. 1:3-5REB). He was given an exalted name (Phil. 2:9), which included all the Angelic titles. "His name *will be* called Wonderful [cp. Jud. 13:18], Counsellor [2 Kings 22:20]" (Is. 9:6). Evidently this high position was not possessed by Jesus before His birth and death; the idea of Him being exalted *to* this position rules this out.

Due to his perfect character, Jesus was the manifestation of God in flesh (1Tim. 3:16); He acted and spoke as God would have done had He been a man. He was therefore the perfect reflection of God - "the *image* of the invisible God" (Col. 1:15). Because of this, there is no need for mortal men to physically see God. As Jesus explained, "He who has seen Me has seen the Father; so how can you say, 'Show us (physically) the Father?'" (John 14:9). The repeated Biblical emphasis is that God the Father was manifest in Jesus Christ His Son (2 Cor. 5:19; Jn. 14:10; Acts 2:22). The doctrine of the trinity teaches that the Son was manifest or 'incarnate' in Jesus; but the Bible teaches that God was manifest ['incarnate' if we must use the term] in Jesus. The word *became* flesh (Jn. 1:14), rather than the word entering into a fleshly form.

Living in a sinful world, beset by sin and failure in our own lives, it is hard for us to appreciate the totality and immensity of Christ's spiritual supremacy; that a man of our nature should fully reveal the righteousness of God in his character. Believing this requires a more real faith than just accepting the theological idea that Christ was God Himself; it is understandable that the false doctrine of the trinity is so popular.

Christ willingly gave his perfect life as a gift to us; he showed his love for us by dying "for our sins" (1 Cor. 15:3), knowing that through his death he would gain us eventual salvation from sin and death (Eph. 5:2,25; Rev. 1:5; Gal. 2:20). Because Jesus was perfect in character he was able to overcome the result of sin by being the first person to rise from the dead and be given immortal life. All those who identify themselves with Christ through baptism and a Christ-like way of life therefore have hope of a similar resurrection and reward.

In this lies the glorious significance of Christ's resurrection. It is the "assurance" that we will be resurrected and judged (Acts 17:31), and if we have been truly like him, share his reward of immortal life, "*knowing* (confidently) that He who raised up the Lord Jesus will also raise us up with Jesus" (2 Cor. 4:14; 1 Cor. 6:14; Rom. 6:3-5). As sinners, we deserve eternal death (Rom. 6:23). Yet, on account of Christ's perfect life, obedient death and his resurrection, God is able to offer us the *gift* of eternal life, completely in accord with all His principles.

To displace the effects of our sins, God "credits righteousness" (Rom. 4:6NIV) to us through our faith in His promises of salvation. We know that sin brings death, therefore if we truly believe that God will save us from it, we must believe that He will count us as if we are righteous, although we are not. Christ was perfect; by being truly *in* Christ, God can count us as if we are perfect, although personally we are not. God made Christ "who had no sin, to be sin for us, so that *in* him we might become the righteousness of God " (2 Cor. 5:21NIV), i.e. being *in* Christ through baptism and a Christ-like life. Thus for those "in Christ Jesus", he is "become for us ... righteousness and sanctification and redemption" (1 Cor. 1:30,31); the following verse therefore encourages us to praise Christ for the great things he has achieved: "In the Gospel a righteousness from God is revealed, a righteousness that is by faith" (Rom. 1:17 NIV).

All this was made possible through Christ's resurrection. He was the "firstfruits" of a whole harvest of human beings who will be made immortal through his achievement (1 Cor. 15:20), "the firstborn" of a new spiritual family who will be given God's nature (Col.1:18,19 cp. Eph. 3:15). Christ's resurrection therefore made it possible for God to count believers in Christ as if they are righteous, seeing that they are covered by his righteousness. Christ "was delivered over to death for our sins and was raised to life for our justification" (Rom. 4:25 NIV), a word meaning 'to be righteous'.

It takes a conscious, meditated faith in these things to really be convinced that we can be counted by God as if we are perfect. Christ can present us at the judgment seat "*faultless* before the presence of His glory", "holy, and blameless, and irreproachable in His sight" (Jude v. 24; Col. 1:22 cp. Eph. 5:27). Given our constant spiritual failures, it takes a firm faith to really believe this. Just putting our hand up at a 'crusade' or making an academic assent to a set of doctrines is not related to this kind of faith. It is a proper understanding of Christ's resurrection which should motivate our faith: "God... raised Him from the dead ... *so that* your faith and hope (of a similar resurrection) are in God" (1 Pet. 1:21).

It is only by proper baptism into Christ that we can be "in Christ" and therefore be covered by his righteousness. By baptism we associate ourselves with his death and resurrection (Rom. 6:3-5), which are the means of our deliverance from our sins, through being 'justified', or counted righteous (Rom. 4:25).

The marvellous things which we have considered in this section are quite out of our grasp unless we have been baptized. At baptism we associate ourselves with the blood of Christ shed on the cross; believers wash "their robes and (make) them white in the blood of the Lamb" (Rev. 7:14). Figuratively, they are then clothed in white robes, representing the righteousness of Christ which has been counted ('credited') to them (Rev. 19:8). It is possible to make these white clothes dirty as a result of our sin (Jude v. 23); when we do this after baptism, we must again use the blood of Christ to wash them clean through asking God for forgiveness through Christ.

It follows that after baptism we still need to strive to remain in the blessed position which we then entered. There is a need for regular, daily self-examination, with constant prayer and seeking of forgiveness. By doing this we will always be humbly confident that, due to our covering with Christ's righteousness, we really will be in the Kingdom of God. We must seek to be found abiding *in* Christ at the day of our death or at Christ's return, "not having (our) own righteousness ...but that which is through faith in Christ, the righteousness which is from God by faith" (Phil. 3:9).

The repeated emphasis on *faith* resulting in imputed righteousness, shows that in no way can we earn salvation by our works; salvation is by grace: "For by grace you have been saved through faith, and that not of yourselves; it is the gift of God, not of works" (Eph. 2:8,9). As justification and righteousness are 'gifts' (Rom. 5:17), so, too, is salvation. Our motivation in doing any works of Christian service should therefore be that of gratitude for what God has done for us - counting us as righteous through Christ, and thereby giving us the way to salvation. It is fatal to reason that if we do works we will then be saved. We will simply not succeed in gaining salvation if we think like this; it is a *gift* which we cannot earn, only lovingly respond to in deep gratitude, which will be reflected in our works. Real faith produces works as an inevitable by-product (James 2:17).

9.2   The Blood Of Jesus

It is very often stated in the New Testament that our justification and salvation is through the blood of Jesus (e.g. 1 John 1:7; Rev. 5:9; 12:11; Rom. 5:9). To appreciate the significance of Christ's blood, we must understand that it is a Biblical principle that "the life of every creature is its blood" (Lev. 17:14 NIV). Without blood a body cannot live; it is therefore symbolic of life. This explains the aptness of Christ's words, "Unless you eat the flesh of the Son of Man and drink His blood, you have no life in you" (John 6:53).

Sin results in death (Rom. 6:23),i.e. a pouring out of the blood, which carries the life. For this reason the Israelites were expected to pour out blood each time they sinned, to remind them that sin resulted in death. "... according to the law (of Moses) almost all things are purged (cleansed mg.) with blood, and without shedding of blood is no remission (forgiveness mg.)" (Heb. 9:22). Because of this, Adam and Eve's covering of themselves with fig leaves was unacceptable; instead, God killed a lamb to provide skins to cover their sin (Gen. 3:7,21). Similarly, Abel's sacrifice of animals was accepted rather than Cain's offering of vegetables, because he appreciated this principle that without shedding blood there could be no forgiveness and acceptable approach to God (Gen. 4:3-5). Not only did he appreciate it, he *had faith* in that blood, and on this basis God accepted his offering (Heb. 11:4).

These incidents point forward to the supreme importance of the blood of Christ. This was especially foreshadowed in the events of the Passover, at which God's people had to place the blood of a lamb on their doorposts to gain salvation from death. This blood pointed forward to that of Jesus, with which we must cover ourselves. Before the time of Christ the Jews had to offer animal sacrifices for their sins, according to God's law through Moses. However, this shedding of animal blood was only for teaching purposes. Sin is punishable by death (Rom. 6:23); it was not possible that a human being could kill an animal as a substitute for his own death or as a true representative of himself. The animal he offered had no appreciation of right or wrong; it was not fully representative of him: "It is not possible that the blood of bulls and goats could take away sins" (Heb. 10:4).

The question therefore arises, Why did the Jews have to sacrifice animals when they sinned? Paul sums up the various answers to this question in Gal. 3:24: "The law was our tutor to bring us to Christ." The animals which they killed as offerings for sin had to be spotless - without blemish (Ex. 12:5; Lev. 1:3,10 etc.). These pointed forward to Christ, "a lamb without blemish" (1 Peter 1:19). The blood of those animals therefore *represented* that of Christ. They were accepted as sacrifices for sin insofar as they pointed forward to Christ's perfect sacrifice, which God knew he would make. On account of this, God was able to forgive the sins of His people who lived before the time of Christ. His death was "a ransom to set them free from the sins committed under the first covenant" (Heb. 9:15 NIV), i.e. the law of Moses (Heb. 8:5-9). All the sacrifices offered under the law pointed forward to Christ, the perfect sin offering, who "put away sin by the sacrifice of Himself" (Heb. 9:26; 13:11,12; Rom. 8:3 NIV cp. 2 Cor. 5:21).

We explained in Section 7.3 how the whole of the Old Testament, particularly the Law of Moses, pointed forward to Christ. Under that Law the way of approach to God was through the High Priest; he was the mediator between God and men under the Old Covenant as Christ is under the New Covenant (Heb. 9:15). "... the law appoints as high priests men who are weak; but the oath ... appointed the Son, who has been made perfect for ever" (Heb. 7:28 NIV). Because they themselves were sinners, these men were not in a position to gain true forgiveness for men. The animals which they sacrificed for sin were not truly representative of the sinners. What was required was a perfect human being, who was in every way representative of sinful man, who would make an acceptable sacrifice for sin which men could benefit from by associating themselves with that sacrifice. In a similar way, a perfect High Priest was required who could sympathize with the sinful men for whom he mediated , having been tempted just like them (Heb. 2:14-18).

Jesus fits this requirement perfectly - "Such a high priest meets our need – one who is holy, blameless, pure ..." (Heb. 7:26 NIV). He does not need to continually sacrifice for his own sins, nor is he liable to death any more (Heb. 7:23,27) In the light of this, the Scripture comments upon Christ as our priest: "Therefore he is able to save completely those who come to God through him, because he always lives to intercede for them" (Heb. 7:25 NIV). Because he had human nature, Christ, as our ideal High Priest, "can have compassion on those who are ignorant and going astray, since *he himself is* (was) *also* beset by weakness" (Heb. 5:2). This recalls the statement regarding Christ, *"He Himself* likewise" shared in our human nature (Heb. 2:14).

As the Jewish high priests mediated for God's people, Israel, so Christ is a Priest for spiritual Israel - those who have been baptized into Christ, having understood the true Gospel. He is "a high priest over the *house of God* " (Heb. 10:21), which is comprised of those who have been born again by baptism (1 Peter 2:2-5), having the true hope of the Gospel (Heb. 3:6). Appreciating the marvellous benefits of Christ's priesthood should therefore encourage us to be baptized into him; for we must enter into His "house" or family if He is to be our High Priest.

Having been baptized into Christ, we should eagerly make full use of Christ's priesthood; indeed, we have certain responsibilities with regard to this which we must live up to. "By Him let us continually offer the sacrifice of praise to God " (Heb. 13:15). God's plan of providing Christ as our priest was in order that we should glorify Him; we should therefore make constant use of our access to God through Christ in order to praise Him. Heb. 10:21-25 (NIV) lists a number of responsibilities which we have on account of Christ being our High Priest: "We have a great priest over the house of God:

1. Let us draw near to God with a sincere heart in full assurance of faith, having our hearts sprinkled to cleanse us from a guilty conscience and having our bodies washed with pure water". Understanding Christ's priesthood means that we should be baptized into him ("our bodies washed"), and we should never let a bad conscience develop in our minds. If we believe in Christ's atonement, we are made at one with God ('AT-ONE-MENT') by his sacrifice.

2. "Let us hold unswervingly to the hope we profess..." We should not deviate from the true doctrines which have brought about our understanding of Christ's priesthood.

3. "Let us consider how we may spur one another on towards love and good deeds. Let us not give up meeting together". We should be lovingly bound together with others who understand and benefit from Christ's priesthood; this is particularly through meeting together for the communion service, by which we remember Christ's sacrifice (see **Section 11.3.5**).

Appreciating these things should fill us with humble confidence that we really will reach salvation, if we are baptized and abide in Christ: "Let us *therefore* approach the throne of grace *with confidence*, so that we may receive mercy, and find grace to help us in our time of need" (Heb. 4:16 NIV).

Belief In Practice 15:

Christ Died For Me: So What Should I Do?

FREEDOM FROM SIN

And so I too must surrender all, I will willingly strive to do this, for the glorious wonder of knowing this Man who died for me to enable such great salvation. He died and rose so that He might be made Lord of His people (Rom. 14:9); if we believe in His resurrection and subsequent Lordship, He will be the Lord of our lives, Lord of every motion of our hearts. We are yet in our sins, if Christ be not risen (1 Cor. 15:17). But He has risen, and therefore we are no longer dominated by our moral weakness. Because baptism united us with His resurrection, we are no longer in our sins (Col. 2:13). Therefore the baptized believer will not " continue in sin" if he really understands and believes this (Rom. 6:1 and context). Ours is the life of freedom with Him, for He was and is our representative [note that He represents us now, in His freedom and eternal life, just as much as He did in His death].

We died and rose with Christ, if we truly believe in His representation of us and our connection with Him, then His freedom from sin and sense of conquest will be ours; as the man guilty of blood was to see in the death of the High Priest a representation of his own necessary death, and thereafter was freed from the limitations of the city of refuge (Num. 35:32,33). Because Christ really did rise again, and we have a part in that, we must *therefore* abstain from sin, quit bad company and labour with the risen, active Lord (1 Cor. 15:34,58).The representative nature of the Lord's death means that we are pledged to live out His self-crucifixion as far as we can; to re-live the crucifixion process in our imagination, to come to that point where we *know* we wouldn't have gone through with it, and to grasp with real wonder and gratitude the salvation of the cross. " As one has died for all, then all have died, and that He died for all in order to have the living live no longer for themselves but for Him who died and rose for them" (2 Cor. 5:14,15 Moffat). It has been powerfully commented by Fred Barling: "To know oneself to have been involved in the sacrificial death of Christ, on account of its representational character, is to see oneself committed to a sacrificial life, to a re-enactment in oneself of the cross".

Such is the power of a true, lived-out baptism and faith that we have found freedom from sin. If we have really died and resurrected with the Lord, we will be dead unto the things of this world (Col. 2:20; 3:1). This is why Paul could say that the greatest proof that Christ had risen from the dead was the change in character which had occurred within him (Acts 26:8 ff.). This was " the power of his resurrection" ; and it works within us too. The death and resurrection of Jesus of Nazareth aren't just facts we know; if they are truly believed, there is within them the power of ultimate transformation.

TRUE FAITH

Nearly everyone in the first century believed in the God-idea. There were very few atheists. Hence the radical nature of statements like 1 Pet. 1:21: we " through him [Jesus] are believers in God" , because God raised Jesus from the dead. The resurrection of the Lord inspires faith in the Father to such an extent that anyone whose faith in 'God' is not based on the risen Jesus does not actually count as a believer in God.

PREACHING

Paul in 1 Cor. 15 lists ten serious consequences of failing to believe that Christ rose. One of these is that there was no reason for him to constantly risk his life to preach the Gospel if Christ was not risen. It stands to reason that the fact Jesus *has* risen is an inspiration to risk and give our lives, time and again, in an all out effort to spread that good news of freedom from sin to others.

SELFLESS SERVICE

The wonder of the resurrection would totally affect our attitude to asking for things, the Lord taught in Jn. 16:23,26. "In that day [of marvelling in the resurrected Lord], you shall ask me nothing…if you shall ask anything of the Father, he will give it you [RV]…in that day you shall ask in my name…". What are we to make of all this talk of asking and not asking, in the 'day' of the resurrected Lord Jesus? My synthesis of it all is this: Due to the sheer wonder of the resurrection of the Lord, we will not feel the need to ask for anything for ourselves. The gift of freedom from sin is enough. Because if God gave us His Son and raised Him from the dead, we will serve for nothing, for no extra 'perks' in this life; and yet, wonder of wonders, *if* we shall ask, in His Name, we will receive. But we must ask whether the implications and wonder of the fact of the Lord's resurrection have had such an effect upon us…?

GENEROSITY

To put it mildly, our experience of His death for us should lead us to be generous spirited in all ways. In appealing for financial generosity to poorer brethren, Paul sought to inspire the Corinthians with the picture of Christ crucified: " For you know the grace [gift / giving] of our Lord Jesus Christ, that, though He was rich, yet for your sakes He became poor [Gk. a pauper], that you through his poverty might be rich" (2 Cor. 8:9). In the light of this, we should not just be generous from the abundance of what we have; we should become as paupers in our giving. By this I don't mean we should get to the position where there are no rich people amongst us- this is clearly not the church scene imagined in passages like 1 Tim. 6. But the image of the pauper is the one that is impressed upon us. The Lord's giving wasn't financial; it was emotional and spiritual. And so, Paul says, both materially and in these ways, we should likewise respond to our brethren, poorer materially or spiritually than we are. " The very spring of our actions is the love of Christ" (2 Cor. 5:14 Philips; it " urges us on" , NRSV).

LIVING LIKE JESUS

By God's grace, the Lord tasted death *for* (Gk. *huper*) *every man*, as our representative: " in tasting death he should stand for all" (NEB). In His death He experienced the essence of the life-struggle and death of every man. The fact the Lord did this *for us* means that we respond *for Him*. " To you it is given *in the behalf of*(Gk. *huper*) Christ, not only to believe on Him [in theory], but to suffer *for his sake* (Gk. *huper*)" (Phil. 1:29). He suffered *for us* as our representative, and we suffer *for Him* in response. This was and is the two-way imperative of the fact the Lord was our representative. He died *for all* that we should die to self and live *for Him* (2 Cor. 5:14,15). " His own self bare our sins [as our representative] in his own body [note the link " *our* sins" and " his *own* body"] that we being dead to sin, should live unto righteousness" (1 Pet. 2:24,25). We died with Him, there on His cross; and so His resurrection life is now ours. He is totally active for us now; His life now is *for us*, and as we live His life, we should be 100% *for Him* in our living. He gave His life *for* us, and we must lay down our lives *for* Him (1 Jn. 3:16). There are about 130 references to being " in Christ" in the NT. But if any man is truly in Christ, he is a new creature, and the old things pass away; it must equally be true that " Christ [is] in you". If we are in Him, He must be in us, in that we live lives around the principle of " what would Jesus do?". His spirit becomes ours.

Because of the nature and extent of His sufferings and experiences, the Lord is able to meaningfully enter into the human experience of us all. Yet we feel so often helpless as we watch the sufferings of others- as we watch their facial features contort, as we listen to their complaints. We are deeply aware of the huge gulf between us and them. We cannot penetrate their suffering- or so we think. Yet the Lord Jesus, on the basis of the extent of His love and the depth of His experience, *can* make this penetration. And it is not impossible that we ourselves can do far better than we think in achieving deep solidarity with others in their sufferings.

PREACHING

2 Cor. 5:14-21 urges us to preach the salvation in Christ to all men, because He died for us, as our representative. He died *for* [the sake of] all (5:14,15), He was made sin *for* our sake (5:21); and therefore we are ambassadors *for* [s.w.] His sake (5:20). Because He was our representative, so we must be His representatives in witnessing Him to the world. This is why the preaching of Acts was consistently motivated by the Lord's death and resurrection for the preachers. Phil. 2 draws out the parallel between the Name of Jesus, in which all the names of those in Him find a part, and the need to confess this in preaching. By baptism into the name of Jesus, men confess that Jesus Christ is Lord, to the glory of God the Father. There was and is no other name given under Heaven by which men can be saved; "every name" under the whole Heaven must take on the name of Jesus in baptism. This is why Acts associates His exaltation (Acts 2:33; 5:31) and His new name (Acts 2:21,38; 3:6,16; 4:10,12,18,30; 5:40) with an appeal for men and women to be baptized into that Name. Realizing the meaning of the Name of Jesus and the height of His exaltation meant that they realized how "all men" could have their part in a sacrifice which represented "all men". And thus they were motivated to preach to "all men". And thus Paul's whole preaching ministry was a bearing of the Name of Jesus before the Gentiles (Acts 9:15).

9.3 Jesus As Our Representative

We have seen that the animal sacrifices were not completely representative of sinful men. Jesus *was* representative of us, being in all points "made like his brethren" (Heb. 2:17). "He suffered death ... for everyone " (Heb. 2:9 NIV). When we commit a sin - e.g. we are angry - God can forgive us if we are "in Christ" (Eph. 4:32). This is because God can compare us with Christ, a man like us who was tempted to sin - e.g. to be angry - but who overcame every temptation. Therefore God can forgive us our sin - of anger - on account of our being in Christ, covered by his righteousness. Christ being our representative is therefore the means by which God can show us His grace, whilst upholding His own righteous principles.

If Jesus was God rather than being solely of human nature, he could not have been our representative. This is another example of where one wrong idea leads to another. Because of this, theologians have developed many complex ways of explaining Christ's death. The popular view of apostate Christendom is that man's sins placed him in a debt to God which of himself he could not pay. Christ then cleared the debt of each believer by his blood, shed on the cross. Many a Gospel Hall preacher has expressed it like this: "It was as if we were all lined up against a wall, about to be shot by the devil. Jesus then rushed in; the devil shot him instead of us, so we are now free."

These elaborate theories are without any firm Biblical support. There is the obvious contradiction that if Christ died *instead* of us, then we should not die. As we still have human nature, we must still die; salvation from sin and death will finally be revealed at the judgment (when we are granted immortality). We did not receive this at the time Christ died. Christ's death destroyed the devil (Heb. 2:14) rather than the devil destroying him.

The Bible teaches that salvation is possible through Christ's death AND resurrection, not just by his death. Christ "died for us" once. The theory of substitution would mean that he had to die for each of us personally. The English preposition "for" (as in "Christ died for us") has a much wider range of meaning than the Greek word which it translates. If Christ had died *instead* of us, the Greek word *anti* would have been used. But never is this word used in any Bible passage which says that Jesus died for us.

If Christ paid off a debt with his blood, our salvation becomes something which we can expect as a right. The fact that salvation is a gift, brought about by God's mercy and forgiveness, is lost sight of if we understand Christ's sacrifice as being a debt payment. It also makes out that an angry God was appeased once He saw the physical blood of Jesus. Yet what God sees when we repent is His Son as our representative, whom we are striving to copy, rather than we connecting ourselves with Christ's blood as a talisman. Many hymns and songs contain an incredible amount of false doctrine in this area. Most false doctrine is drummed into people's minds by music, rather than rational, Biblical instruction. We must ever be on the watch for this kind of brain-washing.

Tragically, the simple words "Christ died for us" (Rom. 5:8) have been grossly misunderstood as meaning that Christ died instead of us. There are a number of connections between Romans 5 and 1 Cor. 15 (e.g. v. 12 = 1 Cor. 15:21; v. 17 = 1 Cor. 15:22). "Christ died for *us*" (Rom. 5:8) is matched by "Christ died for our *sins*" (1 Cor. 15:3). His death was in order to make a way whereby we can gain forgiveness of our sins; it was in this sense that

"Christ died for us". The word "for" does not necessarily mean 'instead of'; Christ died "for (because of) our sins", not 'instead of' them. Because of this, Christ can "make intercession" for us (Heb. 7:25) - not 'instead of' us. Neither does "for" mean 'instead of' in Heb. 10:12 and Gal. 1:4. If Christ died 'instead of us' there would be no need to carry His cross, as He bids us. And there would be no sense in being baptized into His death and resurrection, willingly identifying ourselves with Him as our victorious representative. The idea of substitution implies a short cut to glorification with Him which simply isn't valid. Understanding Him as our representative commits us to baptism into His death and resurrection, the life of cross-carrying along with Him, and realistically sharing in His resurrection. His resurrection is ours; we were given the hope of resurrection because we are in Christ, who was raised (1 Pet. 1:3). The Lord Jesus lived and died with our nature, in all its waywardness, in order to be able to come close to us and to enable us to identify ourselves with Him. By appreciating this doctrinally, we enable Him to see the result of the suffering of His soul and be satisfied. There is a nice little cameo of this when the Lord dealt with the man whose tongue wasn't functioning properly. Because the tongue controls swallowing, surely the man was frothing in his own spittle. And yet the Lord spits and puts His spittle on that of the man, to show His complete ability to identify with the human condition.

It's interesting to note that there are others who've seen through the 'substitution' theory. John A.T. Robinson, one-time Bishop of Woolwich, wrote: "The New Testament writers *never* say that God punishes Christ. Christ stands as our representative, not as our replacement; his work is always on behalf of us (*hyper*) not instead of us (*anti*); he died to sin, not so that we shall not have to (as our substitute), but precisely so that we can (as our representative)" (*Wrestling With Romans* (London: SCM, 1979), p. 48). See too Dorothee Soelle, *Christ The Representative* (London: SCM, 1967).

9.4   Jesus And The Law Of Moses

Jesus being the perfect sacrifice for sin and the ideal High Priest who could truly gain forgiveness for us, the old system of animal sacrifices and high priests was done away with after his death (Heb. 10:5-14). "The priesthood being changed (from the Levites to Christ), of necessity there is also a change of the law" (Heb. 7:12). Christ "has become a priest not on the basis of a regulation as to his ancestry (i.e. just because a man was a descendant of Levi he could be a priest), but on the basis of the power of an indestructible life", which he was given due to his perfect sacrifice (Heb. 7:16 NIV). Therefore, "the former regulation (i.e. the law of Moses) is set aside because it was weak and useless (for the law made nothing perfect), and a better hope (through Christ) is introduced" (Heb. 7:18,19 NIV).

It is evident from this that the law of Moses has been ended by the sacrifice of Christ. To trust in a human priesthood or to still offer animal sacrifices means that we do not accept the fullness of Christ's victory. Such beliefs mean that we do not accept Christ's sacrifice as completely successful, and that we feel that works are necessary to bring about our justification, rather than faith in Christ alone. "No one is justified by the law in the sight of God ... for, The just(ified) shall live by *faith*" (Gal. 3:11 cp. Hab. 2:4). Our own steel-willed effort to be obedient to the letter of God's laws will not bring us justification; surely every reader of these words has disobeyed those laws already.

If we are going to observe the law of Moses, we must attempt to keep *all* of it. Disobedience to just one part of it means that those who are under it are condemned: "All who rely on observing the law are under a curse, for it is written: 'Cursed is everyone who does not continue to do everything written in the Book of the Law'" (Gal. 3:10 NIV). The weakness of our human nature means that we find it impossible to fully keep the law of Moses, but due to Christ's complete obedience to it, we are freed from any obligation to keep it. Our salvation is due to God's gift through Christ, rather than our personal works of obedience. "For what the law was powerless to do in that it was weakened by the sinful nature, God did by sending his own Son in the likeness of sinful man, to be a sin offering. And so he condemned sin in sinful man ..." (Rom. 8:3 NIV). Thus "Christ has redeemed us from the curse of the law, having become a curse for us" (Gal. 3:13).

Because of this, we are no longer required to keep any part of the law of Moses. We saw in Study 3.4 that the New Covenant in Christ replaced the Old Covenant of Moses' law (Heb. 8:13). By his death, Christ cancelled "the written code, with its regulations, that was against us and that stood opposed to us (by our inability to fully keep the law); he took it away, nailing it to the cross ... Therefore do not let anyone judge you by what you eat or drink, or with regard to a religious festival, a New Moon celebration or a Sabbath day. These are a shadow of the things that were to come; the reality, however, is found in Christ" (Col. 2:14-17 NIV). This is quite clear - because of Christ's death on the cross, the Law was taken away so that we should resist any pressure put on us to keep parts of it, e.g. the feasts and the sabbath. Like the rest of the Law, the purpose of these things was to point forward to Christ. After his death, their typical significance was fulfilled, and there was therefore no further need to observe them.

The early Christian church of the first century was under constant pressure from the Orthodox Jews to keep parts of the Law. Throughout the New Testament there is repeated warning to resist these suggestions. In the face of all these, it is extraordinary that today there are several denominations who advocate partial obedience to the Law. We have earlier shown that any attempt to gain salvation from obedience to the Law must aim to keep the *entire* Law, otherwise we are automatically condemned for disobedience of it (Gal. 3:10).

There is an element within human nature which inclines to the idea of justification by works; we like to feel that we are *doing* something towards our salvation. For this reason, compulsory tithing, wearing a crucifix, reciting set prayers, praying in a certain posture etc. are all popular parts of most religions, Christian and otherwise. Salvation by faith in Christ *alone* is a doctrine unique to true Bible-based Christianity.

Warnings against keeping any part of the Law of Moses in order to gain salvation, are dotted throughout the New Testament. Some taught that Christians should be circumcised according to the Mosaic law, "and keep the law". James flatly condemned this idea on behalf of the true believers: "*we* gave no such commandment" (Acts 15:24). Peter described those who taught the need for obedience to the Law as putting "a yoke on the neck of the disciples which neither our fathers nor we were able to bear. But we believe that through the grace of the Lord Jesus Christ (as opposed to their works of obedience to the law) we shall be saved" (Acts 15:10,11). Under inspiration, Paul is equally outspoken, stressing the same point time and again: "A man is not justified by the works of the law but by faith in Jesus Christ ... that we might be justified by faith in Christ and not by the works of the law; for by the works of the law no flesh shall be justified ... no one is justified by the law ... by (Christ) everyone who believes is justified from all things from which you could not be justified by the law of Moses" (Gal. 2:16; 3:11; Acts 13:39).

It is a sure sign of the apostasy of popular Christendom that many of their practices are based upon elements of the Law of Moses - despite the clear and laboured teaching considered above that Christians should not observe this Law, seeing that it has been done away in Christ. We will now consider the more obvious ways in which the Law of Moses is the basis of present 'Christian' practice:-

PRIESTS

The Orthodox, Catholic and Anglican churches openly use a system of human priesthood. The Roman Catholics see the Pope as their equivalent of the Jewish high priest. There is "*one* Mediator between God and men, the Man Christ Jesus" (1 Tim. 2:5). It is impossible, therefore, that the Pope or priests can be our mediators as the priests were under the

Old Covenant. Christ is now our High Priest in Heaven, offering our prayers to God.

There is absolutely no Biblical evidence that the authority possessed by the Spirit-gifted elders of the first century - e.g. Peter - was passed on to successive generations or to the Pope in particular. Even if the possibility of this were admitted, there is no way of proving that the Pope and priests personally are those upon whom the spiritual mantle of the first century elders has fallen.

The miraculous Spirit gifts having been withdrawn, all believers have equal access to the Spirit-Word in the Bible (see Studies 2.2 and 2.4). They are therefore all brethren, none having any more spiritually exalted a position than another. Indeed, *all* true believers are members of a new priesthood by reason of their baptism into Christ, in the sense that they show forth the light of God to a dark world (1 Peter 2:9). They will therefore become the king-priests of the Kingdom, when it is established upon earth at Christ's return (Rev. 5:10).

The Catholic practice of calling their priests 'Father' ('Pope' means 'father' too) is in flat contradiction to Christ's clear words, "Do not call anyone on earth your father; for One is your Father, He who is in heaven" (Matt. 23:9). Indeed, Jesus warned against granting any fellow man the sort of spiritual respect demanded by modern priests: "But you, do not be called 'Rabbi' (teacher), for One is your Teacher, the Christ, and you are all brethren" (Matt. 23:8).

The ornate robes worn by priests, bishops and other clergymen have their basis in the special clothing worn by the Mosaic priests and high priest. This clothing pointed forward to the perfect character of Christ, and, as with all the Law, its purpose has now been fulfilled. It is indeed heartbreaking, that clothing which was intended to extol the glory of Christ, is now used to advance the glory of the men who wear it - some of whom admit that they do not accept Christ's resurrection or even the personal existence of God.

The Catholic idea that Mary is a priest is grossly wrong. Our requests are in *Christ's* name, not Mary's (Jn. 14:13,14; 15:16; 16:23-26). Christ is our only High Priest, not Mary. Jesus rebuked Mary when she tried to get him to do things for others (Jn. 2:2-4). God, not Mary, brings men to Christ (Jn. 6:44).

TITHING

This, too, was part of the Mosaic Law (Num. 18:21), whereby the Jews were to donate a tenth of their substance to the priestly tribe of

Levi. Seeing that there is now no human priesthood, it can no longer be obligatory to pay a tithe to any church elders. Again, one false idea (in this case concerning priests) has led to another (i.e. tithing). God Himself does not *need* our offerings, seeing that all belongs to Him (Ps. 50:8-13). We are only giving back to God what He has given us (1 Chron. 29:14). It is impossible for us to gain salvation as a result of our material offerings, e.g. in financial terms. In gratitude for God's great gift to us, we should not just offer a tenth of our money, but our whole lives. Paul set an example in this, truly practising what he preached: "... offer your bodies as living sacrifices, holy and pleasing to God -- this is your spiritual act of worship" (Rom. 12:1 NIV).

FOOD

The Jewish Law categorized certain foods as unclean - a practice adopted by some denominations today, especially regarding pork. Because of Christ's removing of the Law on the cross, "... do not let anyone judge you by what you eat or drink" (Col. 2:14-16 NIV). Thus the Mosaic commands concerning these things have been done away, seeing that Christ has now come. It was he to whom the 'clean' foods pointed forward.

Jesus clearly explained that nothing a man eats can spiritually defile him; it is what comes out of the heart which does this (Mark 7:15-23). "In saying this, Jesus declared *all* foods 'clean'" (Mark 7:19 NIV). Peter was taught the same lesson (Acts 10:14,15), as was Paul: "I know and am convinced by the Lord Jesus that there is nothing unclean of itself" (Rom. 14:14). Earlier, Paul had reasoned that to refuse certain foods was a sign of spiritual weakness (Rom. 14:2). Our attitude to food "does not commend us to God" (1 Cor. 8:8). Most incriminating of all is the warning that apostate Christians would teach men, "to abstain from foods which God created to be received with thanksgiving by those who believe and know the truth" (1 Tim. 4:3).

Belief In Practice 16:

The Real Cross

The idea that the Lord Jesus ended the Law of Moses on the cross needs some reflection. That statement only pushes the question back one stage further- how exactly did He 'end' the Law there? How did a man dying on a cross actually end the Law? The Lord Jesus, supremely in His death, was "the end of the law" (Rom. 10:4). But the Greek *telos* ["end"] is elsewhere translated "the goal" (1 Tim. 1:5 NIV). The character and person of the Lord Jesus at the end was the goal of the Mosaic law; those 613 commandments, if perfectly obeyed, were intended to give rise to a personality like that of the Lord Jesus. When He reached the climax of His personal development and spirituality, in the moment of His death, the Law was "fulfilled". He taught that He "came" in order to die; and yet He also "came" in order to "fulfil" the Law (Mt. 5:17).

The risen Christ was and is a living reality. Suetonius records that Claudius expelled Jewish Christians from Rome because they were agitated by one Chrestus; i.e. Jesus the Christ. Yet the historian speaks as if He was actually alive and actively present in person . In essence, He was. All the volumes of confused theology, the senseless theories about the Trinity. would all have been avoided if only men had had the faith to believe that the man Jesus who really died and rose, both never sinned and was also indeed the Son of God. And that His achievement of perfection in human flesh was real. Yes it takes faith- and all the wrong theology was only an excuse for a lack of such faith.

It is in our reflections upon the cross that we see revealed the real nature and quality of our relationship with the Lord Jesus. When we survey the wondrous cross... there ought to be that sense of wonder, of love for Him, of conviction of our personal sins, and also conviction of the reality of His forgiveness. As we survey that wondrous cross, all commentary is bathos. It's like trying to describe the Ninth Symphony in words. It is so much easier, so less challenging, to respond to the cross by seeking to describe it in the words of atonement theory. All the ink pointlessly spilt in this area is indicative of this; there seems an obsession with 'the doctrine of the atonement'. But the essential response to the cross is not any commentary in words; for as I've said, grasping it for what it is convicts us that all commentary is bathos. Not words, not theories of explanation, but feelings, belief deep in the heart, challenge to our habits and traits of character, real, actual, concrete and practical change, a transformation that is empowered by the Man hanging there.

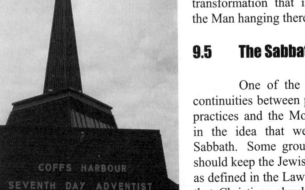

9.5   The Sabbath

One of the most widespread continuities between present 'Christian' practices and the Mosaic Law is seen in the idea that we must keep the Sabbath. Some groups claim that we should keep the Jewish Sabbath exactly as defined in the Law; many others feel that Christians should have a specific day of the week upon which to worship, which they often define as Sunday. The first thing to clarify is that the Sabbath was the last day of the week, when God rested after the six days of creation (Ex. 20:10,11). Sunday being the first day of the week, it would be incorrect to observe this day as the Sabbath. The Sabbath was specifically "a sign between them (Israel) and Me (God), that they might know that I am the Lord who sanctifies them" (Eze. 20:12). As such, it has never been intended to be binding on Gentiles (non-Jews). "... the Lord has given *you* [not all mankind] the Sabbath (Ex. 16:29); "... You [God] made known to them [Israel] Your holy Sabbath" (Neh. 9:14).

The fact God blessed the seventh day (Gen. 2:3) is no reason to think that therefore the Sabbath must be observed-- many centuries went by after creation before God instituted the Sabbath. Jesus once commented on a theological problem: a baby boy had to be circumcised on the eighth day of his life. If this day fell on a Sabbath, then work would have to be done. So which law should be kept, circumcision, or the Sabbath? Jesus replied that circumcision had to be honoured, because this came from the time of Abraham, whereas the Sabbath law was later, from Moses: "Moses therefore gave you circumcision [not that it is from Moses, but from the fathers(*i.e. Abraham)...*]" (Jn.7:22). If the law of circumcision took precedence over that of the Sabbath, how can it be argued by some that the Sabbath law is binding but that of circumcision isn't? Circumcision was the token of the covenant with Abraham, whereas the Sabbath was the token of the law of Moses (Ex. 31:17), and Jesus judged that the covenant with Abraham was more important. The same kind of argument is used by Paul, when he reasons that the new covenant given to Abraham [which included no command about the Sabbath] is something which cannot be *added to* or disannulled. He asks, therefore, why it was that "the law was *added*" (Gal. 3:15,19)? He replies that the law was added, by implication temporarily, seeing that the new covenant cannot really be added to, in order to teach men about sin and lead them to an understanding of Christ, the promised seed of Abraham. Now that Christ has come, we are not under the Law.

Therefore through Christ's death on the cross, the Law of Moses was done away, so that there is now no necessity to observe the Sabbath or, indeed, any festival (Col. 2:14-17). The early Christians who returned to keeping parts of the Mosaic Law, e.g. the Sabbath, are described by Paul as returning "to the weak and miserable principles (NIV) to which you desire again to be in bondage. You observe days (e.g. the Sabbath) and months and seasons and years (i.e. the Jewish festivals). I am afraid for you, lest I have laboured for you in vain" (Gal. 4:9-11). This is the seriousness of attempting to keep the Sabbath as a means to salvation. It is clear that observing the Sabbath is irrelevant to salvation: "One man esteems one day above another (i.e. in spiritual significance); another esteems every day alike. Let each be fully convinced in his own mind. He who observes the day, observes it to the Lord; and he who does not observe the day, to the Lord he does not observe it" (Rom. 14:5,6).

Because of this, it is understandable that we do not read of the early believers keeping the Sabbath. Indeed, it is recorded that they met on "the *first* day of the week", i.e. Sunday: "... on the first day of the week, when the disciples came together to break bread ..." (Acts 20:7). That this was a widespread practice is indicated by Paul advising the believers at Corinth to take up a collection "on the first day of the week" (1 Cor. 16:2), i.e. at their regular meetings on that day. All the believers are described as being priests (1 Peter 2:9) - who were exempt from keeping the Sabbath (Matt. 12:5).

If we are to keep the Sabbath, we must do so properly; we have earlier shown that it is fatal to keep the Mosaic Law partially, because this will result in our condemnation (Gal. 3:10; James 2:10). Salvation is through keeping the law of Christ rather than that of Moses. Israel were not allowed to do any work on the Sabbath: "Whoever does any work on it must be put to death". They were also commanded: "Do not light a fire in any of your dwellings on the Sabbath day", and therefore they were forbidden to prepare food on that day (Ex. 35:2,3; 16:23 NIV). A man who gathered sticks on the Sabbath, presumably in order to kindle a fire, was punished with death for doing so (Num. 15:32-36).

Those denominations who teach that Sabbath-keeping is binding upon their members should therefore punish those members with death when they break the Sabbath. There should be no cooking of food or use of fire in any form - e.g. in driving motor vehicles, using heating systems etc. Orthodox Jews today set an example of the kind of behaviour expected on the Sabbath: they remain indoors all day except for religious reasons, and are not personally involved in cooking, transport etc. Most of those 'Christians' who claim to keep the Sabbath fall far short of this.

It is often argued that keeping of the Sabbath was one of the ten commandments given to Moses, and that, whilst the rest of the Law of Moses was done away, the obligation remains to keep all of the ten commandments. Seventh Day Adventists make a distinction between a 'moral law' of the ten commandments, "the law of God", and a so-called 'ceremonial law', the "law of Moses", which they believe was done away by Christ. This distinction is not taught in Scripture. The Bible uses the terms "law of Moses" and "law of God" interchangeably (Num. 31:21; Josh. 23:6; 2 Chron. 31:3). We have earlier demonstrated that the Old Covenant refers to the Law of Moses, which was replaced on the cross by the New Covenant. It can be shown that the ten commandments, including that concerning the Sabbath, were part of the Old Covenant which was done away by Christ:-

- God "declared to you (Israel) His covenant which he commanded you (Israel) to perform, that is the Ten Commandments; and He wrote them on two tablets of stone" (Deut. 4:13). Again it should be noted that this covenant, based upon the ten commandments, was made between God and *Israel*, not Gentiles of the present day.

- Moses ascended Mount Horeb to receive the stone tablets upon which God had written the ten commandments. Moses later commented concerning this, "The Lord our God made a covenant with us in Horeb" (Deut. 5:2), i.e. through those ten commandments.

- At this time, God "wrote on the tablets the words of the covenant, the Ten Commandments" (Ex. 34:28). This same covenant included details of the so-called 'ceremonial law' (Ex. 34:27). If we argue that keeping the covenant made in the ten commandments is necessary, we must also observe every detail of the entire Law, seeing that this is all part of the same covenant. It is evidently impossible to do this.

- "There was nothing in the ark except the two tablets of stone which Moses put there at Horeb ... the ark, in which is the covenant of the Lord" (1 Kings 8:9,21). Those tablets, on which were the ten commandments, were the covenant.

- Heb. 9:4 speaks of "the tablets of the covenant". The ten commandments were written on the tablets of stone, which comprised "the (old) covenant".

- Paul refers to this covenant as "written and engraved on stones", i.e. on the tablets of stone. He calls it "the ministry of death...the ministry of condemnation ..." that which is "... passing away" (2 Cor. 3:7-11). The covenant associated with the ten commandments can certainly not give any hope of salvation.

- Christ "...cancelled the written code, with its regulations, that was against us..." (Col. 2:14 NIV) on the cross. This alludes to God's handwriting of the ten commandments on the tablets of stone. Likewise Paul speaks of being "released from the law... the old way of the *written code*" (Rom. 7:6 NIV), referring to the letters of the ten commandments which were written on the tablets of stone.

- Just one of the ten commandments is styled "the law" in Rom. 7:7: "The law... said, 'You shall not covet". The preceding verses in Rom. 7:1-6 stress how "the law" has been done away by Christ's death; "the law" therefore includes the ten commandments.

All this makes it clear that the Old Covenant and "the Law" included the ten commandments. As they have been done away by the New Covenant, the ten commandments have therefore been removed. However, nine of the ten commandments have been reaffirmed, in spirit at least, in the New Testament. Numbers 3,5,6,7,8 and 9 can be found in 1 Tim. 1 alone, and numbers 1,2 and 10 in 1 Cor. 5. But never is the fourth commandment concerning the Sabbath repeated in the New Testament as obligatory for us.

The following list of passages documents further how the other nine are reaffirmed in the New Testament:-

1st. - Eph. 4:6; 1 John 5:21; Matt. 4:10
2nd. - 1 Cor. 10:14; Rom. 1:25
3rd. - James 5:12; Matt. 5:34,35
5th. - Eph. 6:1,2; Col. 3:20
6th. - 1 John 3:15; Matt. 5:21
7th. - Heb. 13:4; Matt. 5:27,28
8th. - Rom. 2:21; Eph. 4:28
9th. - Col. 3:9; Eph. 4:25; 2 Tim. 3:3
10th. - Eph. 5:3; Col. 3:5.

The Lord Jesus invites those who follow Him to accept the "rest" which He gives (Mt. 11:28). He uses a Greek word which is used in the Septuagint, the Greek translation of the Old Testament, for the Sabbath rest. Jesus was offering a life of Sabbath, of rest from trust in our own works (cp. Heb. 4:3,10). We shouldn't, therefore, keep a Sabbath one day per week, but rather live our whole lives in the spirit of the Sabbath.

Belief In Practice 17:

The Inspiration Of The Cross In Daily Life

The love of Christ in the cross is to have a continual inspiration upon us- endless love, countless moments of re-inspiration, are to come to us daily *because of the cross*. This is how central it is to daily life. We are to love each other in an ongoing way, as Christ loved us in His death in that once-off act (Jn. 15:12,17). The combination of the present and aorist tenses of *agapan* ['to love'] in these verses proves the point. Thus our obedience *to* Christ in loving each other is exemplified by the obedience *of* Christ (Jn. 15:10). Quite simply, something done 2000 years ago really does affect us *now*. There is a powerful link across the centuries, from the darkness of the cross to the lives we live today in the 21st century. "By his knowledge", by knowing Christ as He was there, we are made righteous (Is. 53:11). As Israel stood before Moses, they promised: "All the words which the Lord hath spoken will we do". When Moses then sprinkled the blood of the covenant upon them- and this incident is quoted in Hebrews as prophetic of the Lord's blood- they said the same but more strongly: "All the words which the Lord hath spoken will we do *and be obedient*" (Ex. 24:3,7). It was as if their connection with the blood inspired obedience. Likewise the communication of God's requirements was made from over the blood-sprinkled mercy seat (Ex. 25:22)- another foretaste of the blood of Christ. Quite simply, we can't face the cross of Christ and not feel impelled towards obedience to that which God asks of us.

The image of soldiers in their time of dying has often been used afterwards as a motivation for a nation: "Earn this" is the message their faces give. And it is no more true than in the death of the Lord. "The love of Christ", an idea elsewhere used of His death (Jn. 13:1; 2 Cor. 5:14,15; Rom. 8:32,34,35; Eph. 5:2,25; Gal. 2:20; Rev. 1:5 cp. 1 Jn. 4:10), *constrains us*; it doesn't force us, but rather shuts us up unto one way, as in a narrow, walled path. We cannot sit passively before the cross of the Lord. That "love of Christ" there passes our human knowledge, and yet our hearts can be opened, as Paul prayed, that we might know the length, breadth and height of it. The crucified Son of God was the full representation of God. The love of Christ was shown in His cross; and through God's enlightenment we can *know* the height, length, breadth of that love (Eph. 3:18,19).

Nothing, whatever, not even life, our sins and dysfunctions of human life, can separate us from the love of Christ towards us in His death (Rom. 8:35). His cross is therefore the constant rallying point of our faith, in whatever difficulty we live through. The resolve and strength we so need in our spiritual path can come only through a personal contemplation of the cross. Do we seek strength to endure unjust treatment and the grace to submit cheerfully to the loss of what we feel is rightfully ours? Be it discrimination in the workplace, persecution from the Government, perceived abuse or degradation by our partner or family...? Let the cross be our endless inspiration: "For it is better, if the will of God be so [a reference to the Lord's struggle in Gethsemane being our struggle], that you suffer for well doing...*for* Christ also hath once suffered for sins, the just for the unjust" (1 Pet. 3:17,18). Remember how under persecution, the faithful love not their lives unto death because of their experience of the blood of the lamb shed for them (Rev. 12:11).

Or do we live in the loneliness of old age or serious illness, fearing death and the uncertainty of our brief future? Again, the cross of Jesus is our rallying point. "For God has not appointed us to wrath, but to obtain salvation by our Lord Jesus Christ, who died for us, that, whether we wake or sleep, we should live together with him" (1 Thess. 5:8-10). Because we are "in Christ", His death was not an isolated historical event. We also are weak with Him (2 Cor. 13:4 RV), such is the identity between us and Him. When Paul reflected upon his own sickness [which the RVmg. calls his stake / cross in the flesh], he could say in all sober truth that he gloried in his weakness, because his identity with the weakness of Christ crucified also thereby identified him with the strength and power of the risen Lord (2 Cor. 11:9).

Do we feel that life is just pointless, an endless round of childcare, working all day doing in essence the same job for 30 years, a trudging through an endless tunnel until our mortality catches up on us? We were redeemed by the precious blood of Christ from the "vain way of life handed down from the fathers" (1 Pet. 1:18), from the frustration of this present life . The word used for "vain" is that used by the LXX for the 'vanity' of life as described in Ecclesiastes, and for idol worship in Lev. 17:7 and Jer. 8:19. We have been redeemed from it all! Not for us the life of endlessly chasing the rainbow's end, slavishly worshipping the idols of ever bigger homes, smarter technology...we were redeemed from the vanity of life "under the sun" by the precious blood of Christ. We were bought out of this slavery, even if in the flesh we go through its motions. Knowing this, we the redeemed, the bought out from vanity, shouldn't spend our hours in front of the television or doing endless crosswords, or frittering away the time of life as the world does. James foresaw that a man could appear to be religious, and yet have a religion that was "vain" (James 1:26)- because he didn't appreciate that the cross had bought him out of vanity. His death was *so that* He might deliver us from this present evil world (Gal. 1:4); because of the Lord's crucifixion, Paul saw himself as crucified unto the world, and the world unto him (Gal. 6:14). The Lord Jesus looked out across the no man's land between the stake and the crowd; He faced the world which crucified Him. We simply *cannot* side with them. To not separate from them is to make the cross in vain for us; for He died to deliver us out of this present world. The pull of the world is insidious; and only sober reflection upon the cross will finally deliver us from it. It's a terrifying thought, that we can make the power of the cross invalid. It really is so, for Paul warned that preaching the Gospel with wisdom of words would make "the cross of Christ...of none effect" (1 Cor. 1:17). The effect of the cross, the power of it to save, is limited in its extent by our manner of preaching of it. And we can make "Christ", i.e. His cross, of "none effect" by trusting to our works rather than accepting the gracious salvation which He achieved (Gal. 5:4).

Do we feel simply not appreciated? As a hassled and harried mother, as a hard working dad who toils to provide for the family he rarely sees, as the person who feels their ideas and abilities are always trashed...? The tragedy of the Lord's death was that when He died, there was nobody to recount His life, as there usually was at a funeral (Is. 53:8 RVmg.). The greatest life that was ever lived was so misunderstood and unappreciated and hated and hurriedly buried, that there was nobody even to give Him an appreciative funeral speech. In our struggle to feel appreciated, we share both His and His Father's sufferings and pain. The cross was the ultimate example of a Man being misjudged and misunderstood and condemned unjustly. When we feel like that, and the nature of our high speed, superficially judging society means that it seems to happen more in this generation than any other [and with deeper consequences]... then we know we are sharing the sufferings of the Lord.

Are we just caught up in our daily work, slave to the corporations who employ us? 1 Cor. 7:23 begs us not to become the slaves of men, because Christ bought us with His blood. Young people especially need to be influenced by this as they choose their career path and employers. Through the cross of Christ, the world is crucified to us (Gal. 6:14 RV).

Do we struggle to live the life of true love, to endure people, even our brethren; are we simply tired of people, and living the life of love towards them? Does the past exist within us as a constant fountain of bitterness and regret? "Let all bitterness, and wrath and anger, and clamour, and evil speaking, be put away from you, with all malice: and be kind one to another, tenderhearted, forgiving one another, even as God for Christ's sake [the sake of His cross] has forgiven you...walk in love, *as Christ also has loved us, and has given himself for us*" (Eph. 4:31-5:2). His cross affects our whole life, our deepest thought and action, to the extent that we can say with Paul, in the silence of our own deepest and most personal reflection: "I live, yet not I, but Christ lives in me: and the life which I now live in the flesh, I live by the faith of the Son of God, who loved me, and gave himself for me" (Gal. 2:20).

Do we find a true unity with our brethren impossible? He died *that* He might gather together into one all God's children (Jn. 11:52). Before His cross, before serious and extended personal meditation upon it, all our personal differences will disappear. A divided ecclesia is therefore one which is not centred upon the cross. Whether or not we must live our church experience in such a context, the barriers which exist within us personally really *can* be brought down by the humbling experience of the cross, and the way in which we are forced to see how that death was not only for us personally. The wonder of it was and is in its universal and so widely-inclusive nature.

Is humility almost impossible for us, lifted up as we may be by our own sense of worth and achievement? Is a true service of *all* our brethren almost impossible for us to contemplate? Consider Mt. 20:26-28: "Whosoever will be great among you, let him be your minister...your servant: even as the Son of man came not to be ministered unto, but to minister, and to give his life a ransom for many". This is our pattern- to give out, with no expectation of appreciation or response. And the cross of Christ alone can inspire us in this.

Do we struggle with some secret vice, in the grip of habitual sin? The cross convicts of sin, for we are impelled by it to follow Christ in going forth "without the camp" (Heb. 13:13), following the path of the leper who had to go forth without the camp (Lev. 13:46). He "his own self bare our sins in his own body on the tree, that *we might die to sin* [Gk.] and live to righteousness" (1 Pet. 2:24). He died for our sins, there all our weakness met their death in His death- so close was the association between Him and our sins. Our response to that is to put those sins to death in *our* bodies, as He put them to death in His on the tree. Speaking of the cross, the Lord said that for our sakes He sanctified Himself [as a priest making an offering], that we might be sanctified in truth (Jn. 17:19). Quite simply, if we behold and believe the cross, we will respond. He mused that if He didn't allow Himself to fall to the ground and die, no fruit could be brought forth (Jn. 12:24). The fact He did means that we will bring forth fruit. It could be that the reference in Jn. 7 to the Holy Spirit being given at the Lord's death (His 'glory'), as symbolized by the water flowing from His side, means that due to the cross we have the inspiration to a holy, spiritual way of life. It is not so that His death released some mystical influence which would change men and women whether or not they will it; rather is it that His example there inspires those who are open to it.

Perhaps we feel that our preaching somehow lacks a sense of power and compulsion of others. Try explicitly telling them about the cross. The apostles recounted the fact of the cross and on this basis appealed for people to be baptized into that death and resurrection. There is an impelling power, an imperative, in the wonder and shame of it all. Joseph saw the Lord's dead body and was compelled to offer for that body to be laid where *his* dead body should have laid. In essence, he lived out the message of baptism. He wanted to identify his body with that of the Lord. He realized that the man Christ Jesus was truly his representative. And so he wanted to identify with Him. And properly presented, this will be the power of response to the preaching of the cross today. "Through one act of righteousness [the cross] the free gift came unto all men to justification of life" (Rom. 5:18)- yet "all men" only receive that justification if they hear this good news and believe it. This is why we must take the Gospel "unto all men" (surely an allusion to the great commission)- so that, in that sense, the wondrous cross of Christ will have been the more 'worthwhile'. Through our preaching, yet more of those "all men" who were potentially enabled to live for ever will indeed do so. This is why the Acts record so frequently connects the preaching of the cross with men's belief. Negatively, men do not believe if they reject the "report" of the crucifixion (Jn. 12:38,39).

Do we struggle to be truly generous to the Lord's cause, and to turn our words and vague feelings of commitment into action? Corinth too were talkers, boasting of their plans to give material support to the poor brethren in Jerusalem, but doing nothing concrete. Paul sought to shake them into action by reminding them of "the grace of our Lord Jesus Christ, that, though he was rich, yet for your sakes he became poor" on the cross (2 Cor. 8:9). Corinth had few wealthy members, but Paul knew that the cross of Christ would inspire in them a generous spirit to those even poorer than they. The richer should be made poor by what the Lord did, Paul is saying- not harmlessly giving of their pocket money. For He gave in ways that hurt Him, ways that were real, meaningful and thereby effective and powerful.

Do we struggle with the ultimate fairness of God? For all we have written about the problem of suffering, it seems to me that no intellectual answer is enough when one personally experiences real tragedy. The sending of Jesus to die in the way that He did was surely one form of God's response to it. In the death of the cross, God showed His entering into our suffering and sense of loss and hurt.

Do we fear that we lack a personal relationship with the Lord Jesus? Do we read of Him, but rarely if ever *feel* Him? Reflection upon His cross should elicit in us an up welling of pure gratitude towards Him, an awkwardness as we realize that this Man loved us more than we love Him...and yet within our sense of debt to Him, of ineffable, unpayable debt, of real debt, a debt infinite and never to be forgotten, we will have the basis for personal response to Him as a person, to a knowing of Him and a loving of Him, and a serving of Him in response. If we feel and know this, we cannot but preach the cross of Christ.

But do we feel ashamed that we just don't witness as we ought to? There is no doubt that the cross and baptism into that death was central to the preaching message of the early brethren. Knowing it, believing it, meant that it just had to be preached. The completeness and reality of the redemption achieved is expressed in Hebrews with a sense of finality, and we ought not to let that slip from our presentation of the Gospel either. There in the cross, the justice and mercy of God are brought together in the ultimate way. There in the cross is the appeal. Paul spoke of "the preaching of the cross", the word / message which *is* the cross (1 Cor. 1:18). Some of the early missionaries reported how they could never get any response to their message until they explained the cross; and so, with our true doctrinal understanding of it, it is my belief that the cross is what has the power of conversion. A man cannot face it and not have a deep impression of the absoluteness of the issues involved in faith and unbelief, in choosing to accept or reject the work of the struggling, sweating, gasping Man who hung on the stake. It truly is a question of believe or perish. Baptism into that death and resurrection is essential for salvation. Of course we must not bully or intimidate people into faith, but on the other hand, a preaching of the cross cannot help but have something compulsive and urgent and passionate about it. For we appeal to men on God's behalf to accept the work of the cross as efficacious for them .Our preaching will then never fail in urgency and entreaty. It will concern the Man who had our nature hanging there perfect, full of love, a light in this dark world....and as far as we perceive the wonder of it all, as far as this breaks in upon us, so far we will hold it forth to this world. The Lord wasn't preaching good *ideas*; He was preaching good *news*. The cross means that we have a faith to share which is a faith to live by all our days; not just a faith to die by, a comfort in our time of dying, as we face the endgame.

The cross alone can shake people out of their indifference, and force them to make some election in this world, instead of sliding dully forward as in a dream. Life is a business we are all apt to mismanage; either living recklessly from day to day, or suffering ourselves to be gulled out of our moments by habits, the TV, life... There is something stupefying in the recurrence of unimportant things. And it is only through the provocations of the Lord and His cross that we are led to take an outlook beyond daily concerns, and comprehend the narrow limits, and great possibilities of our existence. It is the power of the Lord and His cross to induce such moments of clear insight. He, there, is the declared enemy of all living by reflex action. He, there, can electrify His readers and viewers into an instant unflagging activity of service. Those who ignore the challenge of the cross turn to their "own way" (Is. 53:6)- the Hebrew means a custom, habitual way of life. This is what stops us responding to the radical challenge of the cross- our basic conservatism, our love of what we know and are used to. Yet the cross can shake us from this.

Do we feel that our conscience is so dysfunctional and our heart so hardened in some places that nothing much can touch us and motivate us like it used to? The cross can touch and transform the hardest and most damaged heart. Apart from many real life examples around of this, consider the Biblical case of Pilate. Jewish and Roman historians paint a very different picture of Pilate than what we see in the Biblical record. Philo describes him as "ruthless, stubborn and of cruel disposition", famed for "frequent executions without trial" [1]. Josephus speaks of him as totally despising the Jews, stealing money from the temple treasury and brutally suppressing unruly crowds[2]. Why then does he come over in the Gospels as a man desperately struggling with his conscience, to the extent that the Jewish crowds manipulate him to order the crucifixion of a man whom he genuinely believed to be innocent? Surely because the person of the Lord Jesus and the awfulness of putting the Son of God to death touched a conscience which appeared not to even exist.

If the whole drama of the death of Jesus could touch the conscience and personality of even Pilate, it can touch each of us. Just compare the words of Philo and Josephus with how Mark records that Pilate was "amazed" at the self-control of Jesus under trial (Mk. 15:5); how he almost pleads with his Jewish subjects for justice to be done: "Why, what evil has he done?" (Mk. 15:14). Compare this with how Philo speaks of Pilate as a man of "inflexible, stubborn and cruel disposition", famous for "abusive behaviour... and endless savage ferocity". Mt. 27:25 describes how Pilate washes his hands, alluding to the Jewish rite based in Deuteronomy, to declare that he is innocent of the blood of a just man. But Josephus records how Pilate totally despised Jewish religious customs and sensibilities, and appeared to love to commit sacrilege against Jewish things. And in Luke's record, Pilate is recorded as pronouncing Jesus innocent no less than three times.

Do we feel so hurt by others that we find forgiveness impossible, sensing an ever-encroaching bitterness always getting closer to gripping our whole lives? All around this sad world, there seems an endless round of revenge being danced out. The knock someone receives is paid back by them on someone else, and often this ends up in another person being made a scapegoat, someone incapable of defending themselves, who must take all the knocks when they can't pay them back. People subconsciously are obeying a compelling law- to get even. To pay back the hard words the postman gave you with hard words to the girl in the supermarket, and then to scapegoat [say] a child at church for messing up the church service... But the point is, the Lord Jesus is set up as the one and only scapegoat for human sin. On the cross He was the ultimate One who took all the knocks without paying back.

For those who truly believe this to the point of feeling it deep within them, they are freed from the law of revenge- and thus they become free to live life spontaneously, for fun, to not be ashamed of fulfilling life's natural needs. The cycle of revenge and paying back has to be resolved in sacrifice- many societies have shown that. I was a few times in far northern Russia, and it was fascinating to hear the traditions of the Chukchi people. In the past, they say, when a big crime was committed and the criminal convicted, an *innocent* person had to be sacrificed. The study of primitive societies reveals this basic human need for a scapegoat.

There was a psychological value to the Mosaic rite of the scapegoat (Lev. 16:10). All the sins, all the grudges that called for revenge, were to be placed upon that animal, and it was released into the desert. They could watch it scampering away into the bush. This is how we are to understand the placing of human sin- yes, the sins committed against you this day by others- upon the Lord as He hung on the cross. And we must remember that "Vengeance is *mine* [not ours, not the state's], and requital" (Dt. 32:35). That taking of vengeance, that requital, was worked out by God on the cross. There the Lord Jesus was clothed with the 'garments of vengeance' (Is. 59:17); the day of the crucifixion was "the day of vengeance" (Is. 63:4). This is one reason why God doesn't operate a tit-for-tat requital of our sins upon our heads- because He dealt with sin and His vengeance for it in the cross, not by any other way. Hence David calls God the "God of revenge", the one *alone* to whom vengeance belongs (Ps. 94:1,3). Our response to all this is to believe that truly vengeance is God and therefore we will *not* avenge ourselves (Rom. 12:19). I take this to apply to all the micro-level 'takings of vengeance' which we so easily do in our words, body language, attitudes etc., in response to the hurt received from others. The cross alone enables us to break the cycle.

Finally, and, I think, most relevantly. Do we, as men and women all too taken up with our lives, raising families, earning money... lost in the absorption of our daily work, as computer programmers, drivers, factory workers, housewives, business executives...do we in our heart of hearts feel that we just don't have the faith to believe that truly we are forgiven, and will be saved? I know I am talking to the heart of every reader here. Are we like that? I am, and I suspect most of us are. Not that this makes me feel any better about my own inadequacy of faith. Again, let the cross of Christ be our inspiration. For there, "when we were yet without strength, in due time, Christ died for the ungodly". He gave His life there, in the way that He gave it, without any consideration for our personal merits. "God commendeth his love toward us, in that while we were yet sinners, Christ died for us". The Lord gave His all for us, the totally unworthy. And with abounding and matchless logic, Paul continues: "Much more then, being now justified by his blood [i.e. no longer being so worthless and undeserving, but counted as so much better through the atonement He achieved], we *shall be saved from wrath* through him". In this knowledge we can truly have as an helmet the hope of sure salvation. If God gave His Son, and *so* gave His Son, how much more shall He not with Him freely give us all things?

The knowledge and experience of the love of Christ is the end result of all our Bible searching. There's a well known story about the great theologian Karl Barth, who probably penned more words of theology than any other writer in the 20th century. Towards the end of his life, he gave a lecture and invited questions. He was asked something to the effect: 'After a lifetime of Biblical study, what's your single greatest theological insight?'. After a pause he replied, to a hushed audience: 'Jesus loves me, this I know, for the Bible tells me so'. To know that love of Christ, with the full assurance of salvation which it involves, is the end result of all our questioning, our study, our Bible searching, our hunting through concordances, listening to talks, reading studies.

Digression 15: The Crucifix

It is widely believed in Christendom that Jesus Christ was killed on a cross. However, the Greek word 'stauros', which is normally translated 'cross' in English Bibles, really means a stake or pole. Indeed, the crucifix symbol probably has pagan origins. It is fitting that Christ died with hands and arms lifted up above his head, rather than spread out in a crucifix form, seeing that uplifted hands is a symbol of God's promises being confirmed (Ez. 20:5,6,15; 36:7; 47:14), as well as intense prayer (Lam. 2:19; 1 Tim. 2:8; 2 Chron. 6:12,13; Ps. 28:2), which Christ was engaged in on the cross (Heb. 5:7). He said that as the bronze serpent was lifted up on a *pole* when Israel were in the wilderness, so he would be publicly lifted up in his time of dying; thus he associated the 'cross' with the *pole* (John 3:14).

The Roman Catholic Church has attached great mystical significance to the cross. This is completely without Biblical support; it has resulted in the crucifix becoming a talisman, a physical token that God is with us. People have come to feel that by wearing a crucifix or regularly making the sign of the cross, God will be with them. This is mere tokenism; the real power of the cross is through our association with Christ's death by belief and baptism, rather than recalling the physical form of the cross. It is easier, of course, to do the latter than the former.

There is no lack of evidence that the crucifix was a pagan symbol known and used well before the time of Christ. It is yet another piece of paganism, like Christmas trees, which has been mixed into 'Christianity'.

STUDY 9: Questions

1. Why was the death of Jesus, rather than of any other man, required for our salvation?

2. Why were the animal sacrifices of the Law of Moses not sufficient to take away sin?

3. Was Jesus our representative or our substitute when he died?

4. Which of the following statements is true?
   □ Christ died instead of us dying
   □ Christ represented us, so God can forgive us for his sake
   □ Christ was like us but does not represent us
   □ Christ's death meant that God will no longer hold any human being guilty for sin.

5. How can we benefit from the death and resurrection of Jesus?

6. When Christ died on the cross, did he
   □ End the smaller commands of the Law of Moses but not the 10 commandments
   □ End all of the Law of Moses including the ten commandments
   □ End the Law of Moses except for the Jewish feasts
   □ Have no effect on the position of the Law of Moses?

7. Must we keep the Sabbath now in order to be saved?
8. Give reasons for your answer to question 7.

STUDY 10
Baptism Into Jesus

10.1 The Vital Importance Of Baptism

Several times in earlier studies we have mentioned the vital importance of baptism; it is the first step of obedience to the Gospel message. Heb. 6:2 speaks of baptism as one of the most basic doctrines. We have left its consideration until this late stage because true baptism can only occur after a correct grasp of the basic truths which comprise the Gospel. We have now completed our study of these. If you wish to become truly  associated with the great hope which the Bible offers through Jesus Christ, then baptism is an absolute necessity.

"Salvation is of the Jews" (Jn. 4:22) in the sense that the promises concerning salvation were made only to Abraham and his seed. We can only have those promises made to us if we become *in* the seed, by being baptised *into* Christ (Gal. 3:22-29). Then, all that is true of the Lord Jesus becomes true of us. Thus Zacharias quoted prophecies about the seed of Abraham and David as applying to all believers (Lk. 1:69,73,74). Without baptism, we are outside covenant relationship with God. This is why Peter urged: "repent *and* be baptised" in order to receive forgiveness. *Only as many* as have been baptised into Christ are in Him and therefore have the promises of salvation made to Abraham made to them (Gal. 3:27). *If* we share in Christ's death and resurrection through baptism, *then* - and only then - "we also shall be in the likeness of His resurrection…we shall also live with Him" (Rom. 6:5,8).

Jesus therefore clearly commanded his followers: "Go into all the world and preach the gospel (which is contained in the promises to Abraham - Gal. 3:8) to every creature. He who believes *and* is baptised will be saved" (Mk. 16:15,16). Reflection upon this word "and" reveals that belief of the Gospel alone cannot save us; baptism is not just an optional extra in the Christian life, it is a vital prerequisite for salvation. This is not to say that the act of baptism alone will save us; it must be followed by a lifetime of continued openness to God's working in us. Jesus emphasised this: "Most assuredly, I say to you, unless one is born of water and the Spirit, he cannot enter the kingdom of God" (Jn. 3:5). When the barrier of unforgiven sin is removed by grace, when we are 'covered' with Christ's righteousness, then we enjoy a personal covenant relationship with God.

This is an on-going process: "Being born again…through the word of God" (1 Pet. 1:23). Thus it is through our continued response to the spirit word that we become born of the spirit (see Study 2.2).

We are "baptised *into* Christ" (Gal. 3:27), *into* his name and that of the Father (Acts 19:5; 8:16; Mt. 28:19). We can't be "in Christ" without being baptized. Unless we are "washed", we have "no part" in Christ (Jn. 13:8). But note that we are baptised into *Christ* - not into a church or any human organisation. By baptism into him we become a people called by Christ's name, just as Israel were likewise described as having God's name (2 Chron. 7:14). Frequently God warns that the fact Israel carried His name gave them a grave responsibility to act appropriately, as His witnesses to the world. The same is true for us who are baptised into Christ's name. Without baptism we are not "in Christ", and therefore not covered by his saving work (Acts 4:12). Peter weaves a powerful parable around this fact: he likens the ark in the time of Noah to Christ, showing that as the ark saved Noah and his family from the judgment that came upon sinners, so baptism into Christ will save believers from eternal death (1 Pet. 3:20,21). Noah entering into the ark is likened to our entering into Christ through baptism. All those outside the ark were destroyed by the flood; standing near the ark or being a friend of Noah was quite irrelevant. The only way of salvation is, and was, to be inside the Christ/ark. It is evident that the second coming, which the flood typified (Lk. 17:26,27), is nearly upon us. Entry into the Christ/ark by baptism is therefore of the utmost urgency. Human words really do fail to convey this sense of urgency; the Biblical type of entry into the ark in Noah's time is more powerful.

The early Christians obeyed Christ's command to travel preaching the Gospel and baptising; the book of Acts is the record of this. A proof of the vital importance of baptism is to be found in the way that this record emphasises how *immediately* people were baptised after understanding and accepting the Gospel (e.g. Acts 8:12,36-39; 9:18; 10:47; 16:15). This emphasis is understandable once it is appreciated that without baptism our learning of the Gospel is in vain; baptism is a vitally necessary stage to pass through on the road to salvation. In some cases the inspired record seems to highlight how, despite many human reasons to delay baptism, and many difficulties in performing the act, it is so important that people made every effort to overcome all these, with God's help.

The prison keeper at Philippi was suddenly plunged into the crisis of his life by a massive earthquake which completely broke up his high security prison. The prisoners had ample opportunity to escape - something which would have cost him his life. His faith in the Gospel then became real, so much so that "the same hour of the night he was baptised...immediately" (Acts 16:33). If anyone had an excuse to delay baptism it was him. The threat of execution for neglect of duty hung over his head, yet he saw clearly what was the most important act to be performed in his entire life and eternal destiny. Thus he overcame the immediate problems of his surrounding world (i.e. the earthquake), the pressures of his daily employment and the intense nervous trauma he found himself in - to be baptised. Many a hesitant candidate for baptism can take true inspiration from that man. That he could make such an act of faith is proof enough that he already had a detailed knowledge of the Gospel, seeing that such real faith only comes from hearing the word of God (Rom. 10:17 cf. Acts 17:11).

In Acts 16:14,15 we read how Lydia heeded "the things spoken by Paul. And when she ... (was) baptised...". It is *assumed* that anyone who hears and believes the Gospel will be baptised - the baptism is seen as an inevitable part of response to the preaching of the Gospel. Good works are not enough - we *must* be baptised as well. Cornelius was "a devout man and one who feared God...who gave alms generously to the people, and prayed to God always", but this wasn't enough; he had to be shown what he *must do* which he hadn't done - to believe the Gospel of Christ and be baptised (Acts 10:2,6).

Acts 8:26-40 records how an Ethiopian official was studying his Bible whilst riding in a chariot through the desert. He met Philip, who extensively explained the Gospel to him, including the requirement for baptism. Humanly speaking, it must have seemed impossible to obey the command to be baptised in that waterless desert. Yet God would not give a command which He knows some people cannot obey. "As they went down the road, they came to some water", i.e. an oasis, where baptism was possible (Acts 8:36). This incident answers the baseless suggestion that baptism by immersion was only intended to be performed in areas where there was ample, easily accessible water. God will always provide a realistic way in which to obey His commandments.

The apostle Paul received a dramatic vision from Christ which so pricked his conscience that as soon as possible he "arose and was baptised" (Acts 9:18). Again, it must have been tempting for him to delay his baptism, thinking of his prominent social position and high-flying career mapped out for him in Judaism. But this rising star of the Jewish world made the correct and immediate decision to be baptised and openly renounce his former way of life. He later reflected concerning his choice to be baptised: "What things were gain to me, these I have counted loss for Christ...I have suffered the loss of all things (i.e. the things he once saw as "gain" to him), and count them as rubbish, that I may gain Christ...forgetting those things which are behind (the "things" of his former Jewish life), and reaching forward to those things which are ahead, I press toward the goal for the prize ..." (Phil. 3:7,8,13,14).

This is the language of an athlete straining forward to break the finishing tape. Such concentration of mental and physical endeavour should characterise our lives after baptism. It must be understood that baptism is the beginning of a race towards the Kingdom of God; it is not just a token of having changed churches and beliefs, nor is it a passive entrance into a relaxed life of easy-going adherence to a few vaguely stated Christian principles. Baptism associates us in an on-going sense with the crucifixion and resurrection of Jesus (Rom. 6:3-5) - occasions full of ultimate dynamism in every way.

As a tired, yet spiritually triumphant old man, Paul could reminisce: "I was not disobedient to the heavenly vision" (Acts 26:19). As was true for Paul, so it is for all who have been properly baptised: baptism is a decision which one will never regret. Repentance is something never repented of, Paul pithily points out (2 Cor. 7:10). All our lives we will be aware that we made the correct choice. Of few human decisions can we ever be so certain. The question has to be seriously answered: 'Why should I not be baptised?'

10.2   How Should We Be Baptised?

There is a widely held view that baptism can be performed, especially on babies, by sprinkling water on their foreheads (i.e. 'christening'). This is in stark contrast to the Biblical requirement for baptism.

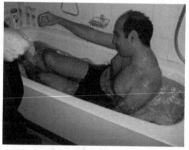

The Greek word 'baptizo', which is translated 'baptise' in the English Bible, does *not* mean to sprinkle; it means to completely wash and immerse in a liquid (see the definitions in the concordances of Robert Young and James Strong). This word is used in classical Greek concerning ships sinking and being 'baptised' (i.e. submerged) in water, or a bucket being submerged in well water. It is also used with reference to a piece of cloth being dyed from one colour to another by 'baptising', or dipping it into a dye. To change the colour of the cloth, it is evident that it had to be fully immersed under the liquid, rather than have the dye sprinkled upon it. Jn. 13:26 uses the Greek *bapto* to describe how the Lord dipped a piece of bread in wine. That immersion is indeed the correct form of baptism is borne out by the following verses:-

- "John also was baptising in Aenon near Salim, because there was much water there. And they came and were baptised" (Jn. 3:23). This shows that "much water" was required for baptism; if it was done by sprinkling a few drops of water, then just one bucket of water would have sufficed for hundreds of people. The people came to this spot on the banks of the River Jordan for baptism, rather than John going round to them with a bottle of water.

- Jesus, too, was baptised by John in the River Jordan - *into* the Jordan (Mk. 1:9 RVmg.). "As soon as Jesus was baptised, he went up out of the water" (Mt. 3:13-16NIV). His baptism was clearly by immersion - he "went up...*out of* the water" after baptism. One of the reasons for Jesus being baptised was in order to set an example, so that no one could seriously claim to follow Jesus without copying his example of baptism by immersion.

- In similar fashion, Philip and the Ethiopian official "went down *into* the water...and he baptised him. Now when they came up *out of* the water..." (Acts 8:38,39). Remember that the official asked for baptism when he saw the oasis: "See, here is water. What hinders me from being baptised?" (Acts 8:36). It is almost certain that the man would not have undertaken a desert journey without at least some water with him, e.g. in a bottle. If baptism were by sprinkling, it could therefore have been done without the need of the oasis.

- Baptism is a burial (Col. 2:12), which implies a total covering.

- Baptism is called a 'washing away' of sins (Acts 22:16). The point of true conversion is likened to a 'washing' in Rev. 1:5; Tit. 3:5; 2 Pet. 2:22; Heb. 10:22 etc. This language of washing is far more relevant to baptism by dipping than to sprinkling.

There are several Old Testament indications that acceptable approach to God was through some form of washing.

The priests had to wash completely in a bath called the 'laver' before they came near to God in service (Lev. 8:6; Ex. 40:7,32). The Israelites had to wash in order to cleanse themselves from certain uncleanness (e.g. Dt. 23:11), which was representative of sin.

A man called Naaman was a Gentile leper who sought to be healed by the God of Israel. As such he represents sin-stricken man, effectively going through a living death due to sin. His cure was by dipping in the River Jordan. Initially he found this simple act hard to accept, thinking that God would want him to do some dramatic act, or to dip himself in a large and well-known river, e.g. the Abana. Similarly, we may find it hard to believe that such a simple act can ultimately bring about our salvation. It is more attractive to think that our own works and public association with a large, well-known church (cf. the river Abana) can save us, rather than this simple act of association with the true hope of Israel. After dipping in Jordan, Naaman's flesh "was restored like the flesh of a little child, and he was clean" (2 Kings 5:9-14).

It is worth noting that most of the early artistic descriptions of baptism in Roman catacombs and sarcophagi show the candidate standing in water, being baptized by immersion.

There should now be little room for doubt that 'baptism' refers to a complete dipping in water after first understanding the basic message of the Gospel. This Bible-based definition of baptism does not make any reference to the status of the person who actually does the baptism physically. Baptism being an immersion in water after belief of the Gospel, it is theoretically possible to baptise oneself. However, because baptism is only baptism by reason of the correct faith which one holds at the time of the immersion, it is definitely advisable to be baptised by another believer of the faith, who can first of all assess the degree of understanding a person has before actually immersing them.

10.3   The Meaning Of Baptism

One of the reasons for baptism by immersion is that going under the water symbolises our going into the grave - associating us with the death of Christ, and indicating our 'death' to our previous life of sin and ignorance. Coming up out of the water connects us with the resurrection of Christ, relating us to the hope of resurrection to eternal life at his return, as well as to living a new life now, spiritually triumphant over sin on account of Christ's victory achieved by his death and resurrection.

"...all of us who were baptised into Christ Jesus were baptised into his death. We were therefore buried with him through baptism into death in order that, just as Christ was raised from the dead through the glory of the Father, we too may live a new life. If we have been united with him like this in his death (by baptism), we will certainly also be united with him in his resurrection" (Rom. 6:3-5NIV).

Because salvation has been made possible only through Christ's death and resurrection, it is vital that we associate ourselves with these things if we are to be saved. The symbolic dying and rising again with Christ, which baptism enacts, is the only way to do this. It should be noted that sprinkling does not fulfil this symbol. At baptism, "our old self (way of life) was crucified" along with Christ on the cross (Rom. 6:6NIV); God "made us alive with Christ" at baptism (Eph. 2:5NIV). However, we still have human nature after baptism, and therefore the fleshly way of life will keep raising its head. The 'crucifixion' of our flesh (human nature) is therefore an on-going process which only *begins* at baptism, hence Jesus told the believer to take up his cross each day and follow him, as it were, in the procession towards Calvary (Lk. 9:23; 14:27). Whilst a life of true crucifixion with Christ is not easy, there is unspeakable consolation and joy through being also united with Christ's resurrection.

Christ brought about "peace through the blood of His cross" (Col. 1:20) – "the peace of God, which surpasses all understanding" (Phil. 4:7). Concerning this, Jesus promised: "Peace I leave with you, My peace I give to you; not as the world gives (peace) do I give to you" (Jn. 14:27). This peace and true spiritual joy more than balances out the pain and difficulty of openly associating ourselves with the crucified Christ. "For as the sufferings of Christ abound in us, so our consolation also abounds through Christ" (2 Cor. 1:5).

There is also the freedom which comes from knowing that our natural self is really dead, and therefore Jesus is very actively living with us through our every trial. The great apostle Paul could speak from his own experience of this. "I have been crucified with Christ; it is no longer I who live, but Christ lives in me; and the life which I now live in the flesh I live by faith in the Son of God" (Gal. 2:20).

"Baptism ... now saves you ... by the resurrection of Jesus Christ" (1 Pet. 3:21NIV) because our association with Christ's resurrection to eternal life gives us access to the same at his return. It is through sharing in this resurrection, then, that we will finally be saved. Jesus stated this in very simple terms: "Because I live, you will live also" (Jn. 14:19). Paul likewise: "We were reconciled to God through the death of His Son ... we shall be saved by His life" (resurrection; Rom. 5:10).

Time and again it is emphasised that by associating ourselves with Christ's death and sufferings in baptism, and our subsequent way of life, we will surely share in his glorious resurrection:-

"If we died with (Christ), we shall also live with Him. If we endure, we shall also reign with Him" (2 Tim. 2:11,12).

"We always carry around in our body the death of Jesus, so that the life of Jesus may also be revealed in our body ... because we know that the one who raised the Lord Jesus ... will also raise us with Jesus" (2 Cor. 4:10,11,14NIV).

Paul shared in "the fellowship of (Christ's) sufferings, being (by his hard experience of life) conformed to His death, if, by any means, I might attain to the resurrection from the dead." as experienced by Christ (Phil. 3: 10,11 cf. Gal 6:14).

10.4   Baptism And Salvation

Baptism associates us with the death of Christ, hence it is only through baptism that we can have access to forgiveness. We are "buried with (Christ) in baptism and raised with him through ... the power of God, who raised him from the dead. When you were dead in your sins ... (God) made you alive with Christ. He forgave us all our sins" (Col.

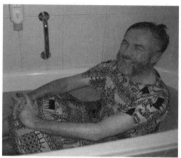

2:12,13NIV). We are "washed...in the name of the Lord Jesus" (1 Cor. 6:11) - i.e. baptism into the name of Jesus is the means by which our sins are washed away. This was typified back in Num. 19:13, where those without the water of purification had to die. We demonstrated in Study 10.2 how baptism is a washing away of sins (cf. Acts 22:16). The descriptions of the believers as being washed from their sins in the blood of Christ therefore refers to their doing this by means of baptism (Rev. 1:5; 7:14; Tit. 3:5 [NIV] speak of this as "the washing of rebirth", referring to our being "born of water" at baptism [Jn. 3:5]).

In the light of all this, it is understandable that Peter's response to the question, "What shall we do?" was, "Repent and be baptised, every one of you, in the name of Jesus Christ *for* the forgiveness of your sins" (Acts 2:37,38NIV). Baptism into Christ's name is *for* the forgiveness of sins; it's that important. There is no salvation except in the name of Jesus (Acts 4:12), and we can only share that name by being baptised into it. This fact means that non-Christian religions can in no way lead to salvation. No true Bible believer can accept that they do; the fact that the wider ecumenical movement do so, is a sad reflection upon their attitude to Holy Scripture.

Christ's resurrection to eternal life was a sign of his personal triumph over sin. By baptism we associate ourselves with this, and therefore we are spoken of as having been raised along with Christ, sin no longer having power over us, as it no longer did over him. Through baptism we are therefore "set free from sin ... sin shall not have dominion over you" after baptism (Rom. 6:18,14). However, after baptism we still sin (1 Jn. 1:8,9); sin is still in a position to enslave us again if we turn away from Christ. We are therefore presently sharing in Christ's death and sufferings, although baptism demonstrates how we are also associated with Christ's resurrection, which we have hope of sharing at his return.

Only in prospect are we free from sin. "He who believes and is baptised *will* be saved" (Mk. 16:16) at Christ's second coming. Ultimate salvation does not occur straight after baptism, but at the judgment seat (1 Cor. 3:13). Indeed, there is no need for the doctrine of the judgment if we receive salvation at baptism, nor should we have to die. "He who endures to the end will be saved" (Mt. 10:22).

Even after his baptism, Paul (and all Christians) had to strive towards salvation (Phil. 3:10-13; 1 Cor. 9:27); he spoke of the *hope* of eternal life (Tit. 1:2; 3:7; 1 Thess. 5:8; Rom. 8:24) and of those who "*will inherit* salvation" (Heb. 1:14). At the judgment seat, the righteous will go *into* eternal life (Mt. 25:46). Paul's marvellous, inspired logic shines through in Rom. 13:11 - he reasons that after baptism we can know that each day we live and endure is one day closer to Christ's second coming, so that we can rejoice that "now our salvation is nearer than when we first believed". Our salvation is therefore not now possessed. Salvation is conditional; we will be saved *if* we hold fast a true faith (Heb. 3:12-14), *if* we remember in faith the basic doctrines which comprise the Gospel (1 Tim. 4:16; 1 Cor. 15:1,2), and *if* we continue in those things which are in keeping with such a great hope (2 Pet. 1:10).

The Greek verb translated "saved" is therefore sometimes used in the continuous tense, showing that salvation is an on-going process which is occurring within us by reason of our continued obedience to the Gospel. Thus the believers are spoken of as "*being* saved" by their response to the Gospel (1 Cor. 1:18; other examples of this continuous theme are in Acts 2:47 and 2 Cor. 2:15). This Greek word for "saved" is only used in the past tense concerning the great salvation which Christ made possible on the cross, and which we can associate ourselves with by baptism (2 Tim. 1:9; Tit. 3:5).

This is all exemplified by God's dealings with natural Israel, which form the basis for His relationship with spiritual Israel, i.e. the believers. Israel left Egypt, representing the world of the flesh and false religion which we are associated with before baptism. They passed through the Red Sea and then travelled through the wilderness of Sinai into the promised land, where they were fully established as God's Kingdom. Their crossing of the Red Sea is typical of our baptism (1 Cor. 10:1,2); the wilderness journey of our present life, and Canaan of the Kingdom of God. Jude v. 5 describes how many of them were destroyed during the wilderness journey: "The Lord, having saved the people out of the land of Egypt, afterward destroyed those who did not believe." Israel were therefore "saved" from Egypt, as all those who are baptised are "saved" from sin. If one of those Israelites had been asked, "Are you saved?" their response could have been, "Yes", but this would not mean that they would *ultimately* be saved.

In the same way as Israel turned back to Egypt in their hearts (Acts 7:39) and reverted to a life of flesh-pleasing and false beliefs, so those who have been "saved" from sin by baptism can likewise fall away from the blessed position in which they stand. The possibility of our doing the same as natural Israel in the wilderness is highlighted in 1 Cor. 10:1-12, Heb. 4:1,2 and Rom. 11:17-21. There are numerous examples in Scripture of those who were once "saved" from sin by baptism, later falling into a position which meant they will be condemned at Christ's return (e.g. Heb. 3:12-14; 6:4-6; 10:20-29). The 'once saved always saved' idea of zealous 'evangelical' preachers is exposed for what it is by such passages - complete flesh-pleasing sophistry.

As with all things, a correct sense of balance is needed in trying to understand to what extent we are "saved" by baptism. By becoming "in Christ" by baptism, we are saved in prospect; we really do have a *sure* hope of being in God's Kingdom if we continue to abide in Christ as we are when we rise from the waters of baptism. At any point in time after our baptism we should be able to have humble confidence that we will certainly be accepted into the Kingdom at Christ's return. We cannot be *ultimately* certain, because we may fall away the next day; we do not know our personal spiritual future in this life.

We must do all we can to maintain the good conscience which we have with God at baptism; to "keep our first love" (Rev. 2:4). Baptism is the "pledge (response mg.) of a good conscience" (1 Pet. 3:21,NIV); the baptism candidate pledges (promises) to keep that clear conscience with God.

Even though baptism is of vital importance to our salvation in Christ, we must be careful not to give the impression that by the one act or 'work' of baptism alone we will be saved. We have earlier shown how that a life of continued fellowshipping of Christ's crucifixion is necessary: "Unless one is born of water *and* the spirit, he cannot enter the Kingdom of God" (Jn. 3:5). A comparison of this with 1 Pet. 1:23 shows that the birth which occurs at a true baptism must be followed by our gradual regeneration by the spirit-word. Salvation is not just due to baptism: it is a result of grace (Eph. 2:8), faith (Rom. 1:5) and hope (Rom. 8:24), among other things. The argument is sometimes made that salvation is by faith alone, and therefore a 'work' like baptism is irrelevant. However, James 2:17-24 makes it clear that such reasoning makes a false distinction between faith and works; a true faith, e.g. in the Gospel, is demonstrated to be genuine faith by the works which it results in, e.g. baptism. "... a man is justified by works and not by faith only" (James 2:24). In several cases of baptism, the believer asked what he must "do" to be saved; the reply always involved baptism (Acts 2:37; 9:6; 10:6; 16:30). 'Doing' the 'work' of baptism is therefore a necessary indication of our belief of the Gospel of salvation. The work of saving us has ultimately been done by God and Christ, but we need to do "works befitting repentance" and believe in this (Acts 26:20 cf. Mk. 16:15,16).

We have earlier shown that the language of washing away of sins refers to God's forgiveness of us on account of our baptism into Christ. In some passages we are spoken of as washing away our sins by our faith and repentance (Acts 22:16; Rev. 7:14; Jer. 4:14; Is. 1:16); in others God is seen as the one who washes away our sins (Ez. 16:9; Ps. 51:2,7; 1 Cor. 6:11). This nicely shows how that if we do our part in being baptised, God will then wash away our sins. Thus the 'work', or act, of baptism is a vital step in taking hold of God's Gospel of grace ('unmerited favour'), which has been offered to us in His Word.

Belief In Practice 18:

The Certainty Of Salvation

Dr. Rene Allendy was a selfless, fine doctor who kept a brutally honest diary to the last day of his long agony of dying (*Journal d'un Medecin Malade*, "Diary of a sick physician"). In the face of death, despite a humanly 'good' life lived, he finally possessed nothing but a hopeless cynicism. I ask you, every reader: In the face of death, what do you have? The true Christian should be able to answer so, so positively.

ASSURANCE AFTER ASSURANCE

The pleasure or will of our loving Father is that we should share His Kingdom (Lk. 12:32), and that pleasure / will prospered through the cross of Jesus (Is. 53:10). God isn't indifferent. He wants us to be there. That's why He gave His Son to die. It's as simple as that. The deepest longings we feel in our earthly lives, as parents, as lovers, are mere flickers of the hungering desire God feels for us. It is a desire that cost Him His very own crucified Son. The Lord Himself knew our basic tendency to disbelieve the certainty of our salvation when He comforted us: "Fear not little flock, it is your Father's good pleasure to give you the Kingdom". God's promises are sure; so sure that they are as good as if they have been fulfilled. Hence the New Testament speaks of our having eternal life right now, even though that promise has not yet been fulfilled. Acts 7:17 speaks of "the time of the promise" drawing near- putting 'the promise' for 'the fulfilment of the promise', so sure are God's promises of fulfilment. "God, willing more abundantly to shew unto the heirs of the promise the immutability of his counsel, confirmed it by an oath: that…we may have a strong consolation, who have fled for refuge to lay hold of the hope set before us; which hope we have as an anchor of the soul, both sure and steadfast" (Heb. 6:17-19). If the hope is an anchor to the soul, the foundation to our innermost thought processes, it must be something more than a mere possibility. "Boldness and glorying in the hope" are the family characteristics of the house / family of Jesus (Heb. 3:6 RV). It is the sureness of the hope that brings us close to God; without such certainty, how can we have the relationship with the Father which He so earnestly intends for us (Heb. 7:19)?

When the Lord taught that "the life is more than the food" which we worry about today (Lk. 12:23 RV), and "the body [which we shall receive] is more than the raiment", He surely means that our hope of eternal life, *the* life, the only real and ultimate life worth having, should eclipse our worries about today's problems of survival. Not worrying about food, drink and clothing, which God will provide, is likely an allusion to His provision for Israel during their wilderness journey to the promised land. And in this context the Lord encourages us: "Seek you the Kingdom of God, and all these things shall be added unto you…fear not, little flock; for it is your Father's good pleasure to give you the Kingdom" (Lk. 12:31,32). If it is God's pleasure to give us the Kingdom, then surely He will give us all basic necessities until that time comes. Our certainty of being there thus greatly relieves us from earthly cares, compared to the person who has no such hope.

The belief that we will be there is the only real anchor in life's uncertain storm. "When the kindness of God our saviour, and his love toward man, appeared, not by works done in righteousness which we did ourselves, but according to his mercy he saved us…that, being justified by his grace, we might be made heirs according to the hope of eternal life…and concerning these things I will that you affirm confidently, to the end that they which have believed God may be careful to maintain good works" (Tit. 3:4-8). The confident, regular reassurance of other believers was to be part of the spiritual diet with which the Cretan brothers and sisters were constantly fed. And this assurance was to be the foundation of ecclesial growth as members individually developed the mind of Christ.

In the end, God gives us our dominant desire. Israel in the wilderness "despised the land of desire, they believed not his word" of promise, that they would enter it (Ps. 106:24 AVmg.). They didn't really desire the land, so they didn't receive it. Israel both despised the land, and they despised their God (Num. 14:11,23,31 RV). Our attitude as to whether or not we want to be in the Kingdom is essentially our attitude to God. This has far reaching implications. Ps. 107:30 likewise speaks of how the faithful are brought to the haven of their desire (RVmg.). All those who truly love the Lord's appearing- with all that implies in practical life and belief- will be accepted (2 Tim. 4:8). And yet Israel didn't have the dominant desire to be in the Kingdom, as Joshua and Caleb had. Why didn't they? It is vital that we understand the reasons for their failure – such an understanding will be a safeguard to help prevent us from making the same mistake (Rom.15:4).

They initially wanted to return to Egypt, and yet it is also true that they sought for a city to live in whilst in the wilderness (Ps. 107:4). They wanted to just stay there in the wilderness. They didn't want to return to Egypt, they didn't really desire the unknown promised land...so, they wanted to just settle there in the wilderness. And so it can be with us. We can be happy with the way to the Kingdom, it can be that the social aspect of the Christian life suits us...we are content with it, and yet it can be that for all that, we lack a real sense of direction towards the Kingdom. We are going some place. The Christian life is but a path leading towards an end, and the end destination is the Kingdom. *If we believe surely that we will be there, we will live lives which reflect this sense of concrete direction and aim.*

OUR MOTIVES

But all this raises the question: Why do I want to be in the Kingdom? What makes this the dominant desire which we will surely receive? David asked to be given "your salvation...that I may see the good of your chosen, that I may rejoice in the gladness of your nation" (Ps. 106:4,5). Paul likewise says that to see the Thessalonians in the Kingdom would be his glory and joy in that day. Both those men had a perspective far bigger than merely themselves. If our sole desire to 'be there' is so that *I* will live for ever, *I* will have a nice level of existence...this, it seems to me, is not only essentially selfish, but our basic dysfunction and tendency to self-abuse and devaluing of ourselves just will not allow us to have the receipt of personal eternity as our dominant desire. We'll be interested in it, but it won't consistently be the thing we desire above all else. But if we see the wider picture, then we will pray for the Kingdom to come so that the things of God's Name may be glorified; because we want to see our dear brethren there in the Kingdom; because we will want to share our Lord's joy and their joy. These things are more than the primitive desire for self-preservation which we all have, and which we can articulate in terms of wanting to personally be in the Kingdom. Thus if our motives are right for wanting to be in the Kingdom, then this will become our dominant desire; and we will be granted the desires of our heart. Really we will be. God's word promises this.

The grace of God guarantees our salvation. Yet we find it so hard to believe- that I, with all my doubts and fears, will really be there. Israel were warned that they were being given the land (cp. salvation) " not for your righteousness, or for the uprightness of your heart...for you art a stiffnecked people" (Dt. 9:5,6). These words are picked up in Tit. 3:5 and applied to the new Israel: "Not by works of righteousness which we have done, but according to his mercy he saved us, by the washing (baptism) of regeneration, and renewing of the Holy Spirit" - by His grace alone.

Our difficulty in believing 'we will be there' is perhaps related to our difficulty in believing that in prospect, we 'are there' right now, through being "in Christ". This most basic truth, that we are "in Christ" through baptism, carries with it very challenging implications. We are well familiar with Paul's reasoning in Romans 6, that through being immersed in water at baptism, we share in the Lord's death and resurrection. As He rose from the dead, so we rise from the waters of baptism. But what happened to Him next? He ascended to Heaven, and sat down at the right hand of the throne of God in glory. And each of those stages is true of us right now. Let Paul explain in Eph. 2:6: "He has raised us up together [Strong: 'to rouse [from death] in company with'], and made us sit together [i.e. Christ and us] in heavenly places in Christ". We are now in 'the heavenlies'; and not only so, but we *sit together* there with Christ. And He now sits upon His throne of glory. Even now we in a sense sit with Him in His Heavenly throne, even though in another sense this is a future thing we await (Lk. 22:30; Rev. 3:21). No wonder Paul goes on to make a profound comment: "That in the ages to come [the aions of future eternity], He might show [Gk.- to indicate by words or act] the exceeding riches of his grace [which was shown through] his kindness toward us through Christ". Throughout the ages of eternity, God will demonstrate to others [the mortal population of the Millennium, and perhaps other future creations] how pure and wonderful His grace was to us in the few brief years of this life- in that, He will demonstrate, He counted us *right now in our mortality* as having resurrected, ascended to Heaven, and reigning / sitting with Christ in glory. The wonder of what we are experiencing now, the height of our present position, is something that will be marvelled at throughout eternity as an expression of God's grace and kindness. And we will be the living witnesses to it.

And we can start that witness right now.

Digression 16: Re-baptism

Some people feel very hesitant to be baptised after having already had what they thought was a 'baptism' of some sort, either by sprinkling as a baby, or by full immersion into "another gospel". Baptism is a once-for-all commitment. Notice the different tenses in the Greek text of Rom. 6:13: 'Don't go on yielding' (present), but rather 'dedicate

yourselves once and for all' (aorist). The death of Jesus for us was a once-for-all commitment to us, and our response in baptism is likewise a once-for-all commitment to Him (Rom. 6:10). This is why *true* baptism is by its very nature unrepeatable (Heb. 6:4).

However, before true baptism there must be repentance and proper belief of the true Gospel (Acts 2:38; Mk. 16:15,16). Baptism is only a true baptism, acceptable to God, when it is undertaken in this way. Mt. 28:19,20 associates baptism with first hearing the teachings of Christ explained. A young child is incapable of repenting or understanding the Gospel; in any case, sprinkling is not baptism. In all Biblical examples, the desire for baptism is purely at the initiative of the person who wants to be baptised (e.g. Lk. 3:10; Acts 2:37; 8:36; 16:30). Parents cannot decide that a young baby can be properly baptised, because they cannot take the initiative for another individual. A swimmer diving into a swimming pool may be immersed in water, but this is not baptism, because the person is not consciously responding to the true Gospel. The same is true of those who are immersed whilst believing "another gospel"; they have been immersed but not baptised.

There is only "one faith", i.e. one set of doctrines which comprises the true Gospel, and therefore only "one baptism" - the baptism which occurs after believing the "one faith". "There is one body (i.e. one true church)... just as you were called in one hope of your calling. One Lord, one faith, one baptism, one God" (Eph. 4:4-6). There are not many hopes, as is believed by those who say that it does not matter how we understand the Christian hope; whether we believe our reward will be in heaven or on earth. There is only "one God" - Jesus is therefore not God. It follows that if, when we were baptised, we failed to understand basic doctrines like the Kingdom of God, the nature of God and Jesus, etc., then our first 'baptism' may not have been valid. At our baptisms, we rose with Christ "through faith in the working of God, who raised Him from the dead" (Col. 2:12). Baptism isn't just immersion in water- it depends upon our faith to make it real and meaningful. And faith comes from believing the one faith, as in the set of teachings that comprise the true Gospel. If we didn't know these at the time of our first immersion, how could we have truly believed?

John the Baptist immersed people, calling upon them to repent, and teaching them certain things about Jesus (Mk. 1:4; Lk. 3:3). However, this was insufficient. Acts 19:1-5 records that some whom John had baptised had to be baptised again because of their incomplete grasp of the true Gospel. Like those whom John baptised, we may feel that at our first dipping we did make a genuine repentance and a new start. This may be true, but it does not take away the need to receive the "one (true) baptism" which can only occur after grasping all the elements of the "one faith".

STUDY 10: QUESTIONS

1. Do you think you can be saved without baptism?

2. What does the word 'baptism' mean?
    - ☐ Commitment
    - ☐ Sprinkling
    - ☐ Belief
    - ☐ Dipping/immersion

3. What is the meaning of baptism as explained in Rom. 6:3-5?

4. When should we be baptised?
    - ☐ After learning the true Gospel and repenting
    - ☐ As a small baby
    - ☐ After getting interested in the Bible
    - ☐ When we want to join a church

5. What are we baptised into?
    - ☐ The church who baptises us
    - ☐ The word of God
    - ☐ Christ
    - ☐ The Holy Spirit

6. Which of the following happens after baptism?
    - ☐ We become part of Abraham's seed
    - ☐ We will never sin again
    - ☐ We are definitely saved for all time
    - ☐ Our sins are forgiven

7. Will baptism alone save us?

STUDY 11
Life In Christ

11.1 Introduction

Baptism brings us into Christ and in Him we have the assured hope of having eternal life in God's Kingdom, as well as enabling us to share in His new life now. The more we believe and appreciate the certainty of this hope and these awesome present blessings which there are in Him, the more evident it becomes that it brings certain responsibilities upon us. These revolve around living a life which is fitting for someone who has the hope of being given God's nature (2 Pet. 1:4), of actually sharing His Name (Rev. 3:12) through being made perfect in every way.

We explained in Study 10.3 that after baptism we are committed to a life of constantly crucifying the evil desires of our mind (Rom. 6:6). Unless we are willing to try to do this, then baptism is meaningless. It should only take place once a person is prepared to accept the responsibilities of the new life which should follow.

In baptism we die to this old, natural way of life, and are figuratively resurrected with Christ. "If then you were raised with Christ (in baptism), seek those things which are above, where Christ is, sitting at the right hand of God. Set your mind on things above, not on things on the earth. For you died ...Therefore put to death ... fornication, uncleanness ... covetousness" (Col. 3:1-5). After baptism we commit ourselves to a life of seeing things from God's heavenly perspective, thinking of heavenly (i.e. spiritual) things, exchanging our worldly ambition for an ambition to overcome our natural human tendencies and thereby to enter God's Kingdom.

The tendency of human nature is to show enthusiasm for obedience to God in fits and starts. God warns against this. God comments upon His own commandments: "which, if a man does, he shall live by them" (Ez. 20:21). If we are aware of God's commands, and begin to obey them in baptism, we should be committed to live a lifetime of obedience to them.

11.2 Holiness

"Holy, holy, holy, is the Lord" (Is. 6:3). The triple emphasis of this verse is one of a multitude of passages which stress the holiness of God. 'Holiness' fundamentally means 'separation' - both separation *from* unholy things, and separation *to* spiritual things. We are asked to be "imitators of God", as His own small children (Eph. 5:1 NIV). Therefore "as He who called you is holy, you also be holy in all your conduct, because it is written, 'Be holy, for I am holy'" (1 Pet. 1:15,16; Lev. 11:44).

Natural Israel was called out of Egypt by their Red Sea baptism to be "a holy nation" (Ex. 19:6). After our baptism, the members of spiritual Israel likewise receive "a holy calling" (2 Tim. 1:9). After baptism we "become slaves of...holiness" (Rom. 6:19,22 and context).

As holiness is such an essential part of God's very being, so it must be a fundamental concern of all those who try to be "imitators of God". If we do this, we will "share in his holiness" when we are granted His nature (Heb. 12:10; 2 Pet. 1:4 NIV). Therefore without holiness in this life, a believer cannot "see the Lord" (Heb. 12:14) - i.e. he will not be able to actually see nor perceive God and relate to Him on a personal level in the Kingdom if he has not demonstrated holiness in this life. True religion is to visit the fatherless and widows (James 1:25-27), to walk humbly with our God (Mic. 6:8).

To have been given such a great hope means that we should be separate from the world around us which does not have this hope, being separated *to* an eternity of sharing God's nature. Our 'separation' should not therefore be something which we feel is being enforced upon us; because of our separation *to* this lofty calling and hope, it should only be natural that we feel separated *from* the things of the world, which is dominated by human principles.

We will now consider some of the things which we should feel separated *from*, and then in Study 11.3 we will study what we are separated *to* in practical terms.

11.2.1   The Christian And The Use Of Force

We are living in a world dominated by sin, in which the strong oppress the weak. We saw in Section 6.1 that human governments can be called 'the devil' because they are organised around sinful human desires, the Biblical 'devil'.

The repeated message of the Bible is that, in the short term, sin and the seed of the serpent will appear to triumph whilst, after temporary suffering in various ways, the seed of the woman will ultimately be justified. For this reason the believer is continually commanded "not to resist an evil person" (Mt. 5:39; Rom. 12:17; 1 Thess. 5:15; 1 Pet. 3:9).

We have seen that evil is allowed, and sometimes brought about, by God (Is. 45:7; Am. 3:6 cf. Study 6.1). Actively to resist evil by force therefore may mean that we oppose God. For this reason Jesus commanded us not to physically resist the forces of evil: "But whoever slaps you on your right cheek, turn the other to him also. If anyone wants to sue you and take away your tunic, let him have your cloak also" (Mt. 5:39,40). Christ is the example in this: "I *gave* My back to those who struck Me ..." (Is. 50:6).

Christ's words associate suing at law with the activities of a world which is opposed to the believer. Doing this is a prime example of resisting evil, and will not be done by anyone who has a firm faith in God's promise that "'Vengeance is Mine, I will repay,' says the Lord" (Rom. 12:19). "Do not say, 'I will recompense evil'; wait for the Lord, and He will save you" (Prov. 20:22 cf. Dt. 32:35). For this reason Paul roundly rebuked the Corinthians for taking others to law (1 Cor. 6:1-7).

In view of the greatness of our hope, we should not be so concerned with the injustices of the present life: "*Dare* any of you, having a matter against another, go to law ... Do you not know that the saints will judge the world?" (1 Cor. 6:1,2). Taking others to law for personal advantage should therefore be unthinkable for the true believer. There is only one judge -- the Lord. We are not therefore to set ourselves up as judges in the sense that He alone is the judge of all the earth.

In order to suppress the forces of evil, as well as (in some cases) to keep evil men in power, military and police forces are used by human governments. These are institutionalised forms of resisting evil, and therefore the true believer should have no part in them. "All who take the sword will perish by the sword" (Mt. 26:52). This is repeating a very early Divine principle: "Whoever sheds man's blood (purposefully), by man his blood shall be shed; for in the image of God He made man" (Gen. 9:6). Any wilful violence against our fellow man is therefore violence against God, unless He has sanctioned it.

Under the New Covenant, we have been told: "Love your enemies, bless those who curse you, do good to those who hate you, and pray for those who spitefully use you and persecute you" (Mt. 5:44; Lk. 6:27). The armed forces and police forces operate in direct contradiction to these principles and therefore the true believer will not seek to be involved with them. Even if not directly involved in committing violence, working within these organisations or involvement in employment connected with them, is evidently inadvisable; indeed, any employment which involves taking an oath of allegiance to such an authority, robs us of our freedom of conscience to obey God's commands. Believers in Christ have therefore always been conscientious objectors to military service, although always willing to take up alternative employment in times of national crisis which will materially benefit their fellow citizens.

11.2.2 The Christian And Politics

A clear understanding of, and firm faith in, the coming of God's Kingdom means that we will recognise that human Government is unable to bring about perfection. Jesus prophesied that things would degenerate from bad to worse in "the last days" just prior to his coming (Lk. 21:9-11, 25-27). It is not possible to believe his words and at the same time hope to radically improve the world's position through human politics. On an individual level, we are simply to do good to all men as opportunity may allow (Gal. 6:10).

The record of the early believers shows them to have been committed to living a spiritual life in anticipation of Christ's return, chiefly manifesting their concern for the surrounding world through preaching to them.

"... the way of human beings is not in their control ... they ... cannot direct their steps" (Jer. 10:23 NRSV); giving these words their weight means that we will recognise that human leadership is something which God's children will never seek. Voting is therefore inconsistent with a true understanding of this. "The Most High rules in the kingdom of men, and gives it to whomever He chooses" (Dan. 4:32). He is the power that is above the high ones of the present governments (Ecc. 5:8 NIV). Human rulers are thus ultimately given their power by God (Rom. 13:1); to vote in a democratic system may therefore involve voting against one whom God has chosen to be in power. Thus it is recorded that God *gave* certain nations into the control of Nebuchadnezzar king of Babylon (Jer. 27:5,6).

Because of our recognition that God has given nations into the hands of their rulers, we should be very careful to be exemplary citizens, abiding by the laws of the country where we live, unless they conflict with the law of Christ.

"Let every soul be subject to the governing authorities ... the authorities that exist are appointed by God ... for because of this you also pay taxes ... render therefore to all their due: taxes to whom taxes are due ... honour to whom honour" is due (Rom. 13:1-7).

The involvement of Christian organisations in forms of political protest and tax boycotts is therefore an indication of their studied disregard of these basic Biblical principles. However, Peter's example of continuing to preach Christ when forbidden by the Government to do so, is an indication of how we can only obey human commands when they do not conflict with the law of Christ: "Whether it is right in the sight of God to listen to you more than to God, you judge " (Acts 4:17-20; 5:28,29).

11.2.3 The Christian And Worldly Pleasures

Due to its lack of a true relationship with God and of a realistic hope for the future, the world has devised countless forms of seeking instant pleasure. Those forms of pleasure which seek to please the sin-prone side of our personalities should be shunned by those who are trying to develop a spiritual mind. "... the sinful nature wants what is contrary to the Spirit, and the Spirit what is contrary to the sinful nature" (Gal. 5:17 NIV). Because of this fundamental opposition, it is impossible to reason that we can legitimately give way to our sinful nature and also claim to be following the Spirit. The world is structured around "the cravings of sinful man, the lust of his eyes and the boasting of what he has and does" (1 Jn. 2:16 NIV). "Whoever therefore wants to be a friend of the world makes himself an enemy of God" (James 4:4). Spending our time, thinking and money on sinful things of the flesh, watching worldly movies etc. is being "a friend of the world". The desires of the world will soon pass away, and those who have sided with the world in this life will pass away with it (1 Jn. 2:15-17). "The world (i.e. society) of the ungodly" will be destroyed by the second coming (2 Pet. 2:5), seeing that "the whole world is under the control of the evil one" (1 Jn. 5:19 NIV). If we are to avoid that destruction, we must be "not of the world" (Jn. 17:16 cf. Rev. 18:4).

Many of the world's ways of getting temporary pleasure involve doing so at the cost of bodily health: hard drug taking and excessive drinking are examples of this. Our physical health, our money, indeed all that we have really belongs to God. We are therefore not free to use these things just as we wish, but must act as stewards of what God has given us. We will be asked to give an account of our management of them at the judgment seat (Lk. 19:12-26). Habits such as drug abuse and alcoholic bingeing are an abuse of both our finances and health. "Do you not know that you are the temple of God and that the Spirit of God dwells in you? If anyone defiles the temple of God, God will destroy him ... your body is the temple of the Holy Spirit who is in you ... you are not your own ...you were bought at a price; therefore glorify God in your body ..." (1 Cor. 3:16,17; 6:19,20). Abuse of the body is therefore a serious matter.

However, it is recognised that if habits like these were formed before conversion, it may not be possible to break them in a moment. What is expected is a recognition of the badness of the habit, and a realistic effort being made to stop it. The stresses of life should increasingly be met by recourse to the Word of God and prayer, rather than to any human form of relaxant.

Underlying all these examples is the fundamental question whether we are allowing our minds to be changed by the influence of Christ working through God's Word. If so, we shall see that all these things, together with dishonesty of any kind, are incompatible with a Christ-like life.

"You, however, did not come to know Christ that way. Surely you heard of him and were taught in him in accordance with the truth that is in Jesus. You were taught, with regard to your former way of life, to put off your old self, which is being corrupted by its deceitful desires; to be made new in the attitude of your minds; and to put on the new self, created to be like God in true righteousness and holiness.

Therefore each of you must put off falsehood and speak truthfully to his neighbour, for we are all members of one body. 'In your anger do not sin': do not let the sun go down while you are still angry, and do not give the devil a foothold. He who has been stealing must steal no longer, but must work, doing something useful with *his own* hands, that he may have something to share with those in need." (Eph. 4:20-28 NIV)

11.3   Practical Christian Life

11.3.1   Bible Study

After baptism, we should bring forth "fruit to holiness", living a life led by the Spirit rather than the sinful nature (Rom. 6:22; 8:1; Gal. 5:16,25). It is through God's Word abiding in us that we bring forth spiritual fruit (Jn. 15:7,8). We have seen that we are led by the Spirit in the sense that God's Spirit is in and works through His Word. Throughout our lives we must keep close to that Word through regular Bible reading and study.

A thoughtful study of God's Word results in a person realising the need for baptism, and therefore performing that act. This process of letting the Word influence our actions and direct our lives should continue; baptism is but the first step in a lifetime of obedience to God's Word. There is a very real danger of familiarity with the Bible and the basic doctrines of the

Gospel, leading us to a position in which the Word no longer influences us: we can read words and they have no practical effect upon us (see Appendix 2). For this reason it is wise to say a brief prayer before each reading of the Scriptures: "Open my eyes, that I may see wondrous things from Your law" (Ps. 119:18).

The Word of God should be our daily food - indeed, our dependence upon it, and natural desire for it, should be even greater than our instinctive appetite for physical food: "... I have treasured the words of his mouth *more* than my necessary food" was Job's feeling (Job 23:12). Jeremiah likewise: "Your words were found, and I ate them, and Your word was to me the joy and rejoicing of my heart" (Jer. 15:16). Making time during each day for regular Bible reading is therefore a vital thing to build into our pattern of daily life. An uninterrupted 30 minutes of Bible study first thing in the morning is bound to start us off each day in the right spiritual gear. Such faith-forming habits are vital.

To avoid the natural tendency to only read those parts of Scripture which naturally appeal to us, the publishers of this book also distribute a programme of reading called "The Bible Companion" (available from the publishers). This gives a number of chapters to be read each day, resulting in the New Testament being read twice and the Old Testament once in the course of a year. As we read the chapters day by day, we can take courage from the thought that thousands of other believers are reading the same chapters. Whenever we meet, we therefore have an immediate bond; the chapters which we have recently been reading should form the basis of our conversation. But let us be aware of the ease of surface level Bible reading. We must let the word really bite in our lives. Jeremiah commented: "My heart within me is broken because of the [words of the] prophets; all my bones shake...I am like a drunken man ... because of the Lord, and because of His holy words" (Jer. 23:9). He paralleled God with His word, and therefore He felt the presence and imperative of God Himself as he read and heard His word.

11.3.2 Practical Christian Life: Prayer

Another vital practice to develop is that of prayer. Having reminded us that there is "one Mediator between God and men, the Man Christ Jesus; who gave Himself a ransom for all", Paul drives home the practical result of understanding Christ's work: "*Therefore* I desire that the men pray every where ... without wrath and doubting" (1 Tim. 2:5-8). "For we do not have a high priest who is unable to sympathise with our weaknesses, but we have one who has been tempted in every way, just as we are -- yet was without sin. *Let us then* approach the throne of grace with confidence, so that we may receive mercy and find grace to help us in our time of need" (Heb. 4:15,16 NIV).

Really appreciating that Christ is our personal High Priest to offer our prayers powerfully to God, should inspire us to regularly pray in faith. However, prayer should not just be a 'wants list' presented to God; thanksgiving for food before meals, for safe keeping on journeys etc. should form an important part of our prayers.

Just placing our problems before the Lord in prayer should, in itself, give a great sense of peace: "...in every thing (nothing is too small to pray about) by prayer ... with thanksgiving, let your requests be made known to God; and the peace of God, which surpasses all understanding, will guard your hearts and minds" (Phil. 4:6,7).

If our prayers are according to God's will, they will surely be responded to (1 Jn. 5:14). We can know God's will through our meditation upon His Word, which reveals His spirit/mind to us. Therefore our Bible study should teach us both how to pray and what to pray for, thus making our prayers powerful. Therefore "If ... my words abide in you, you will ask what you desire, and it shall be done for you" (Jn. 15:7).

There are many examples of regular prayer in Scripture (Ps. 119:164; Dan. 6:10). Morning and evening, with a few short prayers of thanksgiving during the day should be the pattern we adopt and move on from.

11.3.3 Practical Christian Life: Preaching

One of the great temptations which arises from knowing the true God is to become spiritually selfish. We can be so satisfied with our own personal relationship with God, so absorbed in our own personal Bible study and spirituality, that we can neglect to share these things with others - both our fellow-believers and the world around us. The Word of God and the true Gospel which is found in it, is likened to a light or lamp burning in the darkness (Ps. 119:105; Prov. 4:18). Jesus pointed out that no one who has such a light places it under a bucket, but publicly displays it (Mt. 5:15). "You are the light of the world" by reason of being baptised into Christ, "the light of the world" (Mt. 5:14; Jn. 8:12). "A city that is set on a hill cannot be hidden", Christ continued (Mt. 5:14).

If we really live a life according to the true Gospel which we understand, our 'holiness' will be evident to those with whom we live. We will be unable to disguise the fact that we are 'separated to' the hope of the Kingdom, and also 'separated from' their worldly ways.

In a tactful way we should seek to share our knowledge of the Lord with all those with whom we come into contact: turning conversations round to spiritual things; discussing Scripture with members of other churches; distributing tracts, and even placing small advertisements in our local media, are all ways in which we can let our light shine. We should not think that we can leave the work of witnessing to other believers; we each have an individual responsibility. We each, individually, do what we can, largely at our own personal expense.

One of the most successful ways of preaching is through explaining our beliefs to our families and those with whom we are in immediate contact. Those whose partners are not in the faith should clearly explain their beliefs to them, although once this has been done it is unwise to keep raising the issues or exert any pressure upon them. Pressurised converts are not what God wants. Our duty is to witness to the Truth without overdue concern about how much response we achieve. We have a great responsibility to make this witness (Ez. 3:17-21); if Christ comes in our lifetime "two men will be in the field: the one will be taken and the other left" (Lk. 17:36). It would be strange indeed if we had not spoken to our family and work colleagues about our Lord's second coming when this occurs.

11.3.4 Practical Christian Life: Ecclesial / Church Life

So far in this study we have spoken of our personal spiritual responsibilities. However, we have a duty to meet together with others who share our hope. Again, this should be something we naturally

desire to do. We have shown that after baptism we enter a wilderness journey towards the Kingdom. It is only natural that we should desire to make contact with fellow-travellers. It seems we are living in the last days before Christ's coming; to overcome the many complex trials which assail us in these times, we need to fellowship with those who are in the same position: "Let us not give up meeting together .. .but let us encourage one another -- and all the more as you see the Day (of the second coming) approaching" (Heb. 10:25 NIV cf. Mal. 3:16). Believers should therefore make every effort to make contact with each other through letters and travelling to meet with each other to share Bible study, the communion service, and preaching activities.

We have each individually been 'called out' of the world to the great hope of the Kingdom. The word 'saint' means 'a called out person', and can refer to all true believers rather than just to a few notable believers of the past. The Greek word which is translated 'church' in the English Bible is 'ecclesia', meaning 'an assembly of called out ones', i.e. believers. The 'church' therefore refers to the group of believers, rather than the physical building in which they meet. To avoid misunderstanding in the use of this term, some tend to refer to their 'churches' as 'ecclesias'.

Wherever there are a number of believers in a certain town or area, it is logical that they find a meeting place in which to meet regularly. This could be in a believer's house or in a hired hall. Ecclesias meet world-wide in places like community centres, hotel conference rooms, self-built halls or private homes. The purpose of an ecclesia is to help each other on the way to the Kingdom. This is done in a variety of ways such as collective Bible study or witnessing to the world through preaching. A typical schedule for an ecclesia could be something like this:

SUNDAY 11 a.m. - Breaking of Bread service
6 p.m. - Public preaching activity
WEDNESDAY 8 p.m. - Bible study

The ecclesia is part of the family of God. In any close-knit community, each member needs to be sensitive and submissive to the others. Christ himself was the supreme example in this. Despite his evident spiritual supremacy, he acted as the "servant of all", washing the disciples' feet whilst they argued amongst themselves as to who was the greatest among them. Jesus bids us follow his example in this (Jn. 13:14,15; Mt. 20:25-28).

Believers refer to each other as 'brother' or 'sister', being on first-name terms regardless of their differing positions in secular life. This said, it is evident that there should be respect for believers who have known the true God for many years, or who have rapidly matured in spiritual matters through their commitment to God's Word. The advice of believers like this will be greatly valued by those who are seeking to follow God's Word. However, they will only take the advice of other believers insofar as it is an accurate reflection of God's Word.

11.3.5 Practical Christian Life: The Breaking Of Bread

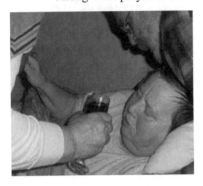

Along with prayer and Bible reading, regular obedience to Christ's command to break bread and drink wine in memory of his sacrifice is vital. "... do this in remembrance of Me", Jesus commanded (Lk. 22:19). It was his wish that his followers should regularly do this until his second coming, when Jesus will share the bread and wine with them again (1 Cor. 11:26; Lk. 22:16-18). The Lord Jesus gave Paul a specific revelation regarding the breaking of bread just as He did concerning the resurrection (1 Cor. 11:23 cf. 15:3); the breaking of bread is that important.

The bread represents Christ's body which was offered on the cross, and the wine his blood (1 Cor. 11:23-27). It does not literally turn into the body and blood of Jesus. When Jesus said "this is My body" (Mt. 26:26) we are to understand that 'this *represents*, this is [a symbol of] my body'. Jesus was clearly referring to what was usually said at the Passover: "This is the bread of affliction which our forefathers ate in the land of Egypt". It wasn't of course literally the same bread. "This is" clearly means 'this represents' in Zech. 5:3,8; Mt. 13:19-23,38; 1 Cor. 11:25; 12:27. In some Bible versions, when we read the word 'means', it is simply a translation of the verb 'to be' (Mt. 9:13; 12:7; Lk. 15:26; Acts 2:12). 'This is' should be read as 'this means / this represents'. The early believers appear to have kept the breaking of bread service frequently (Acts 2:42,46), probably once a week (Acts 20:7). If we truly love Christ, we will obey his commands (Jn. 15:11-14). If we have a true personal relationship with him, we will desire to remember his sacrifice as he has asked, and thereby encourage ourselves at the remembrance of that great salvation which he achieved. A period of quiet reflection upon his sufferings on the cross will make our own trials pale into insignificance when compared with those of our Lord.

The breaking of bread is fundamentally a service of *remembrance*; nothing magical happens as a result of doing it. In this respect it is the equivalent of the Passover feast under the Law of Moses (Lk. 22:15; 1 Cor. 5:7,8). This was a means of remembering the great deliverance from Egypt which God brought about through Moses at the Red Sea. The breaking of bread service takes us back to our salvation from sin through Christ, which was made possible on the cross and to which we became related by baptism.

Keeping this commandment should therefore be something which we naturally want to do.

Physically taking the bread and wine makes the love of Christ for us, and indeed all the things concerning our salvation, become so real once again. Breaking bread about once a week is therefore a sign of a healthy spiritual state. If one cannot do it with fellow-believers of the Truth, it should be done alone. No excuse should be allowed to stop us keeping this commandment. We should make every effort to keep a supply of bread and wine with us for the service, although in extreme circumstances even a lack of these should not prevent us from remembering Christ in the appointed way as best we can. Jesus used "the fruit of the vine" (Lk. 22:18), and we should therefore use red grape wine.

To take the emblems of Christ's sufferings and sacrifice is the highest honour which a man or woman could have. To take them with improper attention to what they represent is nigh on blasphemy, seeing that "as often as you eat this bread and drink this cup, you proclaim the Lord's death ... Therefore whoever eats this bread or drinks this cup of the Lord in an unworthy manner will be guilty of the body and blood of the Lord" (1 Cor. 11:26,27). A breaking of bread service should therefore be held at a time and place where there will not be distractions and interruptions to one's flow of thought. This may involve doing it early in the morning or late at night, in a bedroom or other suitable place. We are further advised, "Let a man examine himself, and *so* (in that humble spirit of self-examination) let him eat of that bread and drink of that cup" (1 Cor. 11:28). We should therefore fix our minds on Christ's sacrifice, perhaps by glancing through the Gospel records of his crucifixion, before we take the emblems. By doing so properly, we will inevitably examine our own conscience towards Christ, too.

A suitable order of service for the breaking of bread is as follows:

1. Prayer - asking for God's blessing upon the meeting; His opening of our eyes to His Word; remembering the needs of other believers; praising Him for His love, especially as shown in Christ, and praying regarding any other specific issues.
2. Do the Bible readings for the day as specified in the "Bible Companion".
3. Meditate upon the lessons to be learnt from them, or read an 'exhortation' - a Bible study upon those chapters which leads us towards the purpose of our service - the remembrance of Christ.
4. Read 1 Cor. 11:23-29.

5. Period of silent self-examination.

6. Prayer for the bread.

7. Break the bread and eat a small piece of it.

8. Prayer for the wine.

9. Take a sip of wine.

10. Concluding prayer.

The whole service should take just over one hour.

11.4   Christian Marriage

We will begin this section by considering the position of those who are single at the point of baptism. We have discussed in Study 5.3 the need to

marry only baptised believers. There are a few passages which encourage those who are single at least to consider the option of remaining single so as to commit themselves totally to the Lord's work (1 Cor. 7:7-9,32-38 cf. 2 Tim. 2:4; Mt. 19:11,12,29; Ecc. 9:9). "But even if you do marry, you have not sinned" (1 Cor. 7:28). Most, if not all, of the apostles were married (1 Cor. 9:5), and marriage as God intended is designed to bring many physical and spiritual benefits. "Marriage should be honoured by all, and the marriage bed kept pure" (Heb. 13:4 NIV). "It is not good that ... man should be alone", unless he can manage a high level of commitment to spiritual things, and therefore God instituted marriage (Gen. 2:18-24). Therefore, "He who finds a wife finds a good thing, and obtains favour from the Lord ...a prudent wife is from the Lord" (Prov. 18:22; 19:14).

We are given a balanced summary of the position in 1 Cor. 7:1,2 NIV: "It is good for a man not to marry. But since there is so much immorality, each man should have his own wife, and each woman her own husband" (cf. v 9).

The implication of these verses is that indulgence of sexual desires outside marriage is fornication. Warnings against fornication (sex between unmarried people), adultery (sex where one or both parties are already married to other partners) and any form of immorality are frequent throughout the New Testament; almost every letter contains them. The following are but some of these: Acts 15:20; Rom. 1:29; 1 Cor. 6:9-18; 10:8; 2 Cor. 12:21; Gal. 5:19; Eph. 5:3; Col. 3:5; 1 Thess. 4:3; Jude 7; 1 Pet. 4:3; Rev. 2:21.

In the light of all this repeated emphasis, to fly in the face of God's clearly expressed will is serious indeed. Whilst God delights to forgive sins of momentary weakness if they are repented of (e.g. David's adultery with Bathsheba), regularly to do these things can only result in condemnation. Paul frequently spelt this out: "... sexual immorality, impurity and debauchery ... and the like. I warn you, as I did before, that those who live like this will not inherit the Kingdom of God" (Gal. 5:19,21 NIV), therefore "Flee from sexual immorality (cf. 2 Tim. 2:22). All other sins that a man commits are outside his body, but he who sins sexually sins against his own body" (1 Cor. 6:18 NIV).

It is becoming accepted almost world-wide that young couples can live together before marriage, enjoying full sexual relationships. The use of the term 'common law marriage' to describe this is a complete misnomer. Marriage for the believer must be marriage according to God's definition of it; we cannot let a definition of marriage created by the sensual world around us have supremacy over God's statements regarding marriage - after all, marriage was instituted by God rather than man. Biblically, marriage is comprised of at least three elements.

1. Some form of marriage ceremony, however simple. The record of Boaz marrying Ruth in Ruth 3:9-4:13 shows that marriage is not a relationship which is just drifted into; there must be a specific moment when one becomes fully married. Christ is likened to the bridegroom and the believers to the bride, whom he will 'marry' at his second coming. There will be "the marriage supper of the Lamb" to celebrate this (Rev. 19:7-9). The relationship between husband and wife typifies that between Christ and the believers (Eph. 5:25-30); as there will be a definite point of marriage between us, so there should be a wedding between believers which begins their marriage, typifying the union of Christ and ourselves after the judgment seat.

2. God's marriage to Israel involved entering into a mutual spiritual covenant of faithfulness to each other (Ez. 16:8), and this should also feature in the marriage of believers.

3. Sexual intercourse is necessary to consummate the marriage (Dt. 21:13; Gen. 24:67; 29:21; 1 Kings 11:2). Because of this, 1 Cor. 6:15,16 explains why intercourse outside of marriage is so wrong. Intercourse signifies, in physical terms, how God has joined a wedded couple together (Gen. 2:24). To be joined as "one flesh" in a temporary relationship is therefore an abuse of the bodies God has given us. He has designed them in order to be able to consummate in physical terms what He has joined together in marriage.

Those who are baptised, whilst their partner is not, should not leave them (1 Cor. 7:13-15), but rather make every effort to love them, and thus show by their manner of life that they have a genuine belief in the true God, rather than just having changed religions. 1 Pet. 3:1-6 encourages those in this position that doing this can, in itself, be a means of converting the unbelieving partner.

The principles governing marriage are epitomised in God's statement regarding it: "a man (shall) leave his father and mother and be joined to his wife, and they shall become one flesh" (Gen. 2:24). This striving for unity between man and wife in as many ways as possible is analogous to our continuous effort for unity with Christ, through overcoming the fundamental sin and selfishness of our natures. This striving is against ourselves rather than against Christ or our partner. The more we succeed in this, the happier and more fulfilling our relationship will be.

However, we are living in a real world of sin and failure, of inability to rise up fully to the supreme standards of holiness which are set us in the Bible, and in the example of the love of God and of Christ. The ideal standard set in Gen. 2:24 is of one man and one woman, living together in total unity for life.

Believers must be prepared to accept that sometimes this standard will not be attained both in their own lives and in those of other believers. Husbands and wives may argue and lose that unity of mind which they should have; it may be physically impossible to consummate the marriage; a man may have several wives, taken before his baptism, if living in a society where polygamy is allowed. In this case he should remain with the wives and care for them, but not take any more. The apostle Paul, in a masterful blend of human sympathy and staunch adherence to Divine principles, advised that separation was possible in extreme cases of incompatibility: "... a wife is not to depart from her husband. *But even if* she does depart, let her remain unmarried ..." (1 Cor. 7:10-11).

This stating of an ideal standard, but willingness to accept a lower standard as long as it does not flout a basic Divine principle (e.g. that adultery is wrong), is quite a common feature of Scripture. Paul's advice in 1 Cor. 7:10-11 is akin to 1 Cor. 7:27,28: "... Are you loosed from a wife? Do not seek a wife (i.e. remain single). *But even if* you do marry, you have not sinned". However, wilful divorce after minor disagreements and with no real effort at the marriage would appear to be an institutionalised flouting of God's principle that man and woman should recognise that He has joined them as one flesh, even if on practical issues they find this hard to put into practice. Christ's words are painfully plain:

"But from the beginning of the creation, God made them male and female. 'For this reason a man shall leave his father and mother and be joined to his wife, and the two shall become one flesh', so then (Jesus emphasises) they are no longer two but one flesh. Therefore what God has joined together, let not man separate (by divorce) ... whoever divorces his wife and marries another commits adultery against her. And if a woman divorces her husband and marries another, she commits adultery" (Mk. 10:6-12).

In this whole area of sexual relations, human nature is adept at making plausible excuses to justify the indulgence of the natural desires. Those who find themselves in particularly tempting situations will only find the strength and spiritual stamina which they need from a repeated meditation upon the verses quoted in this section. Some have sought to justify homosexuality and lesbianism as legitimate, natural desires. However, the basic principle of Gen. 2:24 exposes what's wrong with homosexuality; it is God's intention that man and woman should marry and be joined to each other. God created woman to be a help for Adam, rather than another man. Sexual relations between men are repeatedly condemned in the Bible. This was one of the sins for which Sodom was destroyed (Gen. 18-19); the apostle Paul makes it very clear that persisting in such practices will incur the wrath of God, and exclude from His Kingdom (Rom. 1:18-32; 1 Cor. 6:9,10).

The fact of having once been involved in such things should not make us feel that we are beyond God's help. There *is* forgiveness with God, that He should be given loving reverence by those who experience His forgiveness (Ps. 130:4). The ecclesia at Corinth had its fair share of repentant playboys. "... such were some of you. But you were washed (in baptism), but you were sanctified, but you were justified (by being baptised) in the name of the Lord Jesus ..." (1 Cor. 6:9-11).

The complaint that one has no natural attraction to the opposite sex is effectively an accusation that God is unfair in forbidding us to commit homosexuality, but creates us with that overpowering temptation. God will not let us be tempted above what we can reasonably bear without making a way of escape (1 Cor. 10:13). Through excessive indulgence of any aspect of human desires, one can reach a point where this is naturally what one is like. Thus, an alcoholic or drug addict cannot live without a regular input of certain chemicals; but he is required to change his mental outlook, and with the help of therapy return to a balanced, normal way of living.

Homosexuals must go through the same process. God will confirm men's efforts in this; if they totally give themselves over to the indulgence of their natural desires, God will treat them as He did Israel of old:

"Because of this, God gave them over to shameful lusts. Even their women exchanged natural relations for unnatural ones. In the same way the men also abandoned natural relations with women and were inflamed with lust for one another. Men committed indecent acts with other men, and received in themselves (i.e. in their bodies) the due penalty for their perversion" (Rom. 1:26,27 NIV).

11.5   Christian Fellowship

The Greek words translated 'fellowship' and 'communion' basically describe the state of having something in common: common-union. 'Communion' is related to the word 'communicate'. By reason of knowing and practising God's ways, we have fellowship with Him and with all others who are doing the same through being "in Christ". It is easy to neglect the responsibilities which we have to fellowship with others: "... do not forget to do good and to share (i.e. fellowship)" (Heb. 13:16). Phil. 1:5 speaks of our "fellowship in the Gospel"; the basis of our fellowship is therefore the doctrines and way of life which comprise the true Gospel. For this reason the fellowship enjoyed by true believers is far greater than in any other organisation or church. Because of this fellowship they travel great distances to be with each other and to visit isolated believers. Paul speaks of "fellowship of the Spirit" (Phil. 2:1), i.e. fellowship which is based on our common following of the spirit/mind of God, as revealed in His spirit-word.

One of the greatest expressions of our fellowship is through keeping the breaking of bread service together. The early believers "continued steadfastly in the apostles' doctrine and fellowship, in the breaking of bread, and in prayers ... breaking bread ... with gladness and simplicity of heart" (Acts 2:42,46). The emblems represent the central pivot of our hope and sharing them together should bind us together in "simplicity of heart". "Is not the cup of thanksgiving for which we give thanks a participation in the blood of Christ? And is not the bread that we break a participation in the body of Christ? Because there is one loaf, we, who are many, are one body, for we all partake of the one loaf", i.e. Christ (1 Cor. 10:16,17 NIV). We therefore have an obligation to share the emblems of Christ's sacrifice with all those who benefit from his work, who are "partakers of that one loaf".

John recalls how he shared the Gospel of eternal life with others "that you also may have fellowship with us; and truly our fellowship is with the Father and with His Son Jesus Christ" (1 Jn. 1:2,3). This shows that fellowship is based around a common understanding of the true Gospel, and that this brings us into fellowship both with other true believers, and also with God and Jesus on a personal level. The more we apply the Gospel to our lives, seeking to overcome our sinful tendencies, and the deeper we progress in our living of God's Word, the deeper our fellowship will be with God and Christ.

Our fellowship with God, Christ and other believers does not just depend on our common assent to the truths which comprise the "one faith". Our way of life must be in accordance with the principles which are expressed in them. "... God is light and in Him is no darkness at all. If we say that we have fellowship with Him, and walk in darkness, we lie and do not practise the truth. But if we walk in the light as He is in the light, we have fellowship with one another, and the blood of Jesus Christ His Son cleanses us from all sin" (1 Jn. 1:5-7). Fellowship therefore occurs naturally between those who walk in the light.

'Walking in darkness' must refer to a way of life which is constantly and publicly at variance with the light of God's Word (Ps. 119:105; Prov. 4:18); it does not refer to our occasional sins of weakness, for the next verse continues, "If we say that we have no sin, we deceive ourselves, and the truth (i.e. God's Word – Jn. 17:17; 3:21; Eph. 5:13) is not in us" (1 Jn. 1:8).

From this it should be evident that in practice, meaningful fellowship ceases when a believer starts to teach things, or lives a way of life, which are openly opposed to clear Bible teaching: "Have no fellowship with the unfruitful works of darkness, but rather expose them" (Eph. 5:11). Every effort should be made to win them back after the pattern of the good shepherd seeking the lost sheep (Lk. 15:1-7).

One of the clearest passages concerning fellowship is found in 2 Cor. 6:14-18: "Do not be unequally yoked together with unbelievers. For what fellowship has righteousness with lawlessness? And what communion has light with darkness ... Therefore 'Come out from among them and be separate, says the Lord ... and I will receive you.' 'I will be a Father to you, and you shall be my sons and daughters, says the Lord Almighty'".

We have shown how that the Word of God is light. These verses explain why we should not fellowship with religions which teach false things; why we should not marry those who aren't in Christ, and should shun the ways of the world. If we preach God's truth as we should, it is inevitable that communities which believe heresies like the 'trinity' will themselves exclude us. Doctrine is important because it controls how we live and behave; therefore we must be "pure in the doctrine" if we are to attempt to live a pure life. Our way of life must "be worthy of the gospel" -- a response to the basic Gospel we understand and believe (Phil. 1:27). On account of our separation from the world we have the breathtaking honour of becoming God's very own sons and daughters, part of a world-wide family of others who have this same relationship - our brothers and sisters. There is only one "body", i.e. one true church (Eph. 1:23), which is based upon those who hold the one hope - one God, one baptism and "one faith", i.e. the one true set of doctrines which comprises the one faith (Eph. 4:4-6).

If you have followed these studies carefully, it will be evident by now that there can be no half-way position in our relationship with God. We are either in Christ by baptism into him, or outside of him. We are either in the light, or in darkness. One cannot have a foot in both camps.

Our knowledge of these things gives us a certain degree of responsibility towards God. We do not now walk the streets or go about our daily lives like the average woman or man of the world. God is intensely watching for our response. Both He, the Lord Jesus and all true believers could almost 'will' you to make the right decision. But much as God, Christ and ourselves will do all we can to help you - even in God's case to the extent of having given His only Son to die for us - ultimately your salvation depends upon your own freewill decision to grasp hold of the grace of God and the great Hope of eternity which has now been offered to you.

STUDY 11: Questions

1. What kind of changes should occur in our lives when we are baptised?

2. What does 'holiness' mean?
   □ Having no contact with unbelievers
   □ Being separated *from* sin and *to* the things of God
   □ Going to church
   □ Doing good to others

3. What sort of occupations are unsuitable for a true Christian?

4. What do the words 'saint' and 'ecclesia' mean?

5. Which of the following statements are true about the breaking of bread?
   □ We should do it regularly on a weekly basis
   □ We should do it once a year at Passover time
   □ The bread and wine turn into the literal body and blood of Jesus
   □ The bread and wine represent the body and blood of Jesus

6. Which of the following statements are true about marriage?
   □ We should only marry a true believer
   □ Divorce is permissible for believers
   □ A married believer whose partner is an unbeliever should try to remain with them
   □ In marriage, the man represents Christ and the woman the believers

7. Would you like to be baptised?

If, having finished this book, you'd like to discuss things further or be baptized, please contact any of the addresses shown at the start of the book. You can email us at **info@carelinks.net** .